NATIONAL POLICE LIBRARY

2011555

D0238598

The Collected Courses of the Academy of European Law
Series Editors: Professor Philip Alston and
Professor Gráinne de Búrca,
European University Institute,
Florence

VOLUME XI/1

Rights

The Collected Courses of the Academy of European Law
Edited by Professor Philip Alston and Professor Gráinne de Búrca

This series brings together the Collected Courses of the
Academy of European Law in Florence. The Academy's mission is to
produce scholarly analyses which are at the cutting edge of the two
fields in which it works: European Union law and human rights law.
A 'general course' is given each year in each field, by a
distinguished scholar and/or practitioner, who either examines the
field as a whole through a particular thematic, conceptual or
philosophical lens, or who looks at a particular theme in the context
of the overall body of law in the field. The Academy also publishes
each year a volume of collected essays with a specific theme in each
of the two fields.

Discrimination and Human Rights
The Case of Racism

Edited by

SANDRA FREDMAN

NATIONAL POLICE LIBRARY

Academy of European Law
European University Institute

OXFORD
UNIVERSITY PRESS

OXFORD

UNIVERSITY PRESS

Great Clarendon Street, Oxford OX2 6DP

Oxford University Press is a department of the University of Oxford.
It furthers the University's objective of excellence in research, scholarship,
and education by publishing worldwide in

Oxford New York

Athens Auckland Bangkok Bogotá Buenos Aires Cape Town
Chennai Dar es Salaam Delhi Florence Hong Kong Istanbul Karachi
Kolkata Kuala Lumpur Madrid Melbourne Mexico City Mumbai Nairobi
Paris São Paulo Shanghai Singapore Taipei Tokyo Toronto Warsaw

with associated companies in Berlin Ibadan

Oxford is a registered trade mark of Oxford University Press
in the UK and in certain other countries

Published in the United States
by Oxford University Press Inc., New York

© Sandra Fredman 2001

The moral rights of the author have been asserted
Database right Oxford University Press (maker)

First published 2001

All rights reserved. No part of this publication may be reproduced,
stored in a retrieval system, or transmitted, in any form or by any means,
without the prior permission in writing of Oxford University Press,
or as expressly permitted by law, or under terms agreed with the appropriate
reprographics rights organization. Enquiries concerning reproduction
outside the scope of the above should be sent to the Rights Department,
Oxford University Press, at the address above

You must not circulate this book in any other binding or cover
and you must impose this same condition on any acquirer

British Library Cataloguing in Publication Data

Data available

Library of Congress Cataloging in Publication Data

Data available

ISBN 0–19–924245–3
ISBN 0–19–924603–3(pbk)

1 3 5 7 9 10 8 6 4 2

Typeset in Garamond
by Hope Services (Abingdon) Ltd
Printed in Great Britain
on acid-free paper by
T. J. International Ltd,
Padstow, Cornwall

Acc. no. 2011556

Classmark 344.01133

DISCARDED
NATIONAL POLICE LIBRARY
FRE

Contents

Notes on Contributors

Anneliese Baldaccini holds a Masters degree in the Theory and Practice of Human Rights from the University of Essex. She is a Researcher at the Essex Human Rights Centre on the subject of international human rights responses to racism and racial discrimination. She acts as a consultant to the Human Rights Policy Department of the Foreign and Commonwealth Office, UK, on preparations for the United Nations World Conference Against Racism, August–September 2001.

Kevin Boyle is Professor of Law and Director of the Human Rights Centre at the University of Essex. He has also held academic posts in both parts of Ireland. He is a barrister at law in both Ireland and the United Kingdom with extensive experience of practice before the European Court of Human Rights. He has written widely on international human rights subjects, including on issues of religious discrimination and intolerance as well as on hate speech. His publications include *Freedom of Religion: A World Report* (1997) and *Northern Ireland: The Choice* (1994). He is a member of the International Board of Article 19, the Global Campaign against Censorship, and co- edited, for Article 19, *Striking a Balance: Hate Speech and Freedom of Expression* (1992).

Damian Chalmers is a Senior Lecturer in Law at the London School of Economics and Political Science. His research interests include Law and the European Union, Law and the Environment, and Law and Postnationalism. His recent publications include *European Union Law*, volumes I and II (1998) (volume II with Erika Szyszczak), 'Postnationalism and the Quest for Constitutional Substitutes' 27 *Journal of Law & Society* (2000) 178, 'The Positioning of EU Judicial Politics within the United Kingdom' 23 *West European Politics* (2000) 169.

María Luisa Fernández Esteban is Professor of Constitutional and European Commmunity Law at the Autonoma University of Madrid, and, since June 2001, has been administrator of the Directorate General for Competition of the European Commission in Brussels. She holds a doctoral degree from the European University Institute in Florence. Her main publications include: *El Principio de Subsidiariedad en el Ordenamiento Europeo* (1996), *Nuevas tec- nologías, Internet y Derechos Fundamentales* (1998), and *The Rule of Law in the European Constitution* (1999). She co-authored *Legislacion Electoral del Estado, las Comunidades Autonomas y la Unión Europea* (1999), and 'Incidencia de Internet en los Derechos Fundamentales', in *Derecho de Internet* (2000)

Sandra Fredman is Professor of Law at Oxford University and Fellow in Law at Exeter College, Oxford. She specialises in discrimination law, human rights law, and labour law and has written numerous articles in these fields. Her book, *Women and the Law*, was published by Oxford University Press in December 1997 and she is now completing a book on discrimination law for the Clarendon Law series. She has written a number of articles examining the role of equality, most recently on the new European Union directives on race equality, as well as on affirmative action; pregnancy and parenthood; pensions; and the European Convention on Human Rights. She has also written extensively in the fields of public law and labour law. With Professor Bob Hepple, she co-authors 'Labour Law and Industrial Relations in Great Britain', which is the British section of the *International Encyclopaedia of Labour Relations* edited by Blanpain. She also co-authored, with Gillian Morris, *The State as Employer*.

Christopher McCrudden is Professor of Human Rights Law, Oxford University, and a Fellow of Lincoln College, Oxford. He is also a Visiting Professor at the University of Michigan Law School. He was educated at Queen's University, Belfast (1970–74), Yale Law School (1974–76), and Oxford University (1976–80). He is currently a member of the Northern Ireland Executive's Public Procurement Implementation Group and has acted as specialist Advisor, to the British House of Commons Northern Ireland Affairs Committee (1998–9), and been a Member of the European Commission's Expert Network on the Application of the Equality Directives since 1986. His recent publications include: 'A Perspective on Trade and Labor Rights', 3 *Journal of International Economic Law* (2000) 43 (with Anne Davies); and 'Human Rights Codes for Transnational Corporations: What Can the Sullivan and MacBride Principles Tell Us?', 19 *Oxford Journal of Legal Studies* (1999) 167. He is a member of the editorial board of the *Journal of International Economic Law*.

Dimitrina Petrova is the Executive Director of the European Roma Rights Center in Budapest. Since 1997, she has also been teaching 'Roma Rights' and 'Human Rights politics' at the Central European University. From 1992 to 1996 she was the Chair of the Human Rights Project in Sofia, Bulgaria. In 1995–96 she was a Regional Co-ordinator for Southeastern Europe, and in 1994 a Field Officer at the International Secretariat of the International Helsinki Federation for Human Rights in Vienna. From 1990 to 1991 she was a member of the Bulgarian Parliament, where she participated in the drafting of the 1991 Bulgarian Constitution. She has been teaching and lecturing at various universities and has worked on various fields of human rights movements. She has published extensively on human and minority rights, politics, and public interest law. In 1994 she received the Human Rights Award from the American Bar Association.

Theo van Boven is Professor of International Law at the University of Maastricht. He has served as Director of Human Rights of the United Nations and has been a member of the United Nations Sub-Commission for the Promotion and Protection of Human Rights and of the Committee on the Elimination of Racism and Discrimination. He is President of the Netherlands Association of International Law; Vice-President of the International Commission of Jurists; and a member of the Board of the International Movement against All Forms of Discrimination and Racism. He has written extensively on international human rights and humanitarian law; a selection of his writings has been published in: F. Coomans, C. Flinterman, F.Grünfeld, I. Westendorp, J. Willems (eds.), *Human Rights from Exclusion to Inclusion: Principles and Practice* (2000).

Table of Cases

Table of Treaties and Legislation

Decisions

Directives

H. Netherlands

I. Romania

J. Slovenia

K. Spain

L. South Africa

M. Sweden

N. Turkey

O. United Kingdom

Acts

Statutory Instruments

Motor Cycle (Protective Helmets) Regulations SI No 1279 of 1980 as
amended by SI No 374 of 1981

P. United States

Table of Abbreviations

CEDAW   Convention on the Elimination of All Forms of
          Discrimination Against Women
CERD   Committee on the Elimination of Racial Discrimination
CESCR   Committee on Economic, Social and Cultural Rights
CRC   Convention on the Rights of the Child
DNS   Domain-Name System
ECHR   European Convention on Human Rights
ECJ   European Court of Justice
ECOSOC   Economic and Social Council
ECRI   European Commission Against Racial Discrimination
ERRC   European Roma Rights Centre
EUMC   European Monitoring Centre on Racism and Xenophobia
FETO   Fair Employment and Treatment (NI) Order 1998
HRC   Human Rights Committee
IANA   Internet Assigned Numbers Authority
ICANN   Internet Corporation for Assigned Names and Numbers
ICCPR   International Covenant on Civil and Political Rights
ICERD   International Convention on the Elimination of All Forms of
          Racial Discrimination
ICESCR   International Convenant on Economic, Social, and Cultural
          Rights
ILO   International Labour Organization
NGO   Non-Governmental Organizations
OHCHR   Office of the High Commissioner for Human Rights
OSCE   Organization for Security and Co-operation in Europe
RRA   Race Relations Act 1976
SDA   Sexual Discrimination Act 1975
TEU   Treaty on European Union
TLD   Top-Level Domain
TLDN   Top-Level Domain Names
UDHR   Universal Declaration of Human Rights
UEJF   Union des Etudiants Juifs de France
UN   United Nations
UNESCO   United Nations Educational, Scientific, and Cultural
          Organization
UNHCHR   United Nations High Commissioner for Human Rights
WCAR   World Conference Against Racism, Racial Discrimination,
          Xenophobia, and Other Intolerance

1

Introduction

SANDRA FREDMAN

The opening years of the new century have brought with them a surge of new energy in the struggle to find legal measures to combat racism. The hopes stated in advance of the 2001 World Conference against Racism hold out a glowing ideal of tolerance and diversity as its vision for the twenty-first century. 'Instead of allowing diversity of race and culture to become a limiting factor in human exchange and development,' states the Declaration presaging the conference, 'we must . . . discern in such diversity the potential for mutual enrichment . . . For too long such diversity has been treated as a threat rather than a gift. And too often that threat has been expressed in racial contempt and conflict, in exclusion, discrimination and intolerance.' The World Conference, it is pledged, should provide the standards, structures and remedies to 'ensure full recognition of the dignity and equality of all'.[1] More concrete developments have already occurred in Europe, where, for the first time, the EU has accepted responsibility for enacting legal measures to outlaw discrimination on grounds of race and ethnicity.

The boldness of these sentiments only serves to highlight the dismal reality—a reality not only scarred with the results of past discrimination, but festering with the new and persistent wounds of racial hatred, disadvantage, and intolerance. So how likely is it that new measures will make a real impact? The record of previous attempts tells a sorry tale. Two earlier World Conferences were conspicuously unsuccessful. Even more disappointing has been the operation of international measures against discrimination. And it is not only international law that has been ineffective. Domestic legislation has little more to show for itself.

The contrast between legislative attempts and the reality of racism prompts a closer scrutiny of the legal instruments themselves. Does the problem lie in the goals and purposes of the legislation, or in the substantive provisions, or in the remedial structures? And can we even be sure that the correct answers are being given to the foundational questions: What is race? And what is

[1] 'Tolerance and Diversity: A Vision for the 21st Century' to be found at <http://www.unhchr.ch/html/racism/index.htm>.

racism? It is these fundamental questions which this set of essays attempts to
address. It is increasingly recognized, Fredman argues, that race is itself a
social construct, reflecting ideological attempts to legitimate domination, and
heavily based on social and historical context. Racism is, therefore, not about
objective characteristics, but about relationships of domination and subordination. Nor is there a single racism, but multiple racisms: colour racism must
be examined together with cultural racism, which includes ethnicity, religion,
and language. Racism, it is argued, operates along at least three axes: first, that
of denigratory stereotyping, hatred, and violence; secondly, that of a cycle of
disadvantage; and the third the negation and even obliteration of culture, religion, or language. Policies to combat racism need to address all three, and to
do so in a manner which is specific to the political context and the groups in
question. Indeed, Boyle and Baldaccini argue, agreement on the definition of
racial discrimination should be one of the most important goals of the forthcoming World Conference. Such a definition would need to bring out the difference between discrimination based on colour, which has thus far been the
main focus of international treaties, and discrimination based on other
grounds, such as culture, religion, and language. This in turn requires anti-
discrimination measures to be sensitive to context and history. Van Boven
stresses that the first step in addressing racism is to ascertain the fate of the victims, among them the 'untouchables' in India, indigenous populations, and
the many migrant workers excluded from their 'host' communities despite
their significant economic contribution.

However, even recognition of racism as a problem needing urgent attention
is still not achieved in many states. Both van Boven and Petrova consider the
corrosive influence of denial of racism in its many guises, permitting as it does
the abdication of moral responsibility both by public and private actors.
Indeed, one of the most debilitating features of the operation of international
instruments intended to combat racism has been, as van Boven shows, the
extent to which states have regarded racism as an evil practised by others, to
the extent that the International Convention on the Elimination of All Forms
of Racial Discrimination (ICERD) was perceived as a legal and political
instrument to serve foreign policy interests. Yet, as Boyle and Baldaccini
stress, an international human rights system is inevitably impotent without
the support and commitment of states. The central question for the future,
they suggest, is how to sustain support and commitment from all countries,
not just through changes in the law, but through significant social change.

The need to define race and racism is only the first problematic issue in
developing a human rights structure capable of combating racism. The next
and crucial stage is to formulate the principle of equality itself. As both
Fredman and McCrudden stress, the principle of equality is not monolithic
nor single-dimensional, but can be based on several different conceptual
foundations. In assessing the effectiveness of measures to combat racism, it is

essential to clarify the conceptual underpinnings of particular legal definitions. Thus the concept of direct discrimination primarily reflects a notion of justice as based on consistent treatment, rather than on substantive outcomes. It does not on its own distinguish between treatment which is 'equally bad' and treatment which is 'equally good'. In addition, 'less favourable' treatment can only be established by finding a similarly situated comparator of the 'opposite' race or ethnic group. This means that direct discrimination often requires as a precondition a demonstration of conformity with the comparator. Equally problematically, it assumes that groups have fixed boundaries, and operate in opposition to one another. Thus equality in its most familiar sense, that likes should be treated alike, could well have the effect of collapsing the principle of equality into one of sameness, devaluing difference and endorsing assimilation and conformity.

It is therefore now generally accepted that formal equality should be transcended by principles of substantive equality, often formulated in terms of concepts such as equality of opportunity and equality of results. Such notions appear at first sight to be encapsulated in the principle of indirect or disparate impact discrimination, which forbids equal treatment if it in practice operates as a barrier to disadvantaged groups. Yet indirect discrimination is itself ambiguous as to its aim: while differential impact is accepted as diagnostic of inequality, it is not clear that equality of results is its aim. In any event, more attention needs to be paid to the 'results' referred to in such an analysis: are we focusing on the distribution of jobs, of property, of status, or of representation? The current trend is to go further and articulate explicit values underlying equality, particularly those of dignity and solidarity. Thus harassment, although deemed to be direct discrimination, is now defined as a violation of dignity. But dignity on its own does not provide a determinative set of answers, since it too is compatible with a wide range of political theories. One of the central challenges, therefore, is to fashion a concept of equality which is substantive and transcends the traditional equality–difference dichotomy in that it can encompass positive diversity while at the same time rejecting inferior treatment on racial, religious, or ethnic grounds.

It is this challenge which is central to the most recent attempt to fashion a structure to address race discrimination: the EU race equality directive. Chalmers asks whether the Directive can be correctly viewed as an instrument of intercultural evaluation, based on an acknowledgement of the value of a multicultural society, which respects claims of different collective identities as shared political values. Intercultural evaluation, a concept drawn from the work of Bikhu Parekh, goes further than facilitating the expression of claims by particular groups; it also commits each party to evaluate its own practices in the light of the claims of the other. The EC, according to Chalmers, is in many ways best suited to policing the rules of intercultural evaluation. Even more importantly, in his view, if interpreted in a particular manner, the race equality directive provides the necessary means to do so. Yet the central need to develop and recognize negotiation procedures as a mechanism for inter-cultural evaluation is difficult to meet given the structure of the EC and its decision-making.

International law has likewise developed sophisticated instruments to address racism. Boyle and Baldaccini trace the development of the principle of equality from its beginnings in the United Nations Charter, which was 'rev-olutionary' in insisting that human rights embraced all human beings equally without distinction as to race, sex, language, or religion. This commitment to equality of treatment led to specific international instruments on the main types of discrimination, the most important for our purposes being the ICERD. Indeed, according to Boyle and Baldaccini, it was the search for an effective international response to racism that produced the main compo-nents of the UN human rights regime. At the same time, its effectiveness has been hampered by the fraught political environment into which it was born, and within which it has had to function. Thus the immediate concern with combating colonialism and apartheid has at times obscured the objective of universal elimination of all forms of racial and ethnic discrimination.

However, there are some serious gaps in its coverage, not least of them being the absence of proper protection for non-citizens. Migrant workers, refugees, and asylum seekers are the subjects not just of exploitation, but also of racial hatred, denial of fundamental human rights, and exclusion due to their eth-nicity from education, health, and other services. It is thus troubling, as van Boven notes, that the International Convention on the Protection of the Rights of All Migrant Workers and Members of their Families has only received twelve ratifications and, ten years after its adoption, has not yet entered into force. The international convention itself explicitly allows for distinctions to be made between citizens and non-citizens. The Committee on the Elimination of Racial Discrimination (CERD) has attempted to soften this by requiring that states report on the status of non-citizens, particularly migrant workers and refugees. However, as Boyle and Baldaccini note with regret, despite many evi-dent abuses, the Committee has been constrained in its criticism. In any event, the Committee has no authority to require states to guarantee non-citizens rights comparable to those enjoyed by citizens. This is particularly serious, as these authors stress, since the social inclusion of migrants is crucial if racism and xenophobia are to be successfully combated. This refusal to take responsibility for extending basic protection to non-citizens is reinforced by the newly adopted EU Directive on equality irrespective of race and ethnic origin, which excludes from the scope of its protection discrimination on grounds of nation-ality (except for EU citizens) and permits discrimination against third-country nationals if it arises from the conditions of entry and residence.

The need to clarify the conceptual foundation of equality is particularly important when we come to consider remedies. As McCrudden argues, there is a close connection between the function attributed to anti-discrimination law and the enforcement institutions that are thought to be appropriate and effective. In his chapter he sketches out three models attached to the developing conceptions of equality, and demonstrates how they relate to different enforcement and remedial structures. Firstly, an individual justice model focuses on cleansing the process of decision-making, concentrating on securing fairness for the individual, and reflecting respect for efficiency, 'merit', and achievement. Such a model would yield remedies based on individual justice and individual responsibility, involving, for example, the granting of a civil remedy to an individual victim if the latter has brought a complaint against an alleged perpetrator, and succeeded in proving guilt and causation. Secondly, a group justice model, by contrast, concentrates more on the outcome of decision-making than on the process of making decisions, and seeks as its primary aim to improve the relative position of particular groups. This feeds back into the remedial process, either through adaptations of the individual justice approach, such as the permissibility of class actions and the acceptance of public interest litigators; or by establishing regulatory agencies to create pressures on organizations to produce change often backed up by the state's use of its dominium powers to grant or withhold contracts. Thirdly, a 'participative model' would stress that the primary aim is to give excluded groups an appropriate voice in public affairs and is achieved by a remedial structure which would 'weave policies of equality into the fabric of decision-making across all spheres of government' and which does so by involving the affected groups themselves. Using these models, McCrudden examines and assesses enforcement and remedial structures in international law, particularly in light of the newly defined UN Basic Principle on the right to a Remedy and Reparations, adopted as recently as April 2000. He demonstrates a growing willingness to challenge the idea that national remedies are appropriately left to national discretion, and shows that there is increasingly detailed scrutiny by international bodies of the impact in practice of remedial structures. In the light of this, it is disappointing to find that in the newly adopted race equality directive, the EU has opted for a remedial model which is primarily one based on the individual justice model.

Petrova takes the discussion about the difference between individual and group justice one step further by analysing the notion of group rights more closely. As a start, she distinguishes between group rights which are the sum of the rights of group members (such as a right to political representation of minority groups *per se*) and group rights which are really individual rights which can only be exercised within a group (such as instruction in the mother tongue). The traditional anti-discrimination approach, taking the form of a prohibition on discrimination against individuals, can effectively be served by an individual right, she argues. But if the struggle against racism is to be taken beyond the demand for non-discrimination to one for genuine multiculturalism, is there a need for a notion of group rights such as political representation or preservation of a minority culture? While noting the dangers of some notions of group rights, in particular, the obscuring of conflicts of interest within the group, and the difficulty of defining who constitutes the groups, she nevertheless argues strongly in favour of 'special rights' both for minority members and minority communities, including, where appropriate, the conceptual framework of group rights. Most important is the facilitation of political participation by special group rights empowering disadvantaged minorities.

Among the most important new developments in anti-discrimination law is the imposition of positive duties upon states, not just to provide redress for proven discrimination, but to actively promote equality. Pioneering in this field has been the Northern Ireland fair employment legislation, which has required employers and public bodies to draw up equality schemes to advance equality between different groups. This has been echoed in new race relations legislation in the UK. As Fredman argues, the imposition of positive duties fundamentally alters the architecture of the equality principle. Instead of assuming that redress for discrimination should be provided by the person who is 'at fault' or responsible for the original problem, this 'fourth generation' equality principle places the duty to promote equality on the body best equipped to do so. Proof of fault is therefore replaced by a demonstration of disparate impact, and the resulting duty is proactive rather than reactive. Such a positive duty is in fact contained in the International Convention, which requires states to ensure the adequate development and protection of racial groups. However, as Boyle and Baldaccini show, the precise nature of the duty is unclear and the Committee has done little to elucidate its scope.

Particularly controversial are issues which involve a conflict between the equality right and other rights such as freedom of speech. The requirement in ICERD that hate speech be prohibited is regarded by the Committee as central to the convention, recognizing as it does the power of hate propaganda to foster prejudice and racial discrimination. Yet major state actors on the global scene, such as the United States, regard such prohibitions as a breach of freedom of speech. In a globalized world of communication, such fundamental absence of consensus on the acceptability of hate speech makes any attempt at regulation barely plausible. This is particularly problematic in the light of the dramatic increase in the availability and dissemination of racism propaganda on the Internet. It is this problem which Esteban addresses. The challenges posed by the Internet require an entirely different regulatory approach from that customary in human rights enforcement. Far more powerful than individual state actors are the online intermediaries and content providers, amongst whom self-regulation based on soft law is found to be the most effective approach.

The idealism implicit in the preamble to the World Conference on Racism is essential to keep alive the belief in equality and the abhorrence of racism. However, if we are genuinely to find effective and appropriate measures to combat racism, a great deal of attention needs to be paid both to the principles informing them and the precise tools to achieve them. It is hoped that this book of essays constitutes a constructive contribution to that enterprise.

2

Combating Racism with Human Rights: The Right to Equality

SANDRA FREDMAN

Equality is an ideal to which we all fervently aspire. Attempts to translate it into reality are numerous: all human rights documents, both international and domestic, include an equality guarantee, bolstered in many jurisdictions with statutory provisions. Yet racism in its many guises persists. Racial violence, hate speech, prejudice, and stereotyping are features of everyday life; groups defined by their race or ethnicity remain disproportionately disadvantaged; and minority cultures and religions are silenced or negated.

This imperviousness of racism to equality guarantees prompts us to re-examine the principle of equality itself. Is there something inherent in the conception of equality in human rights contexts which prevents it from achieving real progress in combating racism? Or is it possible to formulate a notion of equality which transcends these limitations? In this chapter, I analyse the principle of equality in order to illuminate its limitations, and to explore whether it is possible to construct alternative conceptions of equality which overcome these difficulties. The chapter begins with an exploration of the issue with which equality is concerned in this context: namely racism itself. In Part II, I examine various conceptions of the principle of equality, before moving on in Part III to the legal application of these different conceptions. In Part IV, I address some of the central challenges facing the attempt to combat racism with equality in a human rights context.

I. RACISM: ITS NATURE AND CONSEQUENCES

Attempts to supply a physiological or evolutionary content to the notion of 'race' are familiar. However, under the guise of 'scientific knowledge', such theories have almost invariably been used to justify exclusion, subordination or even extermination of some 'racial' groups by others. It is therefore increasingly recognized that race is itself a social construct, reflecting ideological attempts to legitimate domination, and heavily based on social and historical context. As Stuart Hall argues,

Black is essentially a politically and culturally constructed category, which cannot be grounded in a set of fixed transcultural or transcendental racial categories and which therefore has no guarantees in Nature. What this brings into play is the recognition of the immense diversity and differentiation of the historical and cultural experiences of black subjects.[1]

Racism is, therefore, not about objective characteristics, but about relationships of domination and subordination, about hatred of the 'Other' in defence of 'Self', perpetrated and apparently legitimated through images of the 'Other' as inferior, abhorrent, even sub-human.

The power of the ideology of racism is not, however, in itself sufficient to explain its tenacity. Crucial too is the extent to which racism serves the needs of advanced capitalism. It is no coincidence that racism has its roots in slavery and colonialism, both driven by economic imperatives. Its modern manifestations, particularly in Europe, are equally based in economic dominance. Thus in Britain, the acute shortage of labour after the war led to the active recruitment of people from the Caribbean; in Germany to the encouragement of Turkish guest workers. This need has, moreover, frequently been highly specific, namely to fill the jobs not wanted by the indigenous population.[2] Policies aimed at ensuring that newcomers remain in such jobs are justified and apparently legitimated by characterizing workers as inferior, not 'fit' for any other work or 'preferring' to remain as they are. The strength of the economic imperative is particularly obvious once the need for 'black' labour disappears, evidenced by the policies of exclusion through immigration laws which have been widespread in Europe. A particularly problematic consequence of the fact that tolerance is only based on economic usefulness is the treatment meted out to families seeking entry to join a worker. The fear of outsiders taking insiders' jobs means that wives of economically active men must be constructed as 'dependents' in order to justify entry; and to prove their dependent status requires humiliation by immigration officers and police.[3] Conversely, British immigration laws at one time excluded husbands of economically active wives. A similar manifestation is in the current attitudes in Britain to asylum seekers. Those seeking refuge in Britain for political reasons, and therefore not viewed as performing an economically useful role, are characterized as 'scroungers', manipulative, and unwelcome intruders. Nor is racism confined to 'outsiders'. The oppression of indigenous

---

[1] Hall, 'New Ethnicities', in J. Donald and A. Rattansi (eds), *Race Culture and Difference* (1992) 254.

[2] Modood, 'Ethnic Diversity and Racial Disadvantage in Employment', in T. Blackstone, B. Parekh, and P. Sanders, *Race Relations in Britain* (1998) 53.

[3] R. Bhavnani, *Black Women in the Labour Market* (1994) ix.

minorities (and even majorities) also manifests as a noxious combination of economic imperatives and legitimating ideologies based on caricatures of inferiority and hate. Economic imperatives range from the deprivation of land and other sources of coveted wealth to marginalization on the grounds of lack of economic usefulness.

The characterization of race as a social construct also makes it clear that, as a target for racism, 'race' encompasses a bundle of personal and social attributes, including religion, culture, nationality, and ethnicity. The inextricable connection between the concept of race and structures of domination is particularly clear in the use of ethnicity as exclusively attached to minorities. The dominant group does not see itself as an ethnic group, but as the embodiment of universal values, which express Truth and Justice in an absolute sense. All other groups can therefore be described as different, where different means deviant and therefore justifies inferior treatment. However, as Young argues, difference is only a relative concept: 'whites' are as different from 'blacks' as 'blacks' are from 'whites'. Once the universality is taken out of the picture, there is no reason to treat any particular culture, colour, or religion as superior to any other.[4]

Because racism is based on a polarization of opposites: 'we' and 'they'; 'white' and 'black'; 'Self' and 'Other', it also has the effect of assuming that there is a uniform, undifferentiated 'Other'. This has several consequences. First, racism is insensitive to diversity between groups. Thus it is common to refer to 'ethnic minorities' as a homogeneous group, without noting the differences between those groups. For example, talk in Britain about ethnic minorities fails to capture the very real differences between people of Afro-Caribbean origin and those from India, which in turn differ from those of Pakistani origin. Secondly, the assumption of an undifferentiated 'Other' assumes that a group has a fixed essence, and that individuals can be wholly defined by their membership of their group. This in turn makes it easy to stereotype individuals, often linking their group identity to denigratory ascriptions. Thirdly, such essentialism creates a rigid and static view of culture, described from the outside, ignoring the dynamic evolution of culture and religion. In addition, while membership of a cultural or religious group is an important aspect of people's lives, many people belong to several different overlapping and intersecting groups. It is therefore more appropriate to speak, not of racism, but of multiple racisms.[5] Indeed, as Modood argues, it is no longer adequate to think that racism is based entirely on colour. Beside 'colour-racism', it has become clear that there is a developing set of 'cultural racisms', which 'use cultural difference to vilify or demand

---

[4] I. M. Young, *The Politics of Difference* (1990) 69.

[5] Bhavnani, *supra* n. 3; Modood, 'Ethnic Diversity and Disadvantage', in T. Modood *et al.*, *Ethnic Minorities in Britain* (1997) 353.

cultural assimilation from groups who also suffer colour racism'.[6] Modood identifies, in particular, anti-Muslim prejudice, a white reaction to the revival of Islamic self-confidence.

Part of the power of racism is its distortion of familiar vocabulary, making it difficult to formulate a language of opposition. Thus 'difference' has come to mean inequality and inequality is synonymous with inferiority, making it problematic to assert difference as positive and egalitarian. This is epitomized by the debate about the use of the word 'black'. Thus one response to racism has been to use the term 'black' specifically as a political construct, to stand for the subordination experienced in common by many different groups, and thereby both to create a sense of solidarity among oppressed groups and to reverse the negative ascriptions of blackness.[7] However, there are now many who argue that despite the self-conscious use of 'black' as a political construct, it falls into the trap of assuming a commonality of experience which obscures reality. In particular, many South Asian groups do not identify themselves as 'black' even in the political sense of the term. Similarly, the attempt to justify blatantly inferior treatment on the grounds that it was 'separate but equal' has made it difficult to assert separateness as a constructive assertion of difference, and to disentangle equality from 'sameness'. This is clearly evidenced in the US cases on segregation of schools. The famous case of *Brown v Board of Education*[8] stood for a crucial and belated recognition that the notion of 'separate but equal' was no more than a pretext for an ideology which used segregation to maintain inferiority both stigmatically and materially. But the terminological equation of segregation with inequality made it seem that equality meant integration, and integration carried with it assimilation. With hindsight, there are many who now criticize *Brown* as based on an assumption of a 'race blind' or 'colour blind' State which in effect was blind to valuable black culture and history; and elevated 'white' culture by assuming it to be universal and neutral.[9] As against Earl Warren's resonant assertion in *Brown* that 'separate educational facilities are inherently unequal',[10] we have Clarence Thomas's complaint: 'It never ceases to amaze me that the courts are so willing to assume that anything that is predominantly black must be inferior. . . . Because of their distinctive histories and traditions, black schools can function as the centre and symbol of black communities and provide examples of independent black leadership, success and achievement.'[11]

An equally problematic consequence of the racist distortion of language has been the equation of group membership with negative stereotyping. This has forced opponents of racism into an unhealthy individualism. Although it has

---

[6] Modood, *supra* n. 5, at 353.   [7] See Bhavnani, *supra* n. 3, at 4–5.

[8] 347 US 483 (1954).

[9] Friedman, 'Brown in Context', in A. Sarat (ed.), *Race, Law and Culture* (1997) 64.

[10] *Brown v Board of Education* 347 US 483 (1954), at 495.

[11] Cited in Sarat, *supra* n. 9, at 3.

been crucial to extract the individual from such stereotypes and insist on individuals being treated on the basis of their real personal qualities, this has been permitted to obliterate the positive, enriching aspect of group membership.

Racism can thus be seen to operate along at least three axes: first, that of denigratory stereotyping, hatred, and violence; secondly, that of a cycle of disadvantage; and thirdly, the negation and even obliteration of culture, religion, or language. Policies to combat racism need to address all three, and to do so in a manner which is specific to the political context and the group in question. Authors have highlighted different types of policy,[12] of which four can be described here.[13] The first is exclusion. This most usually takes the form of immigration controls, which frequently impact most heavily on people from the Third World. Ironically, strict immigration control is often justified as the necessary complement to 'good race relations at home'. Race discrimination legislation in Britain was coincident with the imposition of stricter immigration control, and it may be no accident that the power to legislate against race discrimination at EC level came soon after the agreed imposition of immigration controls around 'Fortress Europe'. The second policy is that of assimilation, a requirement that, as a condition of equal treatment, an individual should conform to the social, cultural, and language structures of the dominant group. This policy is frequently formulated as one of strict 'equality'. But it rests on two problematic assumptions: first, that the dominant culture is not just one of many cultures, but represents universality, truth, and justice; and secondly, that there is no positive value in the culture of the subordinate group. A third, helpfully described by Parekh as a bifurcated approach or partial assimilation, tolerates diversity in the private sphere, but expects conformity or assimilation in respect of the public sphere. This means that assimilation remains a condition of equal participation in political institutions or other aspects of public life.[14] The fourth policy, variously described as pluralism or relational or positive difference, rejects the equation of difference with exclusion or inferiority. Instead, it asserts the positivity of group difference[15] and insists that political and social structures be changed to accommodate and celebrate diversity.[16] But does not this last strategy fall into the trap of essentializing difference? Young addresses this issue directly by arguing that a relational understanding of difference does not entail the presumption of a group 'essence' because it no longer implies that groups are mutually exclusive.

---

[12] See Parekh in *Race Relations in Britain, supra* n. 2; Modood in *Ethnic Minorities in Britain, supra* n. 5.

[13] It should be noted that these are by no means mutually exclusive: indeed they are found in different combinations in many jurisdictions.

[14] Parekh, in *Race Relations in Britain, supra* n. 2, at 18–19.

[15] Young, *supra* n. 4, at 166.

[16] Parekh, in *Race Relations in Britain, supra* n. 2, at 18–19.

To say that there are differences among groups does not imply that there are not overlapping experiences, or that two groups have nothing in common. The assumption that real differences in affinity, culture, or privilege imply oppositional categorization must be challenged. Different groups are always similar in some respects, and always potentially share some attributes, experiences and goals.[17]

II. CONCEPTIONS OF EQUALITY: STRENGTHS AND LIMITATIONS

(i) Historical Background[18]

Equality as an ideal is a relatively modern notion. Classical philosophers regarded order and hierarchy as synonymous with justice. According to Aristotle: 'There is a principle of rule and subordination in nature at large.'[19] This entailed the rightful subordination of many groups to the ruling class of free male citizens. Similarly, feudalism was based on strong notions of hierarchy, according to which each person's destiny was dictated by his or her position in the pre-ordained hierarchy. It was not until the dissolution of feudalism and the advent of mercantile capitalism that notions of individual equality came to the fore. This manifested itself in two ways: economically in pursuit of trade, and politically in the form of a challenge to the supreme authority of the monarch. The liberal ideology which justified the emerging capitalist order was founded on three key concepts: individualism, autonomy, and equality before the law. In the memorable words of Locke: 'Men [are] by Nature all free, equal and independent.'[20]

A closer look at the notion of equality enshrined in early liberalism reveals, however, its paradoxically selective nature. The right to equality was preserved for those designated as right-holders: by deftly excluding women, slaves, and the unpropertied classes from the definition of 'individuals' worthy to be rights-bearers, liberal thinkers were able to justify continued domination. This in turn was legitimated by the argument that only by reason of his rationality could man be a right-bearer. Women, slaves, and others were by definition deemed to be irrational, and therefore excluded from the equality right. Thus the newly ascendant equality principle coexisted with continued and unchallenged relations of domination. Slavery was not outlawed; colonialism flourished and women were denied basic rights such as the franchise, property ownership, and rights over their own children.[21] Thus despite his lofty proclamation that all are equal,

---

[17] Young, *supra* n. 4, at 171.
[18] See generally S. Fredman, *Women and the Law* (1997) ch. 1.
[19] Aristotle, *Politics* (1946) 11.
[20] Locke, *Two Treatises of Government* (P. Laslett (ed.), 1988), 'The Second Treatise', para. 95.
[21] See further Fredman, *supra* n. 18, at chs 1 and 2.

Locke had no trouble describing the family in terms of 'A Master . . . with all these subordinate Relations of Wife, Children, Servants and Slaves.'[22] The equality principle was in any event closely bound up with the dominant ideology of freedom of contract: an emerging market economy required a law of contract based on individuals who were equal only as abstract parties to a contract without regard to realities of bargaining power.

The limitations of the particular conception of equality attached to early liberalism could not prevent the ideal of equality from developing its own momentum. The acceptance of freedom and equality for all individuals gave feminists and other disadvantaged groups the necessary vocabulary to argue for the emancipation of all. It was as a focus for political activism, rather than as a legal concept, that equality began to emerge as a real force for combating sex discrimination and racism. The prohibition on slavery was the first momentous step in this direction; and the real (if painfully slow) expansion of the right to a political voice to include working classes and women continued in this direction. Genocide, anti-Semitism, colonialism, and racist violence forced equality away from its contractual basis into the domain of human rights.

It is against this background that we can begin to dissect the meaning of the concept of equality in the context of racism. To what extent has equality remained a handmaiden of the market, and to what extent does it have genuine transformative potential? It is striking that despite the widespread adherence to the ideal of equality, there is so little agreement on its meaning and aims. Notions of formal equality have now been complemented by more wide-ranging notions of equality of opportunity and equality of results. These in turn skate over the ultimate aims of equality. Possibilities include the redistributive role of alleviating disadvantage, the liberal goal of treating all with equal concern and respect, the neo-liberal goal of market or contractual equality, and the political goal of access to decision-making processes. The earlier discussion of racism has shown that at least three functions are required of equality if it is to begin to combat racism: first, a means of redressing racist stigma, stereotyping, humiliation, and violence; secondly, the redistributive aim of breaking the cycle of disadvantage associated with groups defined by race or ethnicity; and thirdly, the positive affirmation and accommodation of difference as a part of the right to equal concern and respect. In the rest of this section, I consider more closely different notions of equality, considering first formal equality or equality as consistency, and then turning to different types of substantive equality, including equality of opportunity and equality of results.

---

[22] Locke, *supra* n. 20, at 86.

(ii) Notions of Equality

(a) Formal Equality or Equality as Consistency

A basic notion of justice is that likes should be treated alike. Of course, however, this requires an initial judgement as to when two individuals are relevantly alike. One of the biggest leaps in twentieth-century struggles for equality has been the recognition that characteristics based on race, sex, religion, colour, or ethnic origin should not in themselves constitute relevant differences justifying inferior treatment. It was only once the concept of an individual right-bearer could be defined to include those previously excluded that equality could become a meaningful concept. Thus the notion of equality as consistency has played an enormously valuable role in tackling formal, exclusionary rules. Equality as consistency has also been developed into a more general anti-discrimination provision, prohibiting private individuals from discriminating on grounds of race. This allows equality as consistency to make some progress in addressing racial prejudice.

However, a closer look at equality as consistency shows that it is inherently limited. As a start, it has not eradicated all exclusionary rules. Immigration controls remain a central source of race discrimination; yet it is generally accepted that a state has the right to exclude from citizenship anyone who it wishes (provided this does not involve stripping existing citizens of their right to a domicile). This allows the current wave of racism directed against asylum seekers to go unchecked. Measures by various states to restrict immigration have not been open to challenge despite the fact that their primary effect is on black or other minority aspirant entrants.

Even within its scope of operation, equality as consistency is limited. Five main problematic aspects of equality as consistency will be dealt with here. First, equality as consistency is based on an assumption of conformity to a given norm, and therefore of assimilation. Parekh describes a policy of assimilation as one which assumes that a polity cannot be stable and cohesive unless all its members share a common national culture:

The choice before the minorities is simple. If they wish to become part of and be treated like the rest of the community, they should think and live like the latter; if instead they insist on retaining their separate cultures, they should not complain if they are treated differently.[23]

A closer look at the concept of formal equality, or equality as consistency, shows that in many respects, its main impact is to further such a policy. The requirement that likes should be treated alike means that in order to qualify for equal treatment, the claimant must be considered to be 'like' the comparator.

---

[23] Parekh, 'Integrating Minorities', in *Race Relations in Britain, supra* n. 2, at 2.

And if she conforms to this requirement, she may expect only 'like' treatment. In making the first judgement, namely that two individuals are relevantly alike, the law requires us to disregard the race or sex of the parties. Yet in practice only the complainant's race must be disregarded: while her blackness should not count, her comparator's whiteness remains unchallenged. This is not immediately visible because the powerful belief that individuals can be considered in the abstract, apart from their colour, religion, ethnic origins and gender, is unrealistic. In fact, the 'abstract' individual is white, male, Christian, and part of the dominant culture. Thus, the right to equal treatment is reserved to those who conform: who wear Western dress, observe Christian religious holidays and days of rest; speak the dominant language; share common family structures and share common values.

The second problematic aspect of equality as consistency is its treatment of difference. Only 'likes' qualify for equal treatment; there are no constraints on the ways in which those who are different may be treated. This is based on a conceptual framework, derived from Aristotle, which sees the world in terms of moral dichotomies: reason and emotion, soul and body, good and bad, equal and different. In this schema, difference is characterized as the negative partner, legitimating detrimental treatment of those who are different. Nor is there any requirement that people be treated appropriately according to their difference. This contrasts with Young's deliberate reconceptualizing of difference as positive. Indeed, she goes further, and fragments the dichotomy itself, demonstrating that individuals can be members of several groups, and therefore, depending on the focus of comparison, can be both different and equal.

Thirdly, equality as consistency is intensely individualist. Of course, the major contribution of equality has been its insistence that an individual be treated according to her own qualities or merits, and not on the basis of negative stereotypes attributed to her because of her race or sex. However, in rejecting the negative effects of taking group-based characteristics into account, the principle of equality has assumed that all aspects of group membership should be disregarded. Yet, as we have seen, cultural, religious, and ethnic group membership is an important aspect of an individual's identity. Indeed, to attempt to abstract the individual from that context is not to create a universal individual, but simply to clothe him or her with the attributes of the dominant culture, religion or ethnicity. Individualism has also had important limiting effects on the remedial structures created to achieve equality. Most importantly, the correlative of treating a person only on the basis of her 'merit' is the principle that an individual should only be liable for damage for which he or she is responsible. This in turn means that only a respondent who can be proved to have treated the complainant less favourably on grounds of her race can be held liable for compensation. Yet racism extends far beyond individual acts of racist prejudice. It is frequently embedded in the structure of society, and cannot be attributed clearly to any one person. Also significantly limiting has been the fact, found in most legal systems, that it is the individual who is responsible for enforcing the right to equality. This places inordinate burdens on the resources of individual complainants.

The fourth and related problem of equality as consistency is that it creates only negative obligations: i.e. the State, or the individual, is only required to refrain from discriminating on grounds of race. No positive obligations of accommodation are imposed. Yet, one of the main responses to a breach of equality should be a duty to adjust the structures in order to accommodate diversity. This point is related to the other central dichotomy in this area of the law, namely the public private divide. There remains an intense ambivalence within equal rights guarantees as to the extent to which both the public and the private are bound. Constitutional guarantees tend to bind only the public, leaving private discrimination untouched; whereas many statutory guarantees bind private actors too. In the UK, there has until now been a paradoxical situation in which private actors, but not the state are bound. Cutting across this divide is the question of scope: some equality legislation covers only certain aspects of discrimination, such as employment, education, and services.

The final problematic aspect of equality as consistency is the fact that it is no more than a relative concept: it is satisfied so long as likes are treated alike. Once two individuals are found to be relevantly alike, it demands no more than like treatment. Yet the essence of the problem may well be the refusal to recognize the different needs and desires of ethnic, religious, or cultural groups. Moreover, equality as a relative concept has no substantive underpinning. As long as two similarly situated individuals are treated equally, it is irrelevant whether they are treated equally badly or equally well.

It can be seen from the above that formal equality or equality as consistency may play a useful role in prohibiting blatant prejudice. However, at the very least, it must be underpinned by substantive values. Outlawing racist prejudice is a material manifestation of the underlying values of dignity and autonomy. Several constitutions include in a preamble or interpretive section a statement of values to be furthered by the equality guarantee, and most include dignity and autonomy.[24] Such a commitment to the underlying values of human dignity and autonomy prevents equality from operating merely as a relative measure: treatment which is equally bad would not further the basic aim of enhancing the dignity, autonomy, and worth of individuals to improve the position of relatively disadvantaged groups.

(b) Beyond Formal Equality

While formal equality or equality of treatment has a role to play, particularly in eradicating personal prejudice, it is clear from the above that it needs to be

---

[24] Canadian Charter, SA Constitution.

allied to a more substantive approach. Attempts to overcome the limitations of formal equality can be structured in four different, but overlapping ways: equality of results; equality of opportunity; specification of broad values and principles informing discrimination decisions; and a linking of equality to specific substantive rights. Each will be dealt with in turn.

(c) Equality of Results

On this view, the equality principle goes beyond a demand for consistent treatment of likes, and requires instead that the result be equal. Equality of results can be used in three different ways. The first turns the spotlight on the impact on the individual of apparently equal treatment. The second focuses not on the results to the individual, but to the group. In a non-discriminatory environment, any particular body, be it a workforce, an educational establishment or a decision-making body, would include a fair spread of members of different sexes, races, and religions. Therefore, the absence of one group, or its concentration in less lucrative or important areas, is taken as a sign that discrimination is probably taking place. This use of results is therefore diagnostic of discrimination; without specifying an ultimate aim. The third meaning of 'equality of results' would be the more obviously redistributive aim of requiring an equal outcome, for example, equal representation of men and women in a particular grade. Indeed, several jurisdictions have introduced legislation with the explicit aim of increasing the representation of minorities or women in employment or public office.[25] Often, however, it is not equality but proportionality, fairness, or balance which is required. Thus the European Commission is promoting balanced participation of men and women in decision-making, using a figure of 30 per cent as one reflecting a critical mass. Most controversial are duties which require public authorities to achieve their targets by giving preferential treatment to the under-represented group. Such policies are now popular in Germany, where statutes covering local or provincial authorities specify that, if there is an under-representation of women in a particular grade or occupation, preference should be given to women provided they are equally qualified.

Equality of results makes strategic sense, since results are relatively easily quantifiable. However, it has proved highly controversial in principle, largely because it appears to contradict the very principle of equality it purports to advance. This is because preferential treatment of a black person or a woman appears to discriminate against white people or men on grounds of their race or sex. I have dealt with this controversy in detail elsewhere and will not pursue it here.[26]

[25] FETO Art. 4(1); Fair Employment Act 1989; Canadian Employment Equity Act s. 2.
[26] Fredman, 'Reversing Discrimination' 113 *Law Quarterly Review* (1997) 575; Fredman, 'Affirmative Action and the Court of Justice', in J. Shaw (ed.), *Social Law and Policy* (2000) 171.

Even apart from preferential treatment, equality of results is problematic in that its underlying redistributive aims may only be partially achieved. This is because monitoring of results does not necessitate any fundamental re-examination of the structures that perpetuate discrimination. A change in the colour or gender composition of a grade or sector, while to some extent positive, might reflect only an increasingly successful assimilationist policy. Thus women who achieve these positions might have done so by conforming to 'male' working patterns, contracting their child-care obligations to other women, who remain as underpaid and undervalued as ever. Members of ethnic minorities who achieve these positions may similarly be those who had assimilated, whether voluntarily or because of absence of available options, in terms of dress, religious observance, or language. Similarly, the increase in numbers of women or black people doing certain types of jobs might coincide with a decrease in the pay or status of the job in question. Such a pattern has been clearly demonstrated in catering, where women have increased their share of management jobs dramatically. Yet on closer inspection, it is found that the newly feminized managerial positions are relatively low paid (sometimes even less than the national average pay) and to be associated with a correspondingly diminished status. Thus quantifiable change might only partially reflect qualitative change. Most importantly, there is a danger that a focus on equality of results pays too little attention to the equally important notion of equality of diversity; or the duty to accommodate diversity by adapting existing structures.

(d) Equality of Opportunity

An equal opportunities approach steers a middle ground between equal treatment and equality of results. This approach recognizes that discrimination itself can make it inordinately difficult for members of particular groups to fulfil the threshold condition of similarity required to trigger the right to like treatment. Using the graphic metaphor of competitors in a race, it asserts that true equality cannot be achieved if individuals begin the race from different starting points. An equal opportunities approach therefore aims to equalize the starting point, accepting that this might necessitate special measures for the disadvantaged group. On the other hand, it is argued, a results-oriented approach goes too far in subordinating the right to individual treatment to a utilitarian emphasis on outcomes. Once individuals enjoy equality of opportunity, on this view, the problem of institutional discrimination has been overcome, and fairness demands that they be treated on the basis of their individual qualities, without regard to sex or race. This model therefore specifically rejects policies which aim to correct imbalances in the workforce by quotas or targets whose aim is one of equality of outcome.

However, the metaphor of equal starting points is deceptively simple. What measures are required to ensure that individuals are genuinely able to compete equally? Williams distinguishes between a procedural and a substantive sense of equal opportunities. On a procedural view, equality of opportunity requires the removal of obstacles to the advancement of women or minorities, but does not guarantee that this will lead to greater substantive fairness in the result.[27] For example, the abolition of word-of-mouth recruitment or of non-job-related selection criteria remove procedural obstacles and so open up more opportunities, but do not guarantee that more women or minorities will in fact be in a position to take advantage of those opportunities. Those who lack the requisite qualifications as a result of past discrimination will still be unable to meet job-related criteria; women with child-care responsibilities will not find it easier to take on paid work. In the famous words of US President Lyndon Johnson, it is 'not enough to open the gates of opportunity. All our citizens must have the ability to walk through those gates.'[28]

A substantive sense of equality of opportunity, by contrast, requires measures to be taken to ensure that persons from all sections of society have a genuinely equal chance of satisfying the criteria for access to a particular social good.[29] This requires positive measures such as education and training, and family friendly measures. It also requires a reconsideration of existing criteria of merit. As Hepple argues, one is not supplying genuine equality of opportunity if one applies an unchallenged criterion of merit to people who have been deprived of the opportunity to acquire 'merit'.[30]

(e) A Value Driven Approach

Legislatures and courts in several jurisdictions have attempted to articulate broad values or principles informing the equality principle. Three intertwined themes can be discerned. The first, most clearly articulated by the Canadian Supreme Court, stresses the primacy of individual dignity and worth. Thus, according to a recent case, the fundamental values enshrined in the Canadian Charter's equality guarantee are the 'protection and enhancement of human dignity, the promotion of equal opportunity and the development of human potential based upon individual ability'. The purpose of the provision is declared to be 'to prevent the violation of human dignity and freedom through the imposition of limitations, disadvantages or burdens, through the stereotypical application of presumed group characteristics, rather than on the basis of merit, capacity or circumstance'.[31] A second and more outcome-oriented

[27] Williams, 'The Idea of Equality', in P. Laslett and W. G. Runciman, *Philosophy, Politics and Society* (2nd series, 1965) 110 and see Waldron in S. Guest and A. Milne (eds), *Equality and Discrimination* (1985) 97.

[28] Lyndon P. Johnson, Address at Howard University (4 June 1965), cited in Thernstrom, 'Voting Rights, Another Affirmative Action Mess', 43 *UCLA Law Review* (1996) 2031 n. 22.

[29] Williams *supra* n. 27, at 125–6.

[30] Hepple, 'Discrimination and Equality of Opportunity—Northern Irish lessons', 10 *Oxford Journal of Legal Studies* (1990) 408, at 411.

[31] *Miron v Trudel,* 489.

approach is to formulate the aims of equality in terms of participation in society, such as employment, education, or positions of power. Thus the Northern Ireland legislation has as its central and explicit aim the fair participation of Catholics and Protestants in employment, where fair participation has been interpreted as proportional representation. A third aim is openly redistributive, stressing that the aim of equality is to redress historical disadvantage. Thus in the Green Paper containing policy proposals for a new employment equity statute in South Africa, it is stated that the aim of the statute is to redress disadvantages emanating from past racial policies. Some of the Canadian judges have also articulated the aims of the equality guarantee in the Canadian Charter as the protection of groups who suffer social, political, and legal disadvantage.

There are clearly potential conflicts between these values. The emphasis on dignity and worth, while positive in its stress on the value of the individual, may lead to highly inegalitarian results from the perspective of distributive justice. For individuals who can achieve well once the burdens of stereotyping and stigma are removed, this notion holds great promise. But for those whose capacities have themselves been limited by the effects of cumulative disadvantage, an equality conditional on merit might well be a false promise. On the other hand, an emphasis on remedying disadvantage, without bringing in notions of stereotyping and stigma, may well point to policies concerning general welfare, such as social security law, rather than specific anti-discrimination laws. At the same time, it is quite possible, as in the Canadian example, to synthesize several values, achieving a suitable balance.

(f) Equality as Auxiliary to Substantive Rights

One way of overcoming the emptiness of a notion of equality as consistency is to require the consistent application of fundamental human rights. Article 14 of the ECHR epitomizes this approach. Instead of an independent right to equality, Article 14 provides only that the rights contained in the Convention must be applied without discrimination on specified grounds. This makes it impossible to use equality to justify levelling down or an equal deprivation of rights. However, as the case-law of the ECHR shows, it often means that equality has a minimal role to play. This approach is also limited in that it applies only to the rights specified in the Convention. In recognition of this last point, a new protocol extending the equality guarantee to all rights 'set forth by law' as well as to all actions of public bodies has now been opened for signature.[32]

---

[32] Protocol No. 12.

III. CONCEPTS OF EQUALITY IN LEGAL PROVISIONS

(i) Direct Discrimination or Disparate Treatment

The most common formulation of equality at both domestic and international level is that of formal equality or equality as consistency. The principle that 'likes should be treated alike' is translated in legal terms into the requirement that no-one be treated less favourably on grounds of his or her race or sex than a person of the opposite group. Such provisions have played an important role, both educative and in respect of individuals. However, the limitations outlined above have also been evident. Most problematic, in the context of race, has been the assimilationist tendency.[33]

(ii) Indirect Discrimination or Disparate Impact

It has been seen above that equality as consistency, while able to redress the first of the three aims of equality, namely racial prejudice and stereotyping, does little to address the redistributive and restructuring goals of equality. The most important attempt to address these concerns was the development of the concept of indirect discrimination. This principle was first developed by the US courts, to give legal recognition to the realization that apparently equal treatment could entrench disadvantage. This was because discrimination against black people consisted of more than racist prejudice, and extended to structural and institutional factors which perpetuated past disadvantage. The opportunity to formulate and apply the principle arose in the well-known case of *Griggs v Duke Power*,[34] in which an employer had replaced its express policy of excluding black applicants with a requirement that job-seekers have high school qualifications or pass a literacy test. This was despite the fact that the jobs in question were largely unskilled and such qualifications were therefore not strictly necessary for successful performance. The ongoing effects of discrimination against blacks in the education system meant that a disproportionate number failed to achieve the required standard, and the workforce remained almost entirely white. Thus, although blacks and whites were treated equally in that they were subjected to the same test, the result was to entrench disadvantage. In recognition of this pattern, the US Supreme Court held that equal treatment could be discriminatory if the result was that fewer blacks could comply, unless the requirement was necessary for the proper execution of the job in hand.

[33] See *Ahmad v ILEA* Application No. 8160/78 [1981] 4 EHRR 127 (European Commission), discussed below.
[34] 401 US 424 (1971).

This concept rapidly made its way across the Atlantic, first to Britain, then to Europe. Both the SDA 1975 and the Race Relations Act of 1976[35] include statutory formulations of the principle of indirect discrimination. The ECJ in turn adapted the principle to EC sex discrimination law, a development which was crystallized in legislation in the form of the Burden of Proof Directive.[36] This contains probably the most helpful formulation of indirect discrimination, defining it as

an apparently neutral provision, criterion or practice [which] disadvantages a substantially higher proportion of the members of one sex unless that provision, criterion or practice is appropriate and necessary and can be justified by objective factors unrelated to sex.[37]

A modified version has been used in the budding EC race discrimination law.

The concept of indirect discrimination functions as a valuable complement to formal equality, or equality as consistency. While direct discrimination's chief impact is prejudice and racial stereotyping, indirect discrimination makes some progress in the accommodation of diversity. It does this by casting the spotlight on apparently neutral practices and criteria, revealing in fact that they favour the dominant culture or religion. For example, in the landmark case of *Mandla v Lee*,[38] the court held that a school had unlawfully discriminated against a Sikh boy by excluding him from the school when he refused to take off his turban in order to comply with the school rule that boys come bare-headed to school. An apparently neutral rule, applying equally to all pupils, was recognized as in practice requiring conformity to a Christian way of dressing and therefore creating unacceptable barriers to those of different cultures or religions.

Indirect discrimination has, however, been disappointing in its impact. There are four main reasons for this. The first arises from its uneasy combination of group and individual concerns. We have seen that the chief value of indirect discrimination is its recognition that it is not the equality of treatment meted out to the individual that matters but the fact that it has a disparate impact on an individual because of his or her membership of the disadvantaged group. By removing barriers, indirect discrimination helps reduce the cost of retaining group identity. However, the extent to which the group dimension is taken into account remains clumsy. Although indirect discrimination has moved beyond the straightforward 'like for like' comparison, it still requires a comparison to demonstrate that the impact on members of one group is more serious than that on members of the dominant group. Yet it has proved far from straightforward to agree a methodology for establishing such disparate impact. The ultimate figures might differ substantially depending on whether the number of blacks or

---

[35] RRA 1976, s. 1(1)(b) and see also SDA 1975, s. 1(1)(b).
[36] Burden of Proof Directive 97/80/EC.   [37] Ibid., Article 2(2).
[38] [1983] IRLR 209 HL.

women who can comply is taken as a proportion of the appropriately qualified workforce, the number in the particular establishment, or the number in the workforce as a whole. Once this formula has been settled in any particular case, further controversy arises as to whether the difference is sufficient to warrant a finding of indirect discrimination. Is statistical significance enough, or should the difference be 'considerable' in some intuitive sense? These difficulties are strikingly illustrated in the US Supreme Court case of *Wards Cove Packing v Atonio*.[39] This concerned a workforce which was almost wholly segregated, with Filipino and other ethnic minority workers doing all the unskilled work, and whites doing the skilled work. The lower court held that this level of segregation on its own was evidence of discrimination. But the US Supreme Court disagreed, holding that it was not appropriate to compare the number of unskilled Filipinos with the number of whites. Instead, only Filipinos with the requisite qualifications needed to be considered. This of course ignores the contribution of past discrimination in preventing Filipinos from obtaining the necessary skills. In this way, the absence of relevantly qualified Filipinos defeated the claim, rather than giving rise to any redistributive obligations.

The second problematic area concerns the role of a justification defence. Indirect discrimination only requires barriers to be dismantled if they cannot be justified on gender or race neutral grounds. Yet many such exclusionary barriers can indeed be so justified. Criteria which are job related remain legitimate—yet disadvantaged groups, by virtue of their disadvantage, might find it impossible to comply. This is particularly problematic in situations in which qualifications are necessary for a job, but the absence of qualifications is due to past or ongoing discrimination. Thus in a recent British case, training places for management jobs were only available to applicants with previous work experience in Britain. This made it impossible for those who had earlier faced prejudice in the labour market, or who were recent arrivals, to gain a place.[40] This means that the ability of indirect discrimination to achieve its redistributive goals is limited.

The third problematic aspect of indirect discrimination is that a finding of indirect discrimination does not in itself trigger a duty to accommodate diversity or to ensure that applicants are equipped for a job or other benefit. In the above cases, no duty was imposed on the employer to find other means ensuring that relevant experience was available or of preventing the alleged risks. The absence of such positive duties also means that indirect discrimination is limited in its ability to achieve equality of opportunity.

Finally, the remedial structure remains wholly individualistic. It is the individual who must bring the complaint on the grounds that she has suffered damage. The respondent must be individually identified and proved to have

[39] 109 S. Ct. 2115 (1988).
[40] *Ojutiku v Manpower Services Commission* [1982] ICR 661.

been responsible for the damage. In addition, although in practice, a successful claim should lead to the removal of the discriminatory barrier, legally, the
only requirement is to compensate the individual victim.

(iii) Beyond Indirect Discrimination: Positive Duties

The recognition of the limits of both direct discrimination and indirect
discrimination has led law-makers to strike out in a new direction, namely
the imposition of positive duties to promote equality, rather than just the negative requirement to refrain from discriminating. Such a duty has taken diverse
forms, beginning in the US with the imposition of positive duties on government contractors to increase the representation of minorities and of women in
the workforce.[41] More recently, increasingly sophisticated duties have been
imposed both on public authorities and private employers to develop positive
plans to dismantle institutional racism and sexism. Such 'fourth generation'[42]
anti-discrimination provisions address some of the serious weaknesses in the
existing structure of equality legislation. Most importantly, this approach
moves beyond the fault-based model of existing discrimination law. As we have
seen, under existing direct discrimination provisions, only an individual who
can be shown to have treated the complainant less favourably on grounds of
her sex can be held to be legally liable; and then the remedy is usually simply
compensation of the individual victim. Even indirect discrimination requires
proof that an individual employer has imposed a practice or condition which
excludes a disproportionate number of women or blacks. At the root of the
positive duty, by contrast, is a recognition that societal discrimination extends
well beyond individual acts of racist prejudice. This has important implications for both the content of the duty and the identification of the duty-bearer.
The duty becomes that, not just of compensating identified victims, but of
restructuring institutions. Correspondingly, the duty-bearer is identified as the
body in the best position to perform this duty. Even though not responsible
for creating the problem in the first place, such duty-bearers become responsible for participating in its eradication. This reformulation of the basis of the
anti-discrimination law then has effects which ripple out through the whole
remedial structure. Instead of requiring proof of individual prejudice, or of
unjustifiable disparate impact as a result of a practice or condition, the positive
duty is triggered as a result of evidence of structural discrimination, including

----

[41] Executive Order 10925, introduced by President Kennedy in 1961. The current Order
11246, issued by President Johnson in 1964 and amended in 1967 to cover sex and religion,
covers about 300,000 federal contractors, employing about 40 per cent of the working population (see Hepple, Coussey, and Choudhury, *Report of the Independent Review of the
Enforcement of Anti-Discrimination Legislations* para. 3.23).
[42] Hepple, Coussey, and Choudhury, *supra* n. 41.

chronic under-representation in particular types of work or positions of power, inequitable access to the benefits of employment or State provision of services, or the imposition of inordinate costs on those who attempt to maintain religious or cultural preferences which conflict with those of the dominant group. The duty itself is not simply one of providing compensation for an individual victim. Instead, positive action is required to achieve change, whether by encouragement, accommodation, or structural change.

A particularly important dimension of fourth-generation equality laws is their potential to encourage participation by affected groups in the decision-making process itself. Because the duty is prospective, and can be fashioned to fit the problem at hand, it is not a static duty, but requires a continuing process of diagnosing the problem, working out possible responses, monitoring the effectiveness of strategies, and modifying those strategies as required. If participation is built in as a central aspect of such duties, not only is it likely that strategies will be more successful, but the very process of achieving equality becomes a democratic one. Participation rights are particularly important in the context of rights for religious, ethnic, and cultural minorities. It has been argued above that ethnicity should not be regarded as a static notion, but as one that is part of an ongoing dynamic interaction both between those who regard themselves as within the group and between the group and the dominant culture. Thus any attempt to encapsulate the content of minority rights without active participation of the groups in question will be patronizing, erroneous, and unlikely to succeed.

'Fourth generation' equality laws, based on a positive duty to promote equality, rather than simply to refrain from discriminating, are being actively developed in several jurisdictions. At EU level, a powerful boost was given to the effectiveness of sex equality legislation by the adoption of the policy of 'mainstreaming'. Mainstreaming means that equality is not just an add-on or after-thought to policy, but is one of the factors taken into account in every policy and executive decision.[43] 'The reactive and negative approach of anti-discrimination is replaced by pro-active, anticipatory and integrative methods.'[44] At domestic level, the UK race relations legislation included, as far back as 1976, a statutory duty on local authorities to

make appropriate arrangements with a view to securing their various functions are carried out with due regard to the need (*a*) to eliminate unlawful racial discrimination; and (*b*) to promote equality of opportunity and good relations, between persons of different racial groups.[45]

---

[43] Commission of the European Communities, *Incorporating Equal Opportunities for Women and Men into all Community Policies and Activities*, Communication from the Commission COM(96) final, Luxembourg; see generally T. Rees, *Mainstreaming Equality in the European Union* (1998).

[44] Hepple, Coussey, and Choudhury, *supra* n. 41, at para. 3.8.

[45] RRA 1976, s. 71.

However, the vagueness and individual nature of the duty, combined with judicial hostility,[46] made it largely ineffective. Far more focused is the legally binding duty in the Northern Ireland Act 1998, which places a duty on public authorities to have 'due regard to the need to promote equality of opportunity' in carrying out all their functions.[47] The Act goes beyond mere exhortation: each public authority is required to draw up an equality scheme which must state the authority's arrangements for consultation and assessment of the likely impact of policies on the promotion of equality of opportunity; for monitoring any adverse impact of such policies, for publishing results of its assessments, for training staff, and for ensuring public access to information and services. Such schemes must be approved by the Northern Ireland Equality Commission. Positive duties may also be imposed more specifically at local authority level. Thus the recently recreated Greater London Authority has a duty to promote equal opportunity which includes a duty to report annually on the steps it has taken in pursuance of that duty.[48] A similar duty will be imposed in Britain as a whole on all public bodies under the new Race Relations (Amendment) Act 2000.[49] Such duties include first, diagnosis of the problem; second, the promulgation of a targeted plan of action, which must include as an essential element the participation of relevant groups; and finally a mechanism for assessing effectiveness of the strategy. Compliance structures vary: mainstreaming at EC level is not binding but driven by political will; whereas the Northern Ireland Act includes close supervision by the Commission.

As well as general duties of this sort, several jurisdictions have placed specific duties, for example on employers, which are aimed at increasing the participation of under-represented groups and equalizing pay and access to benefits. Such positive duties were pioneered in the USA, where, since 1961, government contractors have been required not merely to abstain from unlawful discrimination but also to take positive measures to increase the representation of racial minorities in their workforces.[50] This requirement, which is estimated to apply to about 300,000 Federal contractors, employing about 40 per cent of the working population, has had a significantly more powerful influence on employers than individual complaint-led investigations. Indeed all the US employers interviewed in a recent study said that they would not have been able to sustain the significant increases in the representation of

[46] *Wheeler v Leicester.*
[47] Northern Ireland Act 1998, s. 75; and see McCrudden, 'The Equal Opportunity Duty in the Northern Ireland Act 1998: An Analysis', in *Equal Rights and Human Rights—Their Role in Peace Building* (Belfast, Committee on the Administration of Justice, 1999), at 11–23.
[48] Greater London Authority Act 1999, s. 33.
[49] See further Fredman, 'Equality: A New Generation?' *Industrial Law Journal* (2001) 145.
[50] Executive Order 10925 (1961). The current Order 11246 (issued in 1964) also covers sex and religion.

women and minorities which had taken place in their organizations without compulsory affirmative action requirements.[51] A similar strategy has been used more recently in Northern Ireland, where legislation introduced in 1989 imposed positive duties on employers to take measures to achieve fair participation in their workforces of Protestant and Roman Catholic employees.[52] Such duties include the duty to monitor the number of existing employees who belong to each Community; to undertake periodic reviews of employment practices; and, where fair participation is not evident, to engage in affirmative action (short of reverse discrimination) to improve the representation of the under-represented group. Enforcement powers are given to a commission, and include the sanction of denial of government contracts or financial assistance. Pioneering positive duties in the field of equal pay between men and women have also been put in place in the Canadian province of Ontario. The structure of the Ontario Pay Equity Act provides a neat contrast to earlier generations of anti-discrimination law. Instead of imposing a duty only in response to individual claims of discrimination, employers must take responsibility for discovering and remedying discrimination. This is a participatory process, incorporating trade unions in the process of drawing up an equity plan to remedy any perceived discrepancies. Compliance takes the form of supervisory powers in the hands of a statutory commission, whose main aim is not to penalize but to keep the process in motion.[53]

The proactive nature of positive duties changes the structure of equality law, but is not itself enough. Positive duties are only meaningful if they are targeted towards particular aims. It is therefore still important to focus on what we are trying to achieve by means of positive action. Which of the three aims outlined above, namely, removal of stigma, redistribution, or accommodation, is being targeted? And which principle of equality is being utilized: formal, equality of results, equality of opportunity or some other substantive value? Many positive duties are formulated in terms of improving the representation of minorities or women in a given sector. This appears to be furthering a redistributive aim, utilizing the principle of equality of results. As such, its limitations should not be ignored, particularly in that there may be no impetus to change underlying distributive structures. Positive duties to be truly effective must amalgamate both equality of opportunity and equality of results notions, requiring substantive improvements not just in the availability of opportunities but the ability to use them; and doing more than just changing the colour or gender make-up of existing structures, but also re-shaping them to accommodate diversity.

---

[51] Hepple, Coussey, and Choudhury, *supra* n. 41, at paras 3.23–3.24; 3.29.
[52] Fair Employment Act 1989, now contained in FETO 1998, Part VII.
[53] Ontario Pay Equity Act, and see A. McColgan, *Just Wages for Women* (1997).

IV. EQUALITY AS A HUMAN RIGHT

How does this analysis translate into human rights protection? In applying equality as a human right, the central challenge is to fashion a concept of equality which transcends the traditional equality–difference dichotomy in that it can encompass positive diversity while at the same time rejecting inferior treatment on racial, religious, or ethnic grounds. This challenge arises in at least three different ways. First, in deciding the reach of the equality concept, it is necessary to decide when a State is *entitled* to differentiate between racial, ethnic, or religious groups, either for overriding extraneous reasons, or deliberately to redress past discrimination and advance substantive equality. Secondly, when is the State *required* to differentiate between groups in order to advance a deeper notion of equality? This question arises in the context of apparently neutral rules which in fact impact on minority racial, ethnic, or religious groups. Thirdly, does there come a point when a State is required to override religious, ethnic, or cultural claims in favour of an apparently universal norm? Should health and safety factors trump manifestations of religious or ethnic, culture, for example in requiring Sikhs to remove their turbans to wear crash helmets on motor cycles? Similarly, it may be arguable that women's rights derive not from their specific culture but from overriding and universal norms, which should trump cultural expressions. Through each of these three basic questions runs the dilemma underlying all human rights adjudication, namely the need to find a democratic rationale for the imposition on democratic legislatures of certain overriding claims, whether they be those of minorities without a full voice in the democratic process, or of women. The correlative democratic argument concerns the extent to which affected individuals should be permitted or encouraged to participate in basic decision-making. Finally, it is questionable whether traditional human rights adjudication is capable of generating the rich concept of equality needed fully to address racism. The individualized nature of human rights adjudication makes it difficult for it to formulate rights which take a group dimension into account. More fundamentally, is it possible for a human rights structure to accommodate fourth generation discrimination law, based primarily on positive duties? The rest of this chapter will address these complex questions.

(i) When is a State Entitled to Differentiate Between Groups?

In most jurisdictions, it has been recognized that not all distinctions are discriminatory. There are many situations in which it is appropriate for a State to differentiate between groups. The challenge then is to distinguish between invidious discrimination and appropriate differentiation. To do this, most jurisdictions have evolved a proportionality test, which requires a government or State to show first that its aims are legitimate and second that the differentiation is appropriate to achieve that aim. A great deal then hangs on the standard of scrutiny which courts are willing to apply to such differentiations, both in deciding which aims are legitimate, and in determining the closeness of the 'fit' between means and ends. This approach is well illustrated by the case-law of the European Court of Human Rights, which has held that a difference of treatment is only discriminatory if it has 'no objective and reasonable justification', that is, it does not pursue a legitimate aim, or if there is not a 'reasonable relationship of proportionality between the means employed and the aim sought to be realised'.[54] In applying this standard, the Court has, notably, begun to create a hierarchy of values. Since the advancement of equality between men and women is said to be a major goal in the member states of the Council of Europe, 'very weighty reasons' would have to be advanced before a difference of treatment on grounds of sex could be regarded as compatible with the Convention.[55] It is not, however, clear whether similarly weighty reasons would be required in the case of differentiation on grounds of race, religion, or ethnicity. This hierarchy is reminiscent of the three-tier set of standards developed by the US Supreme Court albeit with a different order of priority. The most intense or 'strict scrutiny' under US jurisprudence is reserved for racial classifications and requires not just a legitimate State concern, but a compelling interest, as well as proof that the means are 'narrowly tailored' to achieve that end. The least intense standard, by contrast, requires no more than a rational relationship between the means and a legitimate State interest; a standard which applies to most differentiations. The standard applicable to sex, and probably to sexual orientation, religion, and disability, falls somewhere in between.

A particularly interesting approach is that found in the new South African constitution, which explicitly includes the possibility of fair discrimination in the first stage of the inquiry, but alleviates the burden on the complainant by including a presumption that discrimination is unfair unless proved fair. Even unfair discrimination can be justified if the limitation is reasonable and justifiable in an open and democratic society based on human dignity, equality, and freedom, taking into account all relevant factors including the nature of the right; the importance of the purpose of the limitation; the relation between the limitation and its purpose; and less restrictive means to achieve the purpose.[56] However, even the most sophisticated tests depend on judicial application, and it is not always the case that a sufficiently nuanced test has been developed.

---

[54] *Belgian Linguistic Case* 1 EHRR 252 at para. 10; *Marckx v Belgium* 2 EHRR 330 at para. 33; *Abdulaziz v UK* (1985) 7 EHRR 491 at para. 72.

[55] *Abdulaziz, supra* n. 54, at para. 78.   [56] s. 36(1).

'Special' treatment in the form of reverse discrimination to redress the effects of past discrimination is a particularly complex issue, a detailed discussion of which is beyond the scope of this chapter.[57] For these purposes, however, it is worth noting briefly that preferential treatment only appears to breach the concept of equality if a symmetrical approach to equality is sustained. On a symmetrical view, it is equally invidious to discriminate against a white person on grounds of race, as against a black person, even though the measure was intended to alleviate the effects of past discrimination against black people. A view of equality which does not see equality as an end in itself, abstracted from the background of social, political, and economic conditions, but a means to alleviate disadvantage and stigma would make it possible to see preferential treatment as advancing the wider aim of substantive equality.

(ii) When is a State Required to Differentiate Between Groups?

As well as having to decide when explicit differentiation is permitted, courts at national and European level have had to grapple with the question of whether rules which are neutral on their face in fact infringe the equality guarantee. This in turn requires a determination of whether apparent neutrality is really an endorsement of the norms of the dominant group in a particular society. A closer look at the case-law in various jurisdictions reveals that surprisingly little progress has been made in fashioning a concept of equality that can penetrate apparently neutral rules which in fact entrench the dominant norm. This is particularly apparent when the court takes the view that an attempt by a public authority to further the 'public interest' will be obstructed by a more penetrating notion of equality.

Thus the ECHR has been reluctant to hold that immigration laws are discriminatory simply because their impact falls most heavily on would-be immigrants from the New Commonwealth and Pakistan, and therefore affected fewer white people than others. The Court has held that because the rules were applicable to all intending immigrants, irrespective of their race or origin, and because they furthered a legitimate State aim, namely the protection of the labour market at a time of high unemployment, there could be no finding of discrimination on grounds of race.[58] Similarly, despite having itself evolved the principle of indirect discrimination, the US Supreme Court itself moved quickly to limit its reach. In a resurgence of the notion of individual fault and responsibility, the Court held in *Washington v Davis*[59] that only intentional discrimination could violate the equality clause in the Fourteenth Amendment. Disparate impact or indirect discrimination applied

---

[57] See further Fredman, *supra* n. 18, at ch. 9.   [58] *Abdulaziz, supra* n. 54.
[59] 426 US 229 (1976).

only to statutory claims under Title VII of the Civil Rights Act and not to the constitutional equality guarantee contained in the Fourteenth Amendment.

In the context of religious and ethnic identity, formally neutral rules carry a particularly high risk of disguising an endorsement of the dominant norm, particularly where the state asserts that the rule furthers the 'public interest'. A salient example is that of gypsies or Roma people, who have found themselves in breach of planning laws which run counter to the fundamentals of their nomadic lifestyle. The European Court of Human Rights has shown itself to be especially blind to the equation of public interest with that of the dominant groups in society. Thus the eviction of a gypsy from her own land in order to enforce planning regulations against the parking of caravans on land in the area in question was held to be neither a violation of Article 8 of the convention (respect for private and family life) or of Article 8 taken together with Article 14. The majority of the Court 'saw no reason to doubt' that the measures in question pursued the legitimate aims stated by the government of the UK, namely, public safety, the economic well-being of the country, the protection of health, and the protection of the rights of others. Moreover, given that in the exercise of discretion, the domestic authorities have a margin of appreciation, the court found that the measures taken were not disproportionate to the legitimate aim asserted. It did not even recognize that an equality claim under Article 14 was pertinent.[60] The confident assertion by the majority that all was well should be contrasted with that of the dissenting judgments. Thus, in his partially dissenting judgment, Judge Reick pointed out that when

a fundamental right of a member of a minority is concerned, especially a minority as vulnerable as the gypsies, the Court has an obligation to subject any such interference to particularly close scrutiny. In my opinion, the Court has not fully performed its duty as it has not taken into account all the relevant matters adduced by the Commission and was too hasty in invoking the margin of appreciation left to the State.

In particular, he noted that to have allowed the applicant to continue to park her caravans would have had little effect on the countryside, which was already subject to several buildings on neighbouring land. Most importantly, recognizing the importance to gypsies of the desire to travel, he pointed out that she should be permitted to use her land as a safe and stable place to set up home and where her children could go to school. She should also be permitted to retain the option of travelling during school holidays. Judge Lohmus in his partially dissenting opinion cautiously edged towards a more expansive concept of equality than that relied upon by the majority, noting that 'in order to establish equality in fact, different treatment may be

[60] *Buckley v UK* [1996] 23 EHRR 101 ECHR and see P case.

necessary to preserve [minorities'] special cultural existence'.[61] Most piercing was the dissenting opinion of Judge Pettiti. Locating the issue securely within the historical and political context of rejection and exclusion of gypsies, superimposed upon the genocide suffered by gypsies during the Second World War, he asserted emphatically that the purpose of the Convention was to impose a positive obligation on States to ensure that fundamental rights were guaranteed without discrimination. Rejecting the view that planning controls were for the public good, Judge Pettiti recognized instead that the controls were in fact imposed for the greater convenience of the local community, and the extent to which the latter were willing to accept gypsies. These were interests which, in his view, should not be allowed to subordinate respect for family life. They were certainly not necessary in a democratic society as required by the ECHR.

The inability of the ECHR to recognize the extent to which apparently neutral rules entrench the values of the dominant groups in society has also been demonstrated in the context of religious discrimination. A striking example concerns the extent to which working life is structured according to basic Christian assumptions. In particular, the working week leaves little scope for the observance of religious holidays or daily acts of worship by religious minorities. This problem was highlighted in the case of *Ahmad v ILEA*,[62] in which a devout Muslim claimed he was forced to resign his teaching post after his Local Education Authority employer insisted that his attendance at a nearby mosque for Friday prayers was inconsistent with his full-time contract. The UK Court of Appeal took the view that the case fell within the derogation under Article 9(2), which permitted restrictions on the freedom to manifest one's religion for the protection of the rights and freedoms of others. In this case, the rights of the education authority and the pupils were held to be sufficient to override Ahmad's right to freedom of religion. Ahmad took his case to Luxembourg, only to find himself on even less sympathetic territory.[63] The Commission declared the application inadmissible on the basis of a narrow conception of equality. Assuming that only members of other minority religions were in comparable situations, the Commission relied on the proposition that since all minorities had to conform to the norms of the majority religion, the applicant had not proved 'less favourable treatment'. It expressly declined to hold that the relevant comparator was a member of the majority religion. Instead, it deemed it sufficient to observe that 'in most countries, only the religious holidays of the majority of the population are celebrated as public holidays'.[64]

---

[61] *Buckley, supra* n. 60, at 136.   [62] [1978] QB 36 CA.
[63] *Ahmad v ILEA* Application No. 8160/78 [1981] 4 EHRR 127 (European Commission).
[64] Ibid., at para. 28.

In other jurisdictions, courts have been prepared to show somewhat more sensitivity to the real partiality of apparently neutral rules and have begun to develop a concept of equality which required accommodation of diversity. Thus in an early case, the US Supreme Court held that denial of unemployment benefit to a Seventh Day Adventist because she would not work on Saturdays for religious reasons was a denial of the right to free exercise of religion. The majority recognized the rule in question as an apparently neutral one, which denied benefit to anyone intentionally unavailable for work except on a Sunday. However, it was held that the majority could not compel a minority to observe the majority religious scruples.[65] In similar vein, the US Supreme Court held in a later case that the State of Wisconsin was required to make an exception to the law requiring school attendance up to the age of 16 because attendance at 14 and 15 was in conflict with the religious convictions and way of life of the minority Amish community.[66] These robust attempts at an alternative concept of equality have not, however, been sustained in recent Supreme Court decisions. Thus the Court was prepared to uphold the dismissal of a practising Jew from the military for refusing to remove his yarmulke and therefore defying military regulations requiring soldiers to be bare-headed indoors.[67] The concerns of the military for uniformity were held to override particular religious beliefs. Yet, as Brennan J. argued in dissent, the practical effect was to favour Christians under the guise of neutrality and evenhandedness. Particularly worrying was the view voiced by Stevens J. in his concurring opinion, that to permit accommodation of Jewish claims would open the floodgates to claims of other minorities, such as Sikhs and Rastafarians. Instead of this narrowly parochial view, it would have been possible, as Brennan J. argued, that a yarmulke worn with military uniform should be seen as an 'eloquent reminder that the shared and proud identity of US servicemen embraces and unites religious and ethnic pluralism'.

Even more disturbing is the reaction of the US Supreme Court to the adventurous attempt by Congress to give statutory force to the duty of accommodation of religious minorities. The Religious Freedom Restoration Act 1993 prohibited government from substantially burdening a person's exercise of religion by a rule of general applicability, unless the government could demonstrate that the burden was the least restrictive means of furthering a compelling government interest. The Supreme Court struck down the statute on the grounds that it exceeded Congress's power.[68]

This pattern is replicated at international level. Thus the Human Rights Committee of the International Covenant on Civil and Political Rights has concluded, in at least one case, that the guarantee of equality in Article 26 of the ICCPR does not apply to a law which is applied uniformly, regardless of

[65] *Scherbert v Verner* (1963).　　　　[66] *Wisconsin v Yoder* (1972).
[67] *Goldman v Weinberger* (1986).　　[68] *City of Boerne Flores* 117 S. Ct. 2157.

whether it in fact has discriminatory consequences.[69] The International
Convention on the Elimination of All Forms of Racial Discrimination
appears to go further in that it requires State Parties to take 'special and concrete measures to ensure the adequate development and protection of certain
racial groups or individuals belonging to them'. However, it is also stated that:
'These measures shall in no case entail as a consequence the maintenance of
unequal or separate rights for different racial groups after the objectives for
which they were taken have been achieved.'[70] It has been suggested that this
proviso indicates that only measures to combat violations of formal equality
need to be taken.[71]

(iii) When is a State Required to Override the Claims of Minorities in the Interests of Equality?

Perhaps the most complex scenario is that of a conflict between claims of
minorities and other concerns, such as health and safety or gender equality.
These are particularly difficult in that the conflicting claims are themselves
often contested. This is as true for health and safety concerns as it is for sex
discrimination. Thus while it may appear that a ban on the consumption of
such drugs as peyote, hashish, or cannabis is enacted for the universal good of
all the citizens of a country, the belief that these drugs are sufficiently dangerous to warrant banning may on reflection be found to be no more than a
reflection of the dominant culture's views. Minority cultures could for example consider alcohol to be so dangerous as to warrant total prohibition within
their own cultures, while peyote or hashish is considered crucial for religious,
spiritual, or communal purposes. Similarly, while Western women might
regard the wearing of a Muslim head scarf as a discriminatory and oppressive
custom, there are certainly Muslim women who characterize the head scarf as
both essential to their identity and even liberatory. In a different scenario, it
may be that the danger to health and safety is only to the religious individual
himself or herself, and therefore that the state should allow the person the
freedom to choose between his or her religion and safety. The wearing of hard
helmets by Sikhs on motor-bikes or construction sites is such an example. On
the other hand, there are clearly some practices which despite being central to
a culture might legitimately warrant restriction or prohibition. Female geni-
tal mutilation clearly falls into this category. Moreover, it is often misleading
to characterize a minority culture as sexist or inegalitarian. This assumes that
the dominant subgroup within the minority culture may legitimately assert

---

[69] *PPC v The Netherlands* Communication No. 212/1986 (1988) A/43/40 at 244; see Keller,
'Rethinking Ethnic and Cultural Rights in Europe', 18 *Oxford Journal of Legal Studies*, at 55.
[70] Article 2(2).   [71] Keller *supra* n. 69, at 54.

the values of the culture. Yet such views may well be highly contested within the group: women in the group may themselves be voicing a dynamic within the group which has as much of a right to be heard as any other.

All these issues have been played out in the courts, although not always with the sensitivity they deserve. In *Employment Division v Smith*,[72] the US Supreme Court was faced with the question of whether a criminal prohibition on the use of peyote infringed the right to free exercise of religion of members of the Native American Church because it made no exception for religiously inspired use of the drug. Scalia J. for the majority held that government's ability to enforce generally applicable prohibitions of socially harmful conduct should not be subject to individual religious objections, even if those objections could be overridden by proof of a compelling state interest. Far more perceptive was the judgement of O'Connor J. She recognized the acute dilemma facing members of the Native American Church, who had to choose between carrying out ritual embodying of religious beliefs and avoidance of criminal prosecution. At the same time, she acknowledged the legitimate state interest in promoting health, safety, and general welfare. In balancing the two interests, the extent of the potential interference in the free exercise of religion meant that the strictest scrutiny was appropriate, according to which a rule was invalid unless it could be shown to serve a compelling state interest and was narrowly tailored to that interest. While the test is appropriate, its application is, however, highly dependent on judicial perceptions. This is well illustrated by the way O'Connor J. applied the strict scrutiny test. She held that the overriding interest was to prevent harm to the user; that harm occurred regardless of the motivation of the user; and that a uniform application was essential to its effectiveness. Thus, she held, the prohibition passed the strict scrutiny test. Yet all these reasons should themselves be subjected to scrutiny. The 'harm' to the user may need to be defined in spiritual as well as physical terms; and it is not necessarily the case that motivation is irrelevant— consider for example the ritual use of alcohol in church. Nor is it necessarily true that uniform application is essential to effectiveness. Indeed, several other states had enacted exceptions for religiously inspired use of peyote without, it appears, impairing the effectiveness of the rule as a whole.

Health and safety issues have led to similar dilemmas with respect to the compulsory use of crash helmets on motor-bikes and hard hats on construction sites, a requirement which conflicts with the obligation of observant Sikhs to wear turbans. In Britain, a challenge by a Sikh of regulations making it a criminal offence to ride a motor cycle without a helmet was given short shrift by the court. So far as Lord Widgery CJ was concerned:

No-one is bound to ride a motor cycle. . . . The effect of the Regulations no doubt bears on the Sikh community because it means that they will often be prevented

---

[72] 894 US 872.

from riding a motor cycle, not because of the English law, but by the requirements of their religion.[73]

Yet, as Poulter points out, it was clearly not their faith which precluded the riding of motor cycles by Sikhs; but the provisions of English law.[74] A similar response was nevertheless given to the dilemma by the European Commission of Human Rights, which held that any interference with freedom of religion of a turbaned Sikh was justified on grounds that it was necessary for the protection of health.[75] This reaction has been replicated both by the Canadian Supreme court[76] and the UN Human Rights Committee,[77] the latter upholding the decision by the former that the dismissal of a turbaned Sikh for refusing to wear a 'hard hat' in an area designated as a hard hat area was justifiable as reasonably directed towards objective purposes compatible with the ICCPR.

For the UK at least the solution was legislative rather than judicial. Sustained political lobbying eventually produced a statutory exemption for turbaned Sikhs from the requirement of wearing a helmet.[78] It is noteworthy that the British legislature came to the conclusion that an exemption was warranted despite the fact that the cost was not confined to the Sikh motor cyclists: the nationally funded health service would foot the bill for any treatment resulting from the unprotected use of motor cycles. The argument that a special exemption breached the principle of equal applications of the laws was also rejected. Similarly, after heated parliamentary debates, an exemption was provided for turbaned Sikhs from the obligation to wear safety helmets on construction sites. However, the rights to Sikhs to claim compensation in tort in the event of an accident were severely curtailed, reflecting the view that Sikh building workers who wear turbans are deemed to take a substantial part of the risk on themselves.[79] However, care will of course still be provided by public funds through the NHS.

Less sympathetic, however, has been the reaction in circumstances in which the harm alleged is not directly to the Sikh himself, but to others. Thus the courts accepted the argument that refusal by a chocolate factory to employ Sikhs was justifiable because the wearing of beards was prohibited for health and safety reasons. There was little scrutiny in these cases of either the

[73] *R v Aylesbury Crown Court ex p Chahal* [1976] RTR 489.

[74] S. Poulter, *Ethnicity, Law and Human Rights* (1998), at 293.

[75] *X v United Kingdom* (1978) 14 Dec & Rep 234, at 235.

[76] *Bhinder and Canadian Nation Railway Co* (1986) 23 DLR (4th series) 481.

[77] *Bhinder v Canada* Communication 208/1986; *Report of the Human Rights Committee* (1990) II, 50.

[78] Motor Cycle Crash Helmets (Religious Exemption) Act 1976. See now Road Traffic Act 1988, s. 16(2); Motor Cycle (Protective Helmets) Regulations SI No. 1279 of 1980, as amended by SI No. 374 of 1981 reg 4(2)(c).

[79] See Poulter, *supra* n. 74, at 321.

absolute necessity of the 'no-beards' rule; or the availability of alternatives. Thus no attention was paid to the fact that the rule was not enforced in six out of seven of the employer's factories, nor to the possibility of averting danger through the provision of beard nets.[80] More recently, the standard of justification in Britain has been raised, and it is possible that these issues might be given more weight in future cases.[81]

The conflict between gender equality and the rights of minorities is even more acute. Does accommodation and respect for minorities require too the tolerance of gender inequality? I have argued above that it is misleading to regard a group as homogeneous. The internal structures of dominance and subordination within a group should not be ignored. Gender inequality may be asserted by the dominant male sub-groups within the group; but this could well disguise opposition by women within the group. In apparently respecting the rights of the minority to self-determination, the structures of domination within the group are then reinforced. Kymlicka has attempted to resolve these dilemmas by distinguishing between external protections and internal restrictions. He argues that a liberal view requires 'freedom within the minority group and equality between the majority and minority groups'.[82] The reason for protecting cultural membership is that such membership enables informed choice about how to lead one's life. Thus the basic freedom of members of minority groups to question and possibly revise the traditional practices of their own communities should be protected by the wider society against restriction by powerful sections within the group. Gender inequality deprives women of the right to equal participation in their culture, and thus is an area in which the State should intervene.

Courts have had to face such conflicts directly in a series of cases concerning native American or Indian laws tribal ordinances denying basic rights to women who had married out of the tribe and their children, while preserving such rights for men who had married out. The fact that the challenge came from affected women themselves demonstrates that the internal hierarchy was not uncontested. However, courts in both Canada and the US have moved to protect the autonomy of Indian tribes rather than insisting on equality for women. Thus in *Santa Clara Pueblo v Martinez*,[83] the US Supreme Court refused to intervene to invalidate an Indian tribal ordinance denying membership of the tribe to children of women who had married outside the tribe while extending membership to children of men who had done the same. The Court held that Congress was committed to the goal of tribal self-determination, and it was up to tribal courts to adjudicate the dispute. This was against the dissent

---

[80] *Singh v Rowntree Mackintosh Ltd* [1979] ICR 554; *Panesar v Nestle Co Ltd* [1980] ICR 144 CA.

[81] See Poulter, *supra* n. 74, at 312–13.

[82] W. Kymlicka, *Multicultural Citizenship* (1995), at 152.   [83] 436 US 49.

of White J. who held that the Indian Civil Rights Act aimed to ensure that
American Indians are afforded the broad constitutional rights secured to other
Americans. Similarly, the Canadian Supreme Court refused to hold that the
provision of the Indian Act 1970 which prohibited registration as Indians of
women who married non-Indians was overridden by the Canadian Bill of
Rights.[84] However, the UN Human Rights Committee has been far more
receptive to the notion that the rights of the women to enjoy their own culture
are as valid and valuable as those of the men. In the case of *Sandra Lovelace v
Canada*,[85] a Maliseet Indian woman had lost her rights and status as an Indian
because she had married a non-Indian man. Under the relevant Canadian
statute, an Indian man who married a non-Indian woman did not lose his status. It is notable that the Committee chose to deal with the claim under Article
27 of the ICCPR, which states that 'minorities should not be denied the right,
in community with the other members of groups, to enjoy their own culture,
to profess and practice their own religion or use their own language'. Thus
instead of placing the right not to be discriminated against on grounds of sex
in contradistinction to the rights of a minority to profess and practise their culture, the Committee saw the discriminatory act as itself denying her the right
to participate in her culture. Thus restrictions on her right to reside in the
Indian reserve must not only be reasonable and justifiable but must also be consistent with the provisions on non-discrimination.

However, it is not always the case that the dominant view of gender equality is shared by the women in the group itself. There is always a danger that
the apparent upholding of women's rights is in fact an imposition by the dominant group of its own values. One of the key contested sites has concerned
the wearing of headscarves by Muslim girls and women. While some view the
headscarf as a symbol of women's oppression, others, particularly some
Muslim women themselves, see the headscarf as integral to their basic dignity
as Muslim women, having the same religious significance as the yarmulke to
a Jew or a turban to a Sikh. Yet many European countries have reacted fiercely
against the wearing of headscarves, dismissing women teachers and expelling
girls from schools. The conflict is particularly prominent in France and
Turkey, both of which claim the principle of secularity as integral to their constitutional arrangements. The French principle of *laïcité*, or secularity, has
been used to argue for a concept of equality which stresses identity and over-
rides ethnic, religious, or cultural differences except in the domain of private
life. This notion of identity and unity has led France to go so far as to enter a
reservation to Article 27 of ICCPR, which gives the right to enjoy one's own
culture, to profess and practise one's own faith, and to use one's own language.
Indeed, it defended its position by arguing that France was a 'country in

[84] *A-G of Canada v Lavelle* (1974) 38 DLR 3d 481.
[85] Communication No. 24/1977 (30 July 1981) UN Doc CCPR/C/OP/1 at 83 (1984).

which there are no minorities'.[86] In active pursuance of this policy, Muslim schoolgirls were excluded from their secondary school. However, the French Conseil d'État was able to recognize the ease with which a principle of apparent secularism in fact endorsed the majority culture. It therefore advised that the principle of *laicité* was compatible with the right to express religious beliefs, so long as that expression respected the pluralism and freedom of others. In addition, it declared that this right of religion could be limited by education policies which included the guarantees of equality between men and women. These limitations, however, left the position sufficiently vague to permit continued exclusion of girls from schools, and by 1995 as many as 150 had been excluded. The Conseil d'État, while annulling many of these expulsions, has refused to invalidate the government circular which permits only discreet insignia.[87]

Even more problematic has been the response of the ECHR to the prohibition of the wearing of Muslim headscarves in secular universities in Turkey. The case of *Karaduman v Turkey*[88] encapsulates many of the dilemmas associated with the potential clash between values in this area. The applicant in the case was refused a degree certificate because she had supplied a photograph showing her wearing a headscarf, contrary to the rules, which required her to be shown wearing nothing on her head. The Turkish Constitutional Court had recently struck down a legal provision authorizing the wearing of headscarves in higher education establishments on the grounds that the provision in question was contrary to the principle of secularity enunciated in the Constitution. It is noteworthy that, as in France, this principle of secularity is itself far from neutral, but enshrines a particular set of values. However, unlike the situation in France, in which Muslims were a small minority, Muslims are in the great majority in Turkey, and the university claimed that its dress regulations were in fact designed to protect the minority secular culture from the strong pressure of fundamentalist religious movements. In particular, the prohibition was, it was argued, specifically intended to protect women who do not wear headscarves from pressure to conform to the majority norm. The European Commission of Human Rights rejected the applicant's claim of a violation of her freedom of religion under Article 9. The university's objective of protecting non-practising students from the pressures of the majority religion was held to be a legitimate restriction on the applicant's freedom. By choosing to go to such a university, the applicant implicitly accepted its cultural tone. While there is much weight in this argument, it is questionable whether the proportionality doctrine was applied with sufficient rigour. The wearing of a headscarf for a photograph could not in itself create conformist

[86] Poulter ,'Muslim Headscarves in School', 17 *Oxford Journal of Legal Studies* (1997) 43, at 53.
[87] This account is taken from ibid.
[88] European Commission on Human Rights, No. 1627/90 74 DR 93 (1993).

pressures for other students, and indeed the Commission accepted that the certificate was only used for employment purposes. Moreover, there was no claim that she was forced against her will to observe dress regulations during the course of her studies. Thus it is arguable that while the aims of the Turkish state and university were legitimate, the measures used were disproportionately heavy handed.

(iv) Can Human Rights Adjudication Generate a Rich Concept of Equality?

It has been seen that most equality guarantees in human rights documents, whether domestic or international, have been interpreted as extending no further than formal equality. The ECHR in particular has been reluctant to extend the rights in the ECHR to positive duties.[89] Disappointingly, the new Protocol 12, which extends Article 14 to a free-standing equality right, has not been refashioned to bring in the possibility of positive action. To the contrary, the explanatory notes declare that 'such a programmatic obligation would sit ill with the whole nature of the Convention and its control system which are based on the collective guarantee of individual rights which are formulated in terms sufficiently specific to be justiciable'. However, there are provisions in both domestic constitutions and international law which have the potential to develop not just a concept of indirect discrimination, but a duty to take positive steps. The Convention on the Elimination of All Forms of Racial Discrimination requires in Article 2(2) that State Parties should take 'special and concrete measures to ensure the adequate development and protection of certain racial groups or individuals belonging to them'. However, special rights should not be granted after they have achieved their objectives, suggesting that the Article does not require more than redress of past discrimination.[90] In addition, Article 27 of the ICCPR gives a right to members of ethnic, religious, or linguistic minorities, 'in community with other members of their group, to enjoy their own culture, to profess and practise their own religion, or to use their own culture'. Recent policy documents of the UN endorse the principle that states are under a legal obligation to take positive measures to ensure that minority groups enjoy full and effective equality.[91]

Even more focused is the Framework Convention for the Protection of National Minorities. Opened for signature on 1 February 1995, it is already in force in twenty-nine countries and has been signed by a further nine. The

[89] *Belgian Linguistics Case* [1968] 1 EHRR 252.   [90] Keller, *supra* n. 69, at 54.

[91] Declaration on the Rights of Persons belonging to National or Ethnic, Religious and Linguistic Minorities, 32 *International Legal Materials* (1993), at 911; General Comment No. 23 (50) (Article 27, 15 *Human Rights Law Journal* (1994)). See generally Keller, *supra* n. 69, at 55.

Convention expressly addresses some of the difficult dilemmas dealt with above. As a start, it attempts to capture both the individual and the group dimension of ethnic and religious identity. Thus the rights in the Convention may be exercised individually as well as in community with others. The exit option is preserved by giving individuals the right to choose to be treated as a member of a national minority or to choose not to be so treated.[92] Its principle of equality is potentially rich, encompassing both the possibility of equality in diversity, and the obligation to institute positive measures. Thus Article 4, as well as containing the basic principle of formal equality before the law and consistent treatment, imposes the duty on contracting parties 'to adopt, where necessary, adequate measures to promote . . . full and effective equality between persons belonging to a national minority and those belonging to the majority'. Such measures should extend to all areas of economic, social, political, and cultural life, and must take due account of the specific conditions of the persons belonging to the national minorities. It is explicitly provided that such measures should not in themselves be considered as discriminatory. Articles 5 and 6 reinforce this position by requiring Parties to promote the conditions necessary for persons belonging to national minorities to maintain and develop their culture, and to preserve the essential elements of their identity. Parties are required to refrain from policies or practices aimed at assimilation of persons belonging to national minorities against their will and are obliged to protect these persons from any action aimed at assimilation. In addition, Parties are to encourage a spirit of tolerance and intercultural dialogue, and to take effective measures to promote mutual respect and understanding.

However, as has been recently argued, the 'considerable potential' of the document is undermined by some major shortcomings.[93] First, the drafters chose not to define 'national minorities', risking the possibility of entrenching existing arbitrary discrimination between traditional and immigrant minorities to the detriment of the latter.[94] Secondly, the content and aims of the positive duties are not specified. We have seen above that imposing a positive duty is not sufficient: the aims need to be articulated and the content of the duty defined for it to be effective. Its real impact will thus depend on the goodwill of contracting parties and, in the last resort, the monitoring mechanisms. Since positive duties by their nature depart from the notion of an individual right, it is appropriate that the Convention gives no justiciable individually enforceable rights. Instead, State Parties are required to submit, within one year of entry into force of the Convention in the country concerned and every five years thereafter, a report containing full information on legislative and other measures taken to give effect to the Convention. The report is made public and submitted to an Advisory Committee composed of

[92] Article 3.   [93] Keller, *supra* n. 69, at 31.   [94] Ibid., at 43–4.

independent experts for analysis and opinion. In assessing the evidence, the Advisory Committee may receive information from sources other than state reports, and may even invite such information or, with the approval of the Committee of Ministers, hold meetings to gain information from other sources. On receipt of the opinion, the Committee of Ministers considers and adopts its conclusions, and may also adopt recommendations in respect of the Party concerned. This too is made public. Thus far state reports have been received from fifteen countries, and the Advisory Committee has made three visits to countries to seek further information on implementation of the Convention.

This mechanism, while having some important strengths, is entirely dependent on the level of resources allocated to it. The Advisory Committee began work in 1998 with a minimum level of human resources; and it has become clear that the financial and human resources allocated to it are insufficient to allow it to properly carry out its duties, with significant implications for the credibility and effectiveness of the Convention. Even the first set of opinions was postponed because of lack of resources. Although the need for adequate resourcing has been given priority ranking, the only promise given so far is that the Committee of Ministers will consider the matter in its meeting in August 2001.[95]

CONCLUSION

This chapter has shown that the challenges facing the principle of equality are many and complex. If equality is to be reconstructed in a way which can effectively combat racism, then it must move beyond the individualism, symmetry, and dichotomized nature of formal equality. In particular, it must impose positive duties on States to address the stigma, the disadvantages, and the pressures to conform that are the concrete manifestations of equality. In the end result, however, equality cannot single-handedly defeat racism. Deep-seated social and institutional change is the ultimate key to a truly egalitarian future. Equality can then function, as it should, as an important ideal driving change.

[95] This information is gained from the Council of Europe website.

3

Racial Discrimination and the Rights of Minority Cultures

DIMITRINA PETROVA

The denial of racism is fast becoming the most typical and widespread modern manifestation of racist attitudes, opinions, statements, actions, and policies. This chapter examines several ways in which racism is denied and describes the implications. It then explores the implications of acknowledging the presence of racism, the dangers of an acceptance of racism, and the usefulness of legal approaches to racial discrimination. Finally, it suggests improvements in the methods used at the international level to combat racial discrimination.

I. THE RACIST CONSENSUS AND ITS DISGUISES[1]

(i) Denial: The New Phenomenology of Racism

For the purposes of this chapter, it is assumed that (1) all societies are racist to some degree; (2) racism is ubiquitous at least at the level of attitudes, though the presence of racism may not necessarily be visible in social behaviour; (3) the existence of racism is widely denied across cultures, with varying degrees of disguise; and (4) the *acknowledgement* of racism is a prerequisite (but not at all a guarantee, or a bridge) to overcoming it.

The concept, racism, is understood here in the entirety of its broad scope and polysemy or plurality of meaning. 'Racist' can be a description of attitudes (mental states of individuals or groups), of ideologies (sets of socially constructed and politically functional ideas of whole societies, classes, cultures, and so on), of social practices, of institutions. Among these, human rights advocates and international organizations have addressed issues of racism mostly in respect to social practices. This is understandable. While racist beliefs and attitudes may be present in a person's mind with varying

[1] The first part of this chapter builds on an earlier version prepared for the International Council on Human Rights Policy.

degrees of conviction, awareness, scope and intensity, we can define somewhat less vaguely and prohibit by law racist acts which contribute, more or less directly, to ethnic or racial inequality in society.

Critical race theory, a recent legal philosophy, the inception of which can be traced to a 1989 workshop in Madison, Wisconsin, understands racism broadly. Racism is viewed not only as a matter of individual prejudice and everyday practice, but as a phenomenon that is deeply embedded in language and perception. Racism is a ubiquitous and inescapable feature of modern society, and despite official rhetoric to the contrary, race is always present even in the most neutral and innocent terms. Concepts such as 'justice', 'truth', and 'reason' are open to questions that reveal their complicity with power. This extraordinary pervasiveness of unconscious racism is often ignored by the legal system.[2]

There exists a large body of literature on and research into the measurement of racist attitudes in the wake of the classical study by Theodor Adorno and others, *The Authoritarian Personality* (1950), which identifies and measures ethnocentrism, anti-Semitism, fascizoid attitudes, and susceptibility to anti-democratic propaganda in the United States. That study remains relevant to an understanding of the social psychology of racism today and deserves to be rediscovered by the anti-racist movement.

Adorno's team established the existence of 'an anti-utopian syndrome' in the so-called 'high-scorers'—the individuals who scored high on several scales, registering a more or less stable personality structure, which makes individuals susceptible to anti-democratic propaganda. The analysis of the survey questionnaires and interviews showed that, according to these individuals, there will never be and there should never be a Utopia: 'one has to be realistic'. But, in their case, 'realism' is not meant as the need to judge and decide on the basis of objective, factual insight. It is meant rather in the sense that the overwhelming power of the existing order over the individual and his intentions is taken for granted.

The antipodes of the 'authoritarian personality', the so-called 'low-scorers', usually also display an anti-utopian mind-set, but in an entirely different way. While 'high-scorers' share in the official optimism, which is accompanied by more deeply lying motives of contempt for human nature and by a basic cynicism, 'low-scorers' more readily express negative facts and are less affected by the conventional cliché that 'everything is fine', but they demonstrate, at a deeper level of opinion, a much greater trust in the innate potentialities of the human race. While 'high-scorers' ultimately do not want Utopia, 'low scorers' are sceptical because they take its realization seriously and are therefore critical of the existing order, even to a point where they acknowledge the threat of

---

[2] S. Vago, *Law and Society*, 6th edn. (2000), at 68.

existing conditions to ruin just those human potentialities that they bank upon in the depth of their souls.[3]

Can we talk of racism in an historic sense? Was there 'racism' in slave owning, or in feudal societies? Or is racism a phenomenon of modern history that emerged with the rapid expansion of biological, evolutionary, and genetic descriptions of the living order?

Here, the observations are limited to one point: having accepted a very broad definition of racism and fully aware of the risks of anachronisms, we might benefit today from a survey of racist attitudes throughout history. In ancient Greece and Rome, we may then say, racism was typical in the treatment of slaves and *metekoi* (foreigners residing in the city) and reached extreme forms of expression in such places as the Greek *ergasterion*, that special prison in which slaves—as a rule ethnically different from the locals—were engaged in carrying out the hardest labour. The preference for this approach evident in this Chapter is politically based: beyond the historically constructed terms of the discourse, there still lie lessons that might be useful to us.

In the orthodoxy of Stalinist Marxist textbooks, racism was regarded under the rubric 'Nature and Society'. Racism was denounced as a reactionary doctrine the theoretical defect of which consisted in the 'naturalization' of social phenomena, processes, and properties.[4] 'Race' was regarded as a biological concept, while discrimination on racial grounds was denounced. However, racial discrimination and racism were applicable, from the point of view of communist ideology, to cases such as the treatment of blacks in the US, apartheid in South Africa and similar 'black and white' issues, whereas neither racism, nor racial discrimination were acknowledged as a possibility in the context of 'socialist society'. This political localization of racism was at odds with the more general and certainly much more sophisticated Marxist treatment of the relationship between nature and society/culture; a divorce between the universality of the theoretical claim and the limited political impositions of the theory was typical of Marxist ideology as, indeed, of any 'ideology' in the sense of Mannheim.[5]

---

[3] T. W. Adorno, Else Frenkel-Brunswick, Daniel J. Levinson, and R. Nevitt Sanford, *The Authoritarian Personality: Studies in Prejudice* (1950), at 695–696.

[4] Urison, 'Racism', 4 *Filosofskaya Entsiklopedia* (in Russian).

[5] The reference here is to the rich tradition of interpreting 'ideology' which presents ideas as functions of social positions and one of the founders of which was Karl Mannheim, himself influenced by Marx's interpretation of ideology as 'false consciousness' (see, e.g. K. Mannheim, *Ideology and Utopia* (1954). According to Mannheim, the concept of ideology reflects the first discovery which emerged out of the modern political conflict, namely, that the ruling groups can, in their thinking, become so strongly bound, through their interest, by a given situation that they are simply no longer capable of seeing certain facts that would weaken their sense of domination.

Thus, the societies of post-communist (post-1989) Central and Eastern Europe have been unprepared to accept the more general definition of racial discrimination as found in international law, especially in the UN International Convention on the Elimination of All Forms of Racial Discrimination (ICERD). In the first half of the 1990s, the governments and the political classes of the region were—and in many places still are—out-raged by the very suggestion that one can speak of anti-Roma racism in Eastern Europe.[6] Courts, too, have failed to apply the concepts of 'race' and 'racial discrimination' in the broader sense in which they are construed in the ICERD framework. On 30 October 1995, non-Romani persons on a train in the Czech Republic threatened to beat up and throw from the train four Romani passengers. Two perpetrators were subsequently prosecuted and charged with, *inter alia*, racially motivated violence. On 20 November 1996, the District Court in Hradec Kralove acquitted the defendants, stating that the Romani victims were not a distinct racial group and 'belong(ed) to the same race' as the defendants (ethnic Czechs). In so holding, the Court relied on a narrow biologically rooted definition of race according to which Roma, like Czechs, are members of the same 'Indo-European race'. The Court declined to impose punishment on either defendant.[7]

Cognitively, there can be different grades of consciousness or awareness of racism: from totally explicit awareness to hidden assumptions and merely lived experience or habit. For instance, people may be unable to formulate general racist or ethnocentric principles as such, but they know that they disapprove of facilitating immigration or of preferential job allocation to minorities. Levels of awareness of racist attitudes can also be dependent on whether such attitudes form part of a dominant ideology. As Teun A. van Dijk notes:

Whereas oppositional ideologies by definition will tend to be more explicit and con-scious among group members, dominant ideologies will precisely tend to be implicit and denied, or felt to be 'natural' by their members. Such group members may indeed

[6] Below, there are frequent references to the Roma, Europe's most disadvantaged ethnic minority. In the examples relying on Roma, the chapter draws on the author's experience as Director of the European Roma Rights Centre (ERRC), an international public-interest law organization based in Budapest that defends the rights of the Roma throughout Europe.

[7] On 8 Aug. 1997, acting under an extraordinary procedure for review of unlawful court rulings, the Czech Ministry of Justice filed a motion in the case asking the Czech Supreme Court to declare that the District Court's rationale for acquitting the two defendants was in breach of Czech and international law. The ERRC filed a brief with the Supreme Court. The ERRC argued that the District Court's cramped anthropological interpretation of the concept of 'race' was out of step with international jurisprudence, which has confirmed that 'race' and 'ethnicity' are interrelated and overlapping concepts and are to be interpreted broadly. The Supreme Court heard the case on 9 Oct. 1997, annulled the District Court opinion, and ordered that the case be returned to the District Court for further proceedings.

be unaware of their ideologies (typically so of male chauvinism, racism, etc.) until they are challenged by members of the other group.[8]

Much of Stanley Cohen's discussion of the denial of human rights violations in his 1995 *Denial and Acknowledgement* is highly relevant to the case of the denial of racism. Cohen analyses denial in the sense of 'how people react to the suffering of others'.[9] But what he says about the ways people react to information about the suffering caused by human rights violations applies to the experience of racism and its deeds.

'Denial of racism' is meant below in the sense of the denial of (*a*) the suffering of the victims of racism, (*b*) the existence of attitudes in oneself or society which make this suffering possible, or (*c*) the existence of practices and institutions of racism.

The denial of racism is a reaction to the post-Second World War sanction of racism as a socially unacceptable opinion.[10] Racism's presence appears to be denied more vehemently in those cultures which, since the Second World War, have done more to limit racism and related intolerance. Denial is a manifestation of a certain level of accomplishment in the implementation of a human rights and anti-racism agenda in a society. The more progress a society has made in denouncing racism as a social and political evil, the more vehemently is its continued existence denied. Ironically, the denial of racism is a product of the progress of the struggle against it.

In Western democratic societies, for example, most people who share racist opinions and act accordingly would deny that they are racists because racism is officially and culturally condemned, while tolerance, racial equality, and human rights are dominant ideological values. Thus, racism is now rarely a self-description; increasingly and under the influence of the Western democracies and the international anti-racism movement, it is mostly a label applied to groups or individuals by others. Although explicitly racist groups and parties exist, most of today's 'racists' who hold people of a particular ethnic background in contempt or hostility at the same time oppose being described as 'racists'. Austria's Freedom Party experienced a dramatic rise in popularity following a change of leadership in the mid-1980s that brought

---

[8] T. A. Van Dijk, *Ideology: A Multidisciplinary Approach* (1998), at 98. According to van Dijk, the concept of ideology is neutral as regards relations of power and domination and is not limited to those views that reflect the stable and lasting aspects of the status quo. Mannheim's 'utopia', that is, the mind-set opposite to 'ideology', is, according to van Dijk, also a kind of 'ideology'. Van Dijk speaks instead of 'good' and 'bad' ideologies: the latter deny, conceal, legitimate, or monitor social inequality and are exemplified by racism, sexism, and class domination.

[9] S. Cohen, *Denial and Acknowledgement: The Impact of Information about Human Rights Violations* (1995), at 1. The concept of denial is analysed in ch. 2, pp. 19–58.

[10] For an examination of the denial of racism, see van Dijk, 'Discourse and the Denial of Racism', 3 *Discourse and Society* (1992) 87.

the charismatic demagogue Jorg Haider to the top position in the party and, along with him, a reinvigorated populist, anti-foreigner language and a renewed belittling of Austria's complicity in the racist crimes of the Third Reich. Nevertheless, most of the party members and supporters deny the party's racist character.

Since the Second World War and as a direct result, at least in Western cultures, racist prejudice has sunk deeper down the layers of the pre-predicative judgment and has metamorphosed into a set of more subtle assumptions. Most types of contemporary racism make no reference to biology, but take the form of 'cultural racism', though the latter label is, of course, also denied by the proponents. A prominent example of this development is the work of Dinesh D'Souza. In his book *The End of Racism*,[11] we find a forceful rejection of any form of affirmative action, repudiation of egalitarian values, extensive blaming of the victims, and emphasis on the 'pathologies' of black culture. His views have also been characterized as 'symbolic racism'.[12] Thus, at the academic and intellectual-ideological level, 'cultural racism' is a form of denial, insofar as its proponents are trying to avoid the stigma of being called 'racists', while still holding views that perpetuate or worsen racial and ethnic inequality.

An illustration of the way in which racism can manifest itself in seemingly race-neutral policies is the justifications offered by the European Union and Western countries for restrictions on immigration. The Western political class has been pushing marketization and, with it, support for the free movement of capital and goods. But it has baulked at the idea of a free movement of labour and has increasingly been trying to restrict the movement of people across borders. At face value, the current EU policy of erecting obstacles to immigration is race neutral, and its justification may sound legitimate from the point of view of the need to protect domestic labour, national security, national culture, and so on. However, at a deeper level, the policy operates on a foundation of unchallenged racist presumptions and, moreover, is applied in a racist way.

In 1911 the US Congress commissioned a study to document the 'deterioration' of the 'American stock' due to immigration; in the 40-volume report, the contribution of Franz Boas was the only one that argued against racial determinism. At least we can register progress in that the EU today is engaging in a different sort of prevention in terms of immigration. The so-called 'Budapest process', which started in 1994 and which involves to date around forty states and ten international organizations, has as its purpose to 'harmonize' pan-European policies in an effort to avoid illegal migration. The currently sensitive

[11] D. D'Souza, *The End of Racism: Principles for a Multiracial Society* (1995).

[12] On 'symbolic racism' and related forms of 'modern', 'everyday', or 'new' racism, see M. Barker, *The New Racism* (1981); J. F. Dovidio and S. L. Gaertner (eds), *Prejudice, Discrimination and Racism* (1986); P. J. M. Essed, *Understanding Everyday Racism: An Interdisciplinary Theory* (1991).

issue of Roma migration has been closely tied to the enlargement process in the European Union. In several cases in the past few years, groups of Roma numbering from around 20 to over 1,000, have travelled to EU member states, the US, and Canada and applied for asylum. In some instances, governments have responded by reintroducing visa obligations against the relevant associated states, such as Slovakia. On the other hand, it has been suggested at EU fora that 'also the *fear* of a sudden "exodus" of Roma is one of the main reasons why e.g. Romanians still need visas to enter the EU. And EU visa regimes will indeed be maintained in all cases where there is a justifiable fear of irregular migration.'[13]

Racist presumptions become evident in the case of seekers of political asylum who come from countries where there is civil and political unrest and in which entire ethnic groups are denied basic rights. These people, even though they may also be simultaneously victims of extreme and institutionalized poverty, are often genuine victims of persecution in the sense of the definition of 'refugee' contained in Article 1(A)(2) of the 1951 Geneva convention relating to the status of refugees. But if the number of refugees is perceived as significant by Western authorities, then the refugees are rejected by being categorized as mere 'economic migrants' or on other grounds.

What is so frightening about the prospect of the settlement of persecuted ethnic groups from outside Europe (or, by the same token, of Roma from Eastern Europe who seek asylum in Western countries) in the calm and clean cities of the West? At first glance, the claim that they would bring down the fortifications of social welfare by offering cheap labour may seem convincing to those who are unwilling or unable to think beyond the trivialities of a populist agenda. The additional claim that these ethnic immigrant groups would disintegrate the national culture of the host country, insofar as they would not be able or willing to integrate (read, 'assimilate'), meets with the immediate sympathy of large segments of Western society.

Let us assume, for the sake of argument, that it is true that an influx of immigrants could seriously threaten a deterioration in some features of the material well-being of an affluent host country or dilute the national culture. There remains a small, but disturbing question: Why is a citizen of Western Europe more anxious about his compatriots' mere welfare and cultural identity than about the severe threats to the physical safety and even the survival of foreign nationals?

It appears in this light that the very frame of reference (the community, the nation) that shapes our sense of responsibility and our opinions is fraught with assumptions of a racist nature. Most of us take for granted that we should contribute chiefly to our own community (neighbourhood, city, clan,

---

[13] See Martijn Pluim, presentation on behalf of the International Centre for Migration Policy Development at the OSCE conference, 'Roma in the EU Candidate Countries: Challenges of Integration' (Vienna, 26 Sep. 2000), at 2.

nation), even though we would admit that 'outsiders' have suffered more because of more serious violations of human rights than have the members of our own community.

The priorities of the Western majority's concerns thus do not correspond very well with a list of priorities that might have been drawn up if the sole grounds of judgement had been humanitarian or if they had been linked to the seriousness of the human rights violations involved. The conclusion seems unavoidable that the discrepancy—the difference in the *realpolitik*—of the priorities—one set revolving mainly around issues of domestic prosperity, and the other revolving around significant human rights and humanitarian concerns—has become possible precisely because racism is interfering with judgement. Anti-racist movements, on the other hand, are a challenge levelled against the nation-state, in essence if not in their proclaimed goals.

Eurocentric racism has a long ancestry. As Ascherson argues, it can be derived from the ancient assumption—still widespread in Europe—that settled agriculture and the existence of a crop-growing peasantry represent a huge forward development over an earlier stage of nomadism.

Here pseudo-anthropology feeds the basic European nightmare: a terror of people who move. . . . That nightmare survives in the new Europe after the revolutions of 1989. It survives as Western fear of all travelling people, of the millions pressing against Europe's gates as 'asylum seekers' or 'economic migrants', of a social collapse in Russia which would send half the population streaming hungrily towards Germany.

The origins of Euro-racism are traced back to the construction of 'Europe' by the ancient Greeks.

On the shores of the Black Sea, there were born a pair of Siamese twins called 'civilization' and 'barbarism'. This is where Greek colonists met the Scythians. A settled culture of small, maritime city-states encountered a mobile culture of steppe-nomads. People who had lived in one place for unaccounted generations, planting crops and fishing the coastal sea, now met people who lived in wagons and tents and wandered about infinite horizons of grassy prairie behind herds of cattle and horses. This was not the first time in human history that farmers had met pastoralists. Since the Neolithic revolution, the beginning of settled agriculture, there must have been countless intersections of these two ways of life. Nor was it the first witnessing of nomadism by people of an urban culture: that was an experience already familiar to the Chinese on the western borders of Han dominions. But in this particular encounter began the idea of 'Europe', with all its arrogance, all its implications of superiority, all its assumptions of priority and antiquity, all its pretensions to a natural right to dominate.[14]

Considering racism from the point of view of denial is relevant in the struggle against racism, since it immediately conveys the paradigmatic limitations

---

[14] See N. Ascherson, *Black Sea* (1996), at 49. On Eurocentrism as a racist view, see also Joseph, Reddy and Searle-Chatterjee, 'Eurocentrism in the Social Sciences', 31 *Race and Class* (1990) 1.

of the Enlightenment ('education can do everything') as a strategy. The discussion of denial dissipates any illusion that knowledge alone is sufficient as a motive of action whether at the individual or collective level. Even if people clearly *know* the facts about racial abuse, they do not take prompt or adequate action. Why? The problematic of denial seeks the answer in the justifications and rationalizations of the racist status quo.

Moreover, the concept of denial questions knowledge as such, showing that the options 'they knew' and 'they did not know' are neither simple, nor exhaustive. In laying out the phenomenology of racism today, we thus find ourselves describing a broad range of the phenomena of denial.

(ii) Types of Denial of Racism

Many of the types of denial identified by Stanley Cohen in *Denial and Acknowledgement* are highly relevant to the specific case of the denial of racism. Following Cohen's distinctions, we can make a distinction among various forms of denial with respect to the truth-value awareness of the subject(s):

- Denial in good faith, whereby the subject honestly believes she is telling the truth.
- Denial as outright lying, whereby the truth of racist abuse is known, but denied as in the case of deliberate deception at the individual level or the spread of disinformation, manipulation, or cover-up at the political level.
- All other cases of partial knowing, whereby the 'denying' subject is in neither of the above mental states.

Both in theory and in practice, the most challenging case is the third one. Several schools of philosophical thought and social science have addressed the experience of 'knowing without knowing that you know', the lack of the Kantian 'transcendental apperception', or self-consciousness accompanying the mental 'possession' of the 'object'. The psychoanalytic metaphor of the 'subconscious', the phenomenological theories of perception as a constitution of the object, and the existential idea of the self are all possible frameworks for discussing the transcendental possibility of denial.

The psychoanalytical tradition, which is apparently the one most familiar to the general public in the West, insists that denial—in our case the denial of the existence or the significance of racist abuse—is a sort of unconscious defence mechanism for coping with disturbing mental contents. This view has limitations due to the very assumptions that make the concept of denial possible. One such assumption holds that, if they are not prevented from doing so by the various barriers raised by the imperatives of survival and well-being, people would see the 'denied' as 'existing'. Thus, any person, in principle, should be able to grasp the simple truth that people belonging to different racial or ethnic groups are equal as humans and possess dignity and rights. The fact that individuals 'deny' this simple truth is due to a need to avoid suffering if the 'truth' presents itself clearly in one's mind. Yet, why should we assume, together with the psychoanalysts, that, unhindered by any preconceptions, people should see the 'truth' of each state of affairs; specifically, why should they see the principle of basic human rights as a clear and universal truth? In most cultures throughout history, 'truths' about human life and society are not 'unveiled', but, rather, are 'developed'.

Furthermore, why should we assume, with the psychoanalysts, that people suffer when they see the unjust suffering of other people? The definition of denial as developed by Cohen and as applied herein is based on the universal validity of human rights and on an understanding of human nature as emotionally responsive to the suffering of others. It ignores or, in the case of this chapter, deliberately brackets the possibility that, for example, the deepest and most basic emotions of people are not altruistic, but are organically and inherently consistent with their own 'interests'. Thus, if someone does not notice racist practices, this may be due not to the attempt by the individual to avoid the suffering that would accompany acknowledgement, but to a more holistic reaction based on the individual's life interests. 'Not noticing' might be the human equivalent of the animal's supposed indifference to biologically irrelevant stimuli. Could it be that the psychoanalytical perspective endows us with more 'humanity' than we really bear? Could it be that our idealized 'humanity' is a normative, moral idea rather than a psychological and social reality? While these are philosophical speculations and therefore might lead to morally undesirable results, we should keep all theoretical options open be it as a matter of principle or simply as a matter of curiosity. The test of the socio-psychological hypotheses might depend on an understanding of the *mechanisms of shaming*, especially at the social and political levels, and these have not been the subject of much research.

Cohen's distinction among the literal, interpretative, and implicatory denials of human rights violations[15] is highly relevant to the denial of racism as well. Literal racist denial is as widespread as negative governmental reactions to human rights reports and is expressed in such statements as 'your reports are exaggerated', 'your position is alarmist, sensationalist, harmful', or 'we work on issues constructively, while your way of exposing things is destructive'. Interpretative denial is being applied when the facts are not disputed, but the interpretation of the facts is meant to disguise a racist approach. Thus, the 'clarifications' that 'the police action was not a punitive expedition, as human rights advocates called it, but a legitimate search for suspects in the Romani neighbourhood; it is true that force was used, but police acted in self-defence' or that 'this was not ethnic cleansing, but only

---

[15] Cohen, *supra* n. 9, at 23–5.

an anti-guerrilla action to isolate militant separatists' would not be easily accepted by public opinion if the subject of the 'search' or of the 'action' had been a neighbourhood or a home identical ethnically, economically, and socially to the majority in the nation.

'Implicatory' denial represents the toughest challenge in dealing with racist denial. In this case, the subject—individual or collective—inserts a shield of rationalizations between the facts and the moral responsibility the facts call for. A witness of racist abuse, for example the beating of Romani street children by police in Bucharest or Sofia, might acknowledge the facts of the case. The witness might say:

This is racist and outrageous, but it has nothing to do with me, especially since I am in a hurry to catch a plane. I can't correct all the world's evils. I have a right to do other important things. Actually, I am too busy doing other important things, important to the community and not egoistically to myself. Even if I would stop and intervene here, what can one ordinary person like me do? Finally, there must be people, and I am sure there are people somewhere whose job it is to handle this problem of the street children and the brutality against them. Oh, yes, I know of that organization working on the issue. So, let me hurry to the airport.

Implicatory denial—whereby the facts and their interpretation as racist abuse are both acknowledged, but the implications are denied—is a daily reality for many of us. As Cohen himself notes *en passant*, innocently, as if the remark does not turn the whole inquiry upside down, 'the problem is not to explain how people "deny", but how anyone ever pays any attention' (p. 30).

A further useful set of distinctions in Cohen revolves around individual denial, official denial (sponsored by the state), and cultural denial. This last is again the most serious challenge in addressing the issue of racist denial: society members, without being told what to think, reach a silent consensus about what can be publicly acknowledged. For example, there is a broad consensus in EU countries that the tightening of controls on immigration is good and that they cannot therefore be described as racist.

'[T]he mass media coverage of wars, atrocities and human rights stories is the most important arena to observe the mutual dependency between official and cultural denial,' writes Cohen.[16] This interdependency was evident in the anti-Serb bias of the mainstream Western media in the Kosovo War of 1999. ('Another busy night for our pilots over Yugoslavia,' stated a correspondent on a US-based CNN news broadcast heard one morning in late April 1999. As one author wrote, in a way typical in the spring of 1999, 'The cream of Serbian society has largely emigrated, and most of those who remain have lost touch with reality'.) Similarly, in the aftermath of the NATO bombing of Yugoslavia, the way in which the destruction of the Kosovo Roma community was presented in

---

[16] Ibid., at 27.

the mainstream media was an example of wholesale cultural denial. Rather than presenting the process as ethnic cleansing, the media stressed the 'understandable' aspect of revenge due to alleged Roma complicity with 'the Serbs'.

In conclusion, in no particular order, a brief description of several rhetorical forms of racist denial follows. The descriptions focus on the situation of the Roma, who are perhaps the most disadvantaged people in Europe on account of their race-ethnicity. The forms of denial listed below have been encountered repeatedly by the staff of the European Roma Rights Centre in discussions and in publications concerning Roma issues. The list could easily be expanded.

(1) *Race and ethnicity are presented as social or economic problems.* Government officials in Eastern Europe have been saying, 'We are not racist and do not discriminate. We have no problem with the race or ethnicity of the Roma, but this group is economically and socially weak. The fact that its members are of the same, namely Romani ethnicity, is unimportant (irrelevant, accidental, or other).' In this case, the government is creating an excuse for not dealing with race discrimination as an urgent issue. The government's obligation is reduced to improving, slowly and where it can, the material conditions, educational status, and so on of the ethnic group in question, depending on the availability of resources. That the group is also socially disadvantaged, marginalized, or excluded is evident, but this truth is twisted around so that it can be used to deny the racist reality.

(2) *The 'equality before the law' argument.* Somewhat contrary to denial through the presentation of race as solely a socio-economic problem, this argument stresses the alleged existence of equal protection before the law. The claim is that 'racial minority members are equal before the law or are entitled to equal protection by the law and therefore do not suffer discrimination in my country; anything that would favour them over others is unfair'. Sometimes, there may be a conflict between the requirement of equality before the law and the need to foster social justice with respect to ethnic minorities. In this case, special programmes for particular groups have been developed to compensate the disadvantage ('affirmative action' in the US, 'positive action' in Europe). In certain contexts, the stress on legal equality as a sufficient guarantee of race equality can be a seemingly legitimate and highly disguised form of denial.

(3) *The 'equal opportunity' (meritocratic) argument.* This argument is similar to the 'legal equality' argument. In this case, the claim might take the following form: 'The members of the Roma ethnic group enjoy equal opportunities with everyone else in our society. How they use these opportunities is up to them. The fact that they do not make good use of the opportunities is not our fault. People ultimately get what they deserve.' This form of denial sometimes verges on blaming the victims: 'The Roma must have done something wrong, if not the current generation, then previous ones;

otherwise they would not have ended up in such misery [or in prison, on the street, and so on].'

(4) *The limitation of the struggle against racism to prohibition and penalization.* Many people think that they have challenged racism in society sufficiently if (the most egregious forms of) racial discrimination is outlawed and access to justice and to adequate legal remedy is provided to the victims. In essence, this has been the anti-racism strategy reflected in the major conventions and projects of the United Nations to date. While this strategy of making race discrimination illegal and bringing lawsuits in cases of abuse is indispensable, it cannot alone eradicate or even substantially reduce racist practices (let alone attitudes) in society. Just as the removal or reduction of crime cannot be accomplished only via the criminal justice system, no matter how well developed this is, so the removal or reduction of racism is impossible if strategies to combat racism are limited to passing laws. Litigation is not a universal and sufficient response to racism. A society based on the rule of law may also be a society of racist complacency. This is especially true when litigation tends to be too expensive and beyond the reach of most victims.[17]

(5) *Recasting differences in race as mental disability.* An illustration of this form of denial might be the *de facto* racial segregation of Roma children in the school system in the Czech Republic, whereby these children may be sent to so-called 'special schools' for the mentally handicapped. The policy is built on the stereotype that Roma are inferior and that 'Romani children are not ready for normal school'. The result has been a denial of equal educational opportunity for most Romani children. The evidence documented by the ERRC shows that, in the city of Ostrava, for example, a Romani child is over twenty-seven times more likely than a non-Romani child to be enrolled in a 'special school'. Although Roma represent fewer than 5 per cent of all primary school-age pupils in Ostrava, they constitute around 50 per cent of the special school population. Nationwide, as the Czech government itself concedes, approximately 75 per cent of Romani children attend special schools, and more than half of all special school students are Roma.[18] This extraordinary racial disparity constitutes what the UN Committee on the Elimination of Racial Discrimination condemned in 1998 as '*de facto* racial segregation' in the field of education, and it is inconsistent with the Czech government's obligations

---

[17] In acknowledgement of this obstacle and in order to overcome it, public interest law has rapidly developed in the area of racial discrimination in the US, the UK, and elsewhere, enabling victims to obtain remedy even if their formal access to justice is rendered vacuous by the cost. On the prospects of a similar development of public interest law in Central and Eastern Europe, see Petrova, 'Political and Legal Limitations to the Development of Public Interest Law in Post-Communist Societies', 3 *The Parker School Journal of East European Law* (1996).

[18] For more details, see European Roma Rights Centre, 'A Special Remedy: Roma and Schools for the Mentally Handicapped in the Czech Republic', in *Country Reports*, no. 8, June 1999.

under international law. Many Czech politicians and educationalists deny vehemently that sending Roma to special schools is a racist policy. However, race-neutral factors (such as lack of language skills or poverty) fail alone to explain the gross racial overrepresentation in the schools.

(6) *Recasting differences in race as behavioural disorder.* According to the 'private student' arrangement in Hungary, if their behaviour disrupts their own work or that of others, pupils can be removed from school and transferred to a private study scheme, which does not involve school attendance. This seemingly race-neutral arrangement has, in effect, led to the exclusion of a number of Romani pupils from regular schooling. Because these pupils are still expected to take final exams, many of them drop out of school entirely. A similar form of recasting has been reported in the UK in the case of black Caribbean boys who have been removed from school due to bad behaviour.

'Black Caribbean boys are around six times more likely to be permanently excluded from UK schools than white boys, according to Department for Education and Employment Statistics. While there has been a lot of media interest in soaring school exclusion rates in England and Wales, the statistic no longer appears to shock. Yet for black Caribbean families it amounts to a crisis in the education of their children. With an estimated 10,000–14,000 permanent exclusions during 1995–6, schools are dumping the population of a small town each year. This suggests bad practice and possible unlawful discrimination in managing behaviour in schools. Exclusion from school often means the denial of the child's right to education; once excluded a pupil has only a 15 per cent chance of returning to mainstream schooling.'[19]

(7) *Duties are emphasized as preconditions for the enjoyment of rights.* The logic in this case is, 'If Roma do not fulfil their duty, x, they cannot claim their right, y.' Such was the communist approach to rights: rights were conditioned on the fulfilment of corresponding duties. The respective sections in communist constitutions were usefully titled 'Rights and Duties of the Citizen'. One often hears that the high dropout rate among Roma primary school pupils is due to the fact that Romani parents do not fulfil their parental duties. Hence, the overrepresentation of Romani children among those children who have been institutionalized without parental consent: a phenomenon which reflects the societal racist perception of Roma parents as incompetent parents. Absent in this case is the ability or willingness to understand rights as entitlements that are not dependent on the past, present, or future behaviour of the subject. This lack of a human rights perspective is evident in the overwhelmingly paternalistic social care approaches towards Roma issues, whereby Roma are seen as passive recipients of help, rather than as subjects of rights. In Italy,

---

[19] Osler, 'School Exclusions: A Denial of the Right to Education', 18 *Human Rights Education Newsletter* (Autumn, 1997).

for example, numerous charities are spending public funds to provide social work services to Roma in the insane world of the 'nomadic camps'.

(8) *The denial by 'positive example' argument.* 'Look at those members of a minority who have made it to the top of society [the company, and so on].' Such statements, in social practice, reflect a policy of tokenism that is used to counter allegations of racism and discrimination.

(9) *Denial by disclaimer.* This is the classic 'some of my best friends are Jews [Roma, blacks]' argument, also obvious in negative statements of the 'most Jews [Roma, blacks] are such and such, though, of course, there are exceptions' type. The personal disclaimer is so typical of most contemporary racist discourse that it can be considered an ideological marker. Actually, the above statements (with regard to Jews) were included in the questionnaires in Adorno's 1950 inquiry into prejudice; they produced clear clustering among the answers of high-scorers and low-scorers.

(10) *Individualization and self-exclusion from the mainstream.* 'I love my black neighbour, and her friendship is more dear to me than that of others; such personal links are more important than race relations in the larger society.' Similarly, 'I can't be racist, because in my building there was a Romani family, and I had a very good relationship with them.' (The latter statement was made by the current (as of October 2000) chairperson of a parliamentary commission on human rights in an East European country in response to accusations of racism; this particular public official has, in fact, displayed a variety of markedly racist attitudes in his approach to policy.)

(11) *The romanticizing stereotype.* A romantic stereotype is almost surely accompanied by a negative stereotype in the case of many ethnic groups, such as the Roma, the blacks and native Americans in the US, or the Australian indigenous people. The romantic stereotype of Roma includes such 'characteristics' as musical and dancing talent, capacity for passionate love and other strong emotions, spontaneity, free and spiritual personality, a magical relationship with nature, and the ability to enjoy themselves.[20]

(12) *The overstatement of historic optimism.* This argument is based on reference to historical progress in race relations. Statements such as 'compare and

---

[20] Here is an intriguing point on the origins of romanticizing practice, found in Ascherson: 'The Greek tragedians, when they had invented the barbarians, soon began to play with the "inner barbarism" of Greeks. Perhaps part of the otherness of barbarians was that, unlike the civilized, they were morally all of a piece—not dualistic characters in which a good nature warred with a bad, but whole. . . . Barbarians were homogeneous; civilized people were multiform and differentiated. The Greek tragedians thought this might be true about minds as well as bodies. If it was, they were not sure that the contrast between Greek and barbarian psychology—the first complex and inhibited, the second supposed to be spontaneous and natural— was altogether complimentary to the Greeks. Somewhere here begins Europe's long unfinished ballad of yearning for noble savages, for hunter-gatherers in touch with themselves and their ecology, for cowboys, cattle-reivers, gypsies and Cossacks, for Bedouin nomads and aboriginals walking their song-lines through the unspoiled wilderness', Ascherson, *supra* n. 14, at 148.

consider how much has changed in the last 20 years; see how much the situation of minority, x, has improved' are typical of this argument.

(13) *The normalization shrug.* On visiting a Romani ghetto somewhere in Europe, someone might say, shrugging, 'That's just what it's always like in places like this.'

(14) *Interpretative denial by downplaying the injury.* 'No serious damage has occurred. Roma were indeed treated not very gently by the police, but they don't feel abused or humiliated, because they're used to violence. They understand only the language of coercion.'

(15) *Condemning the condemners.* Certain Central European politicians presently in office have been heard to say: 'The Western governments are condemning us only because they want to put pressure on us. They are not really concerned with ethnic equality and their criticism is a geopolitical game.'

Almost none of the above rhetorical forms of racist denial, taken in isolation, would be sufficient to describe a racist attitude. Racist statements are contextual. We can describe an attitude as racist only if we can identify a set of opinions, a more or less clear bias or stereotype. Otherwise, we would have difficulty in differentiating racism from innocent, morally neutral remarks, such as 'The Spanish are bad drivers'.

Most forms of denial are characterized by a deceptively easy availability. They appear whenever needed as comments on the causes of racially based disadvantage, occasions for which, at the level of non-reflective everyday discourse, are never in short supply. For example, a person might say, 'Roma drop out of school because they are poor' and then add a minute later without understanding the circular argument he is making, 'They are poor because they don't study well'. Being 'logical' is not among the qualities of 'ideological' thought. Only upon reflection might one understand that racist rationalizations are not quite rational and often rotate in a vicious circle.

(iii) After Acknowledgement

The discussion of denial of racism should be accompanied by a discussion of *acknowledgement*. To become aware of the existence of denial and to acknowledge the presence of racism may become the beginning of a transformation at a personal level, as well as at a political level and a cultural level. Acknowledgement may lead to a reduction of racist attitudes and to antiracist action. But it may also lead to *acceptance*. This second option is so disturbing that it deserves a few comments.

It is possible that racist prejudice is clearly present in a social or political actor, that it is not denied or masked in any way, and that the actor admits and accepts it. Rather than denial, acceptance would now be our challenge. Acceptance is more dangerous to the public interest than are the various phenomena of denial. With denial in place in a society, anti-racist culture has already traversed part of the path to racial justice insofar as denial can be subsequently resolved through a more or less painful catharsis of acknowledgement that can be the starting point for practical work to eliminate racism. But consider a different case, in which the subject suggests that he is simply not good enough or strong enough to deal with his racist bias.

Racism is definitely a shame, and we have absolutely no excuse not to address it promptly and adequately. Yet, life is hard. We people are fallible, and we should do well to accept ourselves as such. No one is perfect, and we do not live in a perfect world. That I may think racist thoughts should not make me feel guilty, and I should not therefore become anguished and sacrifice my well-being.

This position of full acknowledgement, combined with an acceptance of one's participation in evil or one's weakness, is rare in democratic societies. But it is not implausible to expect that it would resurface in certain political contexts. Even in Western democracies, it may flourish on the soil of the popular 'feel-good-about-yourself' culture, which makes a virtue out of the acceptance of one's self, even one's faults.

II. RACIAL DISCRIMINATION

(i) Racial Discrimination as the Social Practice of Racism

While the acceptance option reveals an essential limitation on the struggle against racist denial and invites analysis of the not always benign practical and political implications of 'acknowledgement', it also highlights the strength of another concept, that of racial discrimination. Racism is a vast and vague notion, engaging the realms both of the mind and of reality, and its phenomenology is quite Protean. However, 'racial discrimination' has been defined in a clearer way and has been given a legal value, notably in Article 1 of the ICERD.[21]

Unlike racism as such, racial discrimination is understood in human rights law as a violation of human rights. The right to be free from discrimination on the basis of race (including ethnicity) is characterized by the universality, inalienability, and democratic nature of fundamental rights. By concluding ICERD, the states parties have in effect made it possible for

---

[21] Article 1 of ICERD defines racial discrimination as 'any distinction, exclusion, restriction, or preference based on race, colour, descent, or national or ethnic origin which has the purpose or effect of nullifying or impairing the recognition, enjoyment, or exercise, on an equal footing, of human rights and fundamental freedoms in the political, economic, social, cultural, or any other field of public life'.

practical measures to be adopted to reduce racism and even to overtake public opinion if the latter is moving at slower speeds. The concept of racial
discrimination takes the issue of racism beyond its dependence on acknowledgement. It makes room for the possibility that societies, as well as persons, may not learn to be mentally free of racist bias before practical steps
have been taken to eliminate racial discrimination. The best textbook from
which to learn anti-racism may be the lived experience of witnessing the
effects of the enforcement of anti-discrimination laws and policies.

Such a definition of racial discrimination has guided the UN Committee
on Racial Discrimination in its quest to identify forms of discrimination
which are objectively identifiable and therefore legally justiciable, regardless of
whether acknowledgement is present in governmental reports or policies.
However, the justiciability of racial discrimination cases has remained largely
rudimentary in the UN approach.

More recently, European Council Directive 43/2000 (29 June 2000)
'implementing the principle of equal treatment between persons irrespective
of racial or ethnic origin' has opened new prospects for anti-discrimination
litigation in European societies. It has done so by focusing on objective, meas-
urable aspects of racist behaviour, characterizing not only direct, but also indirect racial discrimination as a clearly identifiable social phenomenon on
account of the noxious effects and shifting the burden of proof in civil anti-
discrimination cases to the defendant, including non-state actors among perpetrators. Additionally, Protocol 12 of the European Convention on Human
Rights (ECHR), which has been open for ratification since 4 November
2000, brightens the future for anti-discrimination litigation in the European
Court of Human Rights by providing for protection from discrimination on
account of race and ethnicity not only *vis-à-vis* the rights enshrined in the
ECHR, but *vis-à-vis* all domestically protected legal rights.

These developments support the anti-racist movement by strengthening
the 'negative rights' aspect, that is, the ability of the movement to eliminate
racial discrimination. It may now be possible and helpful to foresee the struggle against racism occurring in two stages:

- *Racial equality.* The first stage is the struggle to eliminate all forms of racial
  discrimination; this struggle aims at achieving a situation of stability in
  which non-discrimination is the norm.
- *Racial justice.* During the second stage, which builds on the foundations of
  non-discrimination, the effort to achieve full racial and ethnic justice aims
  at 'the rights of minority cultures', as Will Kymlicka and others have
  employed the term.[22] The term is polyvalent, but here it is used only in reference to rights and to the processes employed to enforce them that go

[22] W. Kymlicka (ed.), *The Rights of Minority Cultures* (1995).

beyond the elimination of racial discrimination and seek the additional empowerment of ethnic and racial groups.

In light of the hierarchy of human rights concerns,[23] one should assume the precedence of the basic civil rights of minority members, such as freedom from discrimination, over special minority rights that extend beyond the securing of non-discrimination. Ethnically or racially motivated violence, ethnic cleansing, violations of due process, or systemic racial segregation in education, for example, are more urgent issues from this perspective than such (positive) rights as the preservation of one's culture, voting rights, or rights related to the self-government of a minority. This precedence should be understood within the framework of the assumption of the universality, indivisibility, and interdependence of human rights.

Human rights are still in search of a theory, as Louis Henkin and many others have stressed. No single comprehensive theory of the relation of the individual to society underlies the international human rights documents or is shared by the signatories. Yet, in an effort to put the right to freedom from racial discrimination in the context of other rights, it should be noted, in the first place, that the democratic nature of human rights implies the equality of humans in the enjoyment of human rights. Therefore, the prohibition of racial discrimination is meant to be valid with regard to all people, regardless of any distinction on whatever basis.

The following distinctions might be considered with a view to identifying a common ground for at least two groups of rights related to the right to freedom from racial discrimination:

- *Some* (a limited number of) rights go to all individuals without distinction of any kind, including without distinction of race or ethnicity. (These are, according to one interpretation, *the* 'human rights'.)
- *All* rights (or, according to a weaker version, all rights that exist as legal rights in domestic law) go to all individuals without distinction of race or ethnicity. (Note that Optional Protocol 12 of the ECHR takes account of this principle, and so does European Council Directive 2000/43 of 29 June 2000. However, neither document offers to extend the protection of rights to cover discrimination on a wider front, thus effectively leaving out discrimination on the basis of, *inter alia*, citizenship.)

These two groups of rights overlap in different ways, according to different criteria. In terms of the bearer of the right, the groups coincide: 'human

---

[23] Moral integrity is impossible without the capacity to arrange one's values and principles in a hierarchy, rather than simply maintaining them ready at hand to be referred to as occasion arises, as is typical of 'ideologies'. This argument has also been applied in another context: the analysis of the human rights dilemmas presented by the NATO bombing during the Kosovo war. See Petrova, 'The War and the Human Rights Community', 8 *East European Constitutional Review* (Summer 1999).

rights' proper (group 1) and non-discrimination rights (group 2) are both enjoyed by all people. In terms of the substance of the right (the answer to the question 'which rights?'), the first are a subset of the second, since few rights, sometimes called 'fundamental' rights, go to all human beings without any distinction on any basis. On the other hand, in terms of the discrimination accounted for, the second are a subset of the first.

It should be noted that international legal norms are currently weak in providing tools that anti-discrimination advocates can use to eliminate discrimination *in effect*. Accordingly, litigation in domestic and international courts in cases of systemic racial discrimination has critically depended on evidence of the intent to discriminate. It seems, however, that public interest lawyers, at least in Europe, may be on the brink of introducing a radical change. Following far-sighted court decisions in the area of gender anti-discrimination and in view of the recently adopted European Council Directive 43/2000 and the venues that will be created once Protocol 12 of the ECHR enters into force, the time may be approaching when courts will be handing down decisions redressing systemic racial discrimination, whereby evidence will be accepted proving effectively disparate results of practices in terms of race, regardless of intent.[24]

(ii) Racial Discrimination and Group Rights

'According to the principle that bad ideas never die but simply reappear in new forms, the group rights notion is now resurfacing, and doing so in rather bizarre habit,' wrote Albie Sachs in South Africa in 1992. 'The claim is made that in order to overcome what is castigated as simple majoritarianism, there should be special representation in the legislature and the executive for political minorities.'[25] Though Albie Sachs calls the whites a '*political* minority' and dismisses any claim to group rights simply by reminding us of the basics of political democracy, the fact is that the minority which was soon to become a political loser roughly coincided with a racial group as well. Yet, in the discussion here, the 'bad idea' of group rights is difficult to avoid. It is preferable, therefore, to face briefly its substance and explore its usefulness in the struggle against racism.

---

[24] A promising test case is the European Roma Rights Centre lawsuit, currently on the docket at the European Court of Human Rights, on behalf of several Romani families from Ostrava, Czech Republic. The applicants seek to eliminate, via a court decision, an entrenched system of segregated schooling that damages the educational opportunities of Romani children and causes further violations of their rights under the ECHR. For details on the litigation, see the ERRC website at <http://www.errc.org/publications/indices/czechrepublic.html>.

[25] A. Sachs, *Advancing Human Rights in South Africa* (1992), at 41.

A first question: Is the concept of group rights helpful in addressing racial discrimination? If the right to be free from discrimination on the basis of race, ethnicity, skin colour, or national origin is understood in a strictly individualistic sense, as solely an individual right, or a right reducible to a sum of individual rights, are we then in a stronger or a weaker position to (*a*) identify racial discrimination practices, (*b*) demonstrate that discrimination exists, or (*c*) obtain remedy in court.

A second question concerns the usefulness of the notion of group rights in taking the struggle against racism beyond non-discrimination. Is there a strategically meaningful usage of the group rights concept when one moves from the guarantee of the fundamental right of freedom from racial discrimination to the formulation of minority rights such as political representation or the preservation of minority culture?

For purposes of the discussion, let us first outline the relevant aspects of the concept of group rights. As Will Kymlicka has pointed out, the distinction between 'non-discrimination' and 'group rights' is a familiar one in the literature. Yet, Kymlicka himself does not appear to insist on the distinction.

'What Walzer calls the "neutral state" can be seen, in effect, as a system of "group rights" that supports the majority's language, history, culture, and calendar,' he states in analysing the positions of Michael Walzer and Nathan Glazer. 'Conversely, what Glazer calls the "group rights" model can be seen, in effect, as a more robust form of non-discrimination.'[26]

It has been argued that the non-discrimination model of the treatment of minorities works in societies where ethnic minorities are immigrant groups, as in the US. 'New World pluralism', which results from the equal treatment of ethnic group members by a 'neutral state', has thus been opposed to 'Old World pluralism', which results from a situation in which ethnic minorities prefer their cultural distinctiveness and are reluctant to integrate in the larger society. In explanations of the latter preference, Old World minority cultures are said to be the result not of a voluntary move from one culture to another, but of involuntary incorporation due to conquest, colonization, or the ceding of territory, whereby minorities are not satisfied with non-discrimination and eventual integration, but demand more, including self-government, proportional political or administrative representation, or different degrees of detachment from the majority polity.

Certainly, one can challenge the above distinction. There are significant cases that do not fit snugly in it. The Roma in Europe are not immigrants who want to integrate. Nor are they found in European nation-states as compact cultural, religious, or linguistic minorities that have appeared as a consequence of forced

---

[26] 'Introduction', in Kymlicka, *supra* n. 22, at 10. See also the literature quoted in this regard by Kymlicka in introducing the views of Michael Walzer and Nathan Glazer to summarize the argument.

incorporation. Nor are they easily compared with other ethnic minorities in Europe who have struggled for greater independence. The picture is more complicated. The Romani agendas are still in flux, and it is unclear whether the integrationist demands based on the achievement of only non-discrimination will prevail over demands for nationhood and for special rights within a 'united Europe'.

Of course, the discussion crucially depends on the way we define 'group rights'. Two possible options are:

- *Group rights are those rights that are irreducible to the sum of the rights of the respective group members.* Concrete rights to the political representation of minorities may be a case in point. In Romania, for example, the constitution guarantees the right of an ethnic minority to one seat in parliament provided the minority candidate has 5 per cent of the votes that are necessary to elect an MP through universal suffrage. The right belongs to the ethnic minority as such in the sense that it is quite difficult to understand it as the sum of the individual rights of all the members of the minority.
- *Group rights are those rights which a group member cannot claim alone.* One way to make sense of the concept of group rights is to apply it to those cases in which an individual group member alone cannot enforce the right, but the rights can only be enforced 'in community with others'. Indeed, if a group right is defined in this way, many rights will turn out to be 'group rights'. Obviously, an isolated individual would hardly succeed in obtaining a positive response to his demand for instruction or for media in his mother tongue without the support of others. Moreover, if the rights are granted, an individual alone cannot expect to enjoy them independently of others. From this point of view, exemptions based on cultural or religious grounds in the observation of certain laws are not group rights: even if there is only one Sikh in a country, he would still rightly be able to enjoy an exemption from the law that cyclists have to wear helmets. In this understanding, group rights are only those rights that can be meaningfully claimed and exercised by a group.

Whatever the theory, in practical terms, while an individual may demand instruction or media in her mother tongue or political participation proportional to the size of her ethnic group, alone she cannot exercise the claimed right without involving other members of the same ethnic group. The notion of *group* is assumed in a number of rights (religious, linguistic, cultural, and so on) in terms of implementation or exercise, though not necessarily in terms of the existence of the right. In other words, we may insist that a certain right (for example, the right to proportional political representation) is due to individuals, but the enjoyment of that right is nonetheless unthinkable without others.

Opponents of group rights have pointed out that limitations on individual rights in the name of group rights obscure the fact that precedence is given to the interests of some individuals over others. This is a crucial observation, and it should be kept in view in examining the usefulness of group rights in the elimination of racism.

In light of the above, the question now becomes: Can we deal effectively with racial discrimination without invoking the concept of group rights? According to Vernon van Dyke,

It would facilitate affirmative action if ethnic communities were accepted as right-and-duty-bearing units. After all, the discrimination for which affirmative action is compensatory was directed against individuals because of their membership in certain communities, and through them against the community as such. The discrimination was in a sense impersonal; it was not that a given person was to be denied certain opportunities and thus be excluded or kept down; it was rather that the whole community was to be kept in its place. The reciprocal of this is to take compensatory action for the whole community and to let individual members benefit even if they have not personally suffered discrimination.[27]

The very concept of racial discrimination implies the existence of groups in society. It is true that *individuals* are victims of discrimination, but they are discriminated against not because of their unique individuality, having a name and a face, but because they are members of a certain more or less negatively perceived group. Discrimination on the basis of race, ethnicity, religion, and so on is a violation of someone's *individual* right to equality of treatment, but one is victimized in one's capacity as a group member. Therefore, the concept of discrimination is based on a preconceptual assumption of membership in a group. Discrimination implies a group. But does it imply a *group right*?

Litigation practices in the United States, England, and elsewhere have demonstrated that remedies to racial discrimination can be achieved entirely within the individual rights paradigm, regardless of the fact that in some cases a group rights approach might also have been effective and probably easier. Similarly, in the litigation of the European Roma Rights Centre challenging the placement of Roma in schools for the mentally handicapped, the individual rights framework has proved sufficient both in the formulation of claims about existing racist practices and in the demand for remedies. Evidence, including statistics, aimed at proving systemic discrimination in the schooling of Romani children was built up by the ERRC without recourse to the concept of a group right.[28] If the victims in a similar case obtain remedy, it will be possible to spell out that remedy in terms of measures aimed at individuals.

[27] Van Dyke, 'The Individual, the State, and Ethnic Communities in Political Theory', in Kymlicka, *supra* n. 22, at 50.
[28] See the ERRC press release of 15 June 1999 on the lawsuit brought by Romani families before the Czech Constitutional Court, <http://www.errc.org/publications/indices/czechrepublic.html>.

In the case of rights to political representation, however, it may be wiser for one to make use of the 'bad notion' of group rights. If not, it may be necessary to twist words around in order to accommodate the issue to the language of the right of an individual member of a group to vote or to live under a government or public administration that is inclusive of her ethnic group. One must only attempt to formulate as an individual right the Romanian constitutional guarantee of the right of ethnic minorities to a seat in parliament, for example, for the difficulty to become apparent. The problem is not necessarily that one cannot perceive every demand of a group in terms of a right of a group member. The point is that, if the unit covered by the right is the group, then the expression of the right becomes more appropriate and reflects more accurately the social reality if it refers to the group rather than merely to the individual.

These comments should not be interpreted to mean that the issue of individual versus group rights is of a verbal nature only. Rather, reality itself is dialectic. The proper question should be: 'Is the term "group right" and the concept underlying it, that is, the concept of irreducible rights, the bearer of which is the group as such, a better framework for the defence of the rights?' Thus, we should be looking at the problem from a conventionalist perspective, similar to that of Henri Poincaré in seeking to understand the status of the concepts of natural science. If we adopt a conventionalist point of view, our approach to the elimination of racism becomes more pragmatic and aims at concrete results rather than at the resolution of metaphysical questions.

III. BEYOND RACIAL EQUALITY: WHAT JUSTICE?

Similar to other human rights, those included in the Universal Declaration of Human Rights for example, the right to non-discrimination on the basis of race or ethnicity applies to the individual as a human being, not as a member of an ethnic or a racial group.[29] However, when seeking to extend the anti-racism agenda beyond anti-discrimination, we articulate rights that are due not to all individuals, but only to certain individuals as members of groups, or even to the groups themselves. The notion of 'special minority rights' can be useful in this regard.

If the struggle against racism can be taken beyond the demand for non-discrimination, should a set of group rights be articulated so as to facilitate the anti-racism agenda? Would the notion of group rights be useful in the effort to take the struggle against racism beyond the achievement of non-discrimination?

---

[29] According to the Universal Declaration of Human Rights, the rights enumerated therein are due to 'everyone . . . without distinction of any kind, such as race, colour, sex, language, religion, political or other opinion, national or social origin, property, birth, or other status'.

More concretely, for instance in the context of Roma rights in Europe, is there a strategically meaningful group rights concept that can be used to shift the focus from the guarantee of the fundamental right to freedom from racial discrimination to the formulation of rights such as the right to political representation or the right to the preservation of minority culture?

These questions cut across two discourses developed in race theory: (1) the discourse on the community-related needs of human beings and (2) the debate over ethnic or racial cultural identity.

'Individuals want freedom and equality, to be sure, but there is also a "quest for community",' van Dyke, for instance, has stated with a view to the former. 'To focus only on the rights of individuals is to focus only on forces making for atomization and estrangement and to ignore primordial collective sentiment and group loyalties.'[30]

Some authors (referred to sometimes as 'communitarians')[31] argue that 'cultural belonging' is a basic human need. Others object by offering a cosmopolitan alternative and denying that the enjoyment of one's culture is an indispensable universal human need. Jeremy Waldron warns that reconciling the two views is practically difficult:

Nor are the citizens of the world, the modernist dreamers of cosmopolis, proposing exactly to destroy minority cultures. Their apartments are quite likely to be decorated with Inuit artifacts or Maori carvings. Still, we know that a world in which deracinated cosmopolitanism flourishes is not a safe place for minority communities. Our experience has been that they wither and die in the harsh glare of modern life, and that the custodians of these dying traditions live out their lives in misery and demoralization.[32]

If we recognize the 'quest for community' as a basic human need, it would then be logical to accept that people—be they members of minority cultures or ethnic groups as such—have rights that are related to the need to preserve their cultures. The preservation of cultures would require from the state more than a passive toleration of minority cultures; it would involve positive action, as indeed international law recommends and sometimes mandates with a view to the elimination of the effects of discrimination. The answer to the question of whether a basic need for a community culture exists or not carries implications: it would have an impact on whether the issues surrounding minority cultures would be pursued in terms of rights or in terms of policy.

[30] Van Dyke, *supra* n. 27, at 49. The term 'quest for community' is borrowed from Nisbet. See R. A. Nisbet, *The Quest for Community* (1953).
[31] See e.g. A. MacIntyre, *After Virtue: A Study in Moral Theory*, 2nd edn. (1984); Taylor 'Atomism', 2 *Philosophical Papers: Philosophy and the Human Sciences* (1985), at 187; M. Walzer, *Spheres of Justice* (1983).
[32] Waldron, 'Minority Cultures and the Cosmopolitan Alternative', in Kymlicka, *supra* n. 22, at 99.

In many cases, it may be easier to achieve certain goals in the empowerment of ethnic groups not through the articulation of group *rights*, but through the formulation and adoption of *policy*. There may be situations in which the difference is blurry, as may be the case of the European Charter on Regional and Minority Languages, which speaks strictly in terms of policy, yet in effect is trying to defend language rights. However, the difference between rights and policy should be insisted upon as an essential one in most cases. Even when it is based on dialogue between state and minority representatives, a policy will always be dependent on the political will of the elite, while rights, including group rights, are perceived as entitlements and therefore are more likely to be sustained during periods of instability or crisis. A right can be seen as a need or an interest for which the interested party has obtained the 'perpetual' passivity of the bearers of the opposite interest. The 'right' signifies the victory over the opposite interest. The 'right' is a fortified interest which has been claimed, recognized, and guaranteed and which is often assigned the character of a moral prerogative. For example, affirmative action in higher education may be easier to defend in terms of policy. Yet, it would represent a greater achievement for the anti-racist movement if the same result could be formulated as a right of minority members or groups.

In the cultural identity discourse, there is a fundamental paradox involved in the identification of the disadvantaged. This paradox has been exposed by, *inter alia*, feminist scholars in respect to gender identity. To challenge anti-women prejudice and the implied reduction from a 'universal' human being to a particular human being (a 'woman'), one must first be able to employ and *pronounce* the particularist term ('woman'). To challenge the reduction from the universal to the particular (a reduction that may be the essence of phenomena such as prejudice and discrimination), one has to assume and to dwell on this reduction in a somewhat self-defeating manner. In order to attack a reality in which there are 'Gypsies' as well as 'non-Gypsies', one has to have first constructed the 'Gypsy-non-Gypsy' dichotomy. One has to construct the 'Gypsy' identity in order to combat anti-Gypsyism. In this effort, 'Roma' (the result of a more recent cultural and historical construction, which has also removed from legitimacy the word 'Gypsy' itself) has 'become' the identity claimed by the members of this far from culturally distinct community. By definition, a claim for a certain degree of ownership of an identity excludes other people (or identities) and at least partially opposes them. We then encounter a curious performative contradiction: those who want to end the racist distinction 'Roma', for example, must first define 'Roma', thereby running the risk of 'essentialization'.[33]

---

[33] For a politically significant illustration, see Kawczynski, 'Report on the Condition of the Roma in Europe' (Report commissioned by the Organization for Security and Cooperation in Europe for presentation at the OSCE Implementation Meeting, October (2000)). The author

Claiming an ethnic or racial identity involves a reinforcement and even fortification of that identity. From that point on, there are at least three possibilities, only one of which effectively restores the fullness of humanity to the disadvantaged identity. The other two lead astray. These possibilities are (*a*) essentialism: the extremist valorization of the ethnic (cultural) identity at the expense of others, (*b*) the deletion of the cultural identity through full assimilation in the majority, (*c*) the pathway forward, the combination of both universality and difference: Roma are universal human beings, equal in dignity and rights, yet enjoying a cultural difference and preserving this difference.

For many authors, the discussion of group rights involves the issue of self-determination. In 1977, van Dyke defended the right to self-determination as a group right, thereby opening up a space for the further examination of this link. He writes:

In some cases the rights that groups exercise are perhaps reducible to individual rights and can thus be brought within the framework of liberal theory, but in other cases the rights belong to groups as corporate units.'[34]

He also contends that

it is preferable to adopt a more complex paradigm permitting individual and group rights, both legal and moral, to exist side by side.[35]

Van Dyke's examples of community rights include the existence in Belgium of a constitutional provision that, with the possible exception of the prime minister, the cabinet must comprise an equal number of French-speaking and Dutch-speaking ministers. Further on, van Dyke cites US case-law in the area of school desegregation, housing legislation, jury selection, and racial gerrymandering. But his examples demonstrate only the inherence of the concept of group in—or the collective nature of—segregation, political representation, and so on, without proving the indispensability of the idea of *group rights*.

Yet, in discussing issues revolving around self-determination, we can hardly escape the group rights approach. An important aspect of the demand for self-determination is its 'moral' character. Van Dyke does not hesitate to introduce the concept of group rights that are not legal, but moral. In 1975, he reminds us, the UN General Assembly adopted a resolution calling for measures 'to

objects to the reduction of humans to 'Gypsies' (p. 5). At the same time, throughout the report, he patrols the borders of the Gypsy identity, making sure that only ethnic Gypsies are allowed to speak on behalf of Gypsies, regardless of the issue under discussion.

[34] Van Dyke, *supra* n. 27, at 32. Given the vast discrepancies in definitions of liberalism, the question of whether certain views are liberal or not is not addressed here.

[35] Ibid., at 37 and at 38: 'Of the various questions that attend these practices, two will be considered here. The first concerns reducibility: whether the communities have rights as units, and whether the rights of the communities are reducible to the rights of individuals as members. The second is whether the legal rights should be thought of as reflecting moral claims. I will argue that the communities have the rights as units, that in some cases the rights are irreducible, and that in principle they may well reflect moral claims.'

enable the Palestinian people to exercise its inalienable national rights'.[36] In this case, it is difficult to see the resolution as a claim to legal rights; rather, the resolution assumes that the 'Palestinian people' have a moral right.

In the case of the European Roma, what is it that they are claiming? Only the right to non-discrimination or more than that? If more, what? Autonomy? Distinction? Self-government? Independence? Recently, Roma have been involved in a lively discussion across Europe regarding their future status. Observers have asked, do Roma want integration in national societies (with minority rights guaranteed) or status as a European non-territorial nation, a status closer to that of citizens of a sovereign nation? If the latter, would the sovereignty of existing states be challenged in any way? During the congress of the International Romani Union in July 2000, representatives adopted a 'non-territorial Roma nation' platform,[37] which is likely to mobilize support and may eventually turn out to be a uniting principle of the Roma movement.

In the case of the Roma at least, the dichotomy between demands for non-discrimination (insisted upon by Roma rights organizations such as the ERRC) and demands for autonomy may be overstated, however. The main Romani organizations, such as the Roma National Congress and the International Romani Union, want both respect for individual rights within nations, including non-discrimination and equal treatment by national authorities, *and* the (seemingly opposed) strengthening of self-government across borders, autonomy, or even sovereignty.

'The Roma are citizens of the countries they are living in, and it is this fact that obliges these countries to let Roma participate equally in the community', says Rudko Kawczynski, who seems to exemplify this double claim.[38] At the same time, he insists on 'the Roma's right of self-determination' (p. 14). He expects the state 'to acknowledge the Romani population as a national minority entitled to recognized political representation' (p. 16). And, blissfully unaware of the theoretical debates about the protection of civil liberties as opposed to (cultural or political) self-determination, he writes: 'In order for social development projects to succeed, Roma must be granted guarantees for the protection of civil liberties. This means a change in the political status of Roma towards political, social and cultural self-determination' (p. 19).

The English and French word 'nation' usually refers to the population of a sovereign state, but the word can sometimes be used to signify a national or ethnic community lacking a national state, as in the Welsh nation, the

---

[36] UN General Assembly Res. 3375(XXX) (1975).

[37] Representatives of the International Romani Union met with Vaclav Havel in October 2000 to explain the organization's demand that Roma be recognized as 'a nation without a state'. 'We do not want our own state,' General-Secretary Christo Kyuchukov of the Union told the Czech Telegraph Agency (CTK) after the meeting. 'We want other states to recognize us as a nation equal to them.' 20 Oct. 2000.

[38] Kawczynski, *supra* n. 33, at 12.

Catalan nation, and so on. By the same token, the Roma nation has now claimed its right to self-determination. Nimni appears correct when he writes that, 'The epistemological requirement locating the national phenomenon within a hierarchical, universal and developmental continuum must be seriously challenged. . . .'[39] Moreover, the serious challenge in the Roma case is likely to arise from movements and platforms, rather than theories.

It is hoped that European governments will react in enlightened ways to the challenge. One positive model of racial justice might be 'multi-culturalism', in the sense developed by the government of Australia, even though the term 'multi-culturalism' itself remains vague and is vigorously debated.

'We reject the argument that cultural diversity necessarily creates divisiveness. Rather we believe that hostility and bitterness between groups are often the result of cultural repression,' stated the Australian government when it adopted its new, more open policy towards immigrant groups.[40]

On the negative side, group rights can easily become a source of conflict when they are claimed by national or ethnic entities that have no clearly defined territorial borders. Thus, former Yugoslav president Milosevic refused, in 1989 and afterwards, to recognize the republics in Yugoslavia as the legitimate units of the federation. He saw only nations as the main constituents and bearers of group rights. He did not want Serbs to live in a number of independent states, but in one state. Those people who did not wish to be part of this state were free to secede, he claimed. However, first, border adjustments would have to be made to reflect the national composition, and, secondly, Serbia would remain the successor state.

To this view of group rights, the concept of 'asymmetrical federation' was developed by the Slovenes in mid-1989 when they amended their republican constitution, an act which precipitated the disintegration of Yugoslavia.[41] Then later, in the summer of 1991, Bosnia's president, Alija Izetbegovic, and the president of Macedonia, Kiro Gligorov, proposed the asymmetrical federation as a model for the constitution of Yugoslavia. The formula envisaged Serbia and Montenegro as the heart of the Yugoslav Federation, Bosnia and Macedonia as semi-detached constituent republics, and Slovenia and Croatia possessing as much autonomy inside the federation as they wanted. In this way, the Serbs' desire for a single state and the Slovene and Croatian aspirations for sovereignty could be accommodated.

Clearly, the danger inherent in the group rights framework is essentially always this: there is no consensus on the answer to the question 'which is the group?'. The reason is that, except in cultural and historical terms, *the group is not* at all a natural phenomenon.

[39] Nimni, 'Marx, Engels, and the National Question', in Kymlicka, *supra* n. 22, at 72.

[40] Commonwealth of Australia, 'Migrant Services and Programmes: Report of the Review of Post-Arrival Programmes and Services for Migrants' (Canberra: AGPS, 1978), at 104–5.

[41] See, e.g. L. Silber and A. Little, *The Death of Yugoslavia* (1995), at 79–81.

Positive action (in US usage, affirmative action) is a policy aimed at reversing racial (or, in different contexts, other prohibited) discrimination and achieving non-discrimination. It does not appear always to presuppose a group right. It can be regarded as a remedy to current discrimination. Owen M. Fiss insists that, with respect to the interpretation of the equal protection clause of the US Constitution, the 'anti-discrimination principle', which relates to the individual, ought to be replaced by the principle of the elimination of group disadvantage.[42] While many forms of positive action can easily be presented as a more consistent and effective means of eliminating racial discrimination, other forms of positive action may be understood in the sense of the 'special measures' required by ICERD, which stipulates that parties

shall, when the circumstances so warrant, take . . . special . . . measures to ensure the adequate development and protection of certain racial groups or individuals belonging to them for the purpose of guaranteeing them the full and equal enjoyment of human rights (ICERD, Article 2(2)).

An example of the first type is the introduction of quotas for disadvantaged minorities in universities or large companies. An example of the second is legislation specifying the rules of political participation for ethnic minorities.

IV. CONCLUSIONS AND RECOMMENDATIONS

The existence and the implications of racism and racial discrimination are broadly denied in democratic cultures. The degrees and types of denial are indicative of the progress made by anti-racist culture. To challenge racism, acknowledgement is the first step, but it should be followed by a human rights offensive against racial discrimination. The legally viable concept of racial discrimination well suits the needs of the agendas of racial and ethnic groups and minorities in fighting racist culture (the racist consensus). However, the strategies required to defeat racism are not exhausted by the achievement of a 'non-discrimination status quo' through the application of tools such as anti-discrimination legislation. Additional strategies to combat racism include 'special rights' for individual members of minorities, as well as minority communities, and in some cases the conceptual framework of group rights is relevant. Positive action may be simply an extension of the principle of non-discrimination, but in the case of voting rights, for example, it can be the core of the protection for special group rights empowering disadvantaged minorities, most notably by providing them with political representation or self-government. Non-discrimination is the first leg of the trip which must be

[42] Fiss, 'Groups and the Equal Protection Clause', 5 *Philosophy and Public Affairs* (Winter 1976), 157.

undertaken to eliminate racist practices. The second leg is represented by the various forms of political participation of racial and ethnic groups.

The World Conference against Racism, Racial Discrimination, Xenophobia, and Other Intolerance (WCAR), scheduled for the summer of 2001, is a good opportunity for the anti-racist movement to advance its agenda. Most of the discussion in this chapter is meant to support a set of practical recommendations that has been adopted by at least one large international NGO forum held in preparation for the conference.[43]

The struggle against racism would benefit greatly from lobbying at the international level for measures to strengthen the role of the United Nations in dealing with racism and racial discrimination, specifically with regard to the work of the UN Committee on the Elimination of Racial Discrimination (CERD), by:

- Ensuring CERD's efficacy as a monitoring body by introducing effective sanctions in cases in which states parties of the International Convention on the Elimination of All Forms of Racial Discrimination do not comply with CERD's 'Concluding Observations' within a reasonable period of time.
- Introducing a mechanism for CERD judicial review by making CERD's decisions with regard to individual complaints against ICERD state parties legally binding, as well as by providing for enforceable sanctions in case of the failure by states to comply with such decisions within a reasonable period of time.

It is recommended that the role of CERD be enhanced by:

- Introducing a transparent process for the appointment of CERD members on the basis of criteria such as proven competence and distinguished achievement in anti-racism and by providing for NGO input into the selection process in each country.
- Providing adequate funding to ensure legal aid to individual complainants.
- Televising all CERD sessions in which country reports are reviewed so that they can be rebroadcast for the purpose of public education and oversight, translating the reports of these sessions into all official UN languages, and recommending that states provide and widely circulate print versions of these proceedings.

---

[43] The author, together with others, drafted and worked to have the recommendations listed herein adopted by the Meeting on NGOs from Central and Eastern Europe (Warsaw, 15–18 Nov. 2000), which formed part of the preparation process for the World Conference Against Racism (WCAR). See 'Statement by the Participants in the Meeting of NGOs from Eastern and Central Europe, Warsaw, November 15–18, 2000, Addressed to the World Conference Against Racism (WCAR)', at <http://www.unhcr.ch/html/racism>.

It is recommended that CERD consider issuing a 'General Comment' to:

- Interpret racial discrimination as constituting 'degrading treatment' within the meaning of Article 3 of the European Convention on Human Rights as construed by the European Court of Human Rights.
- Interpret the concept of 'racial discrimination' to include both 'direct discrimination' and 'indirect discrimination' as this term is defined in European Council Directive 43/2000 (29 June 2000), 'implementing the principle of equal treatment between persons irrespective of racial or ethnic origin'.
- Instruct that, for the purposes of consideration of individual communications pursuant to Article 14 of ICERD, once a complaint sets forth a *prima facie* case of discrimination, the respondent government bears the burden of showing that the challenged law or practice has an objective and reasonable justification.
- Interpret the duty of states to eliminate all forms of racial discrimination, pursuant to Article 2(2) of ICERD, as requiring, in certain cases, positive action to remedy systemic discrimination.

4

The Internet: A New Horizon for Hatred?

MARÍA LUISA FERNÁNDEZ ESTEBAN

There has been a dramatic increase worldwide in bias-related incidents directed towards ethnic, religious, and racial minorities. In parallel, there has also been an increase in all kinds of racist and xenophobic propaganda. The spread of this sort of material over the Internet is a matter of concern for many countries. Thus, the UN General Assembly has called for an assessment of the role of the Internet in the perpetuation or the effort to eliminate racism and racial discrimination.[1] This chapter explores the ways in which this propaganda of hate is spread on the Internet and the initiatives being undertaken to oppose this phenomenon. The response to be adopted to messages of hate and xenophobia on the Internet is not a simple one. The multifaceted nature of the Internet must be taken into consideration.

In the first part of the chapter, the distinctive features of the Internet are examined. An understanding of the structure of the Internet and how it differs from traditional media is necessary if one is to confront the racism and xenophobia being fostered over the web. The analysis then considers the new methods of spreading racism and xenophobia that have appeared because of the Internet. Some experts have begun to talk of an 'electronic community of hate'. The third section outlines traditional strategies for countering hate speech. A clear-cut division seems to be appearing between, on the one hand, countries which oppose a frontal attack on the presentation of any sort of material supporting racial supremacy, denial of the historical reality of the Holocaust and racial ideologies and which may even oppose the criminalization of public incitements to violence based on race, and, on the other hand, countries such as the United States which favour an approach based on the belief that 'more discussion' and the airing of 'counter views' are the most effective strategies for fighting hate speech. The reasons why the nature of the Internet makes national antihate laws difficult to apply or even futile are analysed. The chapter then surveys the efforts of various countries to counteract hate speech on the Internet. Organizations dedicated to the elimination

---

[1] United Nations GA Res. 51/81 (1996), para. 10.

of racial hatred have been developing new methods to fight electronic messages of hatred. However, their task is a difficult one given the current policies
of information and service providers on the Internet. Finally, attention is
given to the key role being played by some Internet information and service
providers in the fight against hate speech.

I. HOW IS THE INTERNET DIFFERENT FROM OTHER MEDIA?

(i) Internet Basics

The Internet is the electronic web of wired and wireless telephone connections which enables individual computers and computer networks each
assigned a unique electronic address to send and receive data and images
among themselves with the assistance of various electronic carriers and con-
necting devices. It was originally developed by the US Department of
Defence for research and military use based upon the simple but powerful
idea that, in case of an attack on the country, the existence of such a network
would help ensure the continued transfer of vital information. Although the
Internet as a medium of electronic information exchange has been available
for at least three decades, it has become more generally widespread and popular because of relatively recent graphic and data transfer enhancements such
as the worldwide web.

Each computer serving the Internet has a unique identifier. A key component of the identifier, the 'domain name', is common to millions of other computers that belong to the same 'branch'. In the domain-name system (DNS),[2]
the root of the system is unnamed. Then, there are the so-called 'top-level
domain names' (TLDNs). These are the generic names, such as 'edu', 'com',
'net', 'org', 'gov', 'mil', and 'int', and the two-letter ISO–3166 country codes.
Under each TLDN, a hierarchy of names is usually created. Generally, many
organizations are registered directly under the generic TLDNs, and the individual organizations may then establish any additional structure. Some of
these individual organizations are proprietary networks called 'Internet service providers'. These allow access to the Internet through network gateways.
They have millions of subscribers and account for a large share of all Internet
users.

Internet service providers can be included in a larger category of actors
operating on the Internet, the online intermediaries. In open networks such
as the Internet, the online intermediaries are those actors which do not take

---

[2] For a general overview of the DNS, see European Commission, 'The Organization and
Management of the Internet: International and European Policy Issues, 1998–2000', COM
(2000) 202, 4 Apr.

part in the creation or selection of the information to be disseminated. Instead, they play various subsidiary roles in the online dissemination of the information provided by the so-called 'content providers'. The different functional roles that can be carried out by online intermediaries are:[3]

- The *network operator* provides the facilities such as cables, routers, and switches for the transmission of data.
- The *access provider* offers access to the Internet. Most individuals connect to the Internet through an access provider's server and commonly also obtain e-mail addresses from this source.
- The *host-service provider* supplies a server through which it rents space to users who wish to host content, for instance a webpage, that can include all kinds of material. Some access providers also give users the opportunity to host pages.
- *Bulletin board operators, news groups,* and *chat room operators* provide space so that users can exchange information and post messages within defined groups.
- *Information location-tool providers* offer tools so that Internet users can find websites where the specific information they seek may be located.

(ii) How the Internet Differs from Traditional Media

The Internet is a vehicle of simultaneous mass communication that exceeds the scale and immediacy of other forms of international information publication, such as print, radio, television, telegraphy, or teleconferencing. Unlike more traditional media, the Internet supports a variety of communication modes. These may be grouped into four categories:[4] (*a*) one-to-one asynchronous communication like e-mail, (*b*) bulletin boards and list servers that require the user to sign up for a service or to log on to access messages grouped around a particular topic, (*c*) synchronous communication which may be one-to-one, like Internet phoning, or one-to-few, or one-to-many, like chat rooms, and (*d*) asynchronous communication that generally requires the user to employ a seek function to access information and that is normally one-to-many, like the search on the worldwide web, gophers, and FTP sites. This is all facilitated by international conventions which have established universal standards allowing the exclusive assignment of unique electronic addresses to individual dial-up sites (the domain names).

---

[3] Julià-Barceló, 'Liability for On-line Intermediaries: A European Perspective', 27028, *ECLIP EP*, 21 Oct. 1999, <http://www.jura.uni-muenster.de/eclip/documents/deliverable_2_1_4_liability.pdf>.

[4] Morris *et al.* 'The Internet as a Mass Medium', 46 *Journal of Communication* (1996) 39, at 42.

A unique characteristic of the Internet is that it functions simultaneously as a medium for publishing and as a medium for communication. An Internet user may 'speak' or 'listen' interchangeably. At any time, a user may become a content provider of his own accord or through a 'reposting' by a third party of the information the user has offered. The Internet therefore radically differs from traditional broadcasting and telecommunication services. The constant shift from 'publishing mode' to 'private communication mode'—governed traditionally by very different legal regimes—constitutes one of the main challenges of Internet regulation.[5]

Another truly original characteristic of the Internet is that it affords any individual the possibility to reach an undetermined number of other Internet users. As the US Supreme Court put it in *Reno, Attorney General of the United States et al. v American Civil Liberties Union:*[6]

The Internet has no parallel in the history of human communication. It provides millions of people around the globe with a low-cost method of conversing, publishing and exchanging information on a vast array of subjects with the worldwide and virtually limitless audience. Never before in history has one person had the power to reach out to the world at large.

The ability of the Internet to afford new powers to do things on a grand scale is what attracts not only the newspaper reporter and human rights activist, but also the terrorist, the child molester, the drug smuggler, the hate-group leader, and the pornographer.[7] There has always been illegal and harmful content in the media, but, because of the specific nature of the Internet, there is no central control and therefore anyone can introduce into the home illegal material or material encouraging criminal behaviour. Because there are no frontiers, the control of the Internet appears quite difficult, if not impossible.

(iii) Internet, Minorities, Haves, and Have-nots

Some authors have pointed out that Internet use is itself skewed along racial lines.[8] Moreover, as a result of lopsided access, it will drive a further wedge between the 'haves' and 'have-nots'. There is an ominous North/South divide

---

[5] European Commission, 'Communication on Illegal and Harmful Content on the Internet', COM (1996) 487 final, 16 Oct. 1996, <http://www.ispo.cec.be/legal/en/internet/communic.html>.

[6] Supreme Court of the United States, *Reno v American Civil Liberties Union et al.*, 117 S. Ct. 2329 (1997), <http://www2.epic.org/cda/cda_decision.html>.

[7] Guzman, 'State of the Internet: Report with a Focus on Racism' (1997), <http://www.unhchr.ch/html/menu2/10/c/racism/guzman.htm>.

[8] Jenkins, 'Erasing e-Racism and Digitalizing Democracy: A Conceptual Response to Combat Racism and Racial Discrimination on the Internet' (1997), <http://www.unhchr.ch/html/menu2/10/c/racism/jenkins.htm>.

emerging. Even within the United States, unintended racial inequities in access to the Internet have a potentially long-term significance. The Internet is becoming an all-encompassing tool in education, commerce, government services, news, entertainment, cultural expression, and interactive communications. Those without access to it will be profoundly handicapped. This may mean that the Internet will encourage some to distort the culture, needs and interests of certain racial and other social groups. In Resolution 51/81, the UN General Assembly expressed concern over the effect of technological developments in communications and computer networks on young people, indigenous people, and migrant workers and their families. The General Assembly urged governments to adopt all necessary measures to combat these and other new forms of racism.

On the other hand, Internet access has allowed indigenous and disadvantaged people to garner worldwide financial and political support by telling their own stories without censors. 'Laptop publishing' is now able to rival the best official propaganda.

According to the European Commission, the information society can play an important role in promoting empowerment and integration, especially by enhancing the ability of citizens fully to participate in democratic processes. However, the use of information society resources can also have negative features, as the worrying growth in hate-sites and the widespread circulation of racist material on the Internet shows.[9]

II. NEW MEDIA, NEW RACISM

The Internet has proved a very effective instrument for the distribution of hate propaganda. The content of the racist messages being spread through the Internet ranges from inflammatory diatribes to pseudo-scientific presentations variously wrapped in the language of genetics, psychology, history, anthropology, archaeology, and biology. In between is a torrent of bigoted e-mails, lurid clip art, and racially provocatory chat rooms.[10]

(i) An Electronic Community of Hate?

Some experts are describing the extremist and racist groups active on the Internet as an 'electronic community of hate'.[11] These groups are highly organized, and they seek out top-level domains where they can install their

[9] European Commission, 'An Action Plan against Racism', COM (1998) 183 final, 25 Mar. 1998.
[10] Jenkins, *supra* n. 8.
[11] Anti-Defamation League, 'Poisoning the Web: Hatred Online' (1999), <http://www.adl.org/publications/sum_poison_web.html>.

webpages. This is the case in the US. Since hate speech is not illegal *per se* under US law, the Internet there has remained open to all kinds of hate groups. Painted in the colours of neo-Nazis or anarchists, these groups are putting up websites, creating international links to hundreds of other sources of hate information, and specifically targeting teenage males with their propaganda.[12] For some authors, the battlefield has changed, and there has been a shift in the rules of engagement with these groups.[13]

According to some experts the use of this new communication technique is leading to fresh forms of racism and racial discrimination. Institutionalized racism is now being supported by a most disconcerting form of modern racism and hatred spread through Internet websites.[14] Members of extremist groups are creating websites on cheap computers in the anonymity of squalid apartments, but, by reaching thousands of people simultaneously, they are giving the impression that they are part of an organized, popular international movement.[15] This inexpensive, instantaneous means of worldwide communication without the need for physical exposure has generated a sense of power among many in the extremist community. The Internet acts as a force-multiplier, enabling racists to have influence far in excess of that normally exercised by such a relatively small number of people.[16]

The rhetoric and the visuals of the hate material on the Internet are not new. What is new is the opportunity the Internet offers to market hate cheaply and directly to a wide audience, particularly the young, who are the main users of cyberspace.[17] Thus, for example, the youth-oriented magazine *Resistance* has announced that Resistance Records, which produces white-supremacist music, plans to have an Internet service that will allow users to download album covers and lyrics produced by the group, which also employs the technology to promote computer hate games.[18]

---

[12] Guzman, *supra* n. 7.

[13] Sheff, 'Yahoo! Internet Live Interview with Rabbi Cooper', Simon Wiesenthal Center, *Cyberwatch*, 8 Jan. 1999, <http://www.wiesenthal.com/watch/yahoo.html>. See also Leadership Conference on Civil Rights, 'The Hate Groups and their Strategies' (2000), <http:// 209.207.129.4/diversity_works/reports/hate_crimes/cause_for_concern/p7.html>.

[14] Special Rapporteur of the UN Commission on Human Rights, 'Report on Contemporary Forms of Racism, Racial Discrimination, Xenophobia and Related Intolerance', UN Doc. A/52/471 (1997).

[15] Weitzman, 'Tecnología y terror: extremismo en Internet', Simon Wiesenthal Center (1999), <http://www.wiesenthal.com/feature/span_tecyterror.html>.

[16] Preparatory Committee of the World Conference against Racism, Racial Discrimination, Xenophobia and Related Intolerance, 'Consultation on the Use of the Internet for the Purpose of Incitement to Racial Hatred, Racial Propaganda and Xenophobia', UN Doc. A/CONF.189/PC.1/5 (2000), <http://www.unhchr.ch/Huridocda/Huridoca.nsf/ TestFrame/2feedaabf88e41ad802568bf0057329a?Opendocument>.

[17] Simon Wiesenthal Center, 'Hate on the Internet', *Cyberwatch* (1999), <http:// www.wiesenthal.com/watch/wpers.html>.

[18] Ibid.

   The number of hate websites has been growing rapidly. Some antihate organizations say this reflects the growing influence of racist groups. According to the Anti-Defamation League, neo-Nazis and other antisemites and racists are using the Internet to open new channels of communication and recruit new members.[19] However, there is no agreement on the number of hate sites. Estimates range from 400 to 1,200, depending on the way the sites are counted. Some of the sites are quite big. For instance, stormfront.org,[20] a 'one-stop' website, hosts several hate sites. The number of 'hits' on some of these increasingly sophisticated hate sites often amount to hundreds per day.

   One of the worst aspects of these pages is that racist groups are using hyperlinks to encourage children to examine more specialized sites.[21] Another worrying aspect is that the Internet is facilitating an exchange and a cross-pollination of ideologies of hatred. Racist groups are now more easily able to share ideas and coordinate their activities.[22]

   However, some experts believe that the Internet strategy of these groups is not as successful as one might think. According to David Goldman, president of HateWatch, a non-profit group that monitors online hate, some extremist groups are abandoning their reliance on huge webpages because they feel the rewards are not sufficient. Indeed, there are no statistics supporting the theory that membership in hate groups is increasing because of the Internet.[23] Personal, face-to-face contact still seems essential for recruitment in most cases.

   Moreover, the Internet is raising the visibility of hate groups. Such groups have always relied on anonymity and secrecy to keep their activities hidden from public scrutiny. But on the Internet, their actions become more exposed and publicized. In addition, hate sites are beginning to promote 'lone wolf' or 'lone shooter' activism, whereby individuals are being encouraged to act on their own. One disadvantage for hate groups is that they may be sued for incitement to commit a hate crime.[24]

   On the other hand, hate speech sells.[25] Behind the hate talk is a market in memorabilia, music, flags, games, clothes, books, and so on. This market is

   [19] Anti-Defamation League, 'Hate Group Recruitment' (1995), <http://www.adl.org/publications/sum_hate_recruit_net.html>.
   [20] <http://www3.stormfront.org/>.   [21] Sheff, *supra* n. 13.
   [22] Applebay 'Police Probe Cyberspace in Hunt for Hate Groups', *The Globe and Mail,* 20 July 1999.
   [23] Chaudhry, 'Hate Sites Bad Recruiting Tools', *Wired News,* 23 May 2000, <http://www.wired.com/news/print/0,1294,36478,00.html>.
   [24] See, for example, the case of Ryan Wilson, who was charged with threatening the life of Bonnie Jouhari, a housing rights activist named on the homepage of Wilson's white supremacist group, Alpha HQ. Chaudhry, 'Slo-Mo Justice against Hate', *Wired News,* 18 Jan. 2000, <http://www.wired.com/news/politics/0,1283,33710,00.html>.
   [25] Owen, 'Hate Speech: The Speech that Kills' (2000), <http://www.indexoncensorship.org>.

also evident on the Internet. As the criminal charges against F. Somm[26] has proved, some online intermediaries know that hate has an audience among Internet users, and more visits means more traffic and more money spent on banners and ads.

(ii) How to Recognize Hate Websites

HateWatch, a nonprofit organization, continuously monitors the Internet in search of hate sites. HateWatch has developed a list of characteristics of such sites.[27] Of course, the main characteristic is that the webpage must advocate unreasonable hostility or violence against a person or group based on race, religion, gender, sexual orientation, or disability. For HateWatch, it is also important to determine if the purpose of the website is to propagandize, recruit, or organize e-commerce. Websites with little or no original content run by a single person are not included in HateWatch's list, since the organization considers such 'cut-and-paste sites' disturbing, but not typical of how the Internet is used by extremist groups to spread their message. Nonetheless, HateWatch pays attention to any features which may be indicative of the evolving nature of online bigotry and give a sense of the state of hate in cyberspace. Some of the elements which HateWatch has identified are:

- The inclusion of an address or post office box so that people can request further information.
- The inclusion of a phone number.
- The use of a registered domain name rather than a page provided through a free web service.
- The affiliation of a site to a larger 'real life' group.
- The inclusion of a list of current events or activities for known hate groups.
- The existence of original content created specifically for the particular website.
- Regular updating.
- Fund-raising or e-commerce carried on through the site.
- The encouragement of acts of harassment or violence or of sympathetic individuals or 'lone wolves'.
- The publication of photographs or personal information on the website owner or sponsoring group.
- Sophisticated or expansive use of technology (such as video, mp3 files, web radio, secure financial transactions).

---

[26] See *Amtsgericht München v F. Somm*, Case number 8340 Ds 465 Js 173158/95, 28 May 1998, <http://www.jura.uni-wuerzburg.de/sieber/somm/somm-urteil.pdf>.

[27] HateWatch, 'Criteria Used to Determine whether a Web Page should be Catalogued as a Hate Site' (2000), <http://www.eu.hatewatch.org/criteriaforhatesites.html>.

- The existence of an e-news list or bulletin.
- The website is also a host or offers links to other online hate groups or racist individuals.

III. TRADITIONAL STRATEGIES TO FIGHT HATE SPEECH

In order to foster an understanding of how the Internet jeopardizes traditional approaches in the fight against hate speech, this section provides a general review of antihate regulations and an analysis of how the peculiar nature of the Internet affects antihate laws.

(i) Hate Speech in International Law

International conventions adhere explicitly to the principle that the exercise of rights cannot be used to destroy other guaranteed rights. International conventions recognize the right to freedom of speech. For example, Article 19 of the Universal Declaration of Human Rights provides that 'everyone has the right to freedom of opinion and expression'. However, it also states, in Article 29(3), that no right may 'be exercised contrary to the purposes and principles of the United Nations'. Article 1 (3) states that a significant role of the United Nations is to promote and encourage respect for human rights and fundamental freedoms without distinction as to race or to sexual, linguistic, or religious orientation. This can reasonably be interpreted as limiting the protection for speech if the speech tends to promote racial, sexual, linguistic, or religious discrimination. Article 5(1) of the Covenant on Civil and Political Rights states that 'Nothing in the present Convention may be interpreted as implying for any state group or person any right to engage in any activity or perform any act aimed at the destruction of any rights and freedoms recognized herein or at their limitation to a greater extent than is provided for in the present Covenant'. One may conclude that, in international law, the rights to, freedom of speech and expression, equality, and non-discrimination have similar weight and are interdependent. International documents on human rights provide safeguards against the conflict between the right to speech and equality rights. The competing interests of society must be balanced.[28]

The International Convention on the Elimination of All Forms of Racial Discrimination is the international community's primary legal instrument for combating racial hatred and discrimination. According to Article 4 of this Convention:

[28] Defeis, 'Freedom of Speech and International Norms: A Response to Hate Speech', 29 *Stanford Journal of International Law* (1992) 57, at 127.

State Parties . . . undertake to adopt immediate and positive measures designed to
eradicate: all incitement to, or acts of, [racial] discrimination and, to this end, with
due regard to the principles embodied in the Universal Declaration of Human Rights
and the rights expressly set forth in Article 5 of this Convention, inter alia:
(*a*) shall declare an offence punishable by law all dissemination of ideas based on
racial superiority or hatred, incitement to racial discrimination, as well as all acts of
violence or incitement to such acts against any race or group of persons of another
colour or ethnic origin, and also the provision of any assistance to racist activities,
including the financing thereof;
(*b*) shall declare illegal and prohibit organizations, and also all other propaganda
activities, which promote and incite racial discrimination and shall recognise participation in such organizations and activities as an offence punishable by law. . . .

By obligating states to punish 'all dissemination of ideas based on racial superiority or hatred', Article 4 goes quite far with respect to articles in other international conventions.

Article 19 of the International Covenant on Civil and Political Rights supports the right to freedom of speech. Restrictions to this right are admitted in
this article provided that they are established by law and are necessary (*a*) to
maintain respect for the rights or reputations of others and (*b*) for the protection of national security, public order, or public health or morals.

Article 20 of this Covenant contains a further limitation. It states that (*a*)
any propaganda for war (war of aggression) shall be prohibited by law and (*b*)
any advocacy of national, racial, or religious hatred that constitutes incitement to discrimination, hostility, or violence shall be prohibited by law.

Since the Covenant makes the spreading of war propaganda and hate propaganda a crime under international law, countries which have ratified the
Covenant without reservation are supposed to enact and enforce laws which,
among other activities, would prohibit the posting of hate speech on the
Internet.

However, in practical terms, extremist groups are setting up webpages and
websites in countries which have not signed the Convention on the
Elimination of Racial Discrimination or have entered a reservation to Article
20 (2). This is the case of the United States, which has made a far-reaching
reservation, stating that 'nothing in the Convention shall be deemed to
require or authorize legislation or other action by the United States of
America incompatible with the Constitution of the United States of America'.

The Committee on the Elimination of Racial Discrimination, as well as
most state parties, agree that the right to freedom of expression is not
absolute, but subject to certain limitations (those in the Covenant, for
instance) and that these limitations reflect the fact that a balance must be
struck between the obligations deriving from Article 4 of the International
Convention and the protection of other fundamental freedoms. Article 4 (a)
and (b) of the Convention are mandatory rules of international law. 'Due

regard' for the rights to freedom of expression cannot be so construed as to justify failure to prohibit or punish the dissemination of ideas of racial superiority or hatred over the Internet or of any other propaganda that promotes or incites racial discrimination.[29]

(ii) Hate Speech and Various National Legal Systems

The main problem in fighting hate speech on the Internet is the fact that different countries define and confront hate speech in different ways. In some countries, hate speech is forbidden and heavily prosecuted. In others, hate speech is treated like other kinds of speech and is protected by law. The varying approaches to hate speech have come about because of differing cultural heritages and historical experiences. Nonetheless, no country in the world accepts a boundless exercise of speech. Even in well-established democracies in which freedom of speech is considered a basic right protected by the constitution, there are limits to this right. Obscenity, defamation, copyright protection, public security, due respect for public institutions, the protection of minors, the protection of public health, consumer protection, and the protection of trade secrets are only a few of the areas in which limits exist on the right of free speech.

(a) Hate Speech in the US

In the United States, the First Amendment to the Constitution guarantees the right of freedom of speech to all Americans. The First Amendment provides that 'Congress shall make no law . . . abridging the freedom of speech, or of the press.' Through its explicit guarantee of freedom of expression, the First Amendment establishes a general rule that neither the federal government nor the governments of the states can criminalize speech (or burden the freedom of speech by imposing civil penalties) on the basis of content. The concept behind the First Amendment is that government must permit the vigorous exchange of (often competing) points of view in the market-place of ideas. One viewpoint cannot be penalized in favour of another. This is the case even when the expression of ideas and opinions may involve speech that a reasonable, fair-minded public might find irrational or even repugnant and reprehensible. The animating principle of First Amendment jurisprudence is that such speech should be challenged not by prosecution, but by the expression of opposing ideas—often described succinctly as 'more speech'—and that citizens could in this way decide for themselves the truth or falsity of the contending viewpoints. First

---

[29] Shahi, 'Prohibition of Racist Propaganda on the Internet: Juridical Aspects, International Measures' (1997), <http://www.unhchr.ch/html/menu2/10/c/racism/shahi.htm>.

Amendment protection has been understood to extend even to speech in support of conduct which itself may be illegal.[30]

Absent from the United States Constitution is a wide-ranging articulation of the responsibilities either of the individual towards society, or of the government towards the individual. A general clause prohibiting the exercise of constitutional rights in such a way as to infringe on other constitutional rights is also absent.[31] Although one Supreme Court canon of the interpretation of the Constitution requires that every clause of the Constitution be given meaning, this rule itself has not been given full meaning, and it has certainly not been interpreted in the sense that First Amendment rights are balanced by the rights guaranteed under the equal protection clause. This implies that freedom of speech occupies a preferred position in a quasi-absolutist manner.[32]

In a recent decision, the Supreme Court has affirmed that the content of Internet 'speech' may not be any more regulated than is speech in traditional areas of expression such as the print media.[33] While courts may take into account the Internet's vast reach and accessibility, they must still approach attempts to censor or regulate online speech within the traditional constitutional framework. Blanket statements expressing hatred of an ethnic, racial, or religious nature are protected by the First Amendment even if they may cause distress. Similarly, the denial of the historical reality of the Holocaust is almost never actionable under US law. Thus, the US Constitution protects the vast majority of extremist websites that disseminate racist or antisemitic propaganda. Only if a bigot's use of the Internet rises to the level of criminal conduct may he become subject to prosecution under a state's hate crime laws.

(b) Hate Speech in Europe

The prohibition in Europe on hate speech has its *raison d'être* in the dramatic historical experience of fascism. Since the Second World War, legal norms against the free expression of ideologies such as white or aryan supremacy or other racial hatred have become accepted as necessary so as to control the spread of the related ideas and materials and thereby avoid any danger of 'repeating history'. The traumatic experience of the Nazi period and the Second World War has led some countries, like Germany and France, to outlaw any kind of

---

[30] Reitinger, 'Legal Aspect of Government-Sponsored Prohibitions against Racist Propaganda on the Internet: The US Perspective' (1997), <http://www.unhchr.ch/html/menu2/10/ c/racism/reitinger.htm>.

[31] Defeis, *supra* n. 28, at 62.   [32] Ibid.

[33] Supreme Court of the United States (1997), *supra* n. 6. For an analysis of the case, see Volokh, 'Freedom of Speech, Shielding Children, and Transcending Balancing', *Supreme Court Review* (1997), <http://www.law.ucla.edu/faculty/volokh/shield.htm>; Fernández Esteban, 'Limitaciones constitucionales e inconstitucionales a la libertad de expresión en Internet', 53 *Revista española de derecho constitucional* (1998) 283.

material supporting racial supremacy, denial of the Holocaust, Nazi ideals, and the like. In many European countries a direct fight against race hatred is a political priority. For example, Article 607.2 of the new Spanish penal code makes it a crime to 'distribute by any means ideas or doctrines which deny or justify [racist crimes] or call for the restoration of institutions or regimes which justified or were based on those ideas'; the article fixes a penalty of one to two years' imprisonment.[34] The previous penal code made no reference to generic hate speech.

The European Commission has issued an 'action plan' for combating racism throughout the European Union.[35] Since the 1995 'Communication on Racism, Xenophobia and Anti-Semitism',[36] the approach of the European Commission has involved the incorporation of antiracism measures within more wide-ranging policy instruments and the launch of initiatives specifically addressing racism.

In 1997 the European Monitoring Centre on Racism and Xenophobia was established in Vienna. The main function of the centre is to study the extent of and trends in racism, xenophobia, and antisemitism in the European Union and to analyse the underlying causes and the consequences.

The Treaty of Amsterdam has provided a significant opportunity to strengthen the Union's fight against racism and xenophobia. Article 13 of the Treaty on the European Community includes a general non-discrimination clause making it possible for the European Council to 'take appropriate action to combat discrimination based on sex, racial, or ethnic origin, religion or belief, disability, age or sexual orientation on the basis of proposals by the Commission'.

Another landmark is a 1996 document on Union action to combat racism and xenophobia.[37] According to this non-binding instrument, each member state should undertake to ensure effective judicial cooperation in respect of offences based on the following types of behaviour and, if necessary for the purposes of this cooperation, make such behaviour punishable as a criminal offence:

- Open incitement to discrimination, violence, or racial hatred in respect of a group of persons or a member of such a group defined by reference to colour, race, religion, or national or ethnic origin.
- Open approval, for a racist or xenophobic purpose, of crimes against humanity and human rights violations.

[34] Ley orgánica 10/1995, 23 Nov. 1995, BOE 3/2/1995, <http://constitucion.rediris.es/codigo/derechos/igualdad/igualdad/lo10-1995.html>.

[35] European Commission, *supra* n. 9.

[36] European Commission, 'Communication on Racism, Xenophobia and Anti-Semitism', COM (1995) 653 final, 13 Dec. 1995.

[37] Joint Action/96/443/JHA, 15 July 1996, adopted by the European Council on the Basis of Article K.3 of the Treaty on European Union, Concerning Action to Combat Racism and Xenophobia, OJ 1996 L 185.

- Open denial as offences of the crimes defined in Article 6 of the Charter of the International Military Tribunal appended to the London Agreement of 8 April 1945 insofar as it includes behaviour which is contemptuous of, or degrading to, a group of persons defined by reference to colour, race, religion, or national or ethnic origin.
- Public dissemination or distribution of tracts, pictures, or other material containing expressions of racism and xenophobia.
- Participation in the activities of groups, organizations, or associations that involve discrimination, violence, or racial, ethnic, or religious hatred.

In the case of investigations into and proceedings initiated as a result of these types of behaviour, each member state should facilitate judicial cooperation and adopt appropriate measures in the following areas:

- The seizure and confiscation of tracts, pictures, or other material containing expressions of racism and xenophobia intended for public dissemination, where such material is offered to the public in the territory of a member state.
- The acknowledgement that the types of behaviour listed above should not be regarded as political offences that would justify a refusal to comply with requests for legal cooperation.
- The provision of information to another member state to enable it to initiate, in accordance with its laws, legal proceedings, or proceedings for confiscation in cases where tracts, pictures, or other material containing expressions of racism and xenophobia are being stored in one member state for the purpose of distribution or dissemination in another member state.
- The establishment of contact points within the member states that would be responsible for collecting and exchanging information which might be useful for investigations into and proceedings against offences based on the types of behaviour listed above.

The EU stance against racism and xenophobia must also be accepted in countries which are negotiating EU accession and in EU candidate countries.[38] The membership of these countries is assessed on the basis of the criteria defined at the European Council meeting in Copenhagen in 1993 whereby candidate countries should have 'stability of institutions guaranteeing democracy, the rule of law, human rights, and respect for and protection of minorities'. In order to prepare the candidate countries for EU membership, it is also possible to involve them in Community programmes, agencies, and activities such as the Action Plan against Racism, the European Monitoring

[38] See European Commission, 'Countering Racism, Xenophobia and Antisemitism in the Candidate Countries: Communication to the Cologne European Council Meeting, 3–4 June 1999', COM (1999) 256 final, 26 May 1999.

Centre on Racism and Xenophobia, the implementation of the Amsterdam Treaty provisions on non-discrimination, and programmes for education, vocational training, youth, and the strengthening of civil society.

Finally, the recent Draft Charter of Fundamental Rights of the European Union[39] of 14 September 2000 does not mention hate speech directly. However, it includes a limitation on all fundamental rights recognized in the Charter which indirectly refers to such behaviour. Under the title 'Prohibition of Abuse of Rights', Article 53 states that '[n]othing in this Charter shall be interpreted as implying any right to engage in any activity or to perform any act aimed at the destruction of any of the rights and freedoms recognised in this Charter or at their limitation to a greater extent than is provided for herein.'

(iii) How the Internet Makes National Antihate Laws Difficult to Apply

Before the Internet, national laws were quite successful in dealing with hate speech. It was quite easy to forbid the distribution of a book, say, *Mein Kampf* in the case of Germany.[40] Books need to be printed, imported, distributed, and sold, and this procedure is relatively easy to control.

Unfortunately, eliminating hate content on the Internet is not so easy. The boundless, global nature of the Internet makes it practically impossible to eradicate all objectionable material or to impede access to that material by anyone with a computer and a modem. Even if the laws in the country in which the content host is located prohibit the distribution of such material, there are multiple ways for the content publisher and users to avoid law enforcement officials. The publisher can obtain a new 'universal resource locator' to disguise the content or he can change the host service provider or Internet service provider and get a new address. It takes only a few seconds to move the objectionable material from one host to another, possibly located in another part of the world (which would mean that the publisher would automatically obtain a new address), or to find a local host with a new domain name. There are also several ways for the user to receive the proscribed material. If the service provider blocks access, he can simply switch provider. If no provider permits access to a certain Internet site, the user can access the site through another site or through another country.[41]

[39] 'Complete Text of the Charter Proposed by the Praesidium Following the Meeting Held from 11 to 13 September 2000 and Based on Charter 4422/00', Convent 47, Charter 4470/00, <http://db.consilium.eu.int/dfdocs/EN/04470En.pdf>.

[40] Pursuant to Article 130(3) of the German penal code, it is forbidden publicly or in a gathering to deny, or to praise, or to play down crimes committed during the Nazi regime in a way which may disturb the public peace. Pursuant to Article 130(4), together with (2), it is forbidden to distribute publicly, show around or *make available in any other way*, to produce, supply, keep in stock, offer, praise, import, or export books with such content.

[41] Lee, 'Basic Internet Technology' (1997), <http://www.unhchr.ch/html/menu2/10/c/racism/lee.htm>.

IV. CAN ANYTHING BE DONE?: GOVERNMENT PROPOSALS
TO FIGHT INTERNET HATE SPEECH

(i) Internet Hate Speech and the United States

Article 4 of the International Convention on the Elimination of All Forms of
Racial Discrimination is as applicable to the distribution over the Internet of
ideas of racial superiority or hatred and other racist propaganda as it is to such
distribution through the press, radio, television, or any other media. Most
state parties to the Convention take this position.

The case of the United States is unique because of the First Amendment,
which guarantees virtually absolute freedom of speech, thereby rendering
online extremism even more enormously difficult to combat. The First
Amendment's protection of free speech shields most extremist propaganda,
and, in the United States, private service providers may freely choose whether
to host extremist sites or not. If a provider chooses not to host such a site, the
site owner can easily migrate to providers with no such scruples.

Furthermore, the size of the web, which contains hundreds of millions of
individual pages, complicates efforts to identify extremist material. Dozens, if
not hundreds of webpages, some of which are not listed by search engines,
contain bombmaking formulas.[42]

Material, including racist and defamatory statements, that is treated as illegal in most other democracies can be presented on the Internet (via United
States postings) and, as a result, becomes accessible to virtually everyone anywhere else around the globe, regardless of existing local laws and mores.[43]
Thus, the United States is a 'safe haven' for racists wishing to spread their
words of hate worldwide over the Internet.

In the landmark decision *Reno, Attorney General of the United States et al. v
American Civil Liberties Union (ACLU)*,[44] the Supreme Court of the United
States declared unconstitutional most of the censorship provisions in the
Communications Decency Act that were aimed at protecting minors by crim-
inalizing 'indecency' on the Internet. The Supreme Court agreed with the
ACLU's argument that the Internet is analogous to the print media, rather
than to the broadcast media, and as such should be afforded full First
Amendment protection. The special features of the broadcast media recognized by the Court in some decisions to justify regulation are not present in
cyberspace. Unlike communications received by radio or television, the

---

[42] Anti-Defamation League, 'Responding to Extremist Speech Online: 10 Frequently
Asked Questions of the Anti-Defamation League' (2001), <http://www.adl.org/issue_
combating_hate/10faq_extremist_online.html>.

[43] Shahi, *supra* n. 29.　　　　　　　[44] See *supra* n. 6.

receipt of information over the Internet requires a series of more deliberate and directed steps than merely turning a dial. Therefore, the Court found the Internet less 'invasive'. Moreover, the Court stated that 'as a matter of constitutional tradition, and in the absence of evidence to the contrary, we presume government regulation of the content of speech is more likely to interfere with the free exchange of ideas than to encourage it'.

The installation of Internet filters on computers at public schools and public libraries in the United States has become a very hot issue. In *Mainstream Loudoun et al. v Loudoun County Library*,[45] the US District Court of the Eastern District of Virginia heard a civil case involving the question of whether a public library could pursue a policy of prohibiting the access of library patrons to certain content-based categories of Internet publications. The plaintiffs were a Loudoun County non-profit organization and individual Loudoun County residents who claimed that their access to Internet sites had been blocked because of the defendant library board's policy. The Court declared the policy illegal. One of the Court's main arguments was that, by restricting the reading material available to adults to a level appropriate for minors, the library was violating the free speech guarantee of the First Amendment and the due process clause of the Fourteenth Amendment. 'Although [the library] is under no obligation to provide Internet access to its patrons, it has chosen to do so and is therefore restricted by the First Amendment in the limitations it is allowed to place on patron access,' the Court added. A possible compromise for public libraries with multiple computers would be to allow unrestricted Internet use for adults, but to provide only supervised access for children. According to the Anti-Defamation League, given the broad free speech rights afforded to students by the First Amendment, it is unlikely that courts would allow school libraries to require filters on all computers available for student use.

The Simon Wiesenthal Center has proposed that certain safeguards which are applied to advertising in the US should also be applied to cyberspace. It suggests that the establishment of guidelines, like the ones set by CNN, could also be applied in cyberspace.[46] A content-monitoring system such as the Federal Trade Commission employs for advertising might also be a reasonable approach to the Internet.

Though hate speech is protected under the US Constitution, the transmission of racist threats against individuals over the Internet is heavily prosecuted. Thus, for example, Richard Machado was found guilty by a federal court of sending racist death threats to fifty-nine Asian students at the University of California on 10 February 1998. He was convicted on two counts: sending threats based on the recipients' race or ethnicity and interfering with the right of individuals to attend the university.

---

[45] Case No. 97-2049-A, 23 Nov. 1998.   [46] Simon Wiesenthal Center, *supra* n. 17.

(ii) The Control of Internet Hate Speech in the European Union

Despite the legal practice in European countries of banning racist speech and neo-Nazi propaganda, European institutions have shunned efforts to regulate content and have favoured instead an approach centred on the education of parents and the establishment of a network of hot lines which people can use to report illegal or indecent websites and newsgroups.

The main goal of the 'action plan'[47] to promote the safe use of the Internet is to create an environment favourable to the healthy development of the Internet industry at the European level (Article 2). The action plan includes a provision aimed at hindering the use of the Internet to commit offences against children or to spread racial discrimination, racial hatred or xenophobic ideologies. The plan is to promote self-regulation by the industry, content-monitoring schemes, filtering tools and rating systems, increasing awareness of such services among users, and support activities, including the assessment of legal issues and the fostering of international cooperation.

The plan represents the most important response so far of the European Union to the need for Internet regulation. It is based on principles stated in the Communication on Illegal and Harmful Content on the Internet[48] and the Green Paper on the Protection of Minors and Human Dignity in Audiovisual and Information Services.[49] Both documents address illegal and harmful content. Not all such content issues involve lawbreaking. Therefore, a variety of legal approaches are required. Illegal material should be dealt through:

• Cooperation among member states for the exchange of information and the establishment of minimum European standards regarding criminal content.
• Clarification of the potential liability of Internet providers (host services and access providers).
• Encouragement for self-regulation among providers.

On the other hand, merely harmful content should be addressed through:

• Encouragement so that the industry supplies filtering tools and rating systems.
• Greater awareness among users, particularly parents, teachers, and children, of appropriate services provided by industry.

---

[47] European Parliament and Council Decision 99/276 of 25 Jan. 1999, whereby an action plan was adopted to promote the safer use of the Internet by combating illegal and harmful content on global networks, OJ 1999 L 33.

[48] European Commission, *supra* n. 5.

[49] European Commission, 'Green Paper on the Protection of Minors and Human Dignity in Audiovisual and Information Services', COM (1996) 483, 23 Jan. 1996.

(a) Self-regulation

For the industry to contribute effectively to restricting the flow of illegal and harmful material, it is important to encourage enterprises to develop a self-regulatory framework. Despite the scepticism of some authors about the effectiveness of codes of conduct, self-regulation of the industry is being promoted through the action plan, and appropriate guidelines are to be developed at the European level.[50] A system of 'quality-site labels' is to be established to assist users in identifying online intermediaries that adhere to the codes of conduct.

Some providers have prohibited the use of their services for hate pages and include this prohibition in their terms of service. For example, Geocities does not allow contractees to 'upload, post or otherwise transmit any content that is unlawful, harmful, threatening, abusive, harassing, tortious, defamatory, vulgar, obscene, libellous, invasive of another's privacy, hateful, or racially, ethnically or otherwise objectionable'.[51] America On Line has adopted similar rules whereby users must agree not to 'upload, post, or otherwise distribute or facilitate distribution of any content . . . that . . . victimizes, harasses, degrades, or intimidates an individual or group of individuals on the basis of religion, gender, sexual orientation, race, ethnicity, age, or disability'.[52]

(b) Filtering

Content filters enable individuals or networks to prevent the reception of or access to materials which contain specifically designated words or phrases. Most of the filtering devices have been developed for the control of pornography and child abuse. The technology is based on pre-scanning and censorship of copy before it is made available for viewing. Some designated words and phrases are pre-screened by the software programmer, but the end-user can also add additional filter-triggering terms at will. Client-based filters must be installed on the client's computer. Net filters are installed on the server or the network control unit.

In addition to the automated screening of content by addresses and by keywords, there have been efforts at blacklisting or whitelisting websites depending on the presence of objectionable material or of recommended content.

Professional rating systems assign labels according to the characteristics of content. Sophisticated examples include Platforms for Internet Content Selection. Among the other non-governmental techniques are proprietary

---

[50] Rutkowsky, 'Elements Relating to Conduct and Good Practices for Internet-Based Materials' (1997), <http://www.unhchr.ch/html/menu2/10/c/racism/rutkowsk.htm>.

[51] <http://docs.yahoo.com/info/terms/geoterms.html>.

[52] <http://www.aol.com/copyright/rules.html>.

software such as Cyber Patrol or Cyber Angels which serve as content monitors to help protect parents and the unsuspecting from unwanted online encounters.[53]

Employing filtering technology can be especially challenging when the laws and values of different countries are involved. Given the international dimension of the Internet, filters cannot always take into account the differences in definitions of infringement. Material that is illegal in one country may be protected in another.[54] On the other hand, experiments have indicated that efficient site labelling may be almost impossible.

(c) Hot Lines

An effective way to restrict the circulation of illegal material is to create a Europe-wide network of hot lines allowing users to report content they come across in their use of the Internet and which they consider questionable or objectionable. For example, the Internet Watch Foundation, an industry-funded entity, has been charged by the UK government with examining 'potentially criminal' hate content in Britain.[55] It was established in 1996 as part of an industry-government agreement that focused on child pornography. The agreement allows the foundation to investigate individual complaints submitted through its hot line. If it determines that the material could be deemed criminal under British law, it asks the service provider to remove the site.[56]

(d) Awareness

The action plan foresees awareness campaigns to contribute to the trust and confidence of parents and teachers in the safer use of the Internet by children. Likewise, the efforts of industry to implement self-regulation, filtering, and rating schemes can bear fruit only if users and potential users are aware of them. A European-wide campaign will be carried out to inform parents and others dealing with children about the best technical and non-technical ways to protect minors from exposure to content that could be harmful to their development. The campaign will include workshops for teachers and the preparation of appropriate printed and multimedia material. Special 'netdays' will also be organized.

(iii) International Cooperation in the Fight against Internet Hate Speech

The fight by national-level law enforcement officials against illegal content on the Internet appears practically futile. Because the Internet is worldwide and

---

[53] Jenkins, *supra* n. 8.   [54] Julià-Barceló, *supra* n. 3, at 20.

[55] Chaudhry, 'British ISPs Crack down on Hate', *Wired News*, 1 Jan. 2000, <http://www.wired.com/news/politics/0,1283,33906,00.html>.

[56] Chaudhry, 'AOL Struggles with Hate Speech', *Wired News*, 25 Oct. 1999, <http://www.wired.com/news/politics/0,1283,33906,00.html>.

because all the information it offers is accessible from every single point of the web means that any attempt to solve the problem of hate speech must involve many countries. Only the cooperative effort of all actors can control the spread of this type of material on the Internet. The UN Third Committee on Social, Humanitarian and Cultural Matters has already addressed the topic of racist and hate material on the Internet on several occasions.[57]

V. THE STRATEGIES OF ANTIHATE GROUPS

(i) Promoting Tolerance

The Internet is a market-place of ideas and information. If it levels the playing field among those who wish to make their views known, the simplest and one of the best antidotes to racism and hate speech on the Internet is the detailed exposure, on the Internet, of the morally and rationally faulty underpinnings of hate speech and the presentation of more compelling speech promoting tolerance. Several civil rights organizations, including the Anti-Defamation League, the National Association for the Advancement of Colored People, the American Civil Liberties Union, and the Simon Wiesenthal Center, are pioneering this process in the United States.

The Simon Wiesenthal Center created the Task Force against Hate[58] in 1991 to confront extremism. The task force offers police agencies specialized training in the complexities of cyberspace, with particular emphasis on hate websites. It has also been instrumental in clarifying issues related to cyberspace and free speech and in presenting pertinent testimony at government hearings. Believing that, because Internet use is popular among young people, it should be considered in any serious public awareness campaign against racism, the Simon Wiesenthal Center has also taken advantage of the opportunity to create the Multimedia Learning Centre and the online Museum of Tolerance on the Internet.[59]

(ii) Negotiating with Online Intermediaries and Content Providers

Some antihate groups negotiate with online intermediaries in an attempt to convince them to uphold their terms of service against bigotry and hatred. For

[57] See UN Press Release, 'Third Committee Hears of Dangers of "Modern Racism and Hatred" Found on Internet Web Sites: Code of Conduct Needed', 22 Oct. 1999, <http://www.un.org/News/Press/docs/1999/1999/1022.gashc3535.doc.htm>.

[58] <http://www.wiesenthal.com/watch/taskforce.html>.

[59] <http://motlc.wiesenthal.com/index.html>. See also 'Conclusions and Recommendations', Seminar on the Role of the Internet with Regard to the Provisions of the International Convention on the Elimination of All Forms of Racial Discrimination, UN High Commissioner for Human Rights, Geneva, 10–14 Nov. 1997.

example, the Anti-Defamation League notified Yahoo! that racist clubs were posting hate messages and racial diatribes that clearly violated Yahoo!'s terms of service agreement, which prohibits users from transmitting content that is deemed 'hateful or racially, ethnically, or otherwise objectionable'.[60] The League received assurances that Yahoo! would be vigilant in its efforts to bar racist and antisemitic clubs from its service. A Yahoo! representative indicated that several such clubs had been removed and that further corrective action would be taken. The provider encouraged the Anti-Defamation League's Internet monitoring unit to report violations and stated that it takes 'very seriously' every allegation of abuse.

With content providers such as the online booksellers Amazon.com and Barnes&Noble.com, the strategy adopted by the Anti-Defamation League has been slightly different. Rather than attempting to challenge the sale of antisemitic publications on the Internet, the League has emphasized instead the need for the booksellers to provide signposts, offer guidance, publish reviews, and otherwise educate site visitors about racist publications. Following extensive discussions, both online booksellers agreed to implement a number of proactive measures, including the placement of a statement from the Anti-Defamation League and making racist books available only after a search by name and not by subject.[61] Where the country regulations so allow, antihate activist organizations have taken a stronger position regarding hate books. Thus, Amazon.com stopped offering Hitler's *Mein Kampf* for sale in Germany after the Wiesenthal Center filed legal complaints against Amazon and other web-based booksellers in 1999.

(iii) Filters and Education Campaigns

The Anti-Defamation League offers a software product, HateFilter,[62] which acts as a gatekeeper, blocking access to websites of individuals or groups that, in the judgement of the League, advocate hatred, bigotry, or racial violence. HateFilter contains a 'redirect' feature that gives users who try to access a blocked site the opportunity to link directly to related Anti-Defamation League educational material.

The United Nations Commission for Human Rights has asked the High Commissioner to develop a campaign of human rights education and awareness over the Internet about experiences in the struggle against racism, xenophobia, and antisemitism.

---

[60] Anti-fascism.org, 'Yahoo! Assures ADL it will Work to Remove Hate Clubs which Violate its Policies', 25 Feb. 2000, <http://www.anti-fascism.org/yahoo.html>.

[61] <http://www.adl.org/frames/front_Online_Booksellers.html>.

[62] HateFilter can be downloaded from the website of the Anti-Defamation League, <http://www.adl.org/hate-patrol/info/default.htm>.

The government of Sweden has introduced the innovative Living History campaign to disseminate information over the Internet about the Holocaust. It has also established a task force to foster international cooperation for Holocaust education and research.

The use of the Internet to distribute information, research, and other materials about immigration and minorities can support efforts against racism, raise awareness, promote understanding, and increase tolerance. Education over the Internet is a bulwark against the use of the web to spread racist and xenophobic ideologies.[63]

(iv) Registering and Purchasing Hate Domain Names

A relatively new strategy among antihate organizations is the purchase of the rights to domain names so as to keep them from being used by racists and hatemongers.[64] Thus, the National Association for the Advancement of Colored People[65] owns every domain name containing any variation on the word 'nigger' in '.com', while the Anti-Defamation League[66] owns, among others, the domains 'kike.com', '.net', and '.org'. However, many feel that buying a few domain names is unlikely to have a significant impact on hate speech, especially over the Internet. Hate groups are readily able to invent new domain names. For example, 'mlking.org', apparently a page devoted to Martin Luther King, is in reality a hate site.

For the registration of hate domain names, the registry policies of the top-level domains (TLDs) are key. We will first study the situation of country-code top-level domain (ccTLD) registers and then the policies (or, rather, the absence of any policy) regarding generic top-level domains (gTLDs).[67]

VI. WHY ARE THERE HATE DOMAIN NAMES?

(i) Country-Code Top-Level Domains and Registration Policy

The Internet Assigned Numbers Authority (IANA) delegates ccTLD registries on the basis of the ISO 3166 standard.[68] In addition to all virtual

---

[63] Preparatory Committee on the World Conference against Racism, Racial Discrimination, Xenophobia and Related Intolerance, *supra* n. 16.

[64] Chaudhry, 'Who Owns the N-Word Dot Com?', *Wired News*, 22 Sept. 1999, <http://www.wired.com/news/culture/0,1284,21873,00.html>.

[65] <http://www.naacp.org>.

[66] <http://www.adl.org>.

[67] For an in-depth discussion of this topic, see P. A. de Miguel Asensio, *Derecho privado de internet* (2000), at 44–54.

[68] ICANN and IANA, 'Internet Domain Name System Structure and Delegation', May 1999, <http://www.iana.org/cctld/icp1.htm>.

national entities, a number of distinct territories, usually islands, are included in the 3166 standard, and the corresponding ccTLDs have been delegated. According to the delegation rules:

The designated manager must be equitable and fair to all groups in the domain that request domain names. Specifically, the same rules must be applied to all requests and they must be processed in a non-discriminatory fashion. The policies and procedures for the use of each TLD must be available for public inspection. . . . While variations in policies and procedures from country to country are expected due to local customs and cultural values, they must be documented and available to interested parties. Requests from for-profit and nonprofit companies and organizations are to be treated on an equal basis.

In 1998 the Internet Corporation for Assigned Names and Numbers (ICANN)[69] was created to manage IP addresses and domain names. The ICANN Governmental Advisory Committee considers the ccTLD registries ultimately subject to the jurisdiction of the relevant public authority or government.[70] According to the rules of delegation, national policies and procedures are expected to vary from country to country, and, provided that the rules are applied in a non-discriminatory fashion, restrictions on the registration of domain names under ccTLD are left to the relevant authority.

ccTLD registries may be managed in four ways. One option is the creation of a non-profit association which governs the operation of the ccTLD. This option permits all principal interest groups involved to participate in the formulation of the registry's policies. Another option is to seek an entirely private, commercial solution for the creation of the registry. The third option is to assign the task to existing public or private organizations. The fourth option is for the competent departments of the public administration to manage the new registry.

In Europe, national registries used to be managed either by a government department, or by a public university. However, nearly all members of the European Union have now reorganized their ccTLD registries and put in place management structures based on the non-profit, cooperative model. ccTLD registry policy has been delegated to the relevant public authority or government entity, which then establishes the rules for the registration of domain names. This will be the approach for the new '.eu' TLD. Although the territorial code 'eu' has not yet become standardized, it has been reserved for this purpose on the list of ISO 3166 codes. New eu ccTLDs will exist side-by-side with national ccTLDs. It will eventually be necessary to determine

---

[69] <http://www.icann.org>. See US Department of Commerce White Paper, 'Management of Internet Names and Addresses', Docket No. 980212036-8146-02,5, 5 June 1998, <http://www.ntia.doc.gov/ntiahome/domainname/6_5_98dns.htm>.

[70] European Commission, 'The Creation of the .EU Internet Top-Level Domain', 2 Feb. 2000, <http://europa.eu.int/comm/information_society/policy/internet/index_en.htm>.

whether certain categories of words, names, or numbers should be excluded from the eu registry. The general public would have access to the new ccTLDs through a large number of competing registrars subject to the general registration policy of the overall registry. The European Commission has initiated a public discussion on these topics.

An example of how a ccTLD functions is offered by the '.es' (Spain) registry. The registry is managed according to the non-profit, cooperative model. The Red Técnica Española de Televisión has been charged with supervising the .es registry. It has been configured as a public service managed by a public company. The registry rules have been defined by regulations issued by the Ministry of Telecommunications.[71] According to the regulations, no domain name contrary to law, mores, or public order can be registered as a ccTLD .es. Thus, the public authorities which manage the ccTLD can impose restrictions in the registry of domain names. These limitations have been accepted by ICANN, provided that they are applied on a non-discriminatory basis, are easily accessible, and are open to public examination. Many countries have introduced such restrictions, which make it very difficult for an Internet user to find a hate website, since it can have only a second-level domain name in a ccTLD. The registration of second-level domain names is within the purview of the owners of the rights to the first-level domain names. For example, 'Yahoo.es' is a first-level domain name registered in the ccTLD .es registry. In turn, Yahoo.es has requirements for the registry of any site hosted on Yahoo.com. Among the terms of its site contracts, Yahoo.es obliges users not to send or make available to others xenophobic or racist material.[72] Any user violating these terms may be barred from reliance on the services offered by Yahoo!. Although in this case, the definition of the terms of contract regarding the acceptable or unacceptable conduct of users is entirely the responsibility of Yahoo.es, some countries, including the countries of the European Union, have rushed to limit the freedom of online intermediaries regarding illegal actions by their clients. The importance of encouraging the self-regulation of online intermediaries and the standardization of the relevant regulations is self-evident.

(ii) Generic Top-Level Domains and (Absent) Registration Policy

There are very few gTLDs. However, from the economic point of view, they are the most important Internet domain names. Of these generic domains, five are international, and two are restricted to use by entities in the United States.

---

[71] 'Orden de 21 de Marzo de 2000 por la que se regula el sistema de asignación de nombres de dominio de Internet bajo el código de país correspondiente a España (.es)', 30 Mar. 2000, BOE 77, <http://www.nic.es/avisos/orden_21demarzode2000.html>.

[72] See terms of contract <http://es.docs.yahoo.com/info/utos.html>.

gTLD.edu was originally intended for all educational institutions. Many universities, colleges, schools, educational service organizations, and educational consortia have been registered under '.edu'.

gTLD.int is reserved for organizations established by international treaty, or for international databases.

gTLD.mil is used by the US military.[73]

gTLD.com is intended for commercial entities, that is, companies. This domain has become very large.

gTLD.org is the miscellaneous TLDN for non-governmental organizations.

gTLD.net is intended to hold only the computers of network providers, the administrative computers, and the network node computers.

gTLD.com, .org, and .net were initially managed by the NSI[74] company under contract from the US Government. The management is currently decentralized, and ICANN maintains a list of accredited registers.[75] There is no limit to the possible number of accredited registers. The domain names under the gTLDs are contained in a centralized register administered by NSI. Domain names with a gTLD are registered on a first-come, first-served basis. To be registered one must accept the Uniform Domain-Name Dispute-Resolution Policy (often referred to as the 'UDRP').[76] This follows the recommendation of a report issued by the World Intellectual Property Organization concerning the advisability of a uniform dispute-resolution policy among all registrars of the .com, .net, and .org TLDs.[77] There is also a restriction regarding the so-called 'seven dirty words'. Official Network Solutions policy prohibits the registration of domain names that include the seven dirty words and their variants, all of which are banned on US radio and television. If someone attempts to register any of these words, an automatic message responds that 'the domain name requested is not accepted due to being inappropriate'. These are the only limitations which are imposed for the registry of a domain name in the gTLDs.

Because nothing is said regarding hate names, hate groups can in theory employ them as domain names. Thus, in the United States, because only commercial and marketing rights are protected by the Anticybersquatting Consumer Protection Act,[78] hate words can be used freely. There seems little the heirs of Martin Luther King can do to stop the excesses of mlking.org.

---

[73] See Postel, 'Domain Name System Structure and Delegation', Mar. 1994, <http://www.isi.edu/in-notes/rfc1591.txt>.
[74] <http://www.networksolutions.com/>.
[75] <http://www.icann.org/registrars/accredited-list.html>.
[76] <http://www.icann.org/udrp/udrp-policy-24oct99.htm>.
[77] <http://ecommerce.wipo.int/domains/process/eng/final_report.html>.
[78] <http://thomas.loc.gov/cgi-bin/query/z?c106:S.1255.IS>.

VII. THE KEY ROLE OF ONLINE INTERMEDIARIES AND CONTENT PROVIDERS

The main judgment in the effort in France to prosecute Internet hate content was handed down on 13 November 1998 by the Chambre Correctionnelle of the Tribunal de Grande Instance de Paris.[79] A certain Faurisson was prosecuted for publishing revisionist ideas on a US-based server.[80] The French Court declared that it was competent in this case according to Article 113.2 of the French penal code. The article authorizes French courts to judge criminal cases involving possible offences committed through the press. The criminal offences are assumed to have been committed anywhere where the material is distributed. Accordingly, French courts are competent since the text was available in France on the Internet. In the end, however, Faurisson was found not guilty since the Court found that it was not sufficiently clear that he had been the author of the illegal writing.

In a recent case in Germany, the highest court for civil suits, the Bundesgerichtshof, ruled that the country's laws against Nazi propaganda can be applied even to websites located outside Germany. The defendant in the case, a certain Töben, was found guilty by a lower court of spreading 'Auschwitz lies' (denying the historical reality of the Holocaust). Töben operates the Adelaide Institute in Australia, which has a policy of denying the historical reality of the Holocaust. The lower court found, however, that Germany's laws against incitement to racial hatred could not be enforced against foreign websites. Töben, who was arrested while visiting Germany in 1999, was subsequently sentenced, because of his printed pamphlets, to ten months in prison on the lesser charge of offending the memory of the dead. He returned to Australia after serving part of his sentence. Overturning the lower court ruling, the Bundesgerichtshof found that German authorities can legally act against foreigners who place illegal material on webservers that are accessible in Germany.[81]

The difficulties in prosecuting the authors of hate material are evident. Once authorship has been proven, enforcement remains complicated. While French or German judges may be considered competent to pass down judgments against the authors of material on any of the thousands of hate sites that are available in France or Germany, judges in the United States or any other hosting country may not be willing or able to enforce these judgments against locally based Internet users or websites. Because hate speech is protected

---

[79] *Jugement correctionnel, Tribunal de Grande Instance de Paris*, Nov. 1998, <http://www.legalis.net/cgi-iddn/certificat.cgi?IDDN.FR.010.0058310.000.R.A.1999.027.41100>.

[80] The text is available at <http://www.legalis.net/legalnet/judiciaire/images/faur1.gif>.

[81] For information on the case, see <http://www.jura.uni-sb.de/Entscheidungen/Bundesgerichte/BGH/strafrecht/bgh95-00.html#top>.

under the First Amendment of the US Constitution, the US authorities cannot extradite a person for engaging in hate speech, though the speech may violate laws elsewhere.

These difficulties have caused plaintiffs to seek to act against Internet service providers, such as host service providers and information location tool providers, based in France, for example, facilitating access to hate speech, though the hate material may have a US origin. Insofar as the (US-based) content provider has selected the material which is published on a website, he can clearly be held responsible for the objectionable material. But it is less clear whether the online intermediaries can or should also be made to respond for these actions of others. Are online intermediaries like broadcasting stations which can be held liable for the content they publish, or are they like telephone companies which cannot be held responsible for the transmissions they facilitate?[82]

(i) The Liability of Online Intermediaries in the US

In the United States, the Communications Decency Act[83] of 1996 provides a broad exemption from liability for online intermediaries for the infringement of any type of law other than copyright law, which is dealt with in the Digital Millennium Copyright Bill of 1998. The relevant portion of §230 of the Communications Decency Act states: 'No provider or user of an interactive computer service shall be treated as the publisher or speaker of any information provided by another information content provider.' Thus, §230 offers federal immunity to service providers in any cause of action seeking to make them liable for information originating with a third-party user of a service. Specifically, §230 prohibits court officers from entertaining claims that would place an Internet service provider in the role of a publisher. This means that lawsuits against an Internet service provider for acts related to the exercise of a publisher's traditional editorial functions—such as publishing, withdrawing, or altering content—are barred. In *Zeran v America Online (AOL)*, the US Fourth Circuit Court decided that the Communications Decency Act 'plainly immunizes computer service providers like AOL from liability for information that originates with third parties'. This judgment clears Internet service providers of any liability for posting racist material.[84]

---

[82] Julià-Barceló, *supra* n. 3. See also Thoumyre, 'Responsabilités sur le web: une histoire de la régleamentation des réseaux numériques', 6 *Lex Electronica*, 1, Spring 2000, <http://www.lex-electronica.org/articles/v6–1/thoumyre.htm>.

[83] Communications Decency Act 47 U.S.C.S.

[84] *Zeran v America Online*, no. 97–1523, 12 Nov. 1997, <http://laws.lp.findlaw.com/4th/971523p.html>. Case cited in Bodard *et al.*, 'Crime on the Internet: A Challenge to Criminal Law in Europe', *Maastricht Journal of European and Comparative Law* (1998) 222, at 255.

(ii) The Liability of Online Intermediaries in the EU

(a) Some Country Examples

In Europe, many countries apply traditional rules on press liability to illegal acts online.

The 1997 German Multimedia Law foresees a with-fault liability standard based on previous knowledge of the illegal act. This means that, if a host service provider knows that illegal or infringing material is on the server it operates and it is technically able and can be reasonably expected to block the objectionable material, but does not do so, then the host service provider may be held liable.[85]

Munich prosecutors thus charged that CompuServe general manager Felix Somm was an accessory in the distribution of pornography and extremist propaganda and that, through his action (or lack thereof), Internet users obtained access to images of Nazi symbols and of Hitler. Somm argued that CompuServe, one of the largest Internet access providers in the world, was like a telephone company, which cannot be held liable for criminal conversations over their lines. Despite his argument, Somm was convicted in May 1998 of spreading the forbidden images via the Internet. The judge held that the defendant, together with CompuServe USA, made access publicly available to material containing violence, child pornography, and bestiality, contrary to Article 184, paragraph 3 of the German criminal code. At any time, CompuServe had been technically able to block access to the news groups containing the images, and, in failing to block access, the defendant acted deliberately, in full knowledge and with a motive of commercial gain.[86]

In Sweden, the law defines the category of bulletin board operators so broadly that the definition appears to be applicable to other online intermediaries as well. The law prohibits the distribution of messages that contain, for example, inflammatory comments against a population group or excessive descriptions of violence. Considering the costs of supervising real-time bulletin boards and chat rooms, the likely consequence of this norm is the closure of offensive bulletin boards.[87]

The publication of revisionist and Nazi theories is a criminal offence in France. On this basis, in March 2000, the Union des Etudiants Juifs de France (UEJF) filed a suit before a court in Nanterre against the service provider

---

[85] Federal Act Establishing the General Conditions for Information and Communication Services (*Informations- und Kommunikationsdienst-Gesetz-IuKDG*), 1 Aug. 1997.

[86] *Amtsgericht München v F. Somm, supra* n. 26. On this case, see McGuire, 'When Speech is Heard around the World: Internet Content Regulation in the United States and Germany', 74 *New York University Law Review* (1999) 750, at 768.

[87] Act (1998/112) on Responsibility for Electronic Bulletin Boards. See also Julià-Barceló, *supra* n. 3, at 11.

Multimania for hosting www.multimania.com/nsdap, an antisemitic and revisionist webpage. The UEJF tried to obtain legal redress from Multimania which, according to UEJF, had not detected that 'nsdap' is the acronym for *Nationalsozialistische Deutsche Arbeiterpartei* (Nazi). However, the Tribunal de Grande Instance de Nanterre decided on 24 May 2000[88] that there is no legal obligation for an Internet service provider either to investigate the identity of its client, or to check the content of the webpages which it is hosting.

But in a parallel case, the Tribunal de Grande Instance de Paris condemned Yahoo! for hosting an auctions page in which Nazi memorabilia were offered in contravention of Article R 645–2 of the French penal code.[89] A Yahoo.com auction site (Ebay) made available for auction hundreds of Nazi, neo-Nazi, and Ku Klux Klan objects, including films, swastikas, uniforms, daggers, photos, and medals. Among the thousands of Nazi items for sale on the site were 'five beautiful, large Nazi death notices' for $40.[90] The defendant, Yahoo!, argued that its English-language Yahoo.com services are physically in the United States, where such auctions cannot be barred because of the constitutional right to freedom of speech. Yahoo!'s French-language portal Yahoo.fr does not host such auctions, but French users, like all others, can switch over to Yahoo.com services with a click of the mouse. Since Yahoo! allows the reception of these pages and the eventual participation in the auction from France, the Court considered French law applicable and decided it was competent to hear the case. (In June 1996, a French court had denied a similar claim on the grounds that such control was technically impossible for access providers. In that case, the plaintiff, the UEJF, sued nine access providers, demanding that they monitor sites and block connections to sites with unlawful content. In June 1997, the decision was confirmed.)[91]

The Court ordered Yahoo! to take all possible measures to dissuade and prevent users from accessing the auction or any other revisionist or Nazi website or service. It also ordered Yahoo! France to inform any users of its services that searches for webpages or forums the name or content of which suggests Nazi propaganda or memorabilia must be immediately interrupted. California-based Yahoo! had to report back to the Court on 24 July 2000 to explain the measures it had taken to comply with the ruling.

---

[88] See <http://www.juriscom.net/archives/informations/avrmai00.htm>. Tribunal de Grande Instance de Nanterre, 1st Chambre, *UEJF v Multimania Production*, 24 May 2000, <http://www.juriscom.net/jurisfr/multimania.htm>.

[89] Tribunal de Grande Instance de Paris, *UEJF et al. v Yahoo! Inc. et Yahoo! France*, 22 May 2000, <http://www.juriscom.net/jurisfr/yahoo.htm#texte>.

[90] Raney, 'Ebay Criticized over Nazi Memorabilia', *New York Times*, 25 Nov. 1999.

[91] *UEJF v Calvacom et al.*, Tribunal de Grande Instance de Paris, 12 June 1996, <http://www.aui.fr/Groupes/GT>RPS/UEJF/ordonance.html>; *UEJF v AlternB*, <http://www.aui.fr/Communiques/commu-proces.html>.

In an interview with the French newspaper *Libération*, Jerry Yang, cofounder of Yahoo!, defied the Court. 'We are not going to change the content of our sites in the United States just because someone in France is asking us to do so,' he said. 'We have a lot of respect for national sovereignty; we also have a lot of respect for the Internet.'[92] In reaction to Yang's words, the French newspaper *Le nouvel observateur* launched a boycott against Yahoo!.[93]

The Tribunal de Grande Instance de Paris confirmed its ruling on 20 November 2000. The Court ordered Yahoo! to conform with the finding of a panel of three web-security experts that a keyword-filter system could block access to the offending sites among 90 per cent of French websurfers. Yahoo! was given 90 days to implement the measures and, failing to do so, was to be fined 100,000 francs for each day thereafter.[94]

This was not the first complaint against Ebay. In November 1999 the Simon Wiesenthal Center, in Los Angeles, asked the company to 'review its policy of . . . marketing items . . . which glorify nazism'. In a letter sent to Ebay, the Center noted that the sale of such items is illegal in Germany, a relevant argument because any user of the worldwide web anywhere can buy from Ebay.

(b) The EU Directive on E-Commerce

A recent directive of the European Parliament and the Council of the European Union seeks to coordinate the principal approaches towards the liability of online intermediaries in Europe.[95] The directive establishes that online intermediaries have no obligation to monitor content. Host service providers can be held liable for damages only if they were aware of facts and circumstances which render the illegal activity apparent, but nonetheless did not act expeditiously to remove the illegal material.

Articles 12, 13, and 14 of the directive list exclusions or limitations on liability for mere 'conduit', 'caching' or 'hosting'. Mere conduit includes the simple provision of access to the Internet and otherwise playing a passive role in the transmission of information provided by third parties. The limitation on liability for caching refers to the practice of storing to a local server copies

[92] See *Excite News*, 'Yahoo! Rejects French Court Ban on Nazi Sites', 16 June 2000, <http://news.excite.com/news/r/000616/08/france-usa-yahoo>; Launet, 'La justice française est très naïve', *Libération*, 16 June 2000, <http://www.liberation.com/multi/actu/20000612/20000616venzc.html>.

[93] Joffrin, 'Boycottons Yahoo!, protecteur des nazis!', *Le nouvel observateur*, 18 June 2000.

[94] See *Excite News*, 'Yahoo! Ordered to Bar French from Nazi Sites', 20 Nov. 2000, <http://news.excite.com/news/r/001120/11/net-france-yahoo-dc>. For full information on the case, see <http://www.legalis.net/jnet/2000/actualite_11_2000.htm>.

[95] Directive 2000/31/EC of the European Parliament and of the Council of 8 June 2000 on Certain Legal Aspects of Information Society Services, in Particular Electronic Commerce, in the Internal Market (Directive on Electronic Commerce), OJ 2000 L 178, <http://europa.eu.int/eur-lex/en/lif/dat/2000/en_300L0031.html>.

of high demand material that originates on remote servers. When the user requires the material, a copy is transmitted from the local server, thereby saving time and reducing the burden on the Internet infrastructure as a whole. Hosting consists of providing, in exchange for a fee, servers with space for webpages, news groups, chat rooms, or other kinds of content.

In general, the directive implicitly recognizes that the limitations on liability apply in both civil and criminal cases. However, Article 14 differentiates between civil and criminal liability in the case of hosting and establishes liability standards which vary according to the type of infringement. Thus, a host service provider is not liable under criminal statutes if he hosts unlawful material posted on the initiative of third parties unless he has actual knowledge of the illegal nature of the content. Likewise, host service providers are not liable for damages in civil cases involving unlawful postings unless they have actual knowledge of the nature of the postings or are aware of facts and circumstances which render the illegal activity apparent. However, even if the host service provider has actual knowledge of the infringement or is aware of facts and circumstances which make the infringement apparent, he may still escape liability if, upon obtaining such knowledge or awareness, he acts quickly to remove the information or to disable access to it. Article 15 adds that mere conduits and host service providers are required neither to monitor the information they transmit or store, nor actively to seek facts or circumstances indicating illegal activity.[96]

The search engine functions performed by information location tool providers are not covered by the directive. On the other hand, the directive does not exempt from liability any activity involving selection, modification, or creation of material by online intermediaries when they are acting as content providers by, for example, directly selling products or offering services such as online bookstores or auctions.[97]

VIII. CONCLUDING REMARKS

In *Being Digital*, Nicholas Negroponte reports a case in the United States in early 1996. A couple were running a bulletin board in Milpitas, California. The bulletin board conformed to community standards, local laws, and state statutes. A person from Tennessee logged into the bulletin board and realized that it violated Tennessee law. The California couple were duly charged, extradited to Tennessee, tried, and found guilty. According to Negroponte,

---

[96] For a thoughtful analysis, see Julià-Barceló, 'On-Line Intermediary Liability Issues: Comparing EU and US Legal Frameworks', *ECLIP EP*, 27028, 16 Dec. 1999, at 6, <http://www.jura.uni-muenster.de/eclip/documents/deliverable_2_1_4_bis_liability.pdf>.
[97] Ibid.

incidents like this show that the law is 'behaving like a dead fish flopping on a dock'.

As this chapter demonstrates, traditional norms can still be valid in cyberspace. However, the peculiar nature of the Internet requires new forms of regulation which must involve the active participation of online intermediaries, organizations, and individuals. Keywords in this process are 'soft' law (self-regulation), terms of service, register policy, hot lines, filtering tools, rating systems, and awareness campaigns.

Differing historical experiences and concerns explain the variety of approaches to the regulation of hate speech in the world. The conceptions of how liberty is best served are often in conflict. While in some countries the prohibition of hate speech appears to be the best way to protect minorities, honour the memory of the victims of racism, and prevent hate crimes, in others such a prohibition would be deemed unconstitutional, and the combat against hate speech and racial hatred is fought through open discussion and tolerance for all points of view.

Because cyberspace is boundless and information moves instantaneously worldwide on the Internet, there is little that a single country can do to counteract hate speech. It is quite clear that white-supremacists, Nazis, and xenophobic groups are benefiting from the possibilities offered by the tolerant approach of some countries to spread their hate propaganda around the globe. International cooperation is required in the struggle against these hawkers of hate.

5

Discrimination and Human Rights Law: Combating Racism

THEO VAN BOVEN

I. EXPLORATION

(i) The Perception of Racism as an Alien Phenomenon

In February 1994 the United Nations Special Rapporteur on contemporary forms of racism, racial discrimination, xenophobia, and related intolerance sent to States Members of the UN a detailed questionnaire with a view to inform them of his mandate and to collect information. In a report submitted in November of the same year to the UN General Assembly the Special Rapporteur stated that thirty States provided information. From among these States a number of Governments, in fact sixteen, affirmed that racism, racial discrimination, and xenophobia did not exist in their territory. The Governments claiming the absence of these phenomena in their countries included those of China, Iraq, Kuwait, Mexico, Myanmar, Pakistan, Saudi Arabia, Ukraine, and Zambia.[1]

The denial of the existence of racism, racial discrimination, and related phenomena and practices is prevalent in many quarters. It is often argued that racism and racial discrimination—and for that matter serious violations of human rights—have been overcome or that they are taking place in foreign lands. Thus, in his review of the early work of the Committee on the Elimination of Racial Discrimination (CERD), the supervisory body established under the International Convention on the Elimination of All Forms of Racial Discrimination (ICERD), Banton, a long-time member of CERD, reminds us how some Committee members were ideologically biased and politically motivated in their assertions of the absence of racial discrimination.[2] Committee members from Eastern Europe argued that certain kinds of economic and social structure, as products of class interest, generated ideologies and policies which encouraged racial discrimination but that the countries of

[1] UN doc. A/49/677, paras. 40, 41, 45 and n. 18.
[2] M. Banton, *International Action Against Racial Discrimination* (1996), at 104–6.

their origin were free from this evil. A Latin American Committee member took the view that the situation in a country of his continent could not be considered in the same manner as the situation in a European country or a developed country in another part of the world. The Committee would be well advised to examine more specifically the situation prevailing in those countries where racial discrimination persisted and where colonialism and imperialism were still rife.[3]

Also other countries were inclined, perhaps not so much on ideological grounds, to regard racism and racial discrimination as an alien problem with roots and rocks elsewhere. This was also the perception in the late 1960s in the Netherlands parliament when it discussed the ratification of the ICERD. Thereafter, the first significant political issue that came up in the Netherlands in connection with ICERD was the requirement of some Arab countries that Dutch companies and individuals, in applying for visas, had to supply declarations of non-Jewish origin. The Dutch authorities considered that such requirement, which reminded of certain practices of the German occupation in the years 1940–5, was seriously at odds with ICERD and they consequently introduced legislation which would have the effect of making the issuance of non-Jewish declarations a criminal offence.[4] Dutch criticism related to a practice that had its origin elsewhere, in Arab countries. Similarly, and in a more pervasive manner, relations with the apartheid regime in South Africa posed problems. Trade relations, financial dealings, export and import of strategic and military commodities led to soul-searching questions of complicity with the apartheid system, vigorously condemned in the United Nations as a crime against humanity.[5] Many governments, institutions, corporations, and individual persons that were engaged in dealings with the apartheid regime of South Africa used to argue that they had no sympathy for apartheid and that in fact this institutionalized system of racism and racial discrimination was practised elsewhere.

It appeared that in many countries and societies the prevailing attitude was to point the finger to elsewhere and consider racism and racial discrimination as an issue of foreign policy and foreign relations rather than as a domestic concern. Thus, ICERD was perceived as a legal and political instrument to serve foreign policy interests.

[3] M. Banton, *International Action Against Racial Discrimination* (1996), at 104–6.
[4] See fifth periodic report of the Netherlands to CERD (UN doc. CERD/C/75/Add.6, part I, section E).
[5] It should be noted that the recent Rome Statute of the International Criminal Court lists the crime of apartheid among the crimes against humanity and further specifies this crime as committed in the context of an institutionalized regime of systematic oppression and domination by one racial group over any other racial group or groups and committed with the intention of maintaining that regime (Article 7, (1) (j) and (2) (h)).

Against this perspective it was not surprising that many countries, notably African states, were eager to adhere to this instrument as a token of solidarity with the anti-apartheid campaign and in support of the movement against colonialism and racism. Initially, after ICERD was adopted and opened for signature and ratification by the UN General Assembly in December 1965,[6] the pace of ratification was high and for quite some time ICERD was the most widely ratified human rights treaty.

The notion of ICERD as a foreign policy instrument was reflected in the fact that many States Parties, in particular those from Eastern Europe and other non-Western countries, nominated active or retired diplomats, foreign ministry officials, former foreign ministers, and similar personalities to serve as members of CERD. One may wonder whether such membership of the Committee, which left its traces up until the present time, is fully consistent with the terms of Article 8(1) of ICERD requiring that the expert members of CERD are of 'high moral standing and acknowledged impartiality' and serve 'in their personal capacity'. Banton correctly observed that while CERD 'benefited' from having a high proportion of diplomats among its members, conditions are changing and that in the future the Committee might benefit from having more members experienced in the implementation of domestic policies against racial discrimination, particularly in the legal field.[7]

Perceptions and conditions are indeed changing. The prevailing attitude in the second half of the twentieth century was to regard racism and racial discrimination as an evil practised by others, and to ignore at the same time the existence of similar or comparable practices on one's own non-domestic scene. This attitude, however, is changing.[8] In spite of past and present denials by important political constituencies, the awareness is growing that no society and no human community is free from racism and racial discrimination. The experience of monitoring institutions, such as CERD and the European Commission against Racial Discrimination (ECRI), bears out that problems of racial discrimination are not only rampant elsewhere, in foreign lands, but that these problems arise everywhere, including within one's own borders. On this score lessons are learnt in Europe, in Australia, in the Americas, and in other continents as well. Racism and racial discrimination is not only a phenomenon of the past, associated with Naziism or colonialism. Neither is it only a phenomenon that manifests itself elsewhere. It is a serious problem everywhere, also in our midst.

It is significant in this context that European institutions and organizations are gradually moving from ignoring the problems of racism and racial

---

[6] G.A. Res. 2106 A (XX), 21 Dec. 1965.   [7] Banton, *supra* n. 2, at 309.

[8] Van Boven, 'United Nations Strategies to Combat Racism and Racial Discrimination; A Sobering but not Hopeless Balance-Sheet', in M. Castermans-Holleman, F. van Hoof, and J. Smith (eds), *The Role of the Nation-State in the 21st Century; Essays in Honour of Peter Baehr* (1998), at 251–64.

discrimination to taking up the matter as an immediate concern. Most welcome is the decision of 27 June 2000 by the Council of Europe Committee of Ministers to adopt the text of protocol No. 12 of the European Convention of Human Rights.[9] An equally welcome development is the adoption on 29 June 2000 by the Council of the European Union of Directive 2000/43/EC based on Article 13 of the Treaty of Amsterdam and implementing the principle of equal treatment between persons irrespective of racial or ethnic origin.[10] These positive developments setting out more comprehensive standards and obligations at the European level will be discussed later in more detail. Other evidence that Europe, at least the European Union, is catching up its efforts to combat racism and racial discrimination is the establishment of the European Monitoring Centre on Racism and Xenophobia (EUMC), based in Vienna, to provide the European Union with comparable, objective, and reliable data on the phenomena of racism and xenophobia and to assist the European Union in its actions against racism.[11]

The struggle against racism and racial discrimination has still a long way to go. It has to cope with widespread fears about loss of identities, deeply rooted prejudices, exclusion and marginalization of ethnically and socially disadvantaged classes of people not sharing in the benefits of the New Economy, and exploitation of ethnic, racial, and religious animosities for political purposes.

(ii) Denial and Acknowledgement

Any strategy of combating racism and racial discrimination should start with the acknowledgement that these phenomena and related practices do exist or may occur. It is on that basis that measures should be devised to prevent and to suppress these wrongs and to afford remedies and redress to the victims. Acknowledgement and denial stand to each other in a dialectical relationship. Only when named and acknowledged can racism be recognized, identified, and addressed effectively.[12] 'Naming and shaming' were qualified by the UN Secretary-General as a transparent and preventive strategy to unmask and expose human rights violations[13] and this applies equally to violations of

[9] Communiqué de Presse of the Council of Europe, 27 June 2000; *European Human Rights Convention: Better Protection Against Discrimination.*
[10] Council Directive on implementing the principle of equal treatment between persons irrespective of racial or ethnic origin, 29 June 2000, OJ 2000, L180/22.
[11] Council Regulation 1035/97, 2 June 1997.
[12] S. Cohen, *Denial and Acknowledgement—The Impact of Information about Human Rights Violations* (1995), at 19–58.
[13] *We the Peoples*, Millennium Report of the UN Secretary-General, United Nations, New York, 2000, at 46.

human dignity as a result of racism and racial discrimination. Denial of history, denial of facts, denial of responsibility are not only obstacles but also calculated and shrewd devices to obstruct the cause of justice. Against this background the International Council on Human Rights Policy developed in a recent publication a 'typology of denial'.[14]

Notorious are the Holocaust denials, deeply offensive to survivors and adding to their suffering. Failure to recognize the distinct culture, lifestyle, and language of certain groups, such as indigenous peoples and minorities (Kurds in Turkey, Turks in Bulgaria, etc.), and forcing them to assimilate to the dominant population and culture also form part of the pattern of denials. The claim by socialist countries of Central and Eastern Europe that racism and racial discrimination were inconsistent with their socio-political ideology of socialism and therefore did not exist in their countries and societies was also a form of self-denial. Another illustration is the denial by certain Asian governments that the caste system is a form of racial discrimination coming under the purview of ICERD, in spite of the fact that the Convention defines racist discrimination in terms of race, colour, *descent*, ethnic, or national origin.[15] The typology of denial is marked by misrepresentations of facts, by euphemisms, by refusal to recognize wrongs committed, and above all by denying responsibility for past and present practices often amounting to grave offences against human dignity and to crimes against humanity. Acknowledgement entails the acceptance of State responsibility, corporate responsibility as well as civil and criminal responsibility of individual persons and further implies the readiness to award reparation to victims and their family members.

II. VICTIMS OF RACIAL DISCRIMINATION

(i) Victims of Deeply Rooted and Entrenched Racism

The effects of racism and racial discrimination are only fully understood in frankly ascertaining the fate of victims. One such category of victims are people who over the centuries have been marginalized and excluded in societies where a particular religion, culture, lifestyle, or socio-political system was predominant. As a result of deeply rooted and entrenched racism people were relegated to the status of non-persons. The right to be recognized as a person before the law (Article 6, Universal Declaration of Human Rights) did not

[14] International Council on Human Rights Policy, *The Persistence and Mutation of Racism* (2000), at 6–8.

[15] See further on this issue the Report of CERD to the 51st session of the UN General Assembly (1996), UN doc. A/51/18, para. 352 and annex IX (letter of the Government of India).

apply to them. Very few outsiders have come to their defence and prospects of improvement of their fate were dim. While all victims of violations of human rights share the misfortune of being ignored and overlooked, the victims of entrenched racism have been suffering in deep silence and their voices found no echo and hardly led to national or international concern. These people were probably not in the minds of the lawyers and diplomats who drafted major human rights instruments such as the International Bill of Human Rights. Only in recent years did international public opinion start to take a modest interest in this category of victims, thanks to interaction between more self-assertiveness on the part of victims and a responsive attitude of human rights monitors, in particular national and international NGOs, treaty bodies, and policy organs of the United Nations, the Organization of American States, the Council of Europe, and the Organization for Security and Cooperation in Europe.

(a) Sinti and Roma

The annual report covering 1999 of the European Commission against Racism and Intolerance (ECRI) notes among the main trends across Europe in the field of racism, xenophobia, anti-semitism, and intolerance that Roma/Gypsies throughout Europe suffer from persisting prejudice and discrimination in many aspects of social and economic life, resulting in damaging social exclusion. They are often the target of violent manifestations of racism and intolerance.[16] In ECRI General Policy Recommendation No. 3 on *Combating Racism and Intolerance against Roma/Gypsies*[17] tribute is paid to the memory of all the victims of policies of racist persecution and extermination during the Second World War, including the considerable number of Roma/Gypsies who perished as a result of such policies. In the same policy document ECRI made a series of important recommendations relating to legal aid, the administration of justice, the media, education (in particular to combat school segregation), the issue of *de jure* and *de facto* access to citizenship, and particular attention was given to the situation of Roma/Gypsy women, who are often the subject of double discrimination.

The CERD held for the first time in its history , in August 2000, a thematic discussion, with participation of various UN bodies and NGOs, on the issue of discrimination against Roma. It subsequently adopted General Recommendation XXVII[18] (a forty-nine-paragraph document) which purports to make the issue of discrimination against Roma an integral part of the monitoring work of CERD and contains recommendations for

[16] Council of Europe doc. CRI (2000) 20, main trends (7–9), at 8.
[17] Council of Europe doc. CRI (1998) 29.
[18] Report of CERD to the 55th session of the UN General Assembly (2000), UN doc. A/55/18, Annex V C.

protection against racial violence, in the field of education, for improving living conditions (employment, housing, health care, access to places and services for the use of the general public), in the field of the media, concerning participation in public life, including all central and local governmental bodies. Important and significant are the recommendations to ensure that legislation regarding citizenship and naturalization does not discriminate against members of Roma communities (para. 4) as well as recommendations to acknowledge wrongs done during the Second World War to Roma communities by deportation and extermination and consider ways of compensating for them (para. 10). These are only first steps which should be followed up by persistent efforts of an alert and vigorous national and international civil society and above all by the empowerment of the Sinti and Roma themselves.

(b) Dalits[19]

The caste system with its age-old and inbred scale of inequality and discrimination has largely escaped attention of the international human rights community. It remained a taboo in the human rights chambers of the United Nations and other international organizations. Those who sit at the very bottom of the hierarchical ladder only hope for a better future in life after death. As was stated in a publication of the International Council on Human Rights Policy, castes have an interest in maintaining the system and are often staunch defenders of their degrees of privilege.[20]

Only in recent times, as part of the monitoring activities of CERD, did the situation of the scheduled castes and scheduled tribes and the ensuing persistent discrimination of untouchables in the Indian society surface as a matter of express concern and as a form of systematic and large-scale racial discrimination. After the examination of the report of India in August 1996, the Committee affirmed, while disagreeing with the position of the Government of India which refused to acknowledge the applicability of the anti-racism convention in this matter, that the situation of the scheduled castes and scheduled tribes falls within the scope of the Convention, in particular in view of the term 'descent' mentioned in Article 1 of the Convention.[21] The Committee recommended that special measures be taken by the authorities to prevent acts of discrimination towards persons belonging to the scheduled castes and scheduled tribes and, in cases where such acts have been committed, to conduct thorough investigations, to punish those found responsible, and to provide just and adequate reparation to the victims. Further, the Committee stressed the importance of the equal enjoyment by members of

---

[19] See M. N. Shrinivas (ed.), *Caste, its Twentieth Century Avatar* (1996).
[20] *Supra* n. 14, at 18.
[21] Report of the Committee on the Elimination of Racial Discrimination to the fifty-first session of the General Assembly, UN doc. A/51/18, para. 352.

those groups of the rights to access to health care, education, work and public places, and services, including wells, cafes, or restaurants.[22] As stated above in the review of the typology of denial, the Government of India persisted in its denial that the caste system comes under the purview of ICERD.[23] It would appear, however, that an irreversible trend is developing to hold caste discrimination, as CERD did, incompatible with the principles and provisions of the International Convention.

(c) Indigenous Peoples

According to the Special Rapporteur on discrimination against indigenous populations:

Indigenous communities, peoples and nations are those which, having a historical continuity with pre-invasion and pre-colonial societies that developed on their territories, consider themselves distinct from other sectors of the societies now prevailing in those territories, or parts of them. They form at present non-dominant sectors of society and are determined to preserve, develop and transmit to future generations their ancestral territories, and their ethnic identity, as the basis of their continued existence as peoples, in accordance with their own cultural patterns, social institutions and legal systems.[24]

Although no such definition of indigenous peoples was formally adopted, the working definition just quoted gives an adequate description of the groups of persons who over the centuries have been victims of exclusion and discrimination and deprived of their basic rights, especially the right to their lands, territories, and resources. Their identity and culture were suppressed and in many cases their very existence was denied. The colonists and invaders occupied their lands as *terra nullius* which implied that the indigenous inhabitants were relegated to the status of nobodies. They were often forced to assimilate or to disappear and even up until recent times children were forcefully separated and taken away from their indigenous parents.[25] In the early years of the United Nations, indigenous representatives made sporadic appeals to the world organization and there was no specific reaction. This changed in the 1970s and early 1980s. Of major importance were the UN study of the Problem of Discrimination against Indigenous Populations[26] (Special Rapporteur Mr Martinez Cobo) and two non-governmental conferences on indigenous issues, in particular land rights, held in Geneva in 1977 and 1981.

---

[22] Report of the Committee on the Elimination of Racial Discrimination to the fifty-first session of the General Assembly, UN doc. A/51/18, para. 352.

[23] *Supra*, n. 15.

[24] *Study of the Problem of Discrimination Against Indigenous Populations*, vol. V—Conclusions, Proposals and Recommendations, para. 379.

[25] See *Report of the National Inquiry into the Separation of Aboriginal and Torres Strait Islander Children from Their Families* (Sydney, Commonwealth of Australia, 1997).

[26] *Supra*, n. 24.

Most instrumental was the establishment in 1982 by the United Nations of the Working Group on Indigenous Populations as a platform of representatives of indigenous peoples and their communities and organizations, with the task to review developments and identify problems and to develop international standards concerning the rights of indigenous peoples.

The legal status of the indigenous peoples, within the context of national states and as emerging and evolving actors in the international society, is still the subject of protracted discussions. The only completed legal instrument adopted and in force (but only with a limited number of States parties)[27] is ILO Convention No. 169 Concerning Indigenous and Tribal Peoples in Independent Countries.[28] The most comprehensive standard-setting exercise relating to the rights of indigenous peoples is embodied in the Draft Declaration on the Rights of Indigenous Peoples, drawn up with the assistance of representatives of indigenous organizations and communities and adopted in 1994 by the UN Sub-Commission on Prevention of Discrimination and Protection of Minorities.[29] Since that time the Draft Declaration is under discussion in a Working Group of the UN Commission on Human Rights which as an inter-governmental body finds it difficult to come to grips with such issues as the right of indigenous peoples to self-determination and their historical land rights, including the right to restitution and compensation for their lost territories.

While the Draft Declaration is still pending as a piece of unresolved business of the Commission on Human Rights, international moral awareness regarding the plight of indigenous peoples is growing. This trend is reflected in the work of CERD which in the examination of country reports and in a General Recommendation on the Rights of Indigenous Peoples (1997)[30] reaffirmed that the provisions of ICERD apply to indigenous peoples. Even though the Draft Declaration has not yet received the endorsement of intergovernmental UN policy organs, notably the Commission on Human Rights and the General Assembly, CERD's General Recommendation draws heavily upon the Draft Declaration and thus recognizes and strengthens its normative value. Noteworthy is the last paragraph which reads:

The Committee especially calls upon States parties to recognize and protect the rights of indigenous peoples to own, develop, control and use their communal lands, territories and resources and, where they have been deprived of these lands and territories

[27] As per 1 January 2000 ILO Convention No. 169 had received thirteen ratifications. See Marie, International Instrument Relating to Human Rights-Classification and Status of Ratifications as of 1 January 2000', 21 *Human Rights Law Journal* (2000) 91, at 102.

[28] See 'Special Issue on the Status and Rights of Indigenous Peoples in Different Regions', 59/2 *Heidelberg Journal of International Law* (1999) 543.

[29] Ibid., at 556–66.

[30] Report of the Committee on the Elimination of Racial Discrimination to the fifty-second session of the General Assembly, UN doc. A/52/18, Annex V.

traditionally owned or otherwise inhabited or used without their free and informed consent, to take steps to return those lands and territories. Only when this is for factual reasons not possible, the right to restitution should be substituted by the right to just, fair and prompt compensation. Such compensation should as far as possible take the form of lands and territories.

(ii) Uprooted People

Over the centuries and up to the present time people are uprooted as a result of foreign intervention and domination, colonial policies, deportation and trade, persecution on political, racial, ethnic, or religious grounds, armed conflicts, and other threats to life and existence. People were victims of slavery and slave trade and also in our days contemporary forms of slavery continue to victimize large groups of persons, such as trafficking of women and children and exploitation for sexual purposes and profit. In the aftermath of colonialism many people, in particular Africans and Asians, moved to metropolitan countries. They still face the adverse consequences and the psychological and material effects of the colonial past. Similarly immigrants, refugees, and asylum seekers—as temporary or permanent residents—encounter hostile sentiments and practices of racism, xenophobia, and intolerance. Some national and local communities have made better efforts than other communities, but the fact remains that virtually no society or community can rightfully claim to be free from racism and racial discrimination in dealing with newcomers from different cultures, religions, and lands.

Migrant workers, notably miners, seasonal workers, and domestic servants, are often at the mercy of their employers and are treated as commodities, attracted when needed and expelled when no longer required. Women migrants are not only subjected to racial discrimination, but often also to discrimination and abuse on the basis of their gender as well.[31] Even where recourse procedures are formally available, they are not utilized out of fear that resort to them would invite retaliation.[32]

The situation of undocumented migrants, the *sans-papiers*, is even more dramatic. They usually belong to ethnic groups different from the 'host' community and they are excluded and discriminated against not only because of their undocumented status but also because of their ethnicity. As so called

[31] See *Discrimination Against Migrants—Migrant Women: In Search of Remedies.* Contribution by the Special Rapporteur on the Human Rights of Migrants, UN doc. A/CONF.189/PC.1/19.

[32] Van Boven, *Common Problems Linked to All Remedies Available to Victims of Racial Discrimination,* background paper for Expert Seminar on Remedies Available to the Victims of Acts of Racism, February 2000, Doc HR/GVA/WCR/SEM.1/2000/BP.5, at 8–9.

'illegal aliens' they are often denied their fundamental human rights and free-doms, including access to education and basic health and social services. Against this background it is troubling that the International Convention on the Protection of the Rights of All Migrant Workers and Members of Their Families, which seeks to protect documented and undocumented migrants, has only received ten years after its adoption twelve ratifications and has not yet entered into force.[33]

The obstacles, inequalities, hostilities, and other serious inconveniences encountered by migrants and other people of different ethnic or national ori-gin are described in detail in the 1999 annual report of ECRI.[34] The main trends vary from region to region and from country to country but the pat-tern as a whole is disturbing and brings out:

- persistent racial and ethnic discrimination in employment, housing, and the provision of services;
- racism and prejudice in the operation of public institutions, including the judicial system and schools;
- racist attitudes and behaviour on the part of law enforcement officers (such as the police and border control personnel);
- incitement to intolerance and racial or ethnic hatred;
- prejudice against Muslim communities (Islamophobia) which manifests itself in violence, harassment, discrimination, general negative attitudes and stereotypes;[35]
- increased use of racist or xenophobic views in politics and the resurgence of the far right.

Many persons who are subject to these disturbing trends are aliens. It must be recalled that as a matter of principle basic human rights apply to every-one, citizens and non-citizens alike.[36] However, certain human rights instru-ments, such as ICERD which states explicitly in Article 1(2) that the Convention shall not apply to distinctions, exclusions, restrictions or prefer-ences as between citizens and non-citizens,[37] are invoked by State authorities to legitimize the treatment of aliens as second-class people, often with racist

---

[33] UN General Assembly resolution 45/158, dated 18 Dec. 1990. See further *supra* n. 27, at 101.

[34] Council of Europe document CRI (2000) 20.

[35] This trend indicates the link between racial discrimination and religious intolerance. See further Abdelfattah Amor, *Racial Discrimination and Religious Discrimination: Identification and Measures,* UN doc. A/CONF.189/PC.1/7.

[36] See *Declaration on the Human Rights of Individuals Who are not Nationals of the Country in which They Live,* adopted by GA Res. 40/144, 13 Dec. 1985.

[37] In similar fashion the recent EU Directive 2000/43/EC, implementing the principle of equal treatment between persons irrespective of racial or ethnic origin, excludes from its scope difference of treatment based on nationality and the legal status of third-country nationals and stateless persons (Article 3(2)).

implications. In Europe such treatment and such attitudes affect in particular people of non-European origin who are visibly distinguishable by their colour of skin. In this regard the words spoken more than ten years ago by Manfred Nowak, a prominent Austrian human rights expert, are still pertinent:

There are millions of migrants workers, refugees and other aliens and ethnic minorities living in Europe as second class human beings. If we believe in the equal rights of all human beings, we should not accept that our societies are split into two major categories of people: in the class of citizens enjoying human rights and in the class of aliens dependent on 'human allowances'. The credibility of European democracies demands that we seriously start to abolish the legal distinction between nationals and aliens.[38]

III. THE ROLE OF THE STATE

(i) General Considerations and Trends

Under international human rights law the State has the duty to ensure, protect, and promote human rights and fundamental freedoms in the civil, political, economic, social, and cultural fields and to carry out policies outlawing discrimination. In this regard the State performs a pivotal role. The obligations undertaken by the State under international human rights conventions relate first and foremost to the persons who fall under the State's jurisdiction but they also constitute commitments *vis-à-vis* other States parties and the international community at large.

With its capacity to legislate and to enforce, with its duty to uphold the rule of law, with its institutions to monitor and to control, with its responsibilities in the areas of teaching, education, culture, and information, with its task to promote social welfare and political justice, the State has a vital role to play in combating racial discrimination and promoting racial equality. In order to meet these obligations the State should be vigorous, effective, well-equipped, and accountable to national constituencies and the international community. I plead for a strong State which at the same time is democratic and accountable.

However, in these days of privatization and globalization of the economy and telecommunication systems, with growing reliance on the forces of the market economy, the role of the State is in decline. Privatization goes even so far as to cover areas which traditionally belonged to the public domain, such as the running of prison institutions, upholding public order and security, law enforcement, and even national defence. The Welfare State is in the process

---

[38] M. Nowak, in *New Expressions of Racism, Growing Areas of Conflict in Europe*, SIM Special No. 7, 17–20, at 19.

of being dismantled. Health care, education, housing, and employment—areas of crucial importance to the racially marginalized and disadvantaged—are increasingly withdrawn from the public domain and transferred to private institutions and corporations which operate for financial gain and economic profit. Consequently, the forces of the market tend to increase inequalities at the detriment of racially and ethnically disadvantaged groups and persons. It is uncertain whether this trend can be reversed, but at least in certain areas measures should be taken to strengthen the capacity of the State to deal more effectively with structural aspects of discrimination, not only discrimination based on racial grounds but also on the grounds of gender, religion, nationality, etc. As was correctly stated: 'Adequate laws, access to court, a willingness to interpret the law broadly and effectively, and a determination on the part of the courts to enforce the law, are all essential prerequisites for the eradication of racism.'[39]

(ii) Legal and Institutional Means

(a) General and Comprehensive Anti-discrimination Legislation

Monitoring bodies, such as CERD and ECRI, have repeatedly called upon States to enact comprehensive anti-discrimination legislation, not only in the criminal sphere to suppress incitement to racial hatred and discrimination and acts of violence (as prescribed by Article 4 ICERD), but also in the area of civil and administrative law. Such legislation is not only needed to direct policies and practices of public authorities and public institutions but also to prohibit racial discrimination by private institutions, enterprises, and individuals with respect to such areas as employment, education, housing, health care, social protection and social security, social benefits, access to the supply of goods and services and to public places as well as access to citizenship.[40]

Such general and comprehensive anti-discrimination legislation, which should also cover the functions of public bodies and authorities in this respect, is clearly encouraged or prescribed by existing provisions and evolving standards at international and European levels. Thus, ICERD requires States parties to prohibit and bring to an end, by all appropriate means, including legislation as required by circumstances, racial discrimination by any person, group, or organization (Article 2(1)(d)) and this obligation is further spelled out in detail in the key provisions of Article 5 ICERD. The adoption of Protocol No. 12 to the European Convention of Human Rights by the

[39] International Council and Human Right Policy, *supra* n. 14, at 15.
[40] See also *All Different, All Equal: From Principle to Practice*, European Contribution to the World Conference against Racism, Racial Discrimination, Xenophobia and Related Intolerance (Strasbourg, 11–13 Oct. 2000), General Conclusions, para. 8.

Council of Europe Ministers on 27 June 2000 will require States which become parties to this new instrument to adopt more far-reaching anti-discrimination legislation.[41] This Protocol provides for a general prohibition of discrimination and aims to remove the limitations of the current non-discrimination provision of the European Convention (Article 14) which only prohibits discrimination of the rights guaranteed by the European Convention (and thus excludes *inter alia* from its scope economic and social rights). Once Protocol No. 12 is widely accepted and States parties have adopted the necessary implementation legislation, the basis is laid for more effective legal means to eradicate racial discrimination and intolerance and to promote equality and non-discrimination on other grounds as well, notably on the grounds of religion or belief and gender.

Another positive legal development in Europe was the adoption on 29 June 2000 of Directive 2000/43/EC by the Council of the European Union.[42] This Directive is based on Article 13 of the Treaty of Amsterdam and implements the principle of equal treatment between persons irrespective of racial or ethnic origin. The Directive covers a wide range of areas of everyday life where the European Community has competence to act: employment and working conditions, social security and health care, education, access to goods and services, including housing (Article 3). Member States must also provide for legal protection for victims and witnesses against retaliation by employers or others (Article 9). In order to improve the implementation of anti-discrimination laws the Directive requires Member States which have not already done so to establish bodies for the promotion of equal treatment, which will provide independent assistance to victims of discrimination, conduct surveys and studies, and publish reports and recommendations (Article 13).

(b) Specialized Bodies to Combat Racism and Racial Discrimination

International monitoring bodies, notably CERD and ECRI, strongly recommend the establishment of national institutions, commissions, or other appropriate bodies to promote equal treatment irrespective of racial or ethnic origin or religious background and to facilitate the effective implementation of national and international standards.[43] Equally, as was noted above, Directive 2000/43/EC requires Member States of the European Union to establish such specialized bodies. No model is prescribed as to the form and nature of these specialized bodies. They may take the form of national

---

[41] *Supra* n. 9.

[42] *Supra* n. 10.

[43] See General Recommendation XVII of CERD on the establishment of national institutions to facilitate the implementation of the Convention (1993) and ECRI General Policy Recommendation No. 2 with the appendix *Basic Principles Concerning Specialized Bodies to Combat Racism, Xenophobia, Antisemitism and Intolerance at National Level.*

commissions for racial equality, ombudsmen against ethnic discrimination, centres or offices for combating racism and promoting equal opportunities, or bodies with wider objectives in the field of human rights.[44]

The specialized bodies may carry out a variety of functions and responsibilities. It is of particular importance that such bodies perform a preventive function and produce remedial effects. In the light of this perspective some of their functions and responsibilities, outlined by ECRI,[45] deserve particular emphasis:

- *Monitoring* the content and effect of legislation and executive acts and making proposals for improving legislation;
- *Advising* the legislative and executive authorities with a view to improving regulations and practice;
- *Providing aid and assistance* to victims, including legal aid;
- *Facilitating recourse* to the courts or other judicial authorities;
- *Hearing and considering complaints* concerning specific cases and seeking amicable settlements or taking binding and enforceable decisions;
- *Providing information and advice* to relevant bodies and institutions;
- *Issuing advice* on standards of anti-discriminatory practice in specific areas;
- *Promoting and contributing to training* of key groups;
- *Promoting the awareness* of the general public to issues of discrimination.

It is obvious that in any review of the responsibility of the State to combat racism and racial discrimination attention has to be paid to the crucial role of the police and other law enforcement officials. The criminal justice system has its distinct function which cannot be overtaken by the various types of specialized bodies just referred to. It is, however, a matter of concern that in many countries the police itself is not free from racist attitudes and that victims of racial discrimination have little confidence in the administration of justice on account of the growing reluctance of many judges to take into account a racist intent or motive in dealing with complaints about racial discrimination.[46] It is further a matter of experience that the police and the prosecution agencies are too indulgent and not vigilant enough in tackling racist crimes. Lack of adequate action by the criminal justice system makes victims or potential victims utterly insecure and vulnerable. One of the means to improve this situation is to provide training courses to law enforcement officials, not only to promote cultural sensitivity and awareness of prejudice but also to ensure that in the performance of their duties law enforcement officials protect human dignity and respect human rights standards.[47] It is also important that in the

---

[44] ECRI, *Basic Principles, supra* n. 43, principle 2.   [45] Ibid., principle 3.

[46] See report of UN Special Rapporteur on contemporary forms of racism, racial discrimination, xenophobia, and related intolerance on his visit to the United States of America, UN doc. E/CN.4/1995/78/Add.1, para. 104.

[47] See General Recommendation XIII of CERD on the training of law enforcement officials in the protection of human rights (1993).

recruitment, promotion, and retention of police staff persons belonging to racially or ethnically targeted groups receive special consideration.

(c) Recourse Procedures

It is the duty of the State to make effective recourse procedures available to victims of racial discrimination. This is essentially the thrust of Article 6 of ICERD, which reads:

States Parties shall assure to everyone within their jurisdiction effective protection and remedies, through the competent national tribunals and other State institutions, against any acts of racial discrimination which violate his human rights and fundamental freedoms contrary to this Convention, as well as the right to seek from such tribunals just and adequate reparation for any damage suffered as a result of such discrimination.

In its practice CERD pays much attention to the implementation of Article 6 of the International Convention; in particular the Committee takes an interest in the availability and effectiveness of remedies and in cases that demonstrate the use of such remedies and that lead to rendering reparation or satisfaction to victims. However, in many instances States fail to provide relevant information on this matter and in other cases CERD identifies special groups of people who are most in need of remedies but who appear to lack the benefit of them as recognized by Article 6. Among groups so identified are aboriginals with respect to their land rights; peasant and indigenous groups suffering from violence; foreign workers including women domestic servants subjected to exploitation; Roma and Jews experiencing racial hatred and acts of violence; indigenous peoples; Afro-Americans and Afro-Latinos; refugees and immigrants lacking access to courts and administrative bodies; undocumented foreigners and temporary residents without entitlement to redress for acts of racial discrimination; internally displaced persons mainly belonging to indigenous and black communities, etc.[48]

Actual practice proves that effective remedies are unavailable or unproductive for those who are most in need of them, in particular the marginalized and the destitute. They lack education; they are ignorant of the law; and in addition, they often distrust the courts. Moreover, certain categories of people, notably undocumented persons (the *sans-papiers*), trafficked women and children, fear intimidation, retaliation, or expulsion and therefore refrain from seeking reparation or satisfaction and improvement of their living conditions. In short, in many countries the picture for victims looks gloomy: lack of protection and remedies, lack of rehabilitation and reintegration, lack of

---

[48] See in more detail T. van Boven, *Common Problems Linked to All Remedies Available to Victims of Racial Discrimination*, Background paper to UN Seminar on Remedies Available to Victims of Racial Discrimination, Geneva, 16–18 Feb. 2000, UN doc. HR/GVA/ WCR/SEM 1/2000/BP.5.

sensitivity on the part of the police authorities and the judiciary, and a climate of fear, intimidation, and retaliation.[49]

In order to improve this unsatisfactory state of affairs, recourse procedures should be more easily accessible, expeditious, and not unduly complicated. In addition, as was stated above in connection with specialized bodies to combat racism and racial discrimination, such bodies are needed to perform the tasks of monitoring, providing aid and assistance to victims, hearing and considering complaints, advising on legislative and other policy measures, and promoting awareness of the general public to issues of discrimination.

Particular attention must be given to means and methods of redress and rehabilitation to persons belonging to targeted groups who have been victims of gender-related crimes, such as rape and other forms of sexual and domestic violence, forced prostitution, and trafficking for the purpose of sexual exploitation. These persons, victims of double discrimination on the grounds of race and gender, a glaring combination of racism and sexism, are in need of effective legal protection and support and empowerment to take action and protection from racism, xenophobia, and intolerance.[50]

IV. THE EUROPEAN CONNECTION

(i) Reticence and Reappraisal

It must be remembered that one of the most vicious, infamous, and fateful doctrines of racism originated in Europe. Point 4 of the programme of the Nazi party, originally established in 1919 and ascending to power in Germany in 1933, read as follows: 'Only a member of the race can be a citizen. A member of the race can only be one who is of German blood, without consideration of creed. Consequently no Jew can be a member of the race . . .'.[51] Persecution and extermination of the Jews became official State practice. Many other people were also killed, in large numbers, on racial, ethnic, and national grounds, including Sinti and Roma. These outrageous policies and practices triggered off broad international action as reflected in the adoption by the UN General Assembly of the Convention on the Prevention and Punishment of the Crime of Genocide and of the Universal Declaration of Human Rights on 9 and 10 December 1948 respectively. These landmark

---

[49] Ibid.

[50] See also *All Different, All Equal, from Principle to Practice*, n. 40, *supra*, General Conclusions, para. 11.

[51] Cited in the Judgment of the International Military Tribunal at Nuremberg and referred to by Hernan Santa Cruz, UN Special Rapporteur on Racial Discrimination, in *Special Study on Racial Discrimination in the Political, Economic, Social and Cultural Spheres*, UN Publication E7.XIV.2 (1971), para. 980.

documents are directly linked with the inhumanities that occurred before and
during the Second World War.

The 'white against black' racism with its historical roots in the slave trade
and in colonialism, in which European countries were heavily implicated, also
spurred international action. It found further expression in public campaigns
such as the civil rights movement in the United States of America and in the
anti-apartheid movement strongly supported by the United Nations and
other organs of international and national society.

Hardly any other subject prompted United Nations organs to produce so
many verbal expressions and statements in the form of legal standards, political resolutions, action plans, and other narratives as the struggle against
racism and racial discrimination.[52] Currently the Third Decade to Combat
Racism and Racial Discrimination is in progress and it was decided, after two
World Conferences to Combat Racism and Racial Discrimination were held
in 1978 and 1983, to convene another World Conference on Racism and
Racial Discrimination, *Xenophobia and Related Intolerance* (emphasis
added),[53] to take place in South Africa early September 2001.

It appears that Europe has never been in the forefront in taking action
against racial discrimination. For historical and present-time considerations
Europe was not very receptive to UN strategies in the matter of racism and
racial discrimination. Certain deeply rooted patterns of racism and racial discrimination are directly or indirectly related to the European colonial past
with its mentality of white supremacy. Many Europeans feel uncomfortable
when taken to task on issues of racism and racial discrimination, both in their
historical and their contemporary dimensions. As noted earlier, Europe's attitude was not convincing in giving effect and weight to UN standards aimed
at the elimination of racial discrimination. Moreover, the principal European
human rights instrument, viz. the European Convention on Human Rights,
set out a limited concept of non-discrimination which only related to the
rights and freedoms set forth in the Convention. An innovative and creative
effort by the European Commission on Human Rights to qualify in certain
circumstances discriminatory treatment on the ground of race as degrading
treatment within the meaning of Article 3 of the European Convention never
got official endorsement in the supervisory system of the European
Convention.[54] The European Court dealt rarely with issues of racial discrimination and, although the lack of much substantive case law in this matter

[52] See in more detail van Boven, *United Nations Strategies, supra* n. 8.

[53] The words in italics are associated with disturbing contemporary manifestations occurring particularly in European countries (see Commission on Human Rights Resolution
1993/20, in particular the preamble).

[54] European Commission on Human Rights, Report of 14 Dec. 1973 (only made public
on 21 Mar. 1994), *East African Asians v United Kingdom,* 15 *Human Rights Law Journal* (1994)
215.

makes it risky to draw general conclusions, it nevertheless appears that the European Court as the custodian of the European Convention follows different interpretations and puts different emphases in weighing issues involving racial discrimination than global bodies such as CERD. Cases in point are the judgments of the European Court of Human Rights relating to the dissemination of racist statements (*Jersild*)[55] and in the matter of immigration laws and policies (*Abdulaziz*).[56] In the first-mentioned case the European Court gave less weight to the protection of racial minorities as envisaged by ICERD, in particular Article 4, than to the freedom of opinion and expression and in the second case the Court only took into account the *intentions and the purposes* of national immigration laws and not their *effects and consequences* as a matter of indirect discrimination which is clearly covered by Article 1(1) of ICERD.[57]

With the adoption and the future entry into force of Protocol No. 12 to the European Convention on Human Rights, it is likely that the European Court of Human Rights will chart new grounds when faced with cases involving racial discrimination. The protection system of the European Convention on Human Rights may thus become more effective and more relevant for victims of racism and racial discrimination in Europe. Furthermore, EU Directive 2000/43/EC implementing the principle of equal treatment between persons irrespective of racial or ethnic origin, requires Member States to adopt laws, regulations, and administrative provisions necessary to comply with the Directive's provisions. Moreover, the Directive will form part of the *acquis communautaire* which applicant countries will have to apply before obtaining Community membership. At the national level the courts as well as bodies specially established or designated to deal with equal treatment and non-discrimination on the grounds of race or ethnic origin and at the Community level the Commission, the European Parliament, and the Council, with the assistance of the European Monitoring Centre on Racism and Xenophobia, each within their sphere of competence, will monitor the application of the Directive.[58] This monitoring task has to be carried out in good consultation and harmony with other monitoring bodies with considerable experience in the matter such as CERD and ECRI. All these mechanisms can mutually reinforce each other and may sooner or later contribute to further convergence of global and European criteria and standards. But it should never be forgotten that at the end of the day public scrutiny and

---

[55] *Jersild v Denmark*, Judgment of 23 Sept. 1994, Publications ECHR, Series A, vol. 298.

[56] *Abdulaziz, Cabales and Balkandali v the United Kingdom*, Judgment of 28 May 1985, Publications ECHR, Series A, Vol. 94.

[57] See for a more detailed discussion of these cases van Boven, 'The Concept of Discrimination in the International Convention on the Elimination of all Forms of Racial Discrimination', in W. Kälin (ed.), *Das Verbot etnisch-kultureller Diskriminierung* (1999) 9, at 20–6.

[58] See Articles 13–17 of the Directive.

public participation determine the effectiveness of national and international supervision.

(ii) Redress and Reparation

The Third World Conference against Racism, to be held from 31 August to 7 September 2001 in South Africa, is now under active preparation. The UN General Assembly and the UN High Commissioner for Human Rights have stressed the need for a grass-roots approach to the preparations for the World Conference, with a focus on national and regional meetings and expert seminars.[59] In her most recent report to the UN General Assembly the High Commissioner highlighted a series of issues for consideration by the World Conference:[60]

- reinforcement of an inclusive national identity;
- addressing both traditional and contemporary forms of racial discrimination, including the issue of trafficking in human beings;
- ensuring effective protection and remedies and the right to seek just and adequate reparation or satisfaction;
- establishing an adequate institutional framework for the effective implementation of anti-discrimination laws;
- combating extreme poverty so as to surmount obstacles that perpetuate racial discrimination;
- combating racial discrimination and gender discrimination not only because of the negative consequences for human development but also for economic development;
- taking preventive measures so as to reduce the potential for the worst manifestations of racial discrimination, such as ethnic conflict and genocide, but also as a means to combat racial discrimination in everyday life;
- education in order to combat ignorance with facts, science, and history;
- promoting policies and practices of ensuring inclusion and not exclusion of all members of society.

This listing of issues constitutes an ambitious plan; it also represents a vision and conveys a sense of direction. Many of these ideas are reflected and further elaborated in documents emerging from regional preparatory meetings, including the European contribution to the World Conference held in Strasbourg (11–13 October 2000) under the theme *All Different All Equal: From Principle to Practice*.[61]

---

[59] Report of the UN High Commissioner for Human Rights to the fifty-fifth session of UNGA, UN doc. A/55/36, para. 81.

[60] Ibid., paras 72–82.

[61] General Conclusions of the European Conference Against Racism, EUROCONF (2000) 7 final, 16 Oct. 2000.

Unfortunately, a disturbing and sharp division of opinion arose between countries belonging to the West, notably the United States and Members of the European Union, and countries of the South in a UN meeting which had to prepare the agenda for the World Conference. One of the themes identified for the agenda is: *Provision of effective remedies, recourses, redress, [compensatory] and other measures, at all appropriate levels, national, regional and international.*[62] The square brackets around the word 'compensatory' reveal a deep cleavage between in particular the Western group and the African group.[63] Although this was not made explicit, it was clearly understood in the minds of the opposing parties that compensatory measures to victims of racial discrimination were to be associated with claims of descendants of the victims of the slave trade and other early forms of slavery. Equally in the minds are claims to make up for past exploitation by colonial powers, claims to repair gross and massive infringements of human dignity and human existence suffered over the centuries by indigenous and aboriginal peoples. Such practices are historically connected with perceptions and manifestations of inequality and discrimination on the ground of race or ethnic origin, with treatment of people as primitive and inferior beings or commodities, resulting in inhuman and degrading treatment, with forced deportations and even extermination. These practices are deeply resented and their effects are felt up to the present day.

This controversial issue of compensation must be seen in relation with victims and survivors becoming more vocal in recent years by pressing for financial claims through political action and in litigating before the courts. This applies to the descendants of the slave trade and other early forms of slavery,[64] the survivors of the Holocaust and their families, the victims of forced labour in Nazi Germany and Japan, the survivors of sexual exploitation by the Japanese army (comfort women),[65] the aboriginals in Australia in connection with their land rights and their forcibly removed children, etc.[66] These claims raise numerous questions of State responsibility, civil responsibility, and also criminal responsibility for crimes against humanity. They raise also questions as to what length redress and reparation can be pursued to make good for historical wrongs and injustices. According to evolving international standards, civil claims relating to reparations for gross violations of human rights, and

---

[62] See Report of the Preparatory Committee on its first session, UN doc. A/CONF.189/ PC.1/21, decision PC. 1/13.

[63] Ibid., para. 30.

[64] I. Hakim *et al.*, *Reparations: The Cure for America's Race Problem* (1994).

[65] G. McDougall, UN Special Rapporteur on *Systematic Rape, Sexual Slavery and Slavery-like Practices in Armed Conflict*, update to final report, UN doc. E/CN.4/Sub.2/2000/21. This document refers to many lawsuits before Japanese courts claiming compensation for war-related injuries and to agreements to compensate Holocaust victims and victims of wartime forced labour under the Nazi regime (paras 71–8).

[66] *Supra* n. 25.

international humanitarian law shall not be subject to statutes of limitations.[67] The complex question remains whether the non-application of statutes of limitations has trans-generational dimensions and to what extent injustices of the past entail prolonged and continuing effects on the life and well-being of people today.

It is undeniable that international human rights bodies have increasingly affirmed and reaffirmed the basic right of victims to reparation, including compensation, for damages suffered by them as a result of gross violations of human rights. For instance, CERD recently did so in four important General Recommendations relating to refugees and displaced persons, indigenous peoples, discrimination against Roma and, more generally, in connection with Article 6 of ICERD.[68] In these General Recommendations CERD envisaged reparations of wrongs and injustices to persons uprooted for reasons of race or ethnicity, to indigenous peoples for loss of their lands, and to Roma for their suffering during the Second World War which remained largely ignored and unacknowledged.

Western countries are obviously apprehensive that the World Conference against Racism will be used as a platform to present them the bill for wrongs committed in the past, with possibly far-reaching financial implications. The present author, in a previous capacity as Special Rapporteur on the right to reparation for victims of gross violations of human rights, was at the time specifically asked to include in his study some views on the question of compensation to the African descendants of the victims of gross violations of human rights by colonial powers, notably the victims of the slave trade and other early forms of slavery. After having struggled with the question, he concluded in his report in 1993:

While it would be difficult and complex to construe and uphold a legal duty to pay compensation to the descendants of the victims of the slave trade and other early forms of slavery, the present Special Rapporteur agrees that effective affirmative action is called for in appropriate cases as a moral duty. In addition, an accurate record of the history of slavery, including an account of the acts and the activities of the perpetrators and their accomplices and of the sufferings of the victims, should receive wide dissemination through the media, in history books and in educational materials.[69]

---

[67] Draft Basic Principles and Guidelines on the Right to Reparation for Victims of Gross Violations of Human Rights and International Humanitarian Law, UN doc. E/CN. 4/1997/104, Appendix, para. 9.

[68] See CERD's General Recommendations XXII (1996), XXIII (1997), XXVI (2000), and XXVII (2000).

[69] Van Boven, *Study Concerning the Right to Restitution, Compensation and Rehabilitation for Victims of Gross Violations of Human Rights and Fudamental Freedoms*, Final Report in UN doc. E/CN.4/Sub.2/1993/8, para. 24.

It may be argued by European governments that we have to deal with the present and to prepare for the future and that this task should not be complicated by burdening each other with evil legacies of the past, but it would appear that such position is not credible. It is true that patterns of racial injustice and racist crimes committed in the past are irreparable in their full extent. Any remedy of redress stands in no proportional relationship to the injury inflicted upon victims. However, for the sake of shaping a new age founded upon a spirit of understanding, tolerance, and friendship among nations and racial or ethnic groups,[70] public acknowledgement of the facts and acceptance of responsibility are essential conditions. As a matter of experience the primary demand of survivors and victims is recognition, acknowledgement, and disclosure of the truth. While the importance of compensation as a means of financial relief and remedy should not be underestimated, compensation must always be considered in conjunction with other forms of reparation, including those of a non-pecuniary nature.

Europe would be ill-advised to persist in an attitude of rejection as to the compensation issue. A forward-looking policy implies that grievances be recognized and acknowledged, that present injustices be redressed, and lessons be learnt from the past. With a view to building and consolidating peace within and among nations, the wrongs of the past need to be repaired, not as a token of generosity but as an expression of diligence and as a matter of right. As noted earlier, reparations may take various forms, pecuniary and non-pecuniary in nature, including public acknowledgement, acceptance of responsibility, accurate accounts in history books, commemorations. Thoughtful and creative approaches and solutions commend themselves rather than denial and refusal.

[70] See Article 7 of ICERD.

6

A Critical Evaluation of International Human Rights Approaches to Racism

KEVIN BOYLE AND ANNELIESE BALDACCINI

I. INTRODUCTION

The focus of the Florence lectures has been on Europe, including the new legal obligations to be undertaken by EU member states on the elimination of racial and ethnic discrimination. The provisions of the Equal Treatment Directives are radical and far-reaching.[1] Yet these same states, with the exception of Ireland, have also been parties to the United Nations International Convention on the Elimination of All Forms of Racial Discrimination (hereinafter 'ICERD'), in most cases for decades.[2] They have been obligated under that treaty to act to eliminate race- or ethnic-based discrimination. The major obligations under the new Directives are paralleled under ICERD. The EU states have submitted many reports to the monitoring committee for the UN Convention. But it is clear that the decades of implementation of the global convention have proved insufficient to force the kind of comprehensive legislative protection against racial and ethnic discrimination now required under the new Directives.

Should one conclude that the UN Convention and other United Nations long-standing efforts to eliminate racism have been in vain? That regional approaches are the only effective way to persuade states to tackle racism? At the least such questions need to be asked. They are particularly appropriate in the context of the forthcoming United Nations World Conference on

---

[1] Council Directive 2000/43/EC of 29 June 2000 implementing the principle of equal treatment between persons irrespective of racial or ethnic origin; Council Directive 2000/78/EC of 27 Nov. 2000 establishing a general framework for equal treatment in employment and occupation.

[2] GA Res. 2106 A (XX) (1965). In United Nations, *A Compilation of International Instruments* (1994), i, Part 1, at 66. For the list of ratifications, accessions, and successions, see Office of the United Nations High Commissioner for Human Rights (OHCHR), *Status of Ratifications of the Principal International Human Rights Treaties,* available on the website of the OHCHR at <http://www.unhchr.ch> (treaty body mechanisms).

Racism.[3] The purpose of that Conference is (or should be) to take stock of achievement and to define what policies and strategies should be pursued for the future. The World Conference takes place against the unpalatable reality that racism, in all its manifestations, is pervasive in the world. Whether expressed in theories of 'natural' racial hierarchy, or in hostility and violence towards different ethnic groups within multiethnic states, or towards migrants and refugees, racism has not only survived the twentieth century's major idea of human rights but threatens its very achievements.[4]

A review of international human rights approaches to the elimination of racism and racial discrimination must begin with the acknowledgement that the world community is a long way from achieving one component of the basic message of human rights—that of the equal dignity of all human beings. At the outset of the new century, the challenge of securing the right to equality promised in the Charter of the United Nations to all individuals remains unfulfilled. Racism and racial discrimination is but one manifestation of the denial of equality. Sex discrimination that feeds violence against women, the hatred and discrimination suffered by people on grounds of their religion, and the suppression of cultural and linguistic minorities are all global facts. There have been advances. In the context of racism, the most important of the last half-century has been the end of colonialism through the achievement of independence and self-determination for millions of people. Another has been the dismantling of institutionalized white racism in Southern Africa and the United States. But fear and rejection of difference, alongside justifications of inequality in the treatment of human beings based on so-called race, ethnic origin, descent or colour, presents a continuing human rights challenge in all societies.[5]

The United Nations Charter gave as one purpose of the new world organization the achievement of international cooperation 'in promoting and

[3] A United Nations World Conference organized by the High Commissioner for Human Rights is to be held in South Africa from 31 Aug. to 7 Sept. 2001. A website devoted to the preparations of the World Conference can be accessed from the OHCHR home page <http://www.unhchr.ch>. See also Part VI *infra*.

[4] For a powerful and sobering analysis of the challenge of contemporary racism, see Report of the International Council on Human Rights Policy, *The Persistence and Mutation of Racism* (1999).

[5] The dilemma involved in using the term race has exercised many concerned with combating racism and racial discrimination. There is only one human race and there is no scientific biological basis as there was once believed to be for classifying human beings into categories called races. Physiological traits and differences of colour between people do not justify racial classifications. The differences between human beings are a function of different ethnic identities. Nevertheless racism constitutes a set of objectively false beliefs that biological differences do exist between humans that are linked to a racial hierarchy. It is the survival of these beliefs that justify discrimination and subordination of others. However, while it is not impossible to abandon completely the language of race used in the international standards, it is desirable to speak of racial or ethnic discrimination rather than racial discrimination. See further n. 77.

encouraging respect for human rights and fundamental freedoms for all without distinction as to race, sex, language or religion'.[6] The United Nations was to be a 'center for harmonizing the actions of nations in the attainment of these common ends'.[7] At the same time, the potential of the UN was deliberately constrained by the limitation imposed through Article 2(7) of the Charter, excluding intervention by the United Nations in matters 'essentially within the domestic jurisdiction of any state'. It has been on these contradictory foundations that international approach to the protection of human rights have been built over the last fifty years. That approach has involved securing agreement on common global human rights standards and having states accept these standards as binding commitments in international law. A crucial part of the international approaches has been to persuade states to accept international supervision in the implementation of such commitments. In addition, the UN has sought to develop its capacity to respond to serious violation of these international human rights standards through investigation and by creating limited avenues of complaint and redress for victims. But it remains an essential feature of the international human rights system that it is virtually impotent without the support and commitment of states. The central question for the future is how to sustain support and commitment from all countries. Elimination of racial, ethnic, and other types of discrimination, as forms of human rights violation, requires significant social change in most if not all societies. It cannot be achieved solely by the enactment of anti-discrimination laws, important as such laws are. There is little evidence that countries understand the full implications of racial or ethnic equality or are yet ready to embrace the long-term changes necessary to achieve it.

With these thoughts in mind this chapter will consider the origins of the international human rights approaches towards racism and racial discrimination. In addition, it will examine the activities and policies pursued at the international level in countering racism and racial discrimination, as well as the institutions through which such activities and policies have been pursued. A full account of international human rights approaches should embrace regional levels as well. These dimensions are covered elsewhere in the volume and this account will concentrate on the global human rights system developed through the United Nations. However, the need for the future to envisage a greater level of integration of national regional and global human rights approaches to the achievement of equality and non-discrimination will be discussed.

---

[6] United Nations Charter, Article 1(3).   [7] Ibid., Article 1(4).

II. THE SIGNIFICANCE OF THE LANGUAGE OF
EQUALITY IN THE UNITED NATIONS CHARTER

International efforts to tackle racism and racial discrimination should be first considered in the context of the UN Charter's endorsement of the principle of human equality. Reference to the human rights language of the UN Charter is often abbreviated to leave out the equally important language of equality. Thus, Article 1(3) of the Charter committed the new international body 'to achieve international cooperation in promoting and encouraging respect for human rights and fundamental freedoms *for all without distinction as to race, sex, language or religion*'.[8]

The revolutionary nature of the Charter was not alone that the promotion and encouragement of human rights was to be one of its purposes, but that that goal embraced all human beings equally 'without distinction as to race, sex, language, or religion'. Language linking the non-discrimination principle with the subject of human rights is to be found throughout the Charter.[9] The rejection of discrimination and the affirmation of the right to equality of treatment in the 1948 Universal Declaration of Human Rights, as well as in all later human rights treaties, underscores that human inclusiveness is a characteristic of the international human rights approach.[10] The early action taken to prepare instruments directed at the elimination of discrimination, in addition to conventions of a general character, is a unique feature of standard setting on human rights at the global level.[11]

Although the dominant approach, after 1945, to the promotion and protection of internationally recognized human rights was to be based on the defence of the rights of individuals, there was also recognition that individuals faced denial of rights because of group characteristics. The distinctions identified in the Charter—race, sex, language, and religion—were at the time seen as the main categories of discrimination or exclusion believed in, practised, and justified throughout the world.

[8] Emphasis added.
[9] See, in addition to Article 1(3), Articles 13(1)(b), 55(c), and 76(c). Other human rights provisions in the Charter are to be found in Articles 62(2) and 68 concerning the functions to be discharged in this field by the Economic and Social Council. See also W. McKean, *Equality and Discrimination under International Law* (1983), at 54–5.
[10] Universal Declaration of Human Rights (UDHR), adopted by GA Res. 217 A (III) (1948). In *International Instruments, supra* n. 2, at 1.
[11] Such early instruments are, for instance, the Convention on the Prevention and Punishment of the Crime of Genocide, GA Res. 260 A (III) (1948); the Convention for the Suppression of the Trafficking in Persons and of the Exploitation of the Prostitution of Others, GA Res. 317 (IV) (1949); the Convention on the Political Rights of Women, GA Res. 640 (VII) (1952); the Supplementary Convention on the Abolition of Slavery, the Slave Trade, and Institutions and Practices Similar to Slavery, GA Res. 608 (XXI) (1956). All in *International Instruments, supra* n. 2, Parts 1 and 2.

The emphasis on equality and the repudiation of discrimination resulted directly from the context in which the United Nations was established. The UN was born in the aftermath of the defeat of Nazism, a racist ideology. The Universal Declaration of Human Rights—the instrument that was to give content to the human rights provisions entrenched in the Charter—was drafted with the perversions of Nazism in mind. The first international human rights convention, the Genocide Convention of 1948, was aimed at stigmatizing as an international crime the ultimate expression of racism, the destruction of national, ethnic, racial, or religious groups.[12] In drafting the Universal Declaration, members of the United Nations Human Rights Commission, while divided over whether the Universal Declaration should be of a binding or declaratory nature, agreed from the outset that prominence was to be given to the principle of equality or the standard of non-discrimination as the starting point of all other liberties.[13] The early establishment of a Sub-Commission on the Prevention of Discrimination and the Protection of Minorities was a crucial reflection of this need for parallel work on the causes and extent of discrimination, as well as the need for new international instruments and standards to combat discrimination.

Article 1 of the Universal Declaration proclaims the positive principle that '[a]ll human beings are born free and equal in dignity and rights'. Article 2 proclaims the entitlement of everyone to the rights and freedoms in the Declaration 'without distinction of any kind such as race, colour, sex, language, religion, political or other opinion, national or social origin, property, birth or other status'. The Declaration thus aimed at the elimination of all forms of discrimination, adding categories not found in the Charter. Article 7 sets forth the principle of equality before the law and the entitlement of all to 'equal protection against any discrimination in violation of this Declaration and against any incitement to such discrimination'.

These principles were also firmly inserted in the subsequent two United Nations Covenants that along with the Universal Declaration of Human Rights make up the International Bill of Human Rights.[14] The two Covenants include a common Article 3 on equality between men and women, as well as prohibitions on discrimination on the grounds first elaborated in Article 2 of the Universal Declaration cited above. In addition, the Civil and Political Covenant in Article 26 sets out a free-standing equality clause based on Article 7 of the Universal Declaration. It was on these foundations, entrenching the norms of equality and non-discrimination, that all other

---

[12] Ibid., Part 2, at 673.

[13] J. Morsink, *The Universal Declaration of Human Rights: Origins, Drafting and Intent* (1999), at 92–116.

[14] International Covenant on Economic, Social and Cultural Rights (ICESCR) and International Covenant on Civil and Political Rights (ICCPR), both adopted by GA Res. 2200 A (XXI) (1966). In *International Instruments, supra* n. 2, at 8 and 20.

international human rights instruments created through the United Nations and the regional systems have been built.

The commitment to equality of treatment led to specific international instruments on the main types of discrimination aimed at their elimination. Racial and ethnic discrimination was one such field. Sex discrimination was another. The International Convention on the Elimination of All Forms of Racial Discrimination came into force in 1969 and the parallel Convention on the Elimination of Discrimination against Women in 1981.[15] Progress on elaborating standards in respect of victims of religious discrimination or discrimination experienced by cultural minorities, including on such grounds as language, proved more difficult. In 1981, the Declaration on the Elimination of All Forms of Intolerance and Discrimination based on Religion or Belief was adopted by the General Assembly.[16] A decade later, the Declaration on the Rights of Minorities was adopted.[17] In neither case has sufficient consensus been found to transform these texts into legally binding instruments. The claim to equality is a dynamic one and new forms of discrimination have been asserted and progressively recognized. The UN Declaration on the Rights of Disabled People 1975 is one example.[18] The proposed Declaration on the rights of Indigenous Peoples is another, as is the emerging concern with discrimination on grounds of sexual orientation.[19]

The links between different forms of discrimination and intolerance, including the links between racial or ethnic discrimination and other forms of discrimination, need for the future to be made more explicit. That can be achieved through a greater emphasis on the right to equality of treatment as a crosscutting concern in international human rights theory and practice. Such an approach can help to end the relative and unproductive isolation in which different international human rights instruments and mechanisms concerned with discrimination appear to operate.

---

[15] Convention on the Elimination of All Forms of Discrimination Against Women (CEDAW), GA Res. 34/180 (1979). In ibid., at 150.

[16] GA Res. 36/55 (1981). In ibid., at 122.

[17] Declaration on the Rights of Persons Belonging to National or Ethnic, Religious and Linguistic Minorities, GA Res. 47/135 (1992). In ibid., at 140.

[18] GA Res. 3447 (XXX) (1975). In ibid., Part 2, at 544.

[19] Draft Declaration on the Rights of Indigenous Peoples. E/CN.4/Sub.2/1994/2/Add.1 (1994). Discrimination against homosexuals has not been the subject of specific norms at the United Nations but has been progressively recognized as a prohibited ground of discrimination in many countries. Under the new Protocol 12 to the European Convention on Human Rights (ECHR) which provides for a 'free-standing' prohibition on discrimination, sexual orientation, while not explicitly mentioned, is included. See, Explanatory Report to Protocol 12, Council of Europe, Directorate General of Human Rights 1999, and *Salgueiro da Silva Mouta v Portugal*, European Court of Human Rights, judgment of 21 Dec. 1999.

III. THE CENTRALITY OF RACIAL DISCRIMINATION IN THE DEVELOPMENT OF INTERNATIONAL HUMAN RIGHTS LAW

The challenge of race and racism has had a profound influence on the international human rights protection system created through the United Nations over the last half century. Indeed, it was largely the search for an effective international response to racism that produced the main components of the UN human rights regime. The United Nations was established in the aftermath of the Holocaust. But it was also born at a time of the colonial empires of European powers that were based on explicit assumptions of racial superiority and inferiority. While the United Nations was centrally involved in the achievement of decolonization, in which the colonial powers for the most part cooperated, these same powers were deeply concerned that racial practices in their colonies would face challenge at the international level. The United States, which did not have colonies but did have racial segregation and disenfranchisement of its black minority in its southern states, had similar concerns with international scrutiny.

Opposition from a number of countries to the United Nations having authority to protect human rights (in addition to the function of encouraging and promoting them) stemmed in part from concern over likely scrutiny of domestic policies on race and immigration. Equally, the exclusion of UN involvement in member states' domestic affairs (Article 2(7) of the Charter) was in large part motivated by an unwillingness of such countries as the United States and the United Kingdom to envisage external scrutiny of their racial practices.[20]

(i) Racial Segregation in the United States

The race question was to prove a major factor in shaping US policy towards accession to the international conventions on human rights promoted through the UN. The importance of the human rights and equality language of the UN Charter was quickly seen by opponents of American apartheid. In 1946, a petition was submitted to the UN by the National Negro Congress expressed to be on behalf of 13 million oppressed Negro citizens.[21] In 1947, the National Association for the Advancement of Coloured People (NAACP)

---

[20] Lauren, 'First Principles of Racial Equality: History and the Politics and Diplomacy of Human Rights Provisions in the United Nations Charter', 5 *HRQ* (1983) 1, at 19.

[21] McDougall, 'Toward a Meaningful International Regime: The Domestic Relevance of International Efforts to Eliminate All Forms of Racial Discrimination', 40 *Howard Law Journal* (1997) 571, at 573.

submitted a similar petition calling for redress.[22] Civil rights lawyers sought to invoke the Charter in domestic challenges to racism with some initial success.[23] In 1950 in *Sei Fuji v State*, a Californian district court of appeal declared a land ownership statute unconstitutional because it discriminated against a Japanese national. The Court relied on the human rights clauses of the Charter in its decision.[24] On appeal, however, the California Supreme Court held that Articles 55 and 56 of the Charter were not self-executing.[25] In an earlier case, also involving discrimination against persons of Japanese origin, the Charter's non-discrimination clauses were raised before the United States Supreme Court.[26] The American Civil Liberties Union argued that the Charter established obligations on the United States government to reject racial discrimination. While the majority of the Court determined the case in favour of the petitioner on other grounds, one judge in a trenchant opinion invoked the Charter and its prohibition of racial discrimination.[27] These cases, although they proved the high water mark of attempts to apply the human rights provisions of the Charter in US courts, did trigger a campaign in the US Congress to restrict the power of the President to enter into human rights treaty commitments. Among the concerns was the likely infringement on the powers of the states and that such treaties would entail international scrutiny of racial segregation. In 1954, the Secretary of State, John Foster Dulles, gave an undertaking to the Senate that the US would not join any international human rights treaty.[28] It has only been in the 1990s that the US has ratified some of the international human rights treaties, including the International Convention on the Elimination of Racial Discrimination.[29]

(ii) South Africa and Apartheid

Notwithstanding the Great Powers' intentions, the race question burst on to the international level at an early point. The coming to power of the

[22] Janken, 'From Colonial Liberation to Cold War Liberalism: Walter White, NAACP and Foreign Affairs, 1941–1955', 21 *Ethnic and Racial Studies* (1998) 1074, at 1982.

[23] Lockwood, 'The United Nations Charter and United States Civil Rights Litigation: 1946–1955', 69 *Iowa Law Rev.* (1984) 900.

[24] 217 P.2d 481 (Cal.Dist.Ct.App. 1950).

[25] 38 Cal.2d 718 (1952). The Court held the Alien Land Act unconstitutional as a violation of the 14th Amendment. Article 56 UN Charter proclaims that '[a]ll Members pledge themselves to take joint and separate action in cooperation with the Organization for the achievement of the purposes set forth in Article 55.' Article 55(c) states that the UN shall promote 'universal respect for, and observance of, human rights and fundamental freedoms for all without distinction as to race, sex, language or religion'.

[26] *Oyama v California*, 332 US 633 (1948).   [27] Lockwood, *supra* n. 23, at 919.

[28] F. Newman and D. Weissbrodt, *International Human Rights Law Policy and Process* (1996), at 34–5.

[29] The US ratified ICERD on 21 Oct. 1994. See *Status of Ratifications, supra* n. 2.

Nationalist Government in the Republic of South Africa in 1948 with an avowedly racist policy of apartheid, and the racist policies in Southern Rhodesia, South West Africa, and the Portuguese colonies, presented the first human rights challenges to the new United Nations.

As early as 1946, when a complaint was lodged by the Indian Government over the treatment of persons of Indian descent in South Africa, that country's racial policies were on the agenda of the major United Nations organs.[30] It was not, however, until 1952 that the 'question of race conflict in South Africa resulting from the policies of apartheid of the Government of the Union of South Africa' was first discussed at the General Assembly. Overruling vehement objection from South Africa that the matter fell essentially within its domestic jurisdiction, the General Assembly voted to establish an ad hoc commission to study the racial situation in South Africa.[31] Reports of the ad hoc commission found that South Africa's racial policies were contrary to the United Nations Charter human rights provisions. The General Assembly noted these findings with 'concern'[32] and 'apprehension'.[33] It was to progressively adopt ever stronger language in condemnation of South Africa's racist policies over the following years.[34]

The resolutions passed by the General Assembly, based on the findings of the ad hoc commission, asserted the right to condemn, and to demand rectification of, breaches of the human rights provisions of the Charter.[35] In particular, the General Assembly determined that governmental policies not directed towards racial equality were inconsistent with Articles 55 and 56 of the Charter.[36] After the outrage provoked by the Sharpeville massacre in 1960, the Security Council joined the General Assembly in condemning South Africa's racial policy, holding implicitly that human rights provisions of the Charter prevailed over the domestic jurisdiction clause.[37] The International Court of Justice upheld the view that the Charter's human rights provisions, far from being simple statements of morality, laid down binding obligations for member states. The challenge of racism played a decisive role in this development. The legal and binding character of the non-discrimination norm enshrined in the

---

[30] Lauren, *supra* n. 20, at 24.   [31] GA Res. 616A (VII) (1952).

[32] GA Res. 721 (VIII) (1953).   [33] GA Res. 820 (IX) (1954).

[34] GA Res. 917 (X) (1955), Res. 1178 (XII) (1957), Res. 1248 (XIII) (1958), Res. 1375 (XIV) (1959). An overview of the General Assembly's early resolutions on South Africa is to be found in Dugard, 'The Legal Effect of United Nations Resolutions on Apartheid', 83 *South African Journal of International Law* (1966) 44, at 44–5.

[35] On the gradual restriction by the General Assembly of states' domestic jurisdiction, see Cassese, 'The General Assembly: Historical Perspective 1945–1989', in P. Alston (ed.), *The United Nations and Human Rights—A Critical Appraisal* (1992) 25, at 32–4. Also R. Higgins, *The Development of International Law Through the Political Organs of the United Nations* (1963), at 58–130.

[36] See *supra* n. 25 for the text of Articles 55 and 56 UN Charter.

[37] Res. S/4300 (1960). On the Sharpeville massacre see further below.

Charter was first tested with respect to the policy and practice of apartheid and racial discrimination.[38] In the *Namibia* case, the International Court of Justice held that racism and racial discrimination constituted a total negation of the purposes and principles of the Charter.[39] It is now established in international law that the prohibition of racial discrimination exists independently of the general obligation to respect human rights and is part of *ius cogens*.[40]

From the 1960s onwards, as a result of the pressure of the newly independent African and Asian countries, which had gained the majority of votes in the General Assembly, critical discussion of apartheid policy gave way to concrete, and over the years successful, attempts at imposing sanctions on South Africa.[41] Condemnation of apartheid led to the adoption, in 1973, of the Convention on the Suppression and Punishment of the Crime of Apartheid.[42] The General Assembly followed this in 1985, with the adoption of the Convention Against Apartheid in Sports.[43]

[38] See the dissenting opinion of Judge Tanaka in the *South West Africa* cases (Second Phase), who referred to Article 55(c) of the Charter to demonstrate that the rule of non-discrimination 'can be regarded as a source of international law'. ICJ Reports (1966), at 293.

[39] The Court stated that 'to enforce distinctions, exclusions, restrictions and limitations exclusively based on grounds of race, color, descent or national or ethnic origin which constitute a denial of fundamental human rights is a flagrant violation of the purposes and principles of the Charter . . .'. *Legal Consequences for States of the Continued Presence of South Africa in Namibia (South West Africa) notwithstanding Security Council Resolution 276 (1970)*, ICJ Reports (1971) 3, at 57. One year before, in *Barcelona Traction, Light & Power Co.*, the Court had referred to the outlawing of, *inter alia*, racial discrimination as obligation *erga omnes*. ICJ Reports (1970), at 3. See Rodley, 'Human Rights and Humanitarian Intervention: the Case Law of the World Court', 38 *ICLQ* (1989) 321, at 321–33.

[40] In 1986, the US (Third) Restatement of the Foreign Relations Law recognized that systematic racial discrimination constitutes a violation of peremptory norms of customary international law. Restatement (Third) § 702, n. 11 (1986).

[41] The first resolution by the General Assembly to call on states to break off diplomatic and economic relations with South Africa was voted in 1962 (Res. 1761 (XVII)). The same resolution requested the Security Council to take appropriate measures and, if necessary, to consider the expulsion of South Africa from the United Nations. A year later the Security Council recommended to the member states an arms boycott against South Africa (SC Res. 181 (1963)). The General Assembly thereafter repeatedly stated that the apartheid policy constituted a threat to international peace and, as early as 1973, it had suspended South Africa from participating in the work of the Organization. The Security Council's endorsement came after much hesitation in 1977 when it imposed sanctions by a binding decision acting under Chapter VII, thus characterizing apartheid as a threat to international peace in the sense of Article 39 of the Charter (SC Res. 418 (1977)). On the international legal and political aspects of apartheid, see Delbrueck, 'Apartheid', in R. Wolfrum (ed.), *United Nations: Law, Politics and Practice* (1995) i, 27, at 34–8.

[42] GA Res. 3068 (XXVIII) (1973). In *International Instruments, supra* n. 2, at 80. Article I(1) declares that apartheid is a 'crime against humanity' and a 'serious threat to international peace and security'. The Convention met objections particularly on the part of Western states because it was said that the vague language used in the definition of various crimes contained in the Convention did not meet the standards required by the rule of law. Delbrueck, *supra* n. 41, at 36.

[43] GA Res. 40/64 (1985). In *International Instruments, supra* n. 2, at 87.

Support in the General Assembly for action against apartheid and racial discrimination in Southern Africa brought a further and least expected change of
policy with respect to domestic jurisdiction. This concerned the treatment of
petitions from individuals over human rights violations. From the outset, it
had been the position of the Commission on Human Rights—the body set up
by the Economic and Social Council (ECOSOC) under Article 68 of the
Charter with the task of promoting human rights—that it had no power to
respond to the stream of petitions over human rights violations throughout the
world received at the UN.[44] This policy suited the colonial powers and the
United States precisely because of the issue of race. It also suited the Soviet
Union, which was equally reluctant that the repressive policies pursued by
Stalin would be ventilated on the international stage.[45] The Soviet Union,
however, was prepared to support as part of the ideological contest the initiative of the African countries to change the Commission's practice on responding to complaints. What both the African countries and the Soviet Union had
in mind was racism and colonialism in Southern Africa. In the event, the
ECOSOC Resolutions 1235 and 1503, which created the mechanisms for
responding to violations, were expressed to be primarily focused on apartheid
and racial discrimination.[46] But the language adopted crucially provided for
competence to consider violations of human rights *wherever they may occur.*[47]
It was on these foundations that the competence of the Commission on
Human Rights and its Sub-Commission to respond to gross violations of
human rights in the world has developed.[48] One response of the Commission
has been to establish special rapporteurs on specific themes of violation. One
such is the Special Rapporteur on Contemporary Forms of Racism and
Related Intolerance appointed in 1993 whose role is discussed below.

[44] What is known as the '1947 Doctrine', following the Commission on Human Rights
adoption, at its first session in 1947, of a self-denying rule to the effect that it would take no
action on individual human rights complaints. See ECOSOC Res. 75 (V). This rule was reaffirmed in 1959 by ECOSOC Res. 728 F (XXVIII).

[45] Alston, 'The Commission on Human Rights', in Alston, *supra* n. 35, 126, at 141.

[46] ECOSOC Res. 1235 (XLII) (1967) authorized the Commission and its Sub-
Commission to 'examine information relevant to gross violations of human rights and fundamental freedoms, as exemplified by the policy of apartheid as practised by the Republic of
South Africa . . . and racial discrimination as practised notably in Southern Rhodesia . . . and
to make a thorough study of situations which reveal a consistent pattern of violation of human
rights, and report, with recommendations thereon, to the Economic and Social Council . . .'.
ECOSOC Res. 1503 (XLVIII) (1970) devises a greatly improved procedure for handling complaints from individuals and non-governmental organizations which appear to reveal a consistent pattern of gross and reliably attested violations of human rights.

[47] See GA Res. 2144 (XXI) (1966), which invited the Council and the Commission 'to give
urgent consideration to ways and means of improving the capacity of the United Nations to
put a stop to violations of human rights *wherever they occur*' (emphasis added).

[48] For an extensive study of the development of these non-treaty procedures, see Alston,
supra n. 45, at 126–210.

(iii) The Pioneering Studies of the Sub-Commission on Prevention of Discrimination and Protection of Minorities

A crucial role in the development of international human rights law and its implementation was played by the Sub-Commission on the Prevention of Discrimination and the Protection of Minorities.[49] The Sub-Commission was set up in 1947 as an advisory body to the Commission on Human Rights.[50] The Commission from its inception was riven by bloc-voting and by the refusal of state delegates to allow their country or other members to be criticized. Members of the Sub-Commission, appointed as independent experts and—at least in theory—less vulnerable to political pressure, proved more willing to act as a human rights body. After contributing to the drafting of the anti-discrimination provisions of the Universal Declaration of Human Rights, the Sub-Commission turned its attention to implementation and enforcement action. Early attempts to pursue an active policy in this respect were, however, challenged by the Commission and ECOSOC. The Sub-Commission thereafter focused on research and standard setting particularly in the field of discrimination.[51]

While the subject of sex discrimination was taken on by the Commission on the Status of Women, the Sub-Commission conducted and forwarded to the Commission on Human Rights a number of studies on the problems of discrimination in other fields. The first such study concerned discrimination in education and became the basis of UNESCO's 1960 Convention on the same subject.[52] A study on discrimination in employment and occupation

---

[49] On the crucial role played by the Sub-Commission in its early years, see Humphrey, 'The United Nations Sub-Commission on the Prevention of Discrimination and the Protection of Minorities', 62 *AJIL* (1968) 869. For an overview on its more recent activities, see Koufa, 'Elimination of Racial Discrimination and the Role of the United Nations Sub-Commission on Prevention of Discrimination and Protection of Minorities', 10 *International Geneva Yearbook* (1996) 44. See also Eide, 'The Sub-Commission on Prevention of Discrimination and Protection of Minorities', in Alston, *supra* n. 35, at 211–64; McKean, *supra* n. 9, at 72–81.

[50] The Sub-Commission was authorized to 'undertake studies, particularly in the light of the Universal Declaration on Human Rights, and to make recommendations to the Commission on Human Rights concerning the prevention of discrimination of any kind relating to human rights and fundamental freedoms and the protection of racial, national, religious and linguistic minorities', *Report of the Commission on Human Rights*, UN Doc. E/1371 (1949).

[51] The difficult relation in the early years of the UN between the Sub-Commission and its referent bodies is well captured in the comment by a notable author that the 'crime of the Sub-Commission was that it had taken its job too seriously'. Humphrey, *supra* n. 49, at 875.

[52] *Study of Discrimination in Education*, by Charles D. Ammoun, appointed Special Rapporteur of the Sub-Commission. UN Doc. E/CN.4/Sub.2/181/Rev.1 (1957). For the UNESCO Convention against Discrimination in Education (1960), see *International Instruments*, *supra* n. 2, at 101.

was entrusted to the International Labour Organization. That also led to an important Convention.[53] Other studies were on discrimination in political rights,[54] on religious rights and practices,[55] on emigration and the right to return,[56] and on racial discrimination in political, economic, social, and cultural fields.[57] These studies were acted upon by the Commission on Human Rights and provided much of the basis for international instruments subsequently adopted in the field of discrimination. This early work of the Sub-Commission was also of enduring value for its analysis of different aspects of discrimination and its development of such concepts as that of indirect discrimination, justified distinctions, and special or positive measures.[58] These concepts were later incorporated in the anti-discrimination treaties.

Although its mandate and functions have considerably expanded, in recent years the Sub-Commission has continued to contribute significantly to work on equality and non-discrimination.[59] Its study on the exploitation of labour through illicit and clandestine trafficking, completed in 1975, led to the International Convention on the Protection of the Rights of All Migrant Workers and Members of Their Families, adopted in 1990.[60]

---

[53] ILO Convention (No. 111) Concerning Discrimination in Respect of Employment and Occupation (1958). In ibid., at 96.

[54] *Study of Discrimination in the Matter of Political Rights*, rapporteur Hernan Santa Cruz. UN Doc. E/CN.4/Sub.2/213/Rev.1 (1962).

[55] *Study of Discrimination in the Matter of Religious Rights and Practices*, rapporteur Arcot Krishnaswami. UN Doc. E/CN.4/Sub.2/200/Rev.1 (1960). This study sharply divided the Commission and despite the General Assembly's decision that there should follow a declaration and a convention on the elimination of religious intolerance, the first saw the light in the 1980s, while the latter never came into existence.

[56] *Study of Discrimination in Respect to the Right of Everyone to Leave Any Country, Including his Own, and to Return to his Country*, rapporteur José D. Inglés. UN Doc. E/CN.4/Sub.220/Rev.1 (1963). Interestingly, the Sub-Commission's intention to include in this study the controversial question of immigration was not accepted by the Council. Humphrey, *supra* n. 49, at 880.

[57] *Special Study of Racial Discrimination in the Political, Economic, Social and Cultural Spheres*, rapporteur Hernan Santa Cruz. UN Doc. E/CN.4/Sub.2/267 (1966).

[58] McKean, *supra* n. 9, at 94–6.

[59] To acknowledge the Sub-Commission's considerably expanded mandate, ECOSOC recently renamed it 'Sub-Commission on Promotion and Protection of Human Rights'. Dec. 1999/256 of 27 July 1999.

[60] GA Res. 45/158 (1990). In *International Instruments, supra* n. 2, Part 2, at 554. Further examples include the report on the rights of persons belonging to ethnic, religious, and linguistic minorities, conducted by Mr Capotorti and completed in 1977, that led to the 1992 UN Declaration on minorities, *supra* n. 17. The study of problems of discrimination against indigenous populations, conducted by Mr Eide in 1983, together with the pioneering work of the Sub-Commission's working group on the indigenous populations, resulted in the draft Declaration on the Rights of Indigenous Peoples, that is currently being considered for adoption by the Commission on Human Rights, *supra* n. 19.

(iv) Standard Setting and Racial Discrimination

As already noted, the late 1950s and early 1960s saw a growing number of newly independent countries taking seats at the United Nations, determined to see the development of new procedures to combat apartheid and racism. The Sub-Commission, as a result, became increasingly concerned with racial discrimination. In 1960, South Africa provoked a horrified international response when its police massacred sixty-nine peaceful protesters in the black township of Sharpeville. In the same year, widespread anti-Semitic incidents in West Germany and other parts of the world provoked a sharp reaction by the Sub-Commission, which was in session. It took the initiative—unprecedented in the UN subsidiary bodies—of adopting a resolution condemning these manifestations of anti-Semitism.[61] In the wake of these events, the need to put in place an effective instrument to combat racial discrimination as well as religious intolerance was widely shared and gave rise to a decision by the General Assembly to draft a declaration to be followed by a convention.[62] The intention had been to draft an instrument embracing both religious and racial discrimination. No consensus could, however, be reached in the Third Committee with regard to religious issues and it was eventually decided to aim at two different instruments, one dealing with religious discrimination and intolerance and one with racial discrimination.[63] The opposition to a joint instrument came from some of the Arab delegations, and the Soviet and Eastern Europe states. Arab countries were concerned over the inclusion of anti-Semitism lest it might be read as a recognition of the state of Israel. The Soviet Union for its own reasons was not prepared to have religious discrimination included but did want a focus on race.[64] Acrimonious controversy over the question of anti-Semitism as constituting racial as well as religious prejudice resurfaced in the Third Committee during the drafting of the Race Convention. As one source of the initiative to draft a Convention had been the outbreak of anti-Semitism some delegations, led by the United States, sought to have a specific reference condemning anti-Semitism, as well as

---

[61] UN Doc. E/CN.4/Sub.2/L.214. Humphrey, *supra* n. 49, at 882.

[62] Literature outlining the history of the adoption of the Race Convention is consistent in tracing its origins back to the events described above. See, among others, Schwelb, 'The International Convention on the Elimination of All Forms of Racial Discrimination', 15 *ICLQ* (1966) 998, at 997–1000. Meron, 'The Meaning and Reach of the International Convention on the Elimination of All Forms of Racial Discrimination', 79 *AJIL* (1985) 283, at 285–6.

[63] Sensitivity over religion had already emerged as a result of the study of discrimination in religious rights and practices conducted by the Sub-Commission's rapporteur, Arcot Krishnaswami, and submitted to the Commission on Human Rights in 1960. See *supra* n. 55.

[64] Schwelb, *supra* n. 62, at 999. Also, N. Lerner, *Group Rights and Discrimination in International Law* (1991), at 46.

apartheid.[65] While a number of delegations did refer in speeches to the Holocaust, Arab political sensitivities resulted in the reference being dropped. But not before the Soviet Union submitted a draft that would have added also a condemnation of Zionism and Nazism.[66]

While controversy over religious issues stranded for more than twenty years a parallel declaration on religious discrimination, the Declaration on the Elimination of Racial Discrimination followed speedily in 1963.[67] It was followed two years later by the Convention on the Elimination of All Forms of Racial Discrimination. That treaty marked the real beginning of the international protection of individual human rights. The UN had begun the treaty approach to combating human rights violations in 1948 with the Genocide Convention, but no progress could be made on the establishment of any international mechanism for the Convention's enforcement. ICERD had enforcement provisions including a procedure for individuals to complain against states, a breakthrough that stemmed from the Sub-Commission.[68] ICERD set an important precedent. It cleared the way for the later adoption of the International Covenants and the development of procedures for monitoring the extent of states' compliance with their human rights treaty obligations.

IV. THE INTERNATIONAL CONVENTION ON THE ELIMINATION OF ALL FORMS OF RACIAL DISCRIMINATION

The centrepiece of the international human rights approach to combating racism and racial discrimination is the International Covenant on the Elimination of All Forms of Racial Discrimination 1966 (ICERD). The Convention entered into force on 4 January 1969 and has therefore now been in force for over three decades. It was, until 1993, when it was overtaken by the Convention on the Rights of the Child, the most widely ratified international human rights treaty.[69]

---

[65] Schwelb, *supra* n. 62, at 1011–14.

[66] Such manœuvres, culminating in the condemnation of Zionism by a resolution of the General Assembly in 1975, have dogged the United Nations over the years and have damaged its credibility considerably. See van Boven, 'United Nations Strategies to Combat Racism and Racial Discrimination: A Sobering but not Hopeless Balance Sheet', in M. Castermans *et al.* (eds), *The Role of the Nation-State in the 21st Century* (1998) 251, at 253 and n. 236 *infra*.

[67] United Nations Declaration on the Elimination of All Forms of Racial Discrimination, GA Res. 1904 (XVIII) (1963). In *International Instruments, supra* n. 2, at 61.

[68] 'the first basic plan for the implementation of the convention was suggested by Judge José Inglés in the Sub-Commission. Had he not taken this initiative, it is unlikely that the General Assembly would ever have adopted measures for implementation of the convention', Humphrey, *supra* n. 49, at 883.

[69] 157 states are to date party to the Convention. See *supra* n. 2 for the status of ratification of the main international human rights treaties.

In assessing the impact of the Convention and its future potential the ideological and political context of its birth requires to be kept in mind. The Convention's provisions, although expressed to be concerned with the elimination of all forms of racial discrimination in all countries, sought at the same time to target colour discrimination and colonialism, in line with the wishes of its African and Soviet sponsors. Thus, the Convention condemns doctrines of racial superiority and singles out apartheid in South Africa, as well as segregation between white and black practised in the European colonies and the United States.[70] The monitoring body established under the Convention, the Committee on the Elimination of Racial Discrimination (hereinafter 'CERD'), was also given a function under Article 15 to comment upon petitions alleging racial discrimination received from the inhabitants of Trust and Non-Self Governing Territories by the Committee on Decolonization.[71]

The tension between the immediate concern with colonialism and apartheid and the objective of universal elimination of all forms of racial and ethnic discrimination finds reflection in the language of the Convention as well as in its interpretation, by both states parties and the Committee. It is a tension that has persisted over the history of the ICERD. The assumption that racism was solely about the consequences of Western imperialism inevitably placed the Convention in a fraught political environment. The other human rights treaties that followed ICERD had also to function in the Cold War years, but none had to function in quite such an emotional and ideological environment as had ICERD.

The ICERD was the prototype for the later international human rights conventions in its scheme of implementation.[72] In addition to fulfilling obligations at the domestic level, states undertake to report periodically to CERD on 'legislative, judicial, administrative or other measures' undertaken to fulfil the Convention's requirements.[73] The Convention scheme of implementation also provides for an inter-state and an individual complaint procedure. However, to date the main vehicle of implementation of the Convention, as with the other international instruments, is through state reporting, and the main activity of CERD is, and has been, the examination of such reports in conjunction with the states parties. Experience with these

[70] As noted above, the serious issue of the resurgence of anti-Semitism was sidelined for political reasons.

[71] For reasons of space this account will not consider the Committee's limited functions under Article 15. With the virtual achievement of decolonization, this always marginal duty of the CERD has accordingly dwindled. See Partsch, 'The Committee on the Elimination of Racial Discrimination', in Alston, *supra* n. 35, 339, at 348.

[72] On the treaty system as a whole, see P. Alston and J. Crawford (eds), *The Future of UN Human Rights Treaty Monitoring* (2000).

[73] Article 9(1) ICERD.

implementation procedures is discussed below as part of an analysis of the work of the Committee. But before considering implementation, the substantive provisions of the Convention require to be set out.

(i) The Definition of Racial Discrimination

At the time of the Convention's adoption most states understood racism politically, applying to cases such as the treatment of the black population of the USA, apartheid in South Africa, and to practices associated with colonialism. The general definition of racial discrimination in ICERD, however, does not focus exclusively on such state policies and practices. It covers all acts of discrimination based on motivations of a racial nature, including acts of individuals or groups, and calls the state to account whenever such activities impinge, either currently or potentially, upon the enjoyment of fundamental human rights.

The drafters of the Convention followed closely the definition of discrimination adopted by the ILO and UNESCO in the Conventions that dealt with discrimination in employment and education, respectively.[74] Article 1(1) defines racial discrimination as

[a]ny distinction, exclusion, restriction or preference based on race, colour, descent, or national or ethnic origin which has the purpose or effect of nullifying or impairing the recognition, enjoyment or exercise, on an equal footing, of human rights and fundamental freedoms in the political, economic, social, cultural or any other field of public life.

The definition is concerned with racial discrimination, not racism as such. Doctrines of racial superiority, however, are condemned in the Convention.[75] Such doctrines at the time were based on biological theories that divided humankind into racial categories according to supposed genetic differences.[76] The efforts undertaken in the post-war era to discredit doctrines of racial

---

[74] The ILO Discrimination (Employment and Occupation) Convention No. 111 (1958), Article 1(a) defines 'discrimination' as including '[a]ny distinction, exclusion or preference made on the basis of race, colour, sex, religion, political opinion, national extraction or social origin, which has the effect of nullifying or impairing equality of opportunity or treatment in employment or occupation', *supra* n. 53. The UNESCO Convention against Discrimination in Education (1960), Article 1, defines 'discrimination' as including 'any distinction, exclusion, limitation or preference which, being based on race, colour, sex, language, religion, political or other opinion, national or social origin, economic condition or birth, has the purpose or effect of nullifying or impairing equality of treatment in education . . .', *supra* n. 52.

[75] See ICERD preambular para. 6 and Article 4.

[76] Racism as a systematic and rationalized hostility based on biological differences is a nineteenth-century phenomenon (Gobineau's *Essay on the Inequality of Human Races* appeared in 1854). See M. Banton, *International Action Against Racial Discrimination* (1996), at 52.

superiority as scientifically false were successful, but did not solve the question as to the nature of difference. Thus, the concept of race, a concept that is at odds with the idea of human unity that the UN intended to promote, survives.[77] While the concept of race could not be dropped altogether from the ICERD definition, it was broadened to include the core mischiefs at which the struggle against racism is aimed—discrimination based on colour, descent, national and ethnic origin.[78] Colour tackles discrimination based on physical criteria. 'Descent', a term unique to ICERD, has been interpreted to include the notion of caste and denotes social origin, while 'national or ethnic origin' refers to prejudice that stems from linguistic, cultural, and historical differences.[79] The definition is thus not limited to objective physical characteristics. It also captures subjective as well as socio-economic variables connected with racism. The definition is capable of addressing past, present, and future expressions of racism: be it white supremacism, casteism, ethnonationalism or what is called neo-racism, a version which no longer presupposes biological difference but emphasizes allegedly insurmountable differences between cultures. It also protects every group that has a defined collective identity and for the purpose of which self-identification is the relevant criterion.[80]

[77] Efforts at UN level to discredit doctrines of racial superiority started as early as 1948, when ECOSOC requested that the UNESCO develop a programme to disseminate scientific facts that would counter commonly held racial prejudices (ECOSOC Res. 116 (VI) B(iii)). UNESCO contributed with its work from the 1950s to the 1970s by convening committees of prominent scientists who were asked to discuss the racial problem and to make known the scientific facts about race. These efforts led to four statements on the concept of race (reprinted in the Encyclopedia of Human Rights (1996) 2nd edn. at 1215–23) and culminated in the adoption, in 1978, of the UNESCO Declaration on Race and Racial Prejudice, which states in the strongest terms that '[a]ll human beings belong to a single species . . . any theory which involves the claim that racial or ethnic groups are inherently superior . . . has no scientific foundation and is contrary to the moral and ethical principles of humanity'. In *International Instruments, supra* n. 2, at 132.

[78] During debates in the Sub-Commission it became clear that 'while, as UNESCO had shown, there was no such thing as race, the term "race" would have to be used in the draft convention', Lerner, *supra* n. 64, at 49.

[79] While the words 'colour', 'descent', and 'ethnic origin' did not represent major difficulties, a serious problem arose with regard to the term 'national origin' due to it being widely used as relating to nationality or citizenship. To avoid any misinterpretation, paragraphs 2 and 3 were added to Article 1 excluding distinctions between citizens and non-citizens from the ambit of the definition, ibid., at 49.

[80] See CERD General Recommendation VIII (38th session, 1990): '[T]he ways in which individuals are identified as being members of a particular racial or ethnic group . . . shall, if no justification exists to the contrary, be based upon self-identification by the individual concerned.' Thus, as a general rule, a group's consciousness of its own separate identity determines whether it is a 'race' for the purposes of the Convention's protections.

(ii) The Scope of the Convention's Substantive Provisions

The Convention's provisions are far-reaching. It obliges states 'to pursue by all appropriate means and without delay a policy of eliminating racial discrimination in all its forms and promoting understanding among races' (Article 2(1)). This general goal is then developed by reference to five objectives for the achievement of which states parties are required

- not to engage directly, or through their public institutions at all levels, in acts or practices of racial discrimination;
- not to sponsor, defend, or support racial discrimination by any persons or organizations;
- to amend, rescind, or nullify legislation which creates or perpetuates racial discrimination;
- to prohibit, by all appropriate means, racial discrimination by any persons, group, or organization;
- to encourage the elimination of barriers through integrationalist multiracial organizations and movements and discourage anything which tends to strengthen racial division.[81]

The prohibition of racial discrimination covers the full range of rights including civil, political, economic, social, and cultural rights. It includes rights pertaining to the private sphere, such as marriage, inheritance, as well as freedom of thought, conscience, and religion—a unique feature in those early days of standard setting.[82] The scope of Article 5, containing a non-exhaustive list of these rights, had to be clarified to allay apprehensions of states entering these obligations. The obligations of the states parties did not refer to the granting of these rights, but only to admitting no racial discrimination in their enjoyment to the extent that they were guaranteed in the domestic law of the states parties.[83] To ensure equality under the law and to guarantee effective protection, Article 6 calls for courts and other state institutions to provide for just and adequate reparation or satisfaction for any damage suffered as a result of racial discrimination.

A number of provisions were, and still are, considered radical in their application and attracted a high number of reservations. Assuring states parties' compliance has proven particularly difficult with regard to Article 4 requiring

---

[81] Article 2(1)(a)–(e) ICERD.

[82] On the drafting history of the substantive provisions of ICERD, see Partsch, 'Elimination of Racial Discrimination in the Enjoyment of Civil and Political Rights', 14 *Texas International Law Journal* (1979) 191.

[83] The Committee debated this issue extensively in 1973, adopting a statement for inclusion in its Report to the General Assembly. See Buergenthal, 'Implementing the UN Racial Convention', 12 *Texas International Law Journal* (1977) 187, at 207.

the prohibition and criminalization of hate speech and the suppression of organizations that incite racial hatred.[84] Article 4 has long been considered by CERD as the key article of the Convention.[85] It recognizes the power of hate propaganda to foster prejudice and racial discrimination. However, the assumption that ideas generate attitudes which can be dispelled mainly by legislation is arguably contradicted by the Convention itself, when it requires states to combat prejudices that lead to racial discrimination through measures in the fields of teaching, education, culture, and information (Article 7). The focus to date in the practice of the Committee on the duty of states to legislate to combat racial discrimination may account for its almost total neglect of Article 7. Yet the latter is the key provision under the scheme of the Convention if states are to address the root causes of racism.[86]

Unsurprisingly, a great deal of the Committee's early efforts to ensure compliance concentrated on what was the priority on the UN's human rights agenda and embodied in Article 3 of the Convention, the condemnation of apartheid and racial segregation. This resulted in the sometimes controversial practice of states being requested to submit information on political matters, i.e. regarding the status of their diplomatic, economic, and other relations with South Africa.[87]

(a) Justified Distinctions: The Case of Non-nationals

The Convention allows for distinctions to be made between citizens and non-citizens (Article 1(2)) and gives due regard to state sovereignty in matters of citizenship, nationality, and naturalization, provided states do not discriminate against categories of foreigners (Article 1(3)). However, other articles have been interpreted to ensure that non-citizens are not completely unprotected under the Convention. CERD's practice therefore has been to construe Article 1(2) narrowly.[88] The inclusion of non-citizens within the reach of Article 4 has never been disputed nor that equality before the law must be guaranteed to 'everyone' without distinction as to race or ethnic

---

[84] A conspicuous number of reservations and/or declarations were entered in respect of Article 4 by states acceding to the Convention. The issue is discussed further below.

[85] See CERD General Recommendation XV (42nd session, 1993), reiterating that '[w]hen [ICERD] was being adopted, Article 4 was seen as central to the struggle against racial discrimination.'

[86] See Farrior, 'The Neglected Pillar: The "Teaching Tolerance" Provision of the International Convention on the Elimination of All Forms of Racial Discrimination', 5 *Journal of International and Comparative Law* (1999) 291.

[87] See CERD General Recommendation III (6th session, 1972). The practice of asking states parties to report under Article 9(1) on their relations with South Africa had been formally endorsed by the General Assembly, which had been pursuing a policy of isolating South Africa since 1962. See *supra* n. 41, and Buergenthal, *supra* n. 83, at 195.

[88] Mahalic and Malahic, 'The Limitation Provisions of the International Convention for the Elimination of All Forms of Racial Discrimination', 9 *HRQ* (1987) 74, at 75.

origin (Article 5). The distinction established in Article 1(2) should have no impact on the implementation of Article 6 and access to remedies. The fact that many non-nationals, such as immigrants, are visibly different from the majority of the population makes them easier targets of racial discrimination and racism. The Convention would be undermined if the protections it affords did not extend to such categories of people.

CERD has recognized that states have the sovereign right to impose distinctions between citizens and non-citizens insofar as their purpose or effect contains no element of discrimination based on race, colour, descent, or national or ethnic origin.[89] It has also held that Article 1(2) 'must not be interpreted to detract in any way from the rights and freedoms recognized and enunciated in other [human rights] instruments . . .'.[90] CERD has been consistent in asking states to report on the status of non-citizens, particularly migrant workers and refugees, who usually belong to a single ethnic group and face hostility, contempt, and social and economic ostracism. Although CERD has no authority under Article 1(2) to require states parties to guarantee non-citizens rights comparable to those enjoyed by citizens, the social inclusion of migrants is pivotal in combating racism and xenophobia. Migrant workers suffer discrimination even when protective legislation is devised for them and their sense of security is seriously endangered by the threat of expulsion common to all aliens. Despite the many instruments adopted at international level to promote their rights and protect them from abuse, there is a stark reluctance to tackle discrimination against migrant workers.[91] None of the instruments has reached a significant number of ratifications and, most disconcertingly, are ignored by the main immigrant-receiving countries—the affluent Western countries.

The treatment of refugees has been discussed primarily under the ambit of Article 1(3). Committee members have asked for statistical breakdowns by race and country of origin of refugees having applied for, been granted, lost, or been refused asylum or citizenship. There have also been inquiries con-

[89] Ibid., at 76.

[90] CERD General Recommendation XI on non-citizens (42nd session, 1993), para. 3. Under international standards of human rights, justified distinctions between citizens and non-citizens are limited. With regard to the non-discrimination standards under ICCPR, see Human Rights Committee General Comment 15 on the position of aliens under the Covenant (27th session, 1986), para. 2: 'The general rule is that each one of the rights of the Covenant must be guaranteed without discrimination between citizens and aliens.'

[91] International protection for migrants is provided by ILO Convention No. 97 (revised) on Migration for Employment and ILO Convention No. 143 on Migrant Workers (Supplementary Provisions). Neither has been widely ratified. The International Convention on the Rights of All Migrant Workers and Members of Their Families, adopted by the General Assembly in 1990, provides more extensive rights than the ILO Conventions, but has not yet entered into force. For the status of ratification of this latter Convention, see Report of the Secretary-General, A/55/205 (2000).

cerning refugees' rehabilitation and resettlement programmes as well as measures to defuse racial tensions resulting from the presence of refugees.[92] States parties' restrictive immigration and asylum policies, including visa systems and other measures aimed at curbing illegal immigration, have been reviewed under this provision. The CERD has sought to assess their disparate impact on people, such as people of colour, or whether discrimination against refugees based on their country of origin was involved. Despite many evident abuses the Committee has been constrained in its criticism.[93] There has also been a reluctance to question naturalization laws, where they grant citizens of favoured nations preferential treatment. Denial to access to citizenship is, however, frequently directed against ethnic minorities, even when legislation does not say so. The absence of clear international norms on acquisition of citizenship complicates the problem considerably.[94] There is scope under the Convention for calling on states to facilitate naturalization of non-nationals as a means of combating prejudices. These are fostered by the legal status of longstanding residents from ethnic or other minority groups as second-class citizens. There is also a need to support and create more opportunities for legal migration and ensuring that international human rights standards are integrated into immigration and asylum policies and practices.

(b) Equality in Fact: Special Measures and Affirmative Action Under the Convention

Racial equality is a free-standing right in the Convention, extending to all human rights and fundamental freedoms, whatever their source.[95] The special feature of the Convention is that it promotes not only equality in law but also equality in fact, in order to allow different ethnic, racial, and national groups the same social development. The goal of *de facto* equality is reflected in several provisions of the Convention, calling for 'special measures' (Article 2(2)), allowing distinctions for the purpose of affirmative action (Article 1(4)), and prohibiting distinctions which have the purpose *or effect* of impairing the recognition, enjoyment, and exercise, 'on an equal footing', of human rights and fundamental freedoms (Article 1).[96] The latter provision addresses

---

[92] Mahalic, *supra* n. 88, at 81.

[93] European states commonly deflect criticism invoking the Schengen Agreement, that results in asylum and immigration policies becoming largely a community matter. See, for instance, at CERD's 56th session the consideration of the 12th, 13th, and 14th report, of France (continued), para. 10–11. CERD/C/SR.1374 of 6 July 2000.

[94] The right to a nationality is enshrined in Article 15(1) UDHR.

[95] Meron, *supra* n. 62, at 286. Cf. Article 14 ECHR (equality as auxiliary to substantive rights). However, the recently adopted Protocol 12 ECHR, which opened for signature on 4 Nov. 2000, provides for a free-standing equality right, *supra* n. 19.

[96] See also Article 2(1)(c) asking states parties to take effective measures to review policies and amend, rescind, or nullify laws and regulations which have the effect of creating or *perpetuating* racial discrimination. On affirmative action, see Fottrell, 'Ever Decreasing Circles:

indirect discrimination, the disproportionate impact of apparently neutral practices on individuals or groups who differ in race, colour, descent, national or ethnic origin from the majority of the population. The Convention thus advocates a notion of equality of outcome, which is sensitive to the starting point of people, to past disadvantages which have created systematic patterns of discrimination in many societies, the effects of which may be continued or even exacerbated by facially neutral policies.

The Convention's purpose of achieving substantive equality in principle goes beyond the formal equality concept where the majority of national constitutions stop and which assumes conformity with the dominant culture. It rather recognizes the need to accommodate diversity and to redress disadvantage emanating from past discriminatory policies and practices, which have developed into structural patterns of injustice. Where racism is institutionalized in society, as is often the case, claims to formal equality are of limited avail.

More effective results may be expected from taking special measures or affirmative action policies with a view of affording opportunities for self-development and advancement of groups who following long periods of persistent racial discrimination and marginalisation, have been denied such opportunities.[97]

The reversal of the effects of historical inequities is a positive duty on states parties. Article 2(2) requires states to take 'when circumstances so warrant' special and concrete measures 'to ensure the adequate development and protection of certain racial groups or individuals, belonging to them for the purpose of guaranteeing them the full and equal enjoyment of human rights and fundamental freedoms'. However, the precise nature of the duty is unclear and CERD has done little to elucidate the scope of affirmative action under the treaty.[98] The lack of precision and standards in ICERD's provision is, however, common to other non-discrimination treaties that envisage affirmative action policies. International human rights bodies, other than stating the existence of the obligation under the relevant treaties, have not to date seriously debated on the merits or modalities of such policies.[99] Moreover, because the benefits of such policies cannot be immediately appreciated—the reversal of historical

---

Affirmative Action and Special Measures under International Law', in D. Fottrell and B. Bowring (eds), *Minority and Group Rights in the New Millennium* (1999) 183.

[97] Van Boven, 'Are Remedies and Reparations Effectively Available to Victims of Racial Discrimination?', 4 *Connect* (Fall 2000) 5.

[98] Fottrell, *supra* n. 96, at 192.

[99] See CEDAW, Article 4(1): 'Adoption by State Parties of temporary special measures aimed at accelerating *de facto* equality between men and women shall not be considered discrimination as defined in the present Convention, but shall in no way entail as a consequence the maintenance of unequal or separate standards; these measures shall be discontinued when the objectives of equality of opportunity and treatment have been achieved', in *International Instruments, supra* n. 15. With regard to the ICCPR, the Human Rights Committee General Comment 18 on non-discrimination (37th session, 1989), para. 10, addresses the question of

inequities being inevitably a long-term process—domestic implementation of affirmative action has exposed the concept to criticism as constituting positive or reverse discrimination, thus rendering it legally contested and politically intractable. The experience of the country which has done most to pursue affirmative action, the United States, is not encouraging in this regard.[100]

Compounding the lack of standards, Article 2(2) provides no safeguards against the use of measures that, in promoting the adequate development of racial groups, constitute assimilationist policies. The ICERD approach is integrationist, as reflected in the provision that the maintenance of separate rights for vulnerable groups is only admitted for a limited period (Article 2(2) second sentence). States are further enjoined under Article 2(1)(e) 'to encourage, where appropriate, integrationalist multi-racial organizations and movements and other means of eliminating barriers between races, and to discourage anything which tends to strengthen racial division'.

These provisions reflect the predominant focus of the Convention on discrimination based on colour. Increased attention to the interests of ethnic minorities has resulted in the adoption of specific international and regional instruments recognizing the right to maintain ethnic identity.[101] In line with these developments, CERD has recently endorsed the importance of recognition by governments of the concrete rights of ethnic or linguistic groups to the preservation of their identity.[102]

special measures, stating that 'the principle of equality sometimes requires states parties to take affirmative action in order to diminish or eliminate the conditions which cause or help to perpetuate discrimination prohibited in the Covenant. For example in a State where the general conditions of a certain part of the population prevent or impair their enjoyment of human rights, the state should take specific action to correct those conditions. Such action may involve granting for a time to part of the population concerned certain preferential treatment in specific matters as compared to the rest of the population. However as long as such action is needed to correct discrimination in fact, it is a case of legitimate differentiation under the Covenant.'

[100] On the legal and political debates in the US, the first country to have undertaken widescale affirmative action programmes over the last thirty years, see Fottrell, *supra* n. 96, at 193–202.

[101] See, e.g., UNESCO 1978 Declaration on Race and Racial Prejudice, *supra* n. 77; UN 1992 Declaration on the Rights of Persons belonging to National or Ethnic, Religious and Linguistic Minorities, *supra* n. 17; Council of Europe 1995 Framework Convention for the Protection of National Minorities, ETS 157. Compare also with Article 27 ICCPR that at least to a modest extent recognizes the interests of ethnic minorities, *supra* n. 14.

[102] CERD General Recommendation XXI (48th session, 1996) on the right to self-determination: 'In accordance with article 2 of the [ICERD] and other relevant international documents, Governments should be sensitive towards the rights of persons belonging to ethnic groups, particularly their right to lead lives of dignity, to preserve their culture, to share equitably the fruits of national growth and to play their part in the Government of the country of which they are citizens. Also, Governments should consider, within their respective constitutional frameworks, vesting persons belonging to ethnic or linguistic groups comprised of their citizens, where appropriate, with the right to engage in activities which are particularly relevant to the preservation of the identity of such persons or groups.'

(c) Public and Private Reach of the Convention

One central provision of ICERD, Article 2(1)(d), provides that '[e]ach state party shall prohibit and bring to an end by all appropriate means, including legislation as required by the circumstances, racial discrimination by any person, group or organization'.

The question of determining the reach of the Convention when non-governmental or private actors are involved has been much debated.[103] Reference is frequently made to the overarching definition of racial discrimination referring to racial discriminatory acts occurring within 'public life'. This appears to exclude private acts from the scope of the Convention. More convincingly, it has been suggested that public life in Article 1 should mean the opposite of private life, rather than referring only to governmental actions.[104] This interpretation is supported by the guarantees contained elsewhere in the Convention, such as the right of access to any place or service intended for the use by the general public (Article 5(f)), the right to work and to housing (Article 5(e)). CERD practice has made it clear that these guarantees extend to employment in private enterprises, to housing provided by private owners, or admission to private clubs. The Committee has stated that 'to the extent that private institutions influence the exercise of rights or the availability of opportunities, the State Party must ensure that the result has neither the purpose nor the effect of creating or perpetuating racial discrimination'.[105]

The issue of the private/public reach of the Convention's provisions is of continuing importance considering the extent to which governments, through programmes of privatization, are divesting themselves from regulating basic public facilities and services and the ever more prominent role played by private actors on a global level.[106] The phenomenon of 'shrinking government' blurs the distinction between spheres of public conduct that are the subject of governmental regulation and spheres of private conduct that are not. Such trends detract from states' accountability and go in the opposite direction to what is needed to counteract racism.

The dichotomy between private and public realms also bears upon other obligations in the Convention, such as the requirement not to 'sponsor, defend and support racial discrimination by any persons or organizations' (Article 2(1)(b)), or to penalize the dissemination of racist ideas and participation in organizations that advocate racial hatred (Article 4). The

---

[103] See, among others, Meron, *supra* n. 62, at 291–5.   [104] Ibid., at 293.

[105] CERD General Recommendation XX (48th session, 1996), para. 5.

[106] For an analysis of these developments, see *Globalization in the Context of Increased Incidents of Racism, Racial Discrimination and Xenophobia*, Working paper submitted to the Sub-Commission by J. Oloka-Onyango as a contribution to the preparation of the World Conference against Racism. E/CN.4/Sub.2/1999/8 (1999).

Convention leaves open the question of how to strike a balance between individual freedom and government restriction in fulfilling these obligations.

(d) Governmental Interference in Private Conduct: Hate Speech

Article 4 requires that states prohibit not only advocacy of hatred, but also 'all dissemination of ideas based on racial superiority or hatred', and the provision of 'any assistance to racist activities, including financing thereof' (Article 4(a)). Organizations which promote and incite racial discrimination are to be declared illegal and prohibited by law, and participation in such organizations or activities is to be made punishable as well (Article 4(b)). Public authorities and institutions at national and local level are enjoined from promoting or inciting racial discrimination (Article 4(c)).

Article 4 mirrors Article 20(2) of the Covenant on Civil and Political Rights (ICCPR) which prohibits any advocacy of national, racial, or religious hatred that constitutes incitement to discrimination, hostility, or violence. But it goes further than Article 20. States must outlaw not only advocacy of hatred, but also 'all dissemination of ideas based on racial superiority or hatred'. The Article requires the suppression of organizations advocating racial hatred. It further requires that incitement be made an offence, as well as the financial support to racist activities of any kind.

CERD has consistently held that Article 4 is mandatory in that it requires comprehensive legislative action to implement its terms.[107] The prohibition of the dissemination of *ideas* based on racial superiority or *hatred* irrespective of intent or consequences has, however, proved in practice to be difficult for governments. In specific cases, proof of an intention to stir up racial hatred or proof that racial hatred was actually stirred up as a result is hard to obtain.[108] The same difficulty emerges with respect to outlawing racist organizations. Legal systems in which criminal intention alone is not sufficient to outlaw an organization before that intention is translated into action face difficulties in implementing the required preventive steps against incitement to racial discrimination.[109]

Criminalizing the expression of views—no matter how despicable—and participation in racist organizations clash with the rights to freedom of expression and association, recognized as fundamental human rights in all major

---

[107] On implementation of Article 4, see CERD General Recommendation I (5th session, 1972), General Recommendation VII (32nd session, 1985), and General Recommendation XV (42nd session, 1993).

[108] Hatred is a feeling, a state of mind and not a clearly established legal interest, as is the case of discrimination. See Lerner, 'Incitement in the Racial Convention; Reach and Shortcomings of Article 4', *Israel Yearbook on Human Rights* (1993) 1, at 8. See also Farrior, 'Molding the Matrix: The Historical and Theoretical Foundations of International Law Concerning Hate Speech', 14 *Berkeley Journal of International Law* (1996) 48.

[109] Lerner, *supra* n. 108, at 13.

human rights instruments.[110] The concern that these requirements for change in domestic law in the proposed Convention would impair freedom of expression and association resulted in the inclusion of the 'due regard' clause. States undertake to adopt immediate and positive measures designed to eradicate all incitement to, or acts of, racial discrimination 'with due regard to the principles embodied in the Universal Declaration of Human Rights and the rights expressly set forth in Article 5 of [the] Convention'.[111] Freedom of expression and association are among the rights to be given 'due regard' in fashioning legislation to implement Article 4. The due regard clause did, however, not dispel the concern among a number of states that Article 4 was too sweeping and a conspicuous number of reservations were entered on this Article upon ratification.[112]

   The interpretation of the due regard clause and Article 4 as a whole is still unsettled. Some states have interpreted it as not imposing on a state party the obligation to take any action impairing the right to freedom of expression (notably, the United States), others have invoked the due regard clause to justify alternative sanctions to criminal liability. CERD considers that the due regard clause must be read in the light of the UDHR as a whole, where the right to free speech and association are not absolute but subject to limitations and arguably greater weight is given to freedom from discrimination.[113] However, the Committee has not always been unanimous with regard to the effects of the due regard clause in Article 4 and with the merits of criminalizing hate speech and racist organizations, recognizing that in some instances

---

[110] See UDHR, Articles 19 and 20(1); ICCPR, Articles 19 and 21; ECHR, Articles 10 and 11; American Convention on Human Rights, Articles 13 and 16; The African Charter on Human and Peoples' Rights, Articles 9 and 10. In I. Brownlie (ed.), *Basic Documents on Human Rights,* 3rd edn. (1992).

[111] ICERD, Article 4, first paragraph.

[112] Some eighteen states parties to ICERD have entered reservations and/or interpretative declarations in respect of Article 4. Interpretative declarations were lodged, among others, by members of the Council of Europe on recommendation of the Committee of Ministers of the Council of Europe. See Resolution (68) 30 adopted by the Ministers' Deputies on 31 Oct. 1968. For the full texts of the reservations and/or declarations, see CERD/C/60/Rev.3, 12 Feb. 1999.

[113] See limitation clauses in the UDHR, Articles 29 and 30. In particular, Article 29(3) provides that the rights and freedoms set forth in the Declaration may in no case be exercised contrary to the purposes and principles of the United Nations. Being one of the purposes, as articulated in Article 1(3) of the Charter, the promotion of human rights for all without distinction, among others, as to race, it follows that under Article 29(3) UDHR no individual or group may exercise their rights to freedom of expression or association in a manner which vitiates the rule against racial discrimination.

   That the right to equality in international human rights law is so basic is confirmed, *inter alia,* by Article 4 ICCPR. While allowing derogation from substantive articles of the Covenant, among which those providing freedom of expression and association, it specifies that any measures taken in derogation of the Convention's provisions (where allowed) may not involve discrimination.

the effect may run counter to the desired goal.[114] Public proceeding in a court may in fact inadvertently provide the offender with the opportunity to publicize his racist views. An organization driven underground by repressive measures might be much more dangerous than one allowed to act openly.

A new challenge comes from the growth of racist propaganda on the Internet.[115] The particular characteristics of communication on the Internet makes state regulation relatively powerless to prevent the misuse of technology even in countries that want to do so. The discussion is largely limited to industrialized countries, where the overwhelming majority of Internet users are concentrated. There is a widening gulf across the Atlantic in attitudes toward curbing the Internet traffic that expresses racist extremism. Web sites banned in Europe, where in broad terms legislation against incitement to racial hatred is being used to cover expression on the Internet, are able to resurface from the haven of the United States, where they are protected under the constitutional guarantee of freedom of speech.[116]

The need for international minimum standards for the legal treatment of racial hatred and xenophobia in cyberspace as well as a draft code of conduct for the Internet community is being widely debated at the international and regional level.[117] Among the measures envisaged to counteract racist

---

[114] Divided comments from CERD members were, for instance, expressed over a hate speech case under the ECHR (*Jersild v Denmark*, ECHR (1978) Series A, No. 19, 1). In that case a television journalist was convicted of aiding and abetting the dissemination of racist speech through broadcasting an interview with young racists. Whilst some members of CERD welcomed the applicant's conviction as 'the clearest statement yet . . . that the right to protection against racial discrimination took precedence over the right to freedom of expression', others considered that 'in such cases the facts needed to be considered in relation to both rights'. In the event, the European Court, in finding that the conviction of the journalist violated Article 10 and the guarantee of freedom of expression, considered its judgment compatible with Article 4 ICERD. See report of the Committee to the General Assembly, A/45/18, p. 21, para. 56.

[115] Technical, legal, juridical aspects relating to the screening and prohibition of racist propaganda on the Internet have been extensively debated at the United Nations *Seminar on the Role of Internet in the Light of the Provisions of the International Convention on the Elimination of All Forms of Racial Discrimination*, Geneva, 10–14 Nov. 1997. See n. 239 *infra*. Moreover, OHCHR has recently conducted consultations with member states, United Nations bodies, specialized agencies, intergovernmental and non-governmental organizations, on the use of the Internet to incite racism, xenophobia, and intolerance. The resulting report has been submitted to the Preparatory Committee for the World Conference against Racism. A/CONF.189/PC.1/5.

[116] For an excellent overview on the legal and technical issues involved in counteracting the dissemination of racist messages via the Internet, see European Commission against Racism and Intolerance (ECRI), *Legal Instruments to Combat Racism on the Internet*, Report prepared by the Swiss Institute of Comparative Law, CRI(2000)27, Strasbourg, Aug. 2000.

[117] See, for instance, the Action Plan on Promoting Safer Use of the Internet, Decision No. 276/1999/EC of the European Parliament and the Council of the European Union of 25 Jan. 1999.

propaganda on the Internet are those which require ISPs (Internet Service Providers) to register web sites and their authors, and the introduction of Internet filtering programs.

(e) Remedies for Victims of Racial Discrimination

The right to a domestic remedy is a basic requirement of the international approach to human rights protection. Article 6 ICERD deals with effective protection and remedies, as well as just and adequate reparation or satisfaction for victims of racism and racial discrimination. The notion of effective remedies entails that recourse procedures should be simple, transparent, and accessible, based on awareness of the vulnerability of victims of racial acts, the fact that they are mostly ignorant of their rights and of linguistic and other barriers they often face in seeking legal remedies. The scrutiny of states' reports by CERD has brought home that in many cases effective remedies so defined are unavailable, particularly where victims belong to the most destitute and marginalized groups of society.[118]

Nevertheless agreement on the priority of establishing practical and effective remedies to victims of racial discrimination—for example by providing for legal aid and assistance, providing standing for non-governmental organizations to assist victims during the legal process, or by alleviating the burden of proof—is a welcome development in current policy recommendations at international and regional level.[119]

A new emphasis is being placed on the role of administrative or other bodies in enforcing anti-discrimination laws. In recent years there has been a growing number of specialized bodies set up in various countries aimed at combating discrimination and promoting equality. These bodies, according to the legal and administrative traditions of the countries in which they are established, have taken different forms—national commissions for racial equality, ombudsmen against ethnic discrimination, centres/offices for combating racism and promoting equal opportunities, or bodies having similar functions within a wider human rights mandate.[120] Their function varies from providing assistance in litigation to taking up the case on behalf of a

---

[118] A comprehensive analysis on the issue of remedies with regard to victims of racial discrimination is provided by a former Committee member, Theo van Boven. See his background paper on 'Common problems linked to all remedies available to victims of racial discrimination' (HR/GVA/WCR/SEM.1/2000/BP.5), prepared for the United Nations *Expert Seminar on Remedies Available to the Victims of Racial Discrimination, Xenophobia and Related Intolerance and on Good National Practices in this Field*, held in Geneva 16–18 Feb. 2000. See n. 239 *infra*.

[119] See, for instance, the report and recommendations of the *Expert Seminar on Remedies* above. A/CONF.189/PC.1/8. At the regional level, see ECRI, *Compilation of ECRI's General Policy Recommendations*, CRI(99)54, Strasbourg, Aug. 1999.

[120] See ECRI, *Good Practices: Specialized Bodies to Combat Racism, Xenophobia, Anti-Semitism and Intolerance at National Level*, CRI(99) 43, Apr. 1999.

victim, or adjudicating complaints through amicable solutions or in binding and enforceable decisions.

This approach shifts the focus from repressive measures and criminal sanctions to conciliatory measures and civil law remedies. It reflects an awareness that the reality of racial or ethnic discrimination is most often experienced in the denial of social and economic rights—especially in the fields of employment, housing, and health care. Alternative civil justice models may prevent the need to bring cases of discrimination to court and are often more effective than criminal prosecution in combating prejudice, promoting understanding and tolerance, and in protecting victims from retaliation.

There is also scope under the Convention for specifically tailored group enforcement mechanisms. Where collective rights are involved—such as the case of indigenous peoples, Roma/Sintis, or other minority groups that are victims of entrenched and deeply rooted racism—individual complaints with a view of obtaining reparation are unlikely to secure structural changes in economic and social life.[121] However, the advocacy of remedial actions of this nature, or of any kind, needs to be accompanied by national educational policies directed at majority communities to promote understanding and tolerance. Such duties, mostly neglected, are set out for states under Article 7 ICERD.

(f) The Need to Address the Root Causes of Racism—Article 7

The struggle against racism and racial discrimination over the history of ICERD has focused on the role of law. Priority has been given under the Convention to legislation intended to suppress propaganda, the dissemination of racist ideas, and the prohibition of organizations that advocate racist violence and hatred. States have been encouraged to rescind discriminatory statutes and regulations, to strengthen legal guarantees and remedies against racial discrimination and, more recently, to take positive or special measures designed to enable disadvantaged racial groups to enjoy their human rights and fundamental freedoms on an 'equal footing'. This approach was and remains an essential foundation. But law alone cannot address the problem of racism at its roots. Combating 'prejudices that lead to racism' is one of the goals of the Convention, which calls upon states 'to adopt immediate and effective measures, particularly in the field of teaching, education, culture and information'.[122] Efforts to implement this article both by the CERD and

---

[121] See, with regard to the rights of indigenous peoples, CERD General Recommendation XXIII (51st session, 1997) addressing the need of fair compensation for indigenous peoples, which should as far as possible take the form of lands and territories.

[122] Article 7 ICERD. Doubts about over-reliance on the impact of legislation in combating racism were forcefully expressed during the drafting process of the Convention by the United Kingdom delegate: 'Using legislation by itself was like cutting down a noxious weed above the ground and leaving the roots intact.' See Banton, *supra* n. 76, at 59.

reporting states have been meagre. After many years of total neglect, guidelines on implementation of Article 7 were developed with assistance from UNESCO, but states' reports have continued to treat it as a marginal issue, as does much of the literature on the Convention.[123]

Article 7 specifies the fields in which states parties are to adopt measures in order to end racial prejudice and promote understanding. The little that states have reported on implementation of Article 7 has tended to focus on the education of schoolchildren.[124] But Article 7 does not address educational measures only in the school setting. It includes broader education and training such as the training of teachers, law enforcement officials, judges, and other public figures.[125] The reference to culture and information addresses persons, associations, and institutions that shape opinions, through, for example, cultural events, in sport and, not least, the media. Article 7 deserves deeper attention both from governments and CERD. The duties it requires of states reflect the thesis that racist ideas are not innate, but are transmitted to the young through others: parents, peers, teachers, politicians, and other opinion leaders. Unless such ideas are tackled at their source, they will continue to be handed down from generation to generation.[126] The importance of full implementation of these provisions for the long-term success of the goals of ICERD and the right to equality cannot be underestimated.

(iii) The Committee on the Elimination of Racial Discrimination

The Committee on the Elimination of Racial Discrimination (CERD) was established in 1970. It comprises eighteen members elected by the states parties from among their nationals. The Convention requires that those elected as members be

experts of high moral standing . . . who shall serve in their personal capacity, consideration being given to equitable geographical distribution and to the representation of the different forms of civilization as well as of the principal legal systems.[127]

---

[123] See Wolfrum, 'The Committee on the Elimination of Racial Discrimination', 3 *Max Planck UNYB* (1999) 489, at 504; Farrior, *supra* n. 86, at 294. CERD issued an early General Recommendation on the implementation of Article 7, but rather than specifying the types of steps states should take, it simply implores states to report on the measures they have taken. CERD, General Recommendation V (15th session, 1977).

[124] See *Joint Working Paper on Article 7 of the International Convention on the Elimination of All Forms of Racial Discrimination*, UN Doc. E/CN.4/Sub.2/1998/4 (1998), para. 46.

[125] See also CERD General Recommendation XIII (42nd session, 1993) on the training of law enforcement officials in the protection of human rights, urging states to include information on implementation of this recommendation in their periodic reports.

[126] See the *Study on the Implementation of Article 7 of the International Convention on the Elimination of All Forms of Racial Discrimination*, prepared by the Special Rapporteur, Mr Georges Tenekides. A/CONF.119/11 (1983).

[127] Article 8(1) ICERD.

Members or experts are elected for a term of four years that can be renewed.[128] The Committee is charged with the task of overseeing the implementation of the Convention and to report on its work to the General Assembly through the Secretary General. It can offer suggestions and general recommendations to the states parties on implementation.[129] It has the competence to receive and respond to complaints from states and individuals.[130]

Study of the Committee has been considerably aided by the existence of a substantial body of literature including the writings of former and serving Committee members.[131] One drawback is that all accounts of the functioning of the Committee have been written by members from Western countries. A fuller assessment would profit from the perspectives of those elected to represent other regional groupings.[132]

How effective has CERD proved to be? Any assessment of an international initiative over a period of thirty years to eliminate racial discrimination of every kind in over 150 states must inevitably be tentative, even speculative. That caveat made, it seems clear that conflicting ideas within the Committee as to the purposes of the Convention, the global geopolitical context in which it developed, and the attributes of Committee members combined to limit its capacities to achieve a great deal. That at least seems to be true for the first twenty years of the Committee's existence. The Committee had permanent members of the Soviet Bloc countries whose governments in their reports insisted that racism was a function of imperialism and colonialism and therefore did not arise in their jurisdictions. Experts from these countries did not question or challenge such submissions. On the other hand the other protagonist in the Cold War, the United States, remained aloof from the Convention while seeking to dismantle its own inheritance of racism and segregation suffered by black citizens through its own internal democratic and constitutional resources.

One of the most perceptive writers on the Committee, and himself a former member, divides its story into the three decades during which it has functioned.[133] During the first decade of the 1970s, states parties and the Committee came to terms with the full implications of the Convention especially for domestic legal change. Research has demonstrated that a substantial number of ratifying countries did incorporate at least some of the Convention's requirements in internal law. Thus, Australia passed the Racial

---

[128] Article 8(5)(a) ICERD.   [129] Ibid., Article 9(2).   [130] Ibid., Articles 11–14.
[131] For a book length study see Banton, *supra* n. 76. Also Banton, 'Decision-taking in the Committee on the Elimination of Racial Discrimination', in Alston and Crawford, *supra* n. 72, at 55–78; Partsch, *supra* n. 71, at 339–68. Wolfrum, *supra* n. 123.
[132] It is regretted that it did not prove possible for reasons of time and resources to interview members of the Committee in preparing these lectures. Advice in conducting our research given by Mr Michael Banton (UK) is gratefully acknowledged.
[133] Banton, *supra* n. 76, at 99–171.

Discrimination Act 1975 prior to ratifying the ICERD and adopted the Convention's definition of racial discrimination in that Act. Costa Rica and Egypt, among others, adopted constitutional changes to incorporate prohibitions on racial discrimination.[134] At the same time, however, other countries insisted that they had ratified the treaty as an act of solidarity with those subject to apartheid and similar practices and saw no need to alter their laws as racial discrimination was unknown in their countries.[135] A review of the first forty-five states' reports submitted found that over half the states in question emphatically denied that any form of racial discrimination existed on their territories.[136]

In the second decade, the 1980s, ICERD, and in particular its Committee, were rendered largely impotent due to the Cold War. There was extraordinary turnover in membership that militated against it achieving much impact through its dialogue with states.[137] The focus on the link between racism and anti-imperialism, both within CERD and the United Nations as a whole, frustrated any modest advances in the procedure and practice of implementation that might have been achieved.[138] ICERD sessions had to be cancelled on a number of occasions due to a lack of funds.[139]

From the end of the Cold War and throughout the 1990s, CERD has been able to recover momentum and to address its mandate with greater commitment and energy.[140] It became more involved with the other treaty bodies through the annual meeting of Chair Persons of the Treaty Bodies and has in consequence implemented a number of reforms and innovations in its work. These changes are reflected in the enhanced quality of discussion of state reports, in the adoption of improved concluding observations,

---

[134] See N. Lerner, *The U.N. Convention on the Elimination of All Forms of Racial Discrimination* (1980), at 165–211.

[135] Banton, *supra* n. 76, at 105.   [136] Ibid., at 106.

[137] Forty-three members occupied the eighteen seats between 1970 and 1978 and forty-one in the ten-year period from 1979 to 1988. The Convention allowed for casual vacancies to be filled by another expert from among the state's experts. There was no provision for election for such vacancies. In contrast, the Human Rights Committee under the ICCPR, which came into force six years after the ICERD, required an election to be held for casual vacancies. The ICCPR also directed that the need for lawyers on the Committee should be factored into the election of eligible Committee members. In the last decade the Committee has increased it effectiveness as a result of a considerably reduced turnover, Banton, *supra* n. 76, at 142.

[138] Banton notes, referring to the first eighteen years of the Committee's existence, that 'CERD was in no position to act against any but a pariah state. Chile and Israel found themselves in such a position and South Africa would have done had that country become a state party. There was insufficient trust within the Committee for it to take decisions other than by consensus and this permitted any small minority to exercise a veto. Many members saw their obligations in diplomatic terms and perhaps could do little else while the opposition between East and West hung over so many of the decisions that had to be taken.' Banton, *supra* n. 76, at 137.

[139] Partsch, *supra* n. 71, at 346.   [140] Banton, *supra* n. 76, at 142.

as well as in the quality of recent General Recommendations adopted under Article 9. The CERD has also fashioned a preventive procedure and, reversing traditional attitudes, has become more open to involvement of non-governmental organizations (NGOs) in its work. Thus in August 2000, the Committee held a two-day seminar on discrimination against Roma in which for the first time NGOs were permitted to attend and make interventions.[141]

(a) Membership of the Committee

One characteristic of the Committee throughout its thirty-year existence has been the practice of many states to appoint civil servants, diplomats, or retired diplomats as members. The practice reflected the assumption of the large number of states, who swiftly ratified the Convention, that it was essentially about apartheid and institutional racism in countries other than their own. While the diplomatic presence has been said to have been useful in the early years of the Committee, especially in bringing governments to understand the nature of the legal obligations they had undertaken, it is also the case that the effective independence of the Committee was in constant question.[142] Concern that committee members, especially country rapporteurs, were subject to pressure from other diplomats led the CERD to adopt a General Recommendation expressing its alarm.[143] At its fiftieth session in 1996, CERD secured majority support from among its members for an amendment to its rules of procedure to ensure for the future that 'as a general rule' experts would not participate in the discussions of their home states' reports. It is current practice to agree the text of Concluding Observations in public session, a change intended to inhibit participation by a member who may be a national of the state under discussion.[144]

The range of professional backgrounds found on the Committee has often been cited a particular strength by its members.[145] However, the expanded range of the Committee's work, such as its focus on ethnic minorities and indigenous peoples, alongside the growing awareness of the complexity of the task of ending discrimination in many countries, suggests that there is a strong case for the appointment of new expertise. Such expertise should include specialists in anti-discrimination law as well as persons experienced in implementing anti-discrimination programmes including in the field of education.

---

[141] The discussion led to the adoption of CERD General Recommendation XXVII (57th session, 2000), outlining a number of measures that governments of relevant states parties should take to improve the situation of the Roma.

[142] Banton, *supra* n. 76, at 101; Partsch, *supra* n. 71, at 340–1; Wolfrum, *supra* n. 123, at 494.

[143] General Recommendation IX (38th session, 1990).

[144] Wolfrum, *supra* n. 123, at 509.   [145] Ibid., at 494.

(b) Committee Procedures

The Committee meets twice a year in March and August to review state reports. Since 1996 it has assessed on average ten reports in each session. A crucial early point of procedure was whether reports would be examined in the presence or absence of the states parties. At the direction of the General Assembly the procedure was settled that states should be present.[146] This decision, followed by the later treaty bodies, allowed what is perhaps the most important feature of the treaty monitoring system to develop, that of dialogue between the Committee and reporting states.[147] It is now hard to envisage that any impact could have been achieved by the CERD without face to face debate between the representatives of states and the experts.

Since 1988 the appointment of special rapporteurs from among its members with responsibility for leading the review of each country report has deepened the quality of the exchange between state representatives and the Committee. The disputed question of access to other information than that provided by governments—in particular information from NGOs—was a source of tension and disagreement as it was to become with other treaty bodies. The entitlement of members to have such access and to refer to it was achieved for CERD through following the precedent of the other human rights treaty bodies.[148] Some members also resisted the acceptance of written information from the specialized agencies, ILO and UNESCO, when dealing with state reports. A solution was found whereby these bodies provided their material to Committee members interested through the Secretariat.[149] ILO and UNESCO representatives attend CERD sessions as observers. It appears that the contribution which is valued by the CERD has been made by the ILO, especially in respect of its Convention on Discrimination in Employment.[150] The potential role of UNESCO in respect of Article 7 could have been considerable. But in practice that has not proved to be the case.[151]

From 1991 the Committee has also adopted a system in step with the reforms proposed by the Independent Expert on the functioning of the treaty bodies, in respect of Concluding Observations following its examination of a state report.[152] This document is now discussed and agreed in public session in the absence of the state party—and a longstanding contentious issue, already noted—without the participation of any Committee member who is

---

[146] A/RES/2783 (XXVI) (1971).   [147] Partsch, *supra* n. 71, at 340–1.
[148] See Decision 1 (XL), 'in examining the reports of States parties, members of the Committee must have access, as independent experts, to all other sources of information, governmental and non-governmental' and Wolfrum, *supra* n. 123, at 507.
[149] Partsch, *supra* n. 71, at 344–5.   [150] Ibid., at 344.
[151] Lerner, *supra* n. 134, at 148.
[152] See *Final Report on Enhancing the Long Term Effectiveness of the United Nations Human Rights Treaty System* (the Alston Report). UN Doc. E/CN.4/1997/74 (1996).

a national of the state in question. The Observations broadly follow a similar layout to the conclusions of the other monitoring committees and are comparable in their focus and quality to those of other treaty bodies.[153] They achieve their purpose of identifying for states exactly where further action has to be undertaken in the implementation of its Convention commitments.

(c) Overdue Reports

The Convention lays down that states parties must report every two years to the CERD.[154] That interval has clearly proved, in the light of the expansion of the treaty system, too onerous on states. The interval provided for periodic reporting by states in the later treaties was longer.[155] Not without hesitation the CERD agreed to a new practice requiring submission of a comprehensive report every four years updated by short reports every two years.[156]

This has been welcomed by states. It has enabled the CERD to reduce the backlog in consideration of reports it has received. But it has not solved the problem of non-submission of reports. ICERD is not alone in having this problem. Delay in the submission of reports by governments is shared with other monitoring committees. However, ICERD is the treaty with the most significant problems (see Fig. 1). Of the 1,235 reports from the main human rights treaties as of 31 March 2000, ICERD accounts for the greatest number.[157] Part of the explanation lies in the cumulative delays of a large number of reports, that are overdue from a number of states (see Fig. 2). Nevertheless, the disproportionate delinquency with regard to ICERD must raise the suspicion that states take their reporting requirement under ICERD less seriously than with respect to the other treaty bodies.

The CERD has taken action. In 1991 it proposed a procedure to the General Assembly that, in the case of states with seriously overdue reports, it would undertake a periodic review based upon the last reports submitted. This initiative was endorsed by the General Assembly and has had positive effects in inveigling some states to submit and to cooperate.[158] The CERD has also pressed that technical assistance be made available to states experiencing difficulties in preparing reports in which the Committee members would participate.[159] Nevertheless the problem remains unresolved and serious.

---

[153] See, for example, 57th Session, Concluding Observations of the Committee on the Elimination of Racial Discrimination: Norway. CERD/C/57/CPR.3/Add.12, 10 Aug. 2000.

[154] Article 9(1) ICERD.

[155] Cf. ICCPR, Article 40(1) 'whenever the Committee so requests'; Convention against Torture (CAT), Article 19(1) 'every four years'; CEDAW, Article 18(1)(b) 'every four years'; Convention on the Rights of the Child (CRC), Article 44(1)(b) 'every five years'.

[156] Partsch, *supra* n. 71, at 367.

[157] See *Recent Reporting History under the Principal International Human Rights Instruments,* HRI/GEN/4 of 27 Apr. 2000.

[158] GA Res. 49/178 (1994), para. 6 and see Banton, *supra* n. 76, at 152.

[159] General Recommendation XI (39th session, 1991).

Treaty	ICESCR	ICCPR	ICERD	CEDAW	CAT	CRC	Total
Overdue reports	160	142	430	236	112	155	1235
State parties	142	144	156	165	119	191	917
Percentage of total	14	12	34	18	12	10	

Figure 1. *Reporting status under the main international human rights instruments*

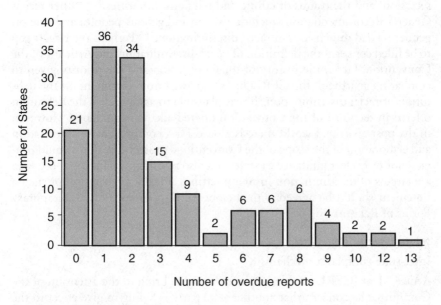

Figure 2. *ICERD overdue reports*

(d) General Recommendations

Under Article 9, paragraph 2, of ICERD the Committee may make suggestions and General Recommendations prompted by its work in examining state reports. Recommendations are to be reported to the General Assembly along with any comments on them from state parties. The Committee over its life has made some twenty-seven General Recommendations.[160] None appear to have provoked a response from the states' parties. As with similar

---

[160] For a compilation of the Committee's General Recommendations, see CERD/C7365 of 11 Feb. 1999.

statements by the other treaty bodies, the recommendations enable it to both indicate to states the Committee's view of the scope of Convention provisions as a guide in their reporting and to offer guidance on the legal interpretation of the Convention.[161] It is accepted that General Recommendations do not bind the states parties, but they do bind the members of the Committee who have agreed them.[162] The recommendations to date cover most provisions under the Convention and in recent years have also dealt with wider issues. In 1994, the CERD called for the establishment of an international tribunal to prosecute crimes against humanity in the light of 'racially and ethnically motivated massacres and atrocities occurring in different parts of the world'.[163] It has also drafted an important statement on self-determination, secession, and the claims of ethnic and religious minorities.[164] Other recent General Recommendations include two on indigenous peoples and one on gender related dimensions of racial discrimination.[165] Perhaps the largest gap to be filled concerns the definition of racial discrimination and Article 1 of the Convention. Given the history of the Convention and the priority given to combating apartheid, the CERD has shied away from comment on the definition of racial discrimination. It was plausible to assume that the definition offered in section I of the Convention offered adequate guidance. However, in the post-apartheid world there is a need for a comprehensive clarification and elaboration of the scope of the Convention's protections. This would provide not only clear guidance to states but also to others, including those who are targets of discrimination in many settings. Ideally, preparation of such a statement should be agreed with the Special Rapporteur on Contemporary Forms of Racism.

(e) Complaint Procedures

Inter-state complaint mechanism

Article 11 of ICERD enables any state party to bring to the attention of the Committee its concern that another state party is failing to give effect to the Convention. The procedure does not require a separate declaration of acceptance by governments.[166] The state-to-state complaint option under

---

[161] The ultimate arbiter of the meaning of the Convention is the International Court of Justice which, under ICERD Article 22, has jurisdiction over disputes between the states parties relating to the 'interpretation or application' of the Convention that are not settled 'by negotiation or by the procedures expressly provided for' by the Convention. Jurisdiction of the ICJ has been excluded via reservation by twenty-two states parties to ICERD. See CERD/C/60/Rev. 3 of 12 Feb. 1999.

[162] Meron, *supra* n. 62, at 285.

[163] General Recommendation XVIII (44th session, 1994).

[164] General Recommendation XXI (48th session, 1996).

[165] See General Recommendation XXIII (51st session, 1997); General Recommendation XXIV (55th session, 1999); General Recommendation XXV (56th session, 2000).

[166] As is the case, for example, with the ICCPR (see Article 41).

Article 11 of ICERD has never been utilized. As with similar procedures in other human rights instruments, it must be regarded, for now at least, as a dead letter. The theory on which it was based, that the states parties have both a collective interest and a responsibility for the elimination of racial discrimination including in other jurisdictions, has not been borne out in practice. The collective involvement of states parties arises only from their participation in elections of members of CERD and in their participation in the General Assembly to which CERD makes an annual report. On occasion the CERD has received notice of what it has termed 'disguised complaints' about other states' actions as part of the periodic report under Article 9 of the Convention.[167] The Committee has suggested in such cases formal resort to the Article 11 procedure but with no results.[168] It has been suggested that the explanation for the failure of states to have resort to the interstate mechanism arises from their awareness that the Committee had no power to legally adjudicate on a state's complaint. The Committee may only recommend a friendly settlement and has no enforcement powers.[169] However, the more likely explanation, as with other state-to-state complaint mechanisms in the major human rights treaties, is political while also reflecting an unwillingness shared by states to empower any quasi-judicial mechanism at the international level.

Individual complaint mechanism

Under Article 14 of the Convention, a state may make a declaration recognizing the competence of the CERD to receive through the Secretary General communications from individuals or groups of individuals within its jurisdiction claiming to be victims of a violation of one of the rights set forth in the Convention.[170] The Article 14 complaint procedure came into force as early as 1982 with acceptance by ten states.[171] However, the increase since that date in the number of states providing recourse to the jurisdiction of the Committee has been minimal. To date thirty out of 156 states parties only have made a declaration under Article 14.[172] As a result there has been a disappointing and limited practice achieved to date. Over the almost two

---

[167] Disguised complaints have included Iraq's claim that it could not report on the operation of the Convention in northern Iraq because of the establishment of safe havens for Kurds during the Gulf War.

[168] See General Recommendation XVI concerning the application of Article 9 of the Convention (42nd session, 1993).

[169] See Wolfrum, *supra* n. 123, at 511. Also Buergenthal, *supra* n. 83, at 202.

[170] On the procedural rules governing Article 14 communications, see M. O'Flaherty, *Human Rights and the U.N. Practice Before the Treaty Bodies* (1996), at 104–7.

[171] Article 14(9) ICERD.

[172] As of 27 Aug. 1999, twenty-eight states had made the declaration under Article 14, A/54/18 paras. 1 and 2. The Yugoslav Republic of Macedonia and Portugal joined in 2000. CERD/C/SR.1372 and CERD/C/SR.1400.

decades the Committee has considered only a dozen communications.[173] All have been from developed Western countries. None have raised s ystemic issues of violation. However, several complaints about alleged racial discrimination in the operation of social security benefits, in housing,[174] or in respect of employment give a clear indication of the considerable potential of the procedure for victims.[175]

The explanation for the low level of acceptance of the individual complaint mechanism can only be a matter of speculation. But it is difficult to avoid the conclusion that states remain unconvinced that the CERD should develop such a quasi-judicial role. This is disappointing for the development of the Convention and international human rights protection as a whole. It could be argued that the individual complaint procedure under the First Optional Protocol to the International Covenant on Civil and Political Rights offers an alternative forum. The Human Rights Committee can address inequalities and racial discrimination under the Protocol. The Committee on Economic, Social and Cultural Rights may also address racial and ethnic discrimination in the future, should the proposed individual complaint mechanism under that Covenant come into effect. But neither body can interpret the ICERD and the duties imposed on states by that Convention. The international treaty system,

---

[173] See *Compilation of Opinions and Decisions Adopted under Article 14 of the Convention*, CERD/C/390 of 5 June 2000.

[174] One case involving, among others, alleged violations of the right to housing (Article 5(e)(iii)) and freedom of residence (Article 5(d)(i)) is *L.K. v The Netherlands* (No. 4/1994), Opinion of 16 Mar. 1993. The case concerned threats of racial violence by local inhabitants hostile to foreigners taking up residence in their neighbourhood. The facts were not disputed and the case focused on the expediency principle, thereby finding that instances of racial discrimination have to be prosecuted with particular attention, *inter alia*, by ensuring the speedy disposal of such cases by domestic judicial instances.

[175] See, for instance, *Yilmaz-Dogan v the Netherlands* (No. 1/1984), Opinion of 10 Aug. 1988, where the Committee found a violation of Article 5(e)(i) concerning equality before the law in respect of the right to work and protection against unemployment. The petitioner's dismissal from employment, after a prolonged period of absenteeism owing to illness and child-birth, was based on the employer's unwillingness to extend sickness-leave benefits to her because of prejudices against foreign women workers. Alleged violations of the right to work under Article 5(e)(i) were also dealt with by the Committee in *Diop v France* (No. 2/1989), Opinion of 18 Mar. 1991; *Z.U.B.S. v Australia* (No. 6/1996), Opinion of 26 Aug. 1999; *Barbaro v Australia* (No. 7/1995), Decision of Admissibility of 14 Aug. 1997; *B.M.S. v Australia* (No. 8/1996), Opinion of 12 Mar. 1999; *D.S. v Sweden* (No. 9/1997), Decision of Admissibility of 17 Aug. 1998. In *Ziad Ben Ahmed Habassi v Denmark* (No. 10/1997), Opinion of 26 Aug. 1999, the CERD found a violation of Article 2.1(d) with respect to the Danish Bank's loan policy *vis-à-vis* foreign residents and that it was necessary to ascertain whether or not the criteria applied involved racial discrimination, within the meaning of Article 1 of the Convention. In *B.J. v Denmark* (No. 17/1999), Opinion of 17 Mar. 2000, that concerned an alleged violation of Article 5(f), the Committee supported the petitioner's request for economic compensation for the humiliation of having been refused access to a place of service for the use of the general public.

as it has evolved, has established a separate role for the anti-discrimination instruments, on racial and sex discrimination, that is complementary to the other human rights conventions.[176] The encouragement of wider acceptance of the Article 14 procedure by states should be a priority for the Convention.[177]

(f) Early Warning and Urgent Procedures

In 1993, following a recommendation of the meeting of chairpersons of the treaty bodies, the CERD adopted new procedures concerned with prevention of violations of the Convention.[178] An early warning procedure was addressed to the prevention of ethnic or racial conflicts and an urgent action procedure was aimed at imminent or actual large-scale problems of serious racial or ethnic discrimination or conflict. In each case, the state in question is placed under the new procedure and remains on the agenda of the Committee at future sessions. These important initiatives have been invoked to date in respect of a range of situations in some fourteen countries, including Bosnia and Herzegovina, Kosovo, the Occupied Palestinian Territories, Algeria, Burundi, and Rwanda.[179]

The actions which the Committee can take under the procedures include requesting the submission of a report, bringing the situation to the attention of others, including the High Commissioner for Human Rights, the Secretary General or indeed the General Assembly and the Security Council. Members have also undertaken Good-Offices missions both to Croatia and Yugoslavia.

It is right that the CERD, given its mandate, should have sought to respond directly to some of the worst episodes of ethnic and racial conflict of the 1990s, such as have occurred in the Balkans and the Great Lakes region of east Africa. It is equally important for the future, given its accumulated knowledge and experience, that it should provide early warning to the international community over threatened ethnic conflict. But its capacity for positive influence on events must be acknowledged to be limited. CERD cannot itself become a vehicle for active conflict resolution. Its role should be rather to develop a more focused approach on the prevention of ethnic and racial discrimination based both on dialogue with reporting states and through the

[176] A proposed optional protocol to the Convention on the Elimination of Discrimination against Women providing for an individual complaint procedure is pending before the UN Human Rights Commission.

[177] A third procedure for monitoring implementation was created by Article 15 of the Convention, providing for cooperation between the Committee and competent United Nations bodies in matters of petitions from and reports concerning Non-Self-Governing Territories. See *supra* n. 71.

[178] UN Doc. A/48/18 paras.15–19 and Annex 3.

[179] For an account of the new preventive procedures, see Wolfrum, *supra* n. 123, at 513. Also Van Boven, 'Prevention, Early-warning and Urgent Procedures: A New Approach by the Committee on the Elimination of Racial Discrimination', in E. Denters and N. Schrijver (eds), *Reflections on International Law from the Low Countries* (1998) 165.

expansion of the individual complaint mechanism. Subject to its primary role as a treaty monitoring body, CERD can best make a contribution in response to gross violation or threatened ethnic violence where it acts as a partner with others, including any relevant national or regional body as well as the UN Human Rights Commission's Special Rapporteur on Contemporary Forms of Racism. However, the prospects of achieving such cooperative action in the short term among all such bodies can only be described as poor given experience to date.

(g) Funding

The capacity of the CERD to function effectively and creatively depends on its budget. That remains in crisis.[180] The finances of the CERD were entrusted under the Convention directly to the states who became parties, not to the UN regular budget. This decision apparently was intended to underscore the independence of the Committee. It has not worked out, however, quite like that. States, although subject to a modest levy, have been late or have failed to pay their contributions. This resulted in a series of sessions being cancelled in the 1980s, only halted when as a stop gap the Secretary General with General Assembly approval provided interim funding. An amendment to ICERD to enable its budget to be paid from the regular UN budget, although approved by the meeting of the states parties and the General Assembly, has still not come into effect.[181] The amendment requires approval in accordance with domestic legal procedures of all states which are parties to ICERD. But a decade later many states have yet to take the necessary steps.

Similar funding concerns afflict the one other UN institution established to respond to racism in the world in addition to ICERD, the Special Rapporteur of the Human Rights Commission, which will next be discussed.

V. THE SPECIAL RAPPORTEUR ON CONTEMPORARY FORMS OF RACISM, RACIAL DISCRIMINATION, XENOPHOBIA, AND RELATED INTOLERANCE

The institution of thematic rapporteurs by the UN Human Rights Commission, tasked with the investigation, analysis and, in some cases, the authority to respond to violation, has been a key innovation in the human rights competence of the United Nations. One such is the Special Rapporteur on Contemporary Forms of Racism, Racial Discrimination, Xenophobia, and

---

[180] ICERD is not alone in its long-term financing problems. All treaty bodies have similar problems. See Schmidt, 'Servicing and Financing Human Rights Supervisory Bodies', in Alston and Crawford, *supra* n. 72, at 481.

[181] This was proposed in the first report on treaty reform of the independent expert, Mr Philip Alston. UN Doc. A/44/668 (1989).

Related Intolerance, first appointed in 1993.[182] The selection of topics of human rights concern by the Commission justifying the appointment of rapporteurs is often infused by political considerations. The need for a thematic rapporteur on racism was pressed by Turkey. Among Turkey's concerns was the treatment of Turkish citizens in Germany. But there was a general concern shared by many developing countries that the focus on human rights violations, including ethnic discrimination in the developing world, should be balanced by attention to racism, especially against immigrants, in the developed world.[183]

The origins of the initiative can be traced to a report reviewing UN Decades against Racism undertaken for the Sub-Commission on Prevention of Discrimination and Protection of Minorities by Asbjorn Eide.[184] His study confirmed the grim reality of the rise of anti-Semitism as well as racism and extreme nationalism in Europe and the developed world as a whole, directed at minorities, indigenous peoples, migrant workers, and other vulnerable groups. The Sub-Commission thereafter sought an overview study from the Secretary General of current trends in racism discrimination, intolerance, and xenophobia.[185] The Secretary General's report, considered at the forty-fourth session (1992) of the Sub-Commission, confirmed the 'resurgence of racism and xenophobia throughout the world and more particularly in Europe, the United States and Australia'.[186]

At its forty-ninth session in 1993, the Commission, acting on a recommendation of the Sub-Commission, approved the appointment for a three-year term of a special rapporteur on contemporary forms of racism.[187] The discussion of the scope of the mandate in the Commission reflected horse-trading between the sponsors (Turkey and Pakistan) and the European Union states. The outcome was a mandate to cover all countries, but with a particular focus on developed countries and the situation of vulnerable groups, especially

---

[182] This account of the Special Rapporteur draws heavily on the research undertaken by Bernhard Schaefer, graduate student. We wish to acknowledge with gratitude his contribution. See Schaefer, 'The United Nations Struggle against Racism and Racial Discrimination—The Contribution of the Special Rapporteur on Contemporary Forms of Racism, Racial Discrimination, Xenophobia and Related Intolerance', *Papers in the Theory and Practice of Human Rights*, University of Essex, 2001 (forthcoming).

[183] According to a report in *The Times* (12 Dec. 1994), the appointment reflected the 'resentment many Third World countries felt at what they saw as the "disproportionate" focus on abuse in the developed world, and the relative silence over race relations in richer, industrialized countries. Turkey, especially, was piqued at the focus on its treatment of Kurds, and wanted more publicity for the treatment of Turkish migrant workers in Germany.' Cited in Banton, *supra* n. 76, at 41.

[184] *Study on the Achievements Made and Obstacles Encountered During the Decades to Combat Racism and Racial Discrimination*, E/CN.4/Sub.2/1989/8/ and Add.1. The UN Decades to Combat Racism are dealt with in Part VI, *infra*.

[185] Sub-Commission Res. 1990/2.   [186] E/CN.4/Sub.2/1992/11, para. 142.

[187] CHR Res. 1993/20.

migrant workers. Mr Robert Dossou (Benin) was initially appointed to the post but on his being made foreign minister, Mr Maurice Glele Ahanhanzo, also from Benin, was appointed on 7 December 1993.

From the perspective of the effectiveness of the UN approach to racism as a whole, it is depressing that this otherwise useful initiative was taken without any consultation with the long established treaty body—the CERD. That the proposal for a special rapporteur was promoted mainly by countries that were not parties to the ICERD is hardly an explanation. The Turkish sponsor stressed the limitations of the treaty mechanism in dealing with the reporting of racist incidents on an ongoing basis. He also argued for the need to monitor developments in countries that had not ratified ICERD.[188] These were legitimate points. The existence of a special thematic rapporteur alongside treaty bodies dealing with the same subject area is not unique.[189] But had the proposal been seen by the CERD and its reactions included in the Commission discussion, the potential contribution of the special rapporteur to a coherent UN human rights strategy towards new forms of racism might have been advanced. In particular, a plan of cooperative and complementary action between both mechanisms could have been endorsed by the Commission. Exchanges have occurred between CERD and the Special Rapporteur on cooperation. But they do not appear to date to have been successful. The question of cooperation is discussed further below.

(i) Anti-Semitism and Islamophobia

The Special Rapporteur's mandate was extended and clarified by the Commission in 1994. It now embraces 'incidents of contemporary forms of racism, racial discrimination, any form of discrimination against Blacks, Arabs, and Muslims, xenophobia, negrophobia, anti-Semitism, and related intolerance'.[190] This language reflects the Arab–Israeli conflict. It was not possible to get agreement to the Western group proposal that would have added anti-Semitism as one focus of the proposed mandate. The same issue had arisen in the same way in the 1960s over the drafting of ICERD.[191] Arab rejection then of a reference to anti-Semitism concerned any implication that it might involve political recognition of Israel.[192] In 1993, with the hopes for the Oslo peace process that began in that year, there appears to have been a change of attitude among states and a preparedness to end the often deliberate confusion between anti-Semitism, anti-Zionism, and other

[188] E/CN.4/Sub.2/1992/SR.11, para. 30–1.
[189] For example, the Special Rapporteur on Torture and the UN Convention Against Torture.
[190] CHR Res. 1994/64, para. 4.   [191] See Part III(iv), *infra.*
[192] Lerner, *supra* n. 134, at 2 and 72.

political disagreements with Israel. The diplomatic solution found for the Special Rapporteur's mandate was to balance the reference to anti-Semitism with other targets of contemporary discrimination, in particular Arabs and Muslims. The result can be criticized in technical terms as inappropriate.[193] Nevertheless on the principles of openness and of naming racism where it occurs or is perceived to occur, the solution has proved to be a positive one.

During the debate on the proposal to create the new position it was pointed out by the representative of the World Jewish Congress that the Commission had never before condemned anti-Semitism.[194] If this was true, the inclusion of anti-Semitism in the mandate constituted condemnation and the Special Rapporteur has in subsequent reports brought to the attention of the Commission the continuing shameful reality of hatred of and violence against Jews.[195] At the same time the Special Rapporteur has been able to also document discrimination against Arabs, a phenomenon captured in the new term 'Islamophobia'.[196] Although he has referred questions of 'discrimination against Muslims' in his mandate to the Special Rapporteur on Religious Intolerance, to avoid overlap he has recognized that, as with the case of anti-Semitism, it is not all that easy to distinguish religious and racially motivated prejudice.[197]

The Special Rapporteur gained some early experience on the sensitivities of discussing the facts and prejudices that inform racism in his first reports. His setting out of what was reported to him about Jews led to expression of concern by several Jewish organizations and the Israeli Government.[198] While praising his work in general, they noted that such statements 'reinforced hateful anti-Semitic stereotypes'. The Rapporteur, in his own defence, noted that he had adopted the same approach in reporting the facts of prejudice against Blacks.[199]

In his next report he set out an extended quotation from the Israeli Government that laid some of the blame for attacks against Jews in Europe at the feet of 'Muslim extremists' and a claim that the same extremists 'were turning to the Qur'an as a primary anti-Jewish source'.[200] This brought a protest from the Organization of the Islamic Conference, an unprecedented condemnation from the Human Rights Commission, and a decision of the Commission requesting its Chairman 'to ask the Special Rapporteur to take

---

[193] Specification can suggest that other forms of discrimination are excluded from the purview of a mandate that is in principle concerned with all contemporary forms of racial and ethnic discrimination.

[194] E/CN.4/1994/SR.9, para. 6. The Sub-Commission condemned anti-Semitism in 1960. See *supra* n. 61, and Banton, *supra* n. 76, at 53.

[195] Anti-Semitism is defined by the Special Rapporteur as 'the despising of Jews' which 'can be considered to be one of the root causes of racial and religious hatred'. A/49/677, para. 149.

[196] E/CN.4/1998/79, para. 39.   [197] A/49/677, para. 17.   [198] A/49/677, para. 111.

[199] A/50/476, paras 10–17.

[200] E/CN.4/1997/71, para. 27 and A/52/471, paras 6–7.

corrective action'.[201] While the Special Rapporteur commented that it was
not for him to censor a government communication, he did delete a sentence
of his report.[202]

This development in turn led to the meeting of special rapporteurs in 1997
at which it was recorded that there was a 'consensus among the participants
that it was inappropriate for the Commission to request a special rapporteur
to amend his report. It was clearly stressed that special rapporteurs were
responsible for the content of their reports and that the Commission could
criticize the substance of a report.'[203]

Professsor van Boven has commented, with no doubt an eye to the forthcoming World Conference on Racism, that 'such discord in the struggle
against racism and racial discrimination is in stark contrast with the unity of
action that the women's movement demonstrated in the process leading to the
World Conference on Human Rights at Vienna in 1993 and the 1995 Fourth
World Conference on Women in Beijing'.[204]

Nevertheless the fact that discord and disagreement exist needs to be faced,
as does the depressing reality of pervasive ethnic and racial hostility in developed and developing world. The contribution of the Special Rapporteur,
whether intentionally or not, has been positive in removing the diplomatic
veil from that reality.

(ii) Assessment

The Special Rapporteur has had his mandate renewed and has been engaged
upon it for six years. He has submitted annual reports to the Commission and
to the General Assembly. He has also undertaken a range of country studies
based on visits to those countries. What assessment can be made on his contribution to date?

There can be no doubt that the work carried out by Mr Glele Ahanhanzo
has been useful. His initial or preliminary report offered some tentative definitions of the broad phenomena he had been asked to report, including
racism, racial discrimination, and xenophobia.[205] Analytical depth may be
wanting but the clear distinction between institutional racism, as reflected in
governmental policies such as apartheid, and the multitude of racist practices
that function without official sanction and despite legal prohibitions is useful
for understanding contemporary racism. His initial reports are also important
in conveying the complexity of racism and its often subtle and covert expression. Thus, while the core idea remains that of belief in a hierarchy of races,

[201] CHR Dec.1997/125 of 18 Apr. 1997.   [202] E/CN.4/1997/Corr.1.
[203] E/CN.4/1998/45, para. 23.   [204] Van Boven, *supra* n. 66, at 255.
[205] E/CN.4/1994/66.

he notes that there has been a shift from biological to cultural explanations among those who espouse such doctrines. At the same time he notes that not all ethnic conflict and discrimination is the working out of belief in racial superiority. Ethnic groups differ and it can be competition over resources and the manipulation of awareness of difference that leads to discrimination, xenophobia, and violence.

(a) Annual Reports

His annual reports presented to the Commission and to the General Assembly provide a limited but undoubtedly authentic view of the reality of racial discrimination, prejudice, and violence experienced by ordinary people in many countries. The most useful function these reports perform is in keeping the Commission and the General Assembly aware of the manifold and ever-changing expressions of racism and racial intolerance. Typically annual reports include a summary of activities, a section on current examples of racism, xenophobia, and related intolerance in different countries, measures taken by governments and public institutions, the initiatives of civil society organizations in combating racism, along with conclusions and recommendations. He reports on incidents of racism and racial discrimination in general, as well as against Blacks and Arabs, and he details information on anti-Semitism, xenophobia, discrimination against women, and migrant workers. Following the appointment of a Special Rapporteur on the human rights of migrants in 1999, Mr Glele Ahanhanzo has dropped this subject from his report.[206] The Rapporteur has also included in his annual reports documentation on other targets of racial discrimination not specified in his mandate, including the Roma and indigenous peoples.

The annual reports lack depth and have other limitations that are related to the failure to provide the human resources the Special Rapporteur needs for his work. Six years into his mandate he has not had the resources he requested to undertake his work. Repeated requests have been made by the Human Rights Commission and the General Assembly to the Secretary General for such support to no avail.[207]A properly resourced mechanism could achieve much more.

(b) Country Missions

The Special Rapporteur has undertaken some eleven country studies to date.[208] These field missions are intended to allow him 'to assess the conditions actually

---

[206] The Special Rapporteur on the human rights of migrants, CHR Res. 1999/44, para. 3. For her first report, see E/CN.4/2000/82.

[207] See, for example, A/49/677, para. 50–1; E/CN.4/1995/78. All special procedures suffer similar administrative, financial, and personnel problems.

[208] In chronological order: USA, Brazil, Germany, France, the United Kingdom, Colombia, Kuwait, South Africa, Hungary, the Czech Republic, and Romania.

prevailing in a country by giving him direct access to first hand reports and to the dialogue established with the authorities of the countries in question and key figures in civil society'.[209] The authority to undertake such country studies deriving from a Special Rapporteur's mandate is one of the distinct advantages of this mechanism. The Special Rapporteur has taken full advantage of the opportunities provided in these missions both to meet governmental and non-governmental representatives, to visit prisons and holding camps, to meet with victims of racial discrimination and with the media.

It is not possible to consider these missions or the reports resulting from them in detail in the confines of this chapter.[210] Only a few will be noted here. The first mission undertaken was to the United States in 1994, producing the first UN study of racism and racial discrimination in that country.[211] The report is noteworthy for its in depth coverage of continued serious questions of racial discrimination, including in respect of the death penalty, the question of police violence, the activities of racist organizations, and the issue of hate speech.

The study resulting from his visit to Brazil deserves mention for the quality of its analysis.[212] As the Rapporteur notes, Brazil is perceived by the international community as a positive example of ethnic and racial integration. While it is true that intermingling of the races—'Whites', 'Blacks', and 'Indians'—has made classification by race difficult, the report shows that nevertheless pervasive and subtle economic and social discrimination persists, based on a 'colour hierarchy'. He was struck, as all observers must be, by the dramatic contrast between the rich and poor in Brazil and the link between poverty and colour.[213]

His reports on Germany, France, and the United Kingdom bring out common concerns over ever more stringent immigration and asylum legislation, as well as issues of anti-Semitism, police violence, and prejudice against racial minorities.[214]

Finally, reference should be made to the Rapporteur's visit to South Africa, a country whose former apartheid governmental system had been the focus of international anti-racism activities for almost half a century. His report records the continuing difficulties of transition to a democratic society, as well as new trends of racism and xenophobia. As regards the latter he noted that the presence of xenophobia directed at 'coloured' immigrants was increasing not only within the white population but also among the black majority.[215]

---

[209] A/49/677, para. 46. [210] See for a detailed account, Schaefer, *supra* n. 182.
[211] E/CN.4/1995/78/Add.1; (A/50/476, paras 18–20).
[212] E/CN.4/1996/72/Add.1. [213] Ibid., para. 74(1).
[214] See Germany, Sept. 1995, E/CN.4/1996/Add. 1; France, Sept.–Oct. 1995, E/CN.4/1996/72/Add.3; United Kingdom, Nov. 1995, E/CN.4/1996/72/Add.4.
[215] Feb. 1995, E/CN.4/1996/72/Add.2.

In so far as one purpose of such visits is to inform the international community in more depth of the issues related to both racial discrimination and the efforts to abate or eliminate it, the country studies certainly succeed in that goal. It should also be noted that the Rapporteur, whose mandate was created primarily to focus on racism in the developed world, has in his country missions as in his annual reports chosen countries from different world regions.

The Special Rapporteur has made efforts to assess the impact of his recommendations and suggestions to governments arising from his country missions in follow up procedures. Given the restraint on resources, these efforts are impressive and the evidence provided on the impact of his work credible.[216]

(c) Cooperation with CERD and Other Bodies

Resolution 1993/20, establishing the mandate of the Special Rapporteur, encouraged him to 'have an exchange of views with the various relevant mechanisms and treaty bodies within the United Nations system in order to further enhance their effectiveness and mutual cooperation'. There have been such exchanges of views with a range of bodies, but they have not led to mutual cooperation or enhanced effectiveness of those working against racial discrimination at the UN level.

An initial meeting between the most relevant other body—the CERD—and the Special Rapporteur was held in March 1995.[217] There was agreement that the two mechanisms should work together in a complementary and reinforcing manner. The key advantages of the Rapporteur were that he had the authority to undertake visits to countries and, in addition, he could gather information on countries that had not ratified the ICERD. Concrete proposals for joint action in, for example, police training and mobilizing youth in the fight against racism were discussed. The Committee proposed that it could alert the Special Rapporteur to emergency situations through its new focus on the prevention of racial discrimination. The Special Rapporteur proposed that he could publicize the ICERD and the work of the Committee in his activities.

Little if anything of this positive thinking has come to pass. CERD has noted that since the 1995 meeting cooperation has 'faltered'.[218] One former member has noted that the Special Rapporteur's reports on Germany, France, the United Kingdom, Kuwait, and Colombia completely ignored the concluding observations of CERD with regard to the very same countries.[219] The

---

[216] On follow up, see A/51/301, paras 8–15 and 47 (field missions implementation of recommendations) and E/CN.4/1996/72, paras 62–5 (provisional evaluation). See also the CHR Res. 1997/74, para. 33, inviting governments that have ratified ICERD and which the Special Rapporteur has visited to include information in their periodic reports on measures they have taken to implement his recommendations.

[217] See A/50/476 and summary records of the meeting CERD/C/SR.1095.

[218] A/52/18, para. 666.   [219] Van Boven, *supra* n. 66, at 261.

Committee concluded in its 1999 report to the General Assembly that the Special Rapporteur 'appears to completely overlook the relevance of the Convention on the Elimination of All Forms of Racial Discrimination and the work of the Committee'.[220]

The Special Rapporteur also participated in a joint meeting of CERD and the Sub-Commission in August 1995.[221] In that year he also met with the Bureau of the European Commission against Racism and Intolerance and UNESCO, in both cases to discuss cooperation.[222] Little evidence is available of any practical outcomes of these contacts in the Special Rapporteur's work.

Some of the explanation for the failure of any synergy to develop with other bodies following the appointment of the Special Rapporteur may be found in the poor internal coordination between the relevant members of the human rights secretariat at the UN, a problem compounded by insufficient staff and funding. Given the seriousness of the human rights challenge that racism offers, it is unacceptable that the few mechanisms charged with responding to that challenge appear to function in isolation, and duplicate each other's role where they might build on their comparative advantages. Something is seriously wrong when, as admitted by the Special Rapporteur, a number of countries from whom he requested information replied by enclosing their periodic reports already submitted under ICERD which contained the information he had requested.[223] It is equally wrong that the Special Rapporteur's mission reports on the countries he has visited ignore data already available in periodic reports under the Convention.[224] As inexcusable is his failure to incorporate in a number of his own reports CERD Concluding Observations in respect of countries he has visited.[225] In contrast it should be noted that CERD members are provided with any relevant reports of the Special Rapporteur when considering a state report.[226] The credibility of the entire international human rights system is put at risk by such self-evident examples of lack of cooperation and of a common strategy.

VI. THE UN PROGRAMME OF DECADES AND WORLD CONFERENCES TO COMBAT RACISM AND RACIAL DISCRIMINATION

The United Nations has pursued an ambitious programme of international action, of Decades and World Conferences over the last thirty years with the

---

[220] A/52/18, para. 666.　　　　[221] See A/50/476, para. 33.
[222] E/CN.4/1996/72, paras 5–10.　　　[223] E/CN.4/2000/16, para. 5.
[224] As noted by the CERD, A/52/18, para. 666.
[225] His reports on Germany, France, United Kingdom, Colombia, and Kuwait ignored the CERD recommendations on those countries.
[226] Van Boven, E.CN.4/1999/WG.1/BP.7, n. 25.

goal of the total and unconditional elimination of racism and racial discrimination throughout the world. The General Assembly, however, has acknowledged in repeated resolutions the failure of this vast programme.[227] On the launch of the Third Decade for Action to Combat Racism and Racial Discrimination in 1993, the Assembly noted with grave concern that 'the principal objectives of the previous two Decades have not been attained and that millions of human beings continue to this day to be victims of varied forms of racism and racial discrimination . . .'.[228] Other resolutions have lamented that 'at various levels . . . [racism is] showing signs of increase'.[229] As the Third Decade draws to an end, little interest or support has been shown by the international community in its fate, as evidenced by the paucity of funds contributed to the Trust Fund for the Decade's Programme of Action.[230]

These global activities stem from an initiative of the former Soviet Union beginning in 1971 when it succeeded in having that year declared the International Year to Combat Racism and Racial Discrimination.[231] As a follow-up to the International Year, the General Assembly designated the ten-year period beginning 10 December 1973 as the Decade for Action to Combat Racism and Racial Discrimination. It also approved a Programme of Action for the Decade calling upon member states to cooperate in every possible way in its implementation.[232] The programme set out activities to be undertaken at national, regional, and international levels, and included the idea of convening a World Conference on combating racism and racial discrimination. That conference was held in 1978.

[227] For the latest such admission, see GA Res. 54/154 of 29 Feb. 2000.

[228] GA Res. 48/91 (1993).

[229] See GA Res. 51/81 (1997); GA Res. 52/11 (1998); GA Res. 52/132 (1999); GA Res. 54/154 (2000).

[230] Lack of resources impeded the implementation of many activities of the Decades. A Trust Fund for the Programme for the Decade of Action was instituted in 1973 in application of para. 17 of the Programme of Action for the first Decade and re-established in 1983, in the framework of the Programme of Action for the second Decade. Contributions to the Fund have been scarce and remained below the levels hoped for, despite repeated appeals to governments (see A/47/77 of 1992 paras 12 and 20, A/50/136 of 1996 para. 22, A/51/81 of 1997 para. 16, A/52/111 of 1998 paras 11 and 12). Finally, A/53/132 of 1999, para. 22, requests the Secretary General to make provisions for financing the activities of the Programme of Action from the UN regular budget as a vital contribution to the World Conference.

[231] See also Resolution VII of the International Conference on Human Rights held in Tehran, Iran, in 1968 calling for the establishment of a new United Nations programme on racial discrimination. For the text of the Proclamation of Tehran, and resolutions, from the Final Act of the International Conference, see UN Doc. A/CONF.32/41. The Proclamation, adopted unanimously at the Tehran Conference, includes a reaffirmation of the Universal Declaration of Human Rights. It thus constitutes the first major endorsement of the UDHR by the Eastern Bloc, that had abstained when it was adopted in 1948, as well as by many newly independent countries.

[232] GA Res. 3057 (XXVIII) (1973) and the Programme of Action for the Decade annexed to the resolution.

A Second Decade (1983–93) was proclaimed on the recommendation of the Second World Conference to combat racism and racial discrimination, which took place in 1983.[233] The purpose of the Second World Conference was to evaluate the work undertaken during the First Decade and to chart new measures where necessary.[234]

Both World Conferences to date crumbled under political controversy. The agenda of both Conferences was dominated by South Africa and the Middle East. Highest priority was given to combating apartheid. Israel, along with South Africa, was singled out for special condemnation.[235] The Israel–Arab conflict was central to the failure not only of the Conferences but also of the Decades as a whole. In 1975 a General Assembly resolution described Zionism as a form of racial discrimination.[236] The 'infamous resolution' provoked the withdrawal of the US and Israel from the Programme for the First Decade. Other Western countries, while remaining involved, opposed what they considered a deliberate diversion from the fight against racism. The Second Decade commenced in 1983 with the international community divided along the same lines of confrontation. The comprehensive and far-reaching measures envisaged in the second Programme of Action—in the field of education, teaching, and training, in the protection of minorities, indigenous populations, migrant workers, and in the establishment of recourse procedures for victims—came to nothing. The Programme did not attract funds from those Western states that contributed most to the UN budget.

The onset of the Third Decade (1993–2003) held out hope of a new approach.[237] The Iron Curtain dividing East and West had fallen, a democratic transition was under way in South Africa, and the peace process in the Middle East had taken off. Discussion in the General Assembly reflected a change in tone, and a shift of focus from condemnation of racist regimes to a recognition that discriminatory practices based on culture, nationality, religion, or language affected states throughout the world. The 1993 World Conference on Human Rights in Vienna had moved the question of equality

[233] GA Res. 38/14 (1983).

[234] A study on the achievements made and obstacles encountered during the First Decade was entrusted by the Sub-Commission to Asbjorn Eide. E/CN.4/Sub.2/1989/8/Add.1 (1989). See *supra* n. 184.

[235] See Reports of the 1978 and 1983 World Conferences to Combat Racism and Racial Discrimination, A/CONF.92/40 and A/CONF.119/26, respectively. Para. 18 of the 1978 Declaration (A/CONF.92/40) states: 'The Conference condemns the existing and increasing relations between the Zionist State of Israel and the racist regime of South Africa, . . .' . Para. 19 expresses deep regret for the situation of Palestinians, calling on Israel to cease all practices of racial discrimination against them. These statements are reiterated, although in a less strong language, in the 1983 Declaration, A/CONF.119/26, paras 18 and 19.

[236] GA Res. 3379 (XXX) (1975), formally revoked by GA Res. 46/86 (1991).

[237] GA Res. 48/9 (1993) and Programme of Action annexed. The Programme of Action was revised by GA Res. 49/146 of 1994 dropping measures related to apartheid.

up the human rights agenda and the conflict in the Former Yugoslavia brought home how racism could lead to such extreme practices as ethnic cleansing.[238]

The new (revised) Programme of Action for the Third Decade reflecting budget constraints is far less ambitious in scope than those that have gone before. But as its pared down programme still depends on voluntary contributions to the Trust Fund there is little scope for optimism. A review of the period 1994–2000 shows that out of a dozen seminars envisaged in the Programme, only five have so far been held.[239] Planned research into the causes of the new manifestations of racism and racial discrimination does not appear to have been undertaken.

The Third Decade may be rescued in its final phase by the momentum generated by the forthcoming (third) World Conference Against Racism, Racial Discrimination, Xenophobia, and Related Intolerance, to be held in South Africa in 2001, to the preparation of which the activities of the Decade's Programme have been focused.[240] The Resolution convening the Conference places emphasis on the need to address in a comprehensive manner all forms of racism and racial discrimination and to focus on action-oriented and practical measures to eradicate racism, including measures of prevention, education, and protection and the provision of effective remedies.[241] It stressed the importance of taking a gender perspective into account

---

[238] See Vienna Declaration and Programme of Action and the text concerning the elimination of racism, A/CONF.157/23 (1993), Part II B.

[239] These are: *Seminar on the Implementation of the International Convention on the Elimination of All Forms of Racial Discrimination with Particular Reference to Articles 4 and 6,* E/CN.4/1997/68/Add.1; *Seminar on the Role of the Internet in the Light of the Provisions of the International Convention on the Elimination of All Forms of Racial Discrimination,* E/CN.4/1998/77/Add.2; *Seminar on Immigration, Racism and Racial Discrimination,* E/CN.4/1998/77/Add.1; *Seminar of Experts on Racism, Refugees and Multiethnic States,* A/CONF.189/PC.1/9; *Expert Seminar on Remedies Available to the Victims of Acts of Racism, Racial Discrimination, Xenophobia and Related Intolerance and on Good National Practices in this Field,* A/CONF.189/PC.1/8. See also the final draft of the Model National Legislation for the Guidance of Governments in the Enactment of Further Legislation Against Racial Discrimination (HR/PUB/96/2). On the non-implementation of the Plan of Action, see also the recent reports submitted to the General Assembly by the Secretary-General, A/52/528 and A/53/305.

[240] The Office of the High Commissioner for Human Rights is to serve as a focal point of coordination. Before the decision of the General Assembly to convene the (third) World Conference against Racism, no focal point existed within the Office of the High Commissioner for Human Rights, which was in charge of the Third Decade. See GA Res. 54/154 (1999) welcoming the establishment of a racism project team within the OHCHR.

[241] GA Res. 52/111 (1998). The first PrepCom (1–5 May, Geneva) adopted the draft provisional agenda based on five major World Conference themes, which are: 1. Sources, causes, forms and contemporary manifestations of racism, racial discrimination, xenophobia and related intolerance; 2. Victims of racism, racial discrimination, xenophobia and related intolerance; 3. Measures of prevention, education and protection aimed at the eradication of racism,

throughout the preparations for and in the outcome of the World Conference. It encourages the organization of regional and national meetings in preparation for the event.[242] Unprecedented attention is given to the role of civil society and non-governmental organizations in contributing to a positive outcome for the Conference.[243] The year 2001 has been designated by the General Assembly as the 'International Year of Mobilization against Racism, Racial Discrimination, Xenophobia, and Related Intolerance'. This decision is intended to draw the world's attention to the objectives of the World Conference and give new momentum to the political commitment to the elimination of racism.[244]

VII. CONCLUSIONS

This chapter has reviewed international human rights approaches to the problem of racism and racial discrimination over the last fifty years. It is a review that must conclude with a mixed verdict in terms of achievement. If success is to be measured in terms of the ending of racist and colonial regimes in the world, then there have been positive results. Apartheid is no more and decolonization is virtually complete. But if success is measured in terms of the global rejection of racist theory or beliefs and the elimination of all forms of racial and ethnic discrimination, the record is dismal.

racial discrimination, xenophobia and related intolerance; 4. Provision of effective remedies, recourse, redress, [compensatory] and other measures at the national, regional and international levels, and; 5. Strategies to achieve full and effective equality, including international cooperation and enhancement of the United Nations and other international mechanisms in combating racism, racial discrimination, xenophobia and related intolerance, and follow-up. See the report of the Commission on Human Rights acting as the Preparatory Committee for the World Conference on its first session (1–5 May 2000), A/55/307 and annexed the decisions adopted by the first PrepCom.

[242] Expert seminars on regional themes were held in Warsaw, Poland (5–7 July 2000), Bangkok, Thailand (5–7 Sept. 2000), Addis Ababa, Ethiopia (4–6 Oct. 2000), Santiago, Chile (25–27 Oct. 2000). Four regional preparatory conferences are also scheduled in Europe, Africa, the Americas, and Asia. The first one—the European Conference against Racism— took place in Strasbourg from 11–13 Oct. 2000. See the General Conclusions of the European Conference against Racism, EUROCONF (2000) 7 final, 16 Oct. 2000.

[243] This is reflected in the appointment in late 1999 of an NGO liaison officer by the Secretariat for the World Conference against Racism, established within the Office of the High Commissioner for Human Rights. Another unprecedented aspect of NGO involvement in the World Conference is the funding of NGOs by OHCHR to support their participation at three of the four regional conferences—the conferences taking place in Santiago for the Americas, Dakar for Africa, and Tehran for Asia. In addition, the OHCHR is funding four networking meetings for NGOs to permit them to plan their input into the NGO Forum which will take place in South Africa just prior to the government conference. On the preparatory process for the World Conference, see A/55/285.

[244] A/53/132 1999, para. 37.

The pressure from the newly independent Asian and African countries, who became in the early 1960s the majority voice in the General Assembly, forced the pace on decolonization and apartheid. That pressure also laid the foundations of what has become the UN human rights system. But there was a cost. The struggle for racial equality and against discrimination became incorporated into the larger political and ideological conflicts of the Cold War. In the aftermath of the Cold War the issue of race threatens to be a continuing ideological battleground between developing and developed world. One indication was the clash at the first PrepCom held in Geneva for the 2001 World Conference, between the Western, African, and Latin American groups on the subject of compensation for the descendants of slaves and for indigenous populations.[245] The prospect of the World Conference reaching the necessary consensus for common action on a global basis towards the elimination of all forms of racial and ethnic discrimination appears remote.

Perhaps the most important if modest goal for the forthcoming World Conference would be the acceptance that new thinking is required. It should start from the premise that the subject is more complex than is often acknowledged and needs a long-term approach. A beginning has been suggested with the proposal that the CERD should agree a statement on the scope of the definition of racial discrimination in the Convention. In particular there is a need to bring out the distinction between discrimination based on colour and other differences, including cultural, which attract hostility and discrimination. Whether it is appropriate to label all forms of ethnic discrimination as racism in a normative definition requires study. Another element of a new approach should be a renewed emphasis on equality as a central component of international human rights law. In concrete terms that would require linking the goal of eliminating racial discrimination with the efforts to eliminate other forms of discrimination. Exploring the common links as well as the overlap between different forms of group discrimination may help to release the subject of racism and racial discrimination from its historical and politicized past. It would also identify the degree of progress or lack of it in removing other dimensions of discrimination, for example discrimination on grounds of religion or belief or sex discrimination.

The political and ideological environment in which the human rights activities directed at combating racial discrimination have been pursued in the past has served to isolate such efforts from other fields of anti-discrimination work. It also appears to have resulted in a distance between, for example, CERD and the bodies implementing the UN Covenants, the Human Rights Committee and the Economic, Social and Cultural Rights Committee. The

---

[245] See n. 241 *supra* and the confrontation over inclusion of the word 'compensatory' in the draft agenda for the World Conference between developed and Western countries, A/CONF.189/PC.1/21, 16 June 2000.

advancement of the international protection of human rights in the twenty-first century in theory and practice should be based on a new alignment between the promotion of equality and non-discrimination and the implementation of substantive human rights. A significant beginning has been made in the case of gender.[246] But there is also a need to address other categories of discrimination and exclusion as mainstream human rights concerns.

New norms strengthening protection against racial and ethnic discrimination are in prospect when the 1990 International Convention on the Protection of the Rights of Migrant Workers and Members of Their Families comes into force. The need for ratification of this Convention will be highlighted at the World Conference. The implementation of this important Convention provides an opportunity for the existing treaty bodies to rethink the relationships between the anti–discrimination treaties and the general human rights instruments. The Convention should not emerge as another unconnected initiative in the international protection of human rights.[247]

The fight against racial discrimination and prejudice needs above all a new emphasis on education. Education will be a topic at the World Conference. It is to be hoped that the need to bring together disparate initiatives in this field will be pursued. Thus, the efforts of the Special Rapporteur on Religious Intolerance to encourage the teaching of tolerance in schools and the activities generated by the current Decade on Human Rights Education (1995–2004) should be linked to any new UN initiatives on anti-racism education.[248] The experience of NGOs and of regional bodies such as the Council of Europe and OSCE in the fields of building tolerance and combating prejudice against minorities must be used in similar programmes at the global level.

The World Conference should also consider whether proclaiming another decade against racism and racial discrimination is called for. The idea behind decades has been to educate world opinion on the evils of racism. They have failed in that purpose. Fresh ideas are needed in the vital battle to involve public opinion on the side of tolerance and rejection of racism and xenophobia.

---

[246] Mainstreaming women's rights in UN activities dates from the Vienna World Conference on Human Rights 1993. See Vienna Declaration and Programme of Action, A/CONF.157/23, Part II B(3), para. 37, providing that '[gender] issues should be regularly and systematically addressed throughout relevant United Nations bodies and mechanisms'.

[247] The call by the Independent Expert, Mr Philip Alston, for radical rethinking of the working of treaty bodies, including his suggestion that the monitoring function for the Migrant Workers Convention ought to be undertaken by an existing treaty body in place of a new committee, is an excellent place to begin such discussion. See *supra* n. 152.

[248] The Special Rapporteur on Religious Intolerance will report on his educational work in an international conference to be held in November 2001 in Madrid. Press Release GA Third Committee 34th Meeting, 25 Oct. 2000. On implementation of the Decade on Human Rights Education see report of the High Commissioner on Human Rights to the General Assembly A/51/506 (1996).

The European experience of concentrating such activities over a year would seem to be a better alternative.[249]

The most important achievement of the international human rights approach to the elimination of racial discrimination has been to establish in international law a prohibition on racism as a state ideology and on the practice of all forms of racial or ethnic discrimination. Not only are these prohibitions part of international customary law but the majority of the world states that have ratified ICERD have embraced a range of duties obligating them to eliminate any such discrimination by legislative, educational, and other means. The encouragement of states in the pursuit of these goals will continue to be the vital and central role of CERD. The monitoring work of that body has expanded beyond discrimination on grounds of colour to include the full range of victims of discrimination, including ethnic minorities, immigrants, and indigenous peoples. CERD needs for the future to work more closely with national and regional anti-discrimination programmes and bodies, as well as to have access to leading research on ethnic relations and inter-cultural education in different parts of the world. CERD's increasingly complex mandate requires more specialist expertise to be added to the Committee's membership if it is to have influence on the policies of states parties. A committee with greater expertise would also in time encourage a wider acceptance by states of the Article 14 individual petition procedure as well as universal ratification of ICERD.

The Vienna World Conference on Human Rights urged the UN bodies to cooperate and avoid overlap in their activities.[250] That has not occurred in the field of racial discrimination. The Commission's Special Rapporteur appears to plough his own furrow without reference to the CERD. It is trite to say that such a situation serves only to undermine the credibility of the entire UN effort to offer leadership in the campaign to eliminate racial discrimination. In particular it makes even more difficult the task of persuading states to fully meet the financial needs of both mandates. It is to be hoped that a coherent United Nations strategy for the future on combating racial discrimination will emerge from the World Conference and that it will provide a coherent role for the Special Rapporteur that reinforces rather than undermines the work of the CERD.

---

[249] The Council of Europe launched a European Youth Campaign against Racism, Xenophobia, Anti-Semitism and Intolerance, which was carried out from 1994 to 1996. See ECRI, *Activities of the Council of Europe with Relevance to Combating Racism and Intolerance*, CRI(99)56 final, Strasbourg, September 1999. Subsequent to this campaign, the European Union declared 1997 the 'European Year Against Racism'. See the report from the Commission on the implementation of the European Year Against Racism (1997), COM(1999)268 final.

[250] See A/CONF.157/23 Part II A.

7

The Mistakes of the Good European?

DAMIAN CHALMERS*

Erro de Português	*Portuguese Mistake*
Quando o português chegou	When the Portuguese arrived
Debaixo duma bruta chuva	In the midst of a wild downpour
Vestiu o índio	He dressed the Indian
Que pena!	What a shame!
Fosse uma manhã de sol	If it had been a sunny morning
O índio tinha despido	The Indian could have undressed
O português.	The Portuguese.
OSWALDÓ DE ANDRADE (1890–1954)	OSWALDO DE ANDRADE (1890–1954)

I. INTRODUCTION

The adoption of Directive 2000/43/EC is a heroic tale.[1] It is a tale of a loose network of non-governmental organizations and Commission officials, with the opportunistic assistance of the Presidency of a small State, the Portuguese, seizing a small 'window of opportunity' against the seemingly insuperable odds of the institutional requirements of Article 13 EC and a context in which many Member States were pressing for less EC legislation not more and in which the most explicitly racist Government in the Union's history had a veto over the adoption of any measure. How this came to pass will undoubtedly be the subject of many policy analyses. Whether, given its unusual circumstances, it can act as a model for the understanding of other legislative contexts is less clear. The most remarkable feature of the saga is not that legislation was adopted, however, but that the legislation adopted was the most wide-sweeping equal opportunities legislation in the Community's history. For the dramatic effects of the measure, both in its remit and its resonance, are not in doubt. The legislation not only extends into the nooks and crannies of national life not covered by any other EC anti-discrimination

---

Note: The author wishes to thank Nathan Barreto and Jill Peay. All errors are the author's.
[1] Directive 2000/43/EC, implementing the principle of equal treatment between persons irrespective of racial or ethnic origin, OJ 2000, L 180/22.

legislation, but it does so on a matter of 'constitutional status'. For all bar three of those Member States with written constitutions contain provisions in these constitutions prohibiting discrimination on grounds of racial or ethnic origin.[2] National constitutional doctrines will have to take on board the Court of Justice's interpretations of the Directive, just as it, one imagines, will be sensitive to existing doctrines and debates within the Member States.

The importance of the Directive transcends the status of the players. Questions about respect for racial and ethnic difference lie at the heart of debates about securing the 'good life' and a 'plural society'. To purloin a phrase, the Directive sets out structures, which not so much dictate that 'Thou shall not oppress a stranger' but rather 'Thou shall treat a stranger as a brother'. The intensity of the demands imposed are searching ones, however. Does this duty require one to treat the stranger like one's own brother or like he treats his brother? In relation to the poem set out above, is the Portuguese required to offer the Indian all the advantages enjoyed by the Portuguese in colonial Brazilian society or is he required to let the Indian run free and naked through the emerging Brazilian cities with no concern for the Catholic mores of the time? The debate is, of course, the old liberal/multicultural debate transferred to a Community context. The premise of one is the right to equal treatment within the framework of a single set of values. The premise of the other is the equal recognition of the values of all different collective identities.[3]

The Community context is a particularly beguiling one for this debate. For, as the first part of this essay traces, the context within which the Directive was negotiated and adopted has led to many of the central structures of both models being present within the Directive. The Directive is, moreover, largely ambiguous over how these fundamental paradoxes are to be resolved. It is argued here that traditional liberalism/multiculturalism debates have been a dialogue of the deaf. Criticisms of the other have led each tradition to ignore its own failings. In this, each mirrors the foundational failings of the other. The danger here, moreover, is not merely one of repetition of this particularly sterile debate. It would also be a failure to rise to the challenge of the Directive, by failing to locate its resources sufficiently within the institutional capabilities and limits of the European Community.

---

[2] The three are Denmark, Finland, and Ireland. The most wide-ranging comparative study of national legislation in the field was the one done by the Swiss Institute of Comparative Law for the Council of Europe in 1997. European Commission against Racism and Intolerance, *Legal Measures to Combat Racism in the Member States of the Council of Europe* (1997, Council of Europe, Strasbourg).

[3] This is, of course, a huge oversimplification of the numerous shades of opinion within each school and the nuances of each school. The central division is that one is premised on a single set of values being hegemonic and the other on the recognition of as many value-systems as collective identities. The liberal/multicultural dichotomy has been used, as, although charged, it does not carry as much baggage as others such as modernist/postmodernist.

In this context, it is argued, in the last part of this chapter, that the European Community has hitherto been remarkably unsuccessful at creating a common political culture premised upon shared political values. It has, by contrast, been rather good at provoking oppositionalities. That is to say at prompting national political settlements to re-evaluate themselves and indeed at prompting reconsideration of questions of governance and territoriality more generally. This suggests that the European Community would be unsuccessful at trying to foster a common culture on race relations or ethnicity. The Directive allows it, by contrast, to impose common structures of intercultural evaluation which require Member States to commit themselves not to fostering the values of individual cultures or universal values, *per se*, but to the value of multicultural diversity. The latter is a good in itself, as it is a perennial on-going reflexive project which is central to the development of liberal values and the learning processes of particular cultural communities.

Styling the Directive as an instrument of intercultural evaluation entails a number of things. It involves acknowledgement of the value of the multicultural society through recognition of a wide variety of collective identities, whose presence is to be valued and protected. Recognition of these collective identities should not give rise to a false equality. Different collective identities have varying levels of resonance and impose differing levels of demand on their members. The inability to map the detailed contours of collective identities should not lead to a 'blindness' to the most salient claims of these communities. These salient claims should be valued and protected as shared political values insofar as they do not create conflicts with the claims of other cultural communities. For the multicultural society implies the ability and value of each community to practise its beliefs where these do not violate the beliefs of others. There is, finally, a principle of intercultural evaluation. This commits cultural communities to negotiate in cases of conflict of beliefs or where a practice is challenged by outsiders as central to a cultural commitment. Such negotiations will be embedded in particular contexts across a wide variety of arenas. They are also agonistic in nature rather than concerned with determining essential truth claims. Nevertheless, the requirement of intercultural evaluation commits each party not only to press its claim but to evaluate its own practices in the light of the claims of the other. This implies a duty to couch one's claims not on one's own terms but using the language of the other party.

The genius of the Directive is that, if interpreted in a particular manner, it provides, through the judicially applicable norms and private governance regimes within it, the institutional machinery to realize these objectives. Such a schema would, moreover, be genuinely *communautaire* in that it is not concerned with truth-finding but with prodding national life-worlds into reconsidering their boundaries and their patterns of inclusion/exclusion. Nevertheless, as a schema, it suggests a common vision, albeit a confined one of the Directive. Unfortunately, common visions are inimical to the chaotic manner in which policy-making usually develops within the Community, with colliding interests pushing their vision of politics in multiple and poorly coordinated arenas. Nevertheless, the demands of the Directive press. Academics would surely fail in their task, if in this area of all areas, they did not suggest structures which allow all those within the European Union the possibility of creating the good life.

II. LIBERAL VISIONS OF RECOGNITION: FROM THE POLITICS OF HONOUR TO THE POLITICS OF DIGNITY

The politics of non-discrimination, the imperative for 'equals to be treated alike', is inseparable from the politics of Dignity. It was the onset of liberalism, as Charles Taylor has observed, which resulted in the latter concept emerging as a replacement for the politics of Honour.[4] Whilst Honour presupposes the existence of certain social hierarchies, as it is necessarily a quality that could not be possessed by everybody, Dignity is, by contrast, a more egalitarian concept. It is both a quality that inheres to everybody and it also implies duties of equal recognition. Not only is my dignity to be respected, but I must respect the dignity of others.[5] This politics of dignity immediately suggested a tension between two poles. My 'right to dignity' first creates a politics of autonomy or agency. There can be no discrimination unless an individual's ability to pursue something has been impaired (e.g. the right to seek education, health care, work, political advancement without discrimination). The non-discrimination principle, as institutional guarantor of the politics of Dignity, therefore sets out a series of entitlements, which protect and enable individual agency. As Kymlicka observed:

we have two preconditions for the fulfilment of our essential interest in leading a life that is good. One is that we lead our life from the inside, in accordance with our beliefs about what gives value to life, the other is that we be free to question those beliefs, to examine them in the light of whatever information and examples and arguments our culture can provide. Individuals must therefore have the resources and liberties needed to live their lives in accordance with their beliefs about value, without being imprisoned or penalised for unorthodox religious or sexual practices etc. Hence the traditional liberal concern for civil and political liberties.[6]

---

[4] Taylor, 'The Politics of Recognition', in A. Gutmann (ed.), *Multiculturalism: Examining the Politics of Recognition* (1994) 25, at 26–7. See also, on this precise point, Berger, 'On the Obsolescence of the Concept of Honour', in S. Hauerwas and A. MacIntyre (eds), *Revisions: Changing Perspectives in Moral Philosophy* (1983).

[5] On this see Habermas's discussion of Hobbes where he argues that any political model of equality cannot be derived from a private law model based on autonomy, but entails a form of sociation within which each agrees to limit her autonomy to accommodate the autonomy of the other. J. Habermas, *Between Facts and Norms* (1996), at 89–94.

[6] W. Kymlicka, *Liberalism, Community and Culture* (1989), at 12–13.

The foundational status given to the principle of individual agency has implications for the *regulatory* reach of the non-discrimination principle. It requires that the State, as a central guarantor of the non-discrimination principle, intervene wherever it is necessary to protect individual choice. As individual agency can be infringed as easily by private as by statal actions, the non-discrimination principle modulates the relationship between state and civil society in a manner that justifies State intervention in a whole series of private relationships. This relationship becomes thereby a paradoxical one, where the invocation of private choice and autonomy is used to legitimate greater bureaucratic management and increased judicial intervention.[7] As a corollary, these powers are to be reflected in corresponding far-reaching duties on the part of State *vis-à-vis* civil society, whereby cases of discriminatory behaviour by private parties also become constructed as cases of regulatory failure whose causal effects lie, in part at least, in either inadequate State resources, management or political will.

The politics of autonomy also has implications for *territorial* reach of the non-discrimination principle. In particular, it pushes for the non-discrimination principle to be regulated at a cosmopolitan level. The bestowal of deontological status upon individual choice results in it being something that precedes and transcends any territorial administrative action. The right to choose, insofar as it does not require extensive consideration of the particular environment which informs that choice, is something that becomes universally acknowledged, and therefore something that is susceptible to global regulation.[8] Moreover, local action can always be construed as something which potentially restricts and threatens individual choice. This inevitably leads to arguments for regulation of the regulators through the creation of new more cosmopolitan layers of government which will assess the extent to which the formers' behaviour restricts choice.

As the imprint of individual agency cannot determine how choice be exercised without robbing the individual of the possibility of dignity, it can do no more than set out conditions enabling the exercise of choice. The consequent disinterest in the question of power, the external manifestation of this exercise of choice, has led to the charge of an insensitivity, on the one hand, to the varying value of these entitlements to different parties. And, on the other, that

[7] In the EC context see the proposal for a new Directorate General to administer human rights policy, Alston and Weiler, 'An "Ever Closer Union" in Need of a Human Rights Policy: The European Union and Human Rights', in P. Alston (ed.), *The EU and Human Rights* (1999) 3.

[8] It has thus been possible to develop UN instruments prohibiting non-discrimination, most notably the International Convention on the Elimination of all Forms of Racial Discrimination 1966, 60 *UNTS* 195; International Covenant on Civil and Political Rights, 999 *UNTS* 171, Article 2; International Covenant on Economic, Social and Cultural Rights 1966, 999 *UNTS* 3, Article 2(2).

it alone can provide no solution for the problem of interdependence, whereby the exercise of one party's choice negates another's.[9] For this reason, many modern, liberal writers place equal emphasis on the other axis within the politics of Dignity—that of the mutual recognition of difference. The requirement that all individuals be accorded equal respect entails recognition of that which allows each individual 'to be true to their own originality'.[10] For it is these structures that enable individuals to develop and project their own identities and, through that, achieve some form of self-fulfilment and self-realization. In this case, it is not agency that is being protected, but the structures, beliefs etc that stabilise and inform identification (e.g. gender, race, sexual orientation, ethnicity, disability, etc.). This transforms the establishment of the non-discrimination principle into a permanent, on-going, unfinished project. A bland statement prohibiting discrimination will not suffice. For there will only be no discrimination when the attributes that go towards establishing that individual's identity are fully recognized and protected. As identity-formation is a dynamic process continually being remade and established through social interaction,[11] it may go unprotected not only as a consequence of some atavistic failure of political will or legal misapplication, but as a result of the evolutionary and unstable nature of this process, which leads to the need for the content of the non-discrimination principle being constantly contested and reconfigured.

This sets in motion countervailing, particularist tendencies to those universalist ones set up by the principle of individual agency. As recognition is based on notions of acquaintance and trust, individuals might recognize certain duties to, and consequently attributes in, those proximate to them that they would not grant universally (e.g. the parent to the child, neighbours to each other, community responsibilities). These structures would, moreover, be particularly central to their idea of 'What am I?' A corollary of this is that if these duties are to be politically regulated, they should be regulated by those governance structures most proximate to the citizen. Within liberal thought, because of its considerable resources, this has traditionally been taken to be the nation-State.[12]

---

[9] The forms of liberalism most vulnerable to these charges are those that focus on liberalism solely as guaranteeing human will or human choice.

[10] Taylor *supra* n. 4, at 31. A similar argument lies at the basis of Walzer's more communitarian theory of multiculturalism. See M. Walzer, *Spheres of Justice: A Defence of Pluralism and Equality* (1983), at 314.

[11] On this aspect of identity-formation see Conover, 'Citizen Identities and Explorations of the Self: An Empirical Exploration', 2 *Journal of Political Philosophy* (1995) 133.

[12] For an advocate of this position, see D. Miller, *On Nationality* (1995). There is obviously an inconsistency here in privileging the nation-State over other more local structures. Seglow, 'Universals and Particulars: the Case of Liberal Cultural Nationalism', 46 *Political Studies* (1998) 963, at 969–70.

This axis between autonomy and dignity is present in all paradigms which acknowledge the distinctness of different types of discrimination—be it race discrimination, sex discrimination, discrimination on grounds of sexual orientation, etc. For acceptance of these different forms is acknowledgement that there are different identities being violated that are worthy of protection. Yet how are the tensions between the two to be mediated? The third feature distinguishing liberal thought is that it considers resort should be had to some ideal of the good life, which is universalizable across time and space. As something universalizable, it becomes a centralized ideal concerned with securing universal respect for an irreducible core of individual autonomy and individual difference based on individuals' biological identity. Certain cultural practices can never be allowed, no matter how central they are to particular individuals, which violates this core.[13]

How this core is articulated varies between writers. For Kymlicka, the value of cultures lies in their providing the structures—be they values, beliefs, attributes or relationships—which enable choice to be informed and monitored.[14] He sees no value in those cultures whose structures or conditions of membership unnecessarily restrict individual autonomy.[15] Whilst Taylor's theory of recognition of multiculturalism is premised upon protecting individual identity rather than individual autonomy, a similar structure is present in his arguments. Taylor sees cultures as providing the contexts and narratives within which individuals can locate themselves in the world. Yet, once again, he only considers that those cultures be supported which both contribute to benign forms of individual identity and are not unnecessarily suppressive or exclusive. A culture must contribute to the 'good life' for it to be supported within a multicultural, liberal society.[16] But, as Zižek has noted, this resort back to some idealized identity inevitably results in the liberal view of multiculturalism and non-discrimination being tainted with a degree of cultural imperialism:

Multiculturalism is a disavowed, self-referential form of racism, a 'racism with a distance'—it 'respects' the Other's identity, conceiving the Other as a self-enclosed 'authentic' community towards which the multiculturalist maintains a distance made possible by his/her privileged universal position. Multiculturalism is a racism which

[13] Classic debates revolve around female circumcision or severe penalties for the publication of certain works. See B. Parekh, *Rethinking Multiculturalism: Cultural Diversity and Political Theory* (2000), ch. 10.

[14] Kymlicka, *supra* n. 6, at 162–78.

[15] Id., *Multicultural Citizenship* (1995), at 152–65.

[16] Taylor, *supra* n. 4, at 51–60. Some authors argue that Taylor's and Kymlicka's work is not necessarily contradictory as the values of cultures are dual, namely that they promote and sustain both individual identity and individual autonomy. This is indeed the gist of Joseph Raz's later work on this debate. J. Raz, *Ethics in the Public Domain: Essays in the Morality of Law and Politics* (1994), at 177–9; 'Multiculturalism: A Liberal Perspective', *Dissent* (1994, Winter) 67. For a strong criticism of this see J. Habermas, *Die postnationale Konstellation* (1998), at 113–14.

empties its position of all positive content (the multiculturalist is not a direct racist; he or she does not oppose to the Other the *particular* values of his or her own culture); none the less he or she retains this position as the privileged *empty point of universality* from which one is able to appreciate (and depreciate) other particular cultures very properly . . .[17]

Thus, whilst there is intuitively something appealing in denying legitimacy to certain forms of malignant belief, such as White Supremacism, which are traditionally Western, liberalism ties itself up in knots over how to deal with traditions that do not fall within well-established, Western pigeon-holes.[18]

Liberalism also holds that individual identity be not tied too closely to collective identities. Appiah, for example, notes that collective identities should not be so tightly scripted that they 'make it hard for those who want to treat their skin and their sexual body as personal dimensions of the self'.[19] On its face, there is once again something very appealing in this. Collective identities are constructed as facilitative in nature—structures which enable individuals to create their own life-histories without their being stereotyped or forced down narrow paths. This, however, betrays a narrow view of identity-formation. Identities constrain as well as facilitate. For they are not merely structures entered into by individuals, but forms of external identification imposed upon them by others. 'Blackness' refers, above all, to an 'imagined community' based upon a tradition of slavery, neo-colonialism and exclusion. Williams has noted, therefore, how:

blacks are defined as those whose expressed humanity is too often perceived as 'taking' liberties, whose submission is seen as a generous and proper 'gift' to others rather than as involving personal cost.[20]

This failure has, in practical terms, led to the liberal paradigm having great difficulties in resolving the question of 'affirmative action'. It is not simply that choosing X in place of a 'better qualified' Y seems to offend the notions

[17] S. Žižek, *The Ticklish Subject* (1999), at 216.

[18] Examples might include the views of certain Islamicists who believe that blasphemous works should not be published or the practices of certain hospital wards in the United Kingdom in areas where there are high proportions of Muslims not to inform parents of the sex of the foetus in the belief that Muslim parents are more likely to terminate the foetus if its sex is female.

[19] Appiah, 'Identity, Authenticity, Survival: Multicultural Societies and Social Reproduction', in A. Gutmann (ed.), *Multiculturalism: Examining the Politics of Recognition* (1994) 149, at 163.

[20] P. Williams, *The Rooster's Egg: On the Persistence of Prejudice* (1995), at 71. In similar vein in relation to gender, Iris Marion Young has stated ' "women" is the name of a series in which some individuals find themselves positioned by virtue of norms of enforced heterosexuality and the sexual division of labour', I. Young, *Inclusion and Democracy* (2000), at 100. See also Young, 'Gender as Seriality: Thinking about Women as a Social Collective', in I. Young (ed.), *Intersecting Voices: Dilemmas of Gender, Political Philosophy and Policy* (1997).

of individual autonomy strongly present within this paradigm, it is that the cognitive blindness of the liberal paradigm prevents it being able to identify, in the first place, the modalities through which asymmetries of power are developed and disseminated.

The fourth feature distinguishing most liberal writing, derived from its high faith in individual agency, is that the individual is construed in terms that are strongly self-determining and self-expressing. She is not something whose qualities are continually being reconfigured and transformed through the networks within which she is located.[21] Instead, the Subject has more or less the same attributes whatever the circumstances She finds herself in. This results in approaches to cultural identity being adopted, which are often 'essentialist' in nature. Attributes are ascribed which are seen as relatively static in nature. They do not change, as the individual's subject-position changes. Furthermore, as these attributes are separated from the individual's agency, they are externalized. They are features that exist as objectivized, observable 'matters of fact' quite separate from the individual's subjectivity. Central to this notion is the nineteenth-century concept of 'type'. A typology of groups is conceived with each group conceived as being essentially and permanently different and being classified through a series of observable, distinguishable, physical, or cultural characteristics.[22] Group-membership involves these attributes being in turn ascribed to the individuals. These attributes can be biological or genetic in nature[23] or they can be 'group-circumscribed values' such as belief in a common descent[24] or identification of the group with a particular language, religion, custom, cuisine, dress, etc.[25] Essentialist approaches adopt the classificatory tools of racist ideologies, but turn these on their head by insisting that the criteria used by the latter as a basis for discrimination are, in principle, not to be used. Certain totems are created which attribute physical patterns or norms of behaviour of the group, and thereby, indirectly of its members. These are used not only as a reference point for gauging actions taken against individual members of the group—resort to these will therefore be considered racist, discriminatory, etc.—but also,

---

[21] The starting point for actor-network theory is B. Latour, *We Have Never Been Modern* (1993). A fine collection of essays exploring its themes can be found in J. Law and J. Hassard (eds), *Actor Network Theory and After* (1999).

[22] M. Banton, *Racial Theories,* 2nd edn. (1998), at 76–81.

[23] The view of some scholars is that this is the 'essence' of racial categorizations. See R. Benedict, *Race and Racism* (1983), at 96–7; Appiah, 'Racisms', in D. Goldberg (ed.), *Anatomy of Racism* (1990); R. Miles, *Racism* (1989), at 71–3.

[24] This has been construed by some as the 'essence' of an ethnic group. T. Eriksen, *Ethnicity and Nationalism* (1993), at 10–12.

[25] Increasingly, debates about the politics of cultural identity have straddled conventional distinctions between race and ethnicity and near hybrid categories, such as 'cultural racism' have been developed which include the above. Goldberg, 'The Semantics of Race', 15 *Ethnic and Racial Studies* (1992) 544.

paradoxically, generate expectations about the behaviour or features of individual members of that group.

Within the liberal model of political economy essentialism has become the dominant paradigm adopted by policy-makers. In particular, it is the central structure behind the famous 1951 UNESCO statement on Race, which conceived of race as a 'physical fact'.[26] It is present in the Convention on the Elimination of Racial Discrimination, the most influential structure in securing the development of race relations legislation across Europe, in which race and ethnicity are considered as discrete, observable categories.[27] It is present even in norms, such as those in Article 3 of the German Constitution, not developed in response to the Convention but in which race is treated as a series of 'shared hereditary characteristics'.[28] In part, this is, undoubtedly, because it fits with more general, liberal views influencing Western governance of the individual as a Universal Subject possessed of an inner core of being, separable from any external attributes used to identify her. In part, it is also, however, that essentialist views on race and ethnicity render these subjects more governable, and therefore facilitate the transformation of these questions into a regulative ideal. Group attributes can be relatively clearly articulated in legislation, thereby allowing clear markers to be provided, which stabilize societal expectations about the limits of acceptable behaviour. Their generalizable nature also allows a political economy of race or ethnicity to be developed. The traditional instruments of government, such as statistics, can be applied, to develop and act on information about questions such as the 'levels' of racism in society, the ethnic mix of society, the behaviour of different groups, interrelations between different groups, etc.

III. THE ARCHITECTURE OF A LIBERAL ETHIC WITHIN EC RACE DISCRIMINATION LAW

The history of the development of Article 13 EC, more generally, and Directive 2000/43 are replete with structures which have served to reinforce the central features of this liberal ethic within both these legal instruments.

(i) Article 13 EC as an Outgrowth of the Discourse of Fundamental Rights

In the institutional history of the EC, it is probably correct to see Article 13 EC emerging as a concrete manifestation of the more general prohibition on

---

[26] On this debate see A. Montagu, *Statement on Race* (1972).

[27] *Supra* n. 8, Art. 1(1).

[28] For discussion of this see European Commission against Racism and Intolerance, *supra* n. 2, at 177.

non-discrimination. It will be remembered that isolated forms of discrimination were prohibited in the EEC Treaty. These operated, variously, in the fields of EU migration,[29] gender,[30] and competitive advantage law.[31] In the 1970s, these were re-rationalized by the Court of Justice as being particular instances of a more general prohibition on non-discrimination.[32] This rationalization allowed, on the one hand, a relationship to be drawn between these different forms of discrimination whereby the similarities were emphasized and the differences diminished. In this way, rather bizarrely, the principles safeguarding women's maternity rights were in some way taken to be comparable to those prohibiting certain forms of national labelling. It also allowed these all to be linked up to the discourse of fundamental rights. For, just as the 'fundamentality' of the principle of freedom of expression has resulted in its tenets being applied to situations as different as political censorship, pornography, advertising, and media concentration, so the 'fundamentality' of the general prohibition on non-discrimination is used to justify its application to equally diverse arenas. The similarity, in all cases, is taken to be the arbitrary restriction on individual agency. This discourse also allowed for the non-discrimination principle to be used as an argument for an extension of EC competencies. If all forms of discrimination were illicit and fundamentally wrong, then it was a failure of EC governance that it prohibited only certain forms of discrimination. In this, the central legitimation for an EC competence in race and ethnicity was tied by its advocates to two quintessentially liberal positions.

The first was that the EC should act to protect it as a fundamental right. The earliest coordinated EC, the Joint Declaration of the Institutions against Racism and Xenophobia, thus condemned such practices on the basis of the 'prime importance for the respect for fundamental rights'.[33] Successive Resolutions of the European Parliament condemned these practices on a similar basis.[34] It was also given as one of the reasons for the need for the creation of the European Monitoring Centre on Racism and Xenophobia.[35] Finally, the Commission initially proposed Directive 2000/43 alongside a package of measures,[36] which included a proposed Action Plan to combat the types of discrimination mentioned in Article 13 EC for the period 2001–6[37] and a proposed Directive to combat all forms of discrimination mentioned in

---

[29] Case 167/76 *Commission v France* [1974] ECR 359.
[30] Case 43/75 *DeFrenne v Sabena* [1976] ECR 455.
[31] Joined Cases 117/76 & 16/77 *Ruckdeschel v Hauptzollamt Itzehoe* [1977] ECR 1753.
[32] Case 2/74 *Reyners* [1974] ECR 631.   [33] OJ 1986 C 158/1, Preamble, alinea 2.
[34] e.g. Resolution B4-0261/94, OJ 1994 C 323/154; Resolution B-4 1239/95, OJ 1995 C 308/140. Most recently see 'Resolution on racism, xenophobia and anti-Semitism and further steps to combat further racial discrimination' OJ 1999 C 98/488.
[35] Regulation 1035/97/EC, OJ 1997 L 151/1, Preamble, alinea 1.
[36] OJ 2000 C 116/12.   [37] OJ 2000 C 116/7, Preamble, alinea 1.

Article 13 EC in the field of employment. Its justification for these measures was that these would reinforce fundamental rights by eliminating variations in the scope, contents, and enforceability of anti-discrimination legislation.[38] Most tellingly, the Portuguese President of the Council issued a statement on adoption of Directive 2000/43/EC that such legislation was an essential part of the Union's being founded on the basis of respect for fundamental human values.[39]

The second was that, as non-discrimination was a universal ideal, any breach was equally egregious. From this it was arbitrary, even discriminatory, for EC social policy to prohibit certain forms of discrimination in the field of gender, but not equivalently egregious acts in the field of race and ethnicity.[40] Directive 2000/43/EC in this sense became no more than a process of rationalization of an on-going process.

(ii) The Emergence of an EU Political Economy of Race

One of the pressures that led to a 'Europeanization' of race and ethnicity was that it provided new regulative resources for the management of these questions. In particular, it allowed national agencies the possibilities to develop new instruments free from the constraints of domestic public spheres.[41] National governments began to instigate the garnering of new resources, mechanisms, and institutions at an EC level, with the traditional administrator, the Commission, not through any lack of formal powers on its part, taking a relatively subsidiary role.[42] In particular, it was the French and German Governments, both concerned, at the beginning of the 1990s, about the rise of xenophobic incidents and the Far Right domestically, who pressed for further EC cooperation in the field of race. This action took a number of forms.

The most wide-reaching legislative instrument was Joint Action 96/443/JHA concerning action to combat racism and xenophobia.[43] This

---

[38] EC Commission Communication, *Certain Measures to Combat Discrimination*, COM (99) 566 final, Introduction.

[39] 2269th Council Meeting on Employment and Social Policy, Press Release 8890/00.

[40] European Council Consultative Commission on Racism and Xenophobia, *Final Report* (1995, Secretariat of the Council of the European Union, Brussels) 59; House of Lords Select Committee on the European Communities, *EU Proposals to Combat Discrimination* (9th Report, Session 1999–2000, SO, London), paras 23–6.

[41] On the related field, in terms of policy actors, of migration on non-EU nationals see Guiraudon, 'European Integration and Migration Policy' 38 *JCMS* (2000) 251.

[42] There are Commission surveys on the question of race relations, but these are few and far between, and quite legalistic in nature, e.g. EC Commission, *Legal Instruments to Combat Racism and Xenophobia: Comparative Assessment of the Legal Instruments Implemented in the Various Member States to Combat all Forms of Discrimination, Racism and Xenophobia and Incitement to Hatred and Racial Violence* (1993, OOPEC, Luxembourg).

[43] OJ 1996 L 185/1.

required Member States to make a number of racist acts punishable as criminal acts or exempt from the principle of double criminality,[44] and to improve judicial and administrative cooperation in the field. The most wide-ranging form of administrative cooperation was the establishment of the Kahn Commission at the Corfu European Council in 1994. A 'Consultative Commission' of high-ranking national civil servants was to develop a Union strategy aimed at combating racist and xenophobic violence, which would encompass the making of recommendations on 'encouraging tolerance and understanding of foreigners' and the training of officials. The influence of the Kahn Commission extended beyond this brief, however. Its opinion that the Community should acquire a competence to combat discrimination in the field was highly influential, based upon its experience and the status of its members, in securing the view that, in regulatory terms, Community action possessed an 'added value' to Member State action.[45] In addition, it was the Kahn Commission who pushed for a problem-solving approach to the field, which called for a panoply of regulatory instruments to be used. In the period prior to the Treaty of Amsterdam, the most far-reaching was the establishment of the European Centre for the Monitoring of Xenophobia and Racism whose central task was:

to provide the Community and its Member States . . . with objective, reliable and comparative data at European level on the phenomena of racism, xenophobia and anti-Semitism in order to help them when they take measures or formulate courses of action within their respective spheres of competence.[46]

The development of Article 13 EC and Directive 2000/43 not only took place against the backdrop of this inheritance, but, with the entry into force of the Treaty of Amsterdam, the same 'problem-solving' ethos to race relations was adopted by the Commission. This is most explicit in the Commission's proposed Action Programme for 2001–6 to combat discrimination. The objectives of this programme are therefore to:

(*a*) improve the understanding of issues related to discrimination through improved knowledge and measurement and through the evaluation of the effectiveness of policies and practice;
(*b*) develop the capacity of target actors (in particular Member States, local and regional authorities, independent bodies responsible for the fight against discrimination, the social partners and non-governmental organizations) to address discrimination effectively, in particular through

---

[44] Broadly these included incitement to discrimination, Holocaust denial, public condoning of crimes against humanity, dissemination of racist literature, and participation in racist groups.
[45] European Council Consultative Commission on Racism and Xenophobia, *Final Report* (1995, General Secretariat of the Council, Brussels) 59.
[46] Regulation 1035/97, OJ 1997 L 151/1, Art. 2(1).

support for the exchange of information and good practice and networking at European level;

(*c*) promote and disseminate the values and practices underlying the fight
against discrimination.[47]

A particular vision of race relations is therefore set out, and the duties for
meeting this imputed to the authorities set out in the Action Plan. All this
posits a liberal relationship between the State and civil society in which the
State is given extensive responsibilities to discipline civil society in this regard
and targets against which to review its success in this regard. It also suggests
the establishment of a single *telos* (or limited number of *teloi*) of welfare and
equality to which all Statal and private resources should be harnessed. In this,
the deployment of the instruments used may be extremely imaginative, but
these will all be directed towards a relatively unitary conception of the politics
of dignity.

(iii) The Qualities of the EC Public Sphere

A third feature that pushed towards the Community adopting a liberal model
were the qualities of those non-Statal agents who pushed for the development
of an EC 'race competence'. The central player in this regard was the Starting
Line Group.[48] Established in 1989, this Group was an umbrella network for
about 200 non-governmental organizations, which pushed for the development of EC anti-discrimination legislation. [49] In addition to extensive lobbying of both the supranational institutions and the national governments, the
central achievement of this Group was the adoption of a draft Directive in
1991.[50]

The Starting Line Group, like any lobby group, enjoyed a symbiotic relationship with the Commission and the Parliament. Commission funding
helped sustain it, and its *raison d'être* was, in a corollary manner, bound to
pushing for EC action in the field. There was a further reason for its liberal
inheritance. This was that the Starting Line Group was, to a large part, a

---

[47] OJ 2000 C 116/7, Art. 3.

[48] This has now dissolved with the adoption of the Treaty of Amsterdam and been replaced
by the European Network against Racism.

[49] On the origins of the group see Iganski, 'Legislating Morality, and competing rights:
legal instruments against racism and anti-semitism in the European Union', 25 *Journal of
Ethnic and Migration Studies* (1999) 509; Chopin, 'The Starting Line Group: A Harmonised
Approach to Fighting Racism and to Promote Equal Treatment', 1 *European Journal of
Migration and Law* (1999) 111.

[50] On this draft, from one of its authors, see Dummett, 'The Starting Line: a proposal for
a draft Community directive concerning the elimination of racial discrimination', 20 *New
Community* (1994) 530.

consequence of 'interest group' spillover. Many of its members were migrants groups, who had arrived in Brussels, concerned that the 1992 project might lead to further exclusion and disempowerment of non-EU nationals. The failure to establish a pan-European front by NGOs on the question of migration of non-EU nationals led some of the proponents of the failed scheme to create, as a substitute, a more politically manageable pan-European effort on the part of race.[51] In all this, it became natural for the links between treatment of non-EU nationals and the problematic of race to be emphasized.

In this, the Starting Line Group tied itself to two liberal beliefs. The first lay in the potential effectiveness of State action. The draft Directive proposed far-reaching State powers of involvement for securing equal treatment in an extensive number of areas[52] and in the economic, political, religious, social, and cultural fields.[53] The second, linked to the very strong tie-in between race and migration, was a cosmopolitan belief that the basis for migration and racist policies being equally egregious was in their denial of the Universal Subject. Neither recognized the universal equality of all Humans, regardless of their race, ethnic, national, or cultural origin. The initial proposed Directive therefore sought to prohibit discrimination on 'grounds of race, colour, descent, nationality, national or ethnic origin'.[54]

It is impossible to gauge, in any precise manner, the liberal influence of the Starting Line Group upon the contents of Directive 2000/43. That there was some seems likely. The draft was adopted by the European Parliament as a model for EC legislation in the area.[55] Furthermore, the Starting Line Group proposal was used as a basis upon which to assess original Commission proposals. In particular, the Commission proposals were criticized that they had a narrower remit than that in the final Directive—in particular, they did not apply to voluntary work, housing, or health care.[56] Whilst the remit of the

[51] The central activists behind the Starting Line Group were Isabelle Chopin and Jan Niessen, both of whom were leaders of migrants' organizations based in Brussels.

[52] These were the exercise of a professional activity, whether salaried or self-employed; access to any job or post, dismissals, and other working conditions; social security; health and welfare benefits; education; vocational guidance and vocational training; housing; provision of goods, facilities, and services, participation in social, cultural, religious, and public life. Starting Line Group, *A Proposal for a Draft Council Directive Governing the Elimination of Racial Discrimination* (1993, Churches Committee for Migrants in Europe, Brussels) Art. 1(1). This draft was amended in 1998, see 'The New Starting Line Proposal' in Chopin, *Campaigning Against Racism and Xenophobia from a Legislative Perspective at European Level* (1999, European Network against Racism, Brussels). For analysis of the latter see Gearty, 'The Internal and External "Other" in the Union Legal Order: Racism, Religious Intolerance and Xenophobia in Europe', in Alston, *supra* n. 7, at 350–5.

[53] Starting Line Group, *supra* n. 52, Art. 1(2).   [54] Ibid., Art. 1(1) and 1(2).

[55] See the following Resolutions in this regard, OJ 1993 C 342/19; OJ 1994 C 323/154, para. 9.

[56] COM (1999) 566 final, Art. 3.

Directive is still not as wide as the Starting Line Group proposal, the final text was extended in these fields to accommodate these concerns.

(iv) The Scaling of Race and Ethnicity by the European Union

The scale of European Union law has been described by de Sousa Santos as 'small-scale legality' in the manner in which it decides which features of any activity are legally meaningful.[57] Small-scale legality is inattentive to the intimate context and detail of a legal dispute, but moves wider considerations to the fore through setting any dispute against a broader backdrop of legal and social relations. This is the scale generated both by the pan-European Union territorial scale of EC law and the diverse number of political, economic, and social relations that any EC text must accommodate.

The poverty of detail and context in small-scale legality pushes towards a liberal view of race and ethnicity. A European Community statement on race cannot be sensitive about the intricacies of every situation. What it is able to do, however, is relate activities to one another—determine that two forms of detriment suffered at opposite ends of the EU are legally identical. It does this precisely through the establishment of generalizations within which there is a direct correlation between the broadness of the generalization and the capacity to draw legal comparisons. Highly totemic imagery—desecrated Jewish cemeteries and burnt-out asylum shelters—were thus used in both the institutional and academic literature to justify an EC race competence,[58] even though the central burdens facing most people facing discrimination involve highly context specific questions of manners, taste, lifestyle, and fit.[59] In similar fashion, EC legal and political instruments frequently relapse into very general and sweeping language on the question of race and ethnicity. It is sufficient in this regard to point to the first and the most recent EC institutional developments.

---

[57] B. de Sousa Santos, *Toward a New Common Sense: Law, Science and Politics in the Paradigmatic Transition* (1995), at 463–4.

[58] Institutional examples include both the Evrigenis and Ford Reports of the European Parliament, European Parliament, *Report Drawn up on Behalf of the Committee of Inquiry into the Rise of Fascism and Racism in Europe* (1985, European Parliament, Luxembourg), and ibid. (1991, OOPEC, Luxembourg). See also EC Commission, *Action Plan against Racism*, COM (1998) 183 final. Academic examples include Alston and Weiler, *supra* n. 7, at 14–15; Gearty, *supra* n. 52, at 327; Bindman, 'When will Europe Act Against Racism?', 2 *European Human Rights Law Review* (1996) 143; Guild, 'EC Law and the Means to Combat Racism and Xenophobia', in A. Dashwood and S. O'Leary (eds), *The Principle of Equal Treatment in EC Law* (1997).

[59] Brief *et al.*, 'Just Doing Business: Modern Racism and Obedience to Authority as Explanations for Employment Discrimination', 81 *Organizational Behaviour and Human Decision Processes* (2000) 72.

The first was the Evrigenis Report of the European Parliament in 1985. Prompted by the election of French Front Nationale MEPs in 1984, the central focus of its wider-ranging comparative study of race relations is acts of physical violence in the Member States. It ends with a call for a 'European policy on inter-community relations'. Such a policy would regulate relations between communities identified by various parameters (e.g. ethnicity, culture, religion) and would:

bring together around a consistent framework of principles and objectives, such strands as what is usually called 'Community policy' on migration, action in defence of fundamental rights and freedoms, some aspects of political cooperation (relations with large immigrant populations) and educational, social and cultural policy.[60]

Beyond being a rhetorical flourish on the importance of fundamental rights, this Report offers little instruction on how the delicate balance between the politics of dignity and the politics of autonomy should be struck. Things had changed little by the time of the adoption of Directive 2000/43/EC. The justifications given for the Directive are therefore placed against the backdrop of two contexts. The first is that as the Union is required by Article 6 TEU to respect fundamental rights and democracy,[61] it should therefore have an anti-discrimination policy as a requisite to its being a democratic polity. The other is that discrimination based on racial or ethnic origin might undermine objectives of the EC Treaty, such as the attainment of a high level of employment and social protection, economic and social cohesion, developing the area of freedom, security, and justice, and raising the standard and quality of life.[62] An instrument thus founded, on the one hand, on providing institutional legitimacy for the EC and, on the other, as instrumental to securing other EC objectives is unlikely to be finely attuned to the contextual complexities of the problematic of race and ethnicity. It will, at best, fall back on general, received conceptions of the problem.

There is a second reason why small-scale legality leads to liberal views of race and ethnicity. Small-scale legality is the scale which requires race relations law to negotiate and accommodate the broadest number of political, economic, and social pressures. In negotiating any text, there is concern that it might be too costly not just upon industry, but particularly small and medium-sized enterprises. Worries occur also about how far it should be imposed upon and how it should be incorporated within the political and social architecture of Member States. Concern will be expressed that it not be too disruptive of existing conceptions of race and ethnicity. The 1996 Joint Action adopted by the Council to combat racism and xenophobia was therefore accompanied by no less than four Declarations by different Member

[60] European Parliament, *Report Drawn up on behalf of the Committee of Inquiry into the Rise of Fascism and Racism in Europe,* PE DOC A 2-160/85 (1985) para. 306.
[61] Ibid., Preamble, alinea 2. [62] Ibid., alinea 9.

States interpreting their own obligations under it.[63] These tensions are also present within the scope of the Directive itself. It not only limits itself to stating that it seeks merely only to establish minimum standards, but many of the conflicts and tensions within the Directive are consciously not resolved. Debates about whether an anti-racism or a multiculturalism strategy should be pursued; the value of affirmative action; the independence of administrative enforcement agencies; the best manner to secure the most effective implementation of the Directive. All these are left open on that a decision on any of these questions would not have been acceptable to at least one national government. All this presses towards a liberal conception of race and ethnicity being adopted simply because this is the least disruptive. It is not simply that most national governments adopt this model and there is most administrative conformity. It also resides in the liberal position being one that tries to secure maximum autonomy for as wide a variety of processes as possible. It therefore sets out a general, stable set of attributes around which it is relatively easy for social, economic, and political relations to adapt.

To be sure, it can be argued that to examine merely the legal texts of EC instruments is misleading. The application of any text in a particular dispute will result in a larger scale being applied. A dispute involving Directive 2000/43, which appears before a national court, will therefore be heavily influenced by the context and details of the dispute. The court will be influenced primarily by the merits of the dispute, and some of the broader questions mentioned earlier will be faded out. Indeed, insofar as the question might be referred up to the Court of Justice, it, and consequently the development of the Directive, will be sensitive to this context. Even if one puts aside concerns about the extent to which the reports of national judges filter out questions of detail during the preliminary reference procedure, it is not clear that, over the *longue durée*, this is so. A ruling of the Court of Justice sensitive to one context is thereby likely to be insensitive to the pressures in numerous other contexts across the Union. These then push to contest the ruling, pressing for the law to take account of their particular circumstances. The result is the development of a process of qualification of the legal text, which permits, over time, the re-entry of the wider social pressures outlined earlier. And with this, as the law tries to take on board a wider number of circumstances and pressures across the Union, comes, of course, a corresponding reduction of scale.

(v) The Reproduction of the Legal Structures of the Nation-State

The final feature that contributes to the adoption of a liberal ethos is that the European Community tends to reproduce legal structures found in

---

[63] *Supra* n. 43. These were the Greek, British, French, and Danish Governments.

nation-State models. This is, in part, because national governments, as important players in the decision-making process, often seek to impose through EC legislation their own national model on the other Member States.[64] The British Government was therefore eager that the Directive require all other Member States to have some equivalent to the British Commission on Racial Equality through the designation of bodies in each Member State charged with promoting equal treatment.[65] Similarly, the French Government insisted that no definition of 'race' be provided within the Directive and that the Preamble reject 'theories which attempt to determine the existence of separate human races'.[66] More architectonically, the Community is also induced to draw upon national structures, however, because these are the central 'cultural frames' in the area. It is these that have informed political understandings and structured debate about expectations about legislation in this area. These will inevitably therefore be the first 'port of call' that the Commission will stop at in developing the content of any proposed legislation.

This has resulted not merely in a transplacement of national forms of institutional machinery to the European level. It is also apparent in how the problematic of 'race' and 'ethnicity' is conceived by the EC. In this, to be sure, the ideologies, histories, and practices that constitute racism differ widely across Europe. As do the national strategies combating racism.[67] Yet all national models converge in their refusal to link the question of racism to the foundations of modern political economy. This is not unproblematic, as such explanations are common in the academic literature. Miles has, for example, suggested that racism stems from a dislocation. The nation-State is, on the one hand, unable to contain the effects of the capitalist mode of production—migration, transnational corporations, international movements of capital—yet at the same time it provides the hegemonic structure within which subjects organize themselves politically and through which they construct themselves as nationalized subjects.[68] Wievorcka, by contrast, links recent forms of racism to the development of post-industrialization. The dislocation produced by the decline in traditional forms of production has led to reorganizations which create future aspirations by reference to symbols of the past. This leads to a renewed prominence for ethnic and racial ideologies.[69]

[64] The phenomenon of competition between law-makers is well documented, A. Héritier *et al.*, *Ringing the Changes in Europe: Regulatory Competition and the Transformation of the State* (1996). The normative implications of this have been less fully discussed in the literature.

[65] *Supra* n. 1, Art. 13(1).   [66] Ibid., alinea 6.

[67] Lloyd, 'Universalism and Difference: The Crisis of Anti-Racism in the UK and France', in A. Rattansi and S. Westwood (eds), *Racism, Modernity and Identity on the Western Front* (1994).

[68] Miles, 'Migration, racism and the nation State in contemporary Europe', in V. Satzewich (ed.), *Deconstructing the Nation: Immigration, Multiculturalism and Racism in '90s Canada* (1992).

[69] Wievorka, 'Racism in Europe: Unity and Diversity', in Rattansi and Westwood, *supra* n. 67.

Such explanations, if adopted, would provoke an existential crisis within the nation-State. This is avoided by the underlying causes of racism being constructed as the responsibility of the individual psyche—to be 'cured' through 'education'.[70] Race relations policy is treated as a reflexive adjustment which addresses the effects rather than the causes of racism. Within this paradigm, law becomes central, as the instrument through which both the individual is ascribed responsibility as the primary source of racism and the State responsibility for dealing with the consequences of racism. Race relations legislation is confined therefore to limiting, monitoring,[71] and punishing the acts of individual legal subjects. This limits its capacities to prompt wider change, as legislation becomes qualified by principles of individuation. Intervention is confined to concrete individual disputes, which come before courts in an ad hoc manner. When this happens, responsibility must be clearly ascribed to specific subjects and such compensation as is given is backward-looking and confined to retribution for individual past wrongs.[72]

IV. THE LIBERAL ETHIC IN DIRECTIVE 2000/43

These pressures are not only likely to influence how the Directive is applied and enforced, but have resulted in the central structures of this liberal ethos crystallizing within the text of the Directive in a number of ways.

(i) The Refrain of Essentialism

The most prominent is in the approach taken as to when discrimination takes place. This regime is intended to be more protective than many national systems. The provisions in Article 2 of the Directive therefore prohibit four types of practice:

Direct discrimination. One person is treated less favourably than another is, has been or would be treated in a comparable situation on grounds of racial or ethnic origin.[73]

Indirect discrimination. An apparently neutral provision, criterion or practice would put persons of a racial or ethnic origin at a particular disadvantage compared with

---

[70] e.g. Resolution by the Council on the Response of Educational Systems to the Problem of Racism and Xenophobia, OJ 1995, C 312/1; Declaration by the Council on respecting Diversity and Combating Racism and Xenophobia, OJ 1998, C 1/1.

[71] Through, for example, stipulating the conditions in which legal subjects can engage in affirmative action.

[72] For more on this generally see Lustgarten and Edwards, 'Racial Inequality and the Limits of the Law', in P. Braham, A. Rattansi, and R. Skellington (eds), *Racism and Antiracism: Inequalities, Opportunities and Policies* (1991).

[73] *Supra* n. 1, Art. 2(2)(a).

other persons, unless these are justified by a legitimate aim and the means used are appropriate and necessary.[74]

Racial harassment. Unwanted conduct related to racial or ethnic origin takes place with the purpose or effect of violating the dignity of a person and of creating an intimidating, hostile, degrading, humiliating or offensive environment.[75]

An instruction to discriminate on grounds of racial or ethnic origin.[76]

Notwithstanding that no definition is provided of racial and ethnic origin, the provision is open to a quintessentially essentialist interpretation in which a finding of discrimination is premised upon the classification and bounding of a racial or ethnic group and the ascribing of attributes to that group. This is most evident in the inclusion of 'covert discrimination' in the prohibition on direct discrimination, whereby illegal discrimination occurs if individuals of a different racial or ethnic group in a comparable situation 'would be' treated differently on grounds of racial or ethnic origin. These involve cases where there is no contemporaneous comparator but there is good reason to believe that if the individual had been of a different ethnic or racial group they would have been treated more advantageously. To prove this, it will generally be insufficient to point to one instance, but will be necessary to point to a recurrent practice against a bounded group. It is also present in traditional interpretations of the indirect discrimination provision. Such interpretations, on the basis of statistically derived data, clump together the attributes of the group. Action is illegal if group members are disadvantaged by reference to criteria that involve those attributes unless there is an objective justification for the use of these criteria.

Essentialist interpretations are supported by the provision on positive action. This allows Member States to maintain general or specific measures to 'prevent or compensate for disadvantages linked to racial or ethnic origin'.[77] Introduced, undoubtedly, to give Member States a free hand with affirmative action programmes, the provision takes a vision of race and ethnicity that is strongly collectivist in nature.[78] As the logic is one of commensurate representation of different groups, where affirmative action is deployed, the merits

---

[74] Ibid., Art. 2(2)(b).

[75] Ibid., Art. 2(3). This is to be defined according to the national laws and practices of Member States.

[76] Ibid., Art. 2(4).

[77] Ibid., Art. 5. It is worth noting that there is one other 'exception' to the principle of non-discrimination. This allows differences of treatment based on racial or ethnic origin where this is a genuine and legitimate occupational requirement for the post, ibid., Art. 4. Language requirements are one example. More famously, practices only allowing members of a particular ethnic group to serve in restaurants serving that ethnic food is another.

[78] This provision was undoubtedly worded such to prevent the Court of Justice reviewing affirmative action programmes in the manner it did in Case C-450/93 *Kalanke v Freie Hansestadt Bremen* [1995] ECR I-3051.

of each individual case are subordinated to the goal of collective equality. Within such a process, there is, indeed, no acknowledgement of individual identities other than as concrete manifestations of bounded, monolithic cultural communities.

(ii) Faith in the Regulatory State

The Directive vests ultimate authority in curbing discriminatory practices with the State. Member States are responsible not merely for ensuring that all legal and administrative provisions comply with the Directive, but also that all forms of private-rule making occurring within their jurisdiction does as well. They are also under duties to police and sanction any discriminatory conduct.[79]

A corollary of these responsibilities for the activities of private actors is that the Directive necessarily has a very wide material reach. It is indeed difficult to conceive of any other EC instrument which provides for such wide-reaching or intrusive intervention in the market-place or in civil society by either national administrative authorities or EC law as Directive 2000/43/EC. The Directive prohibits discrimination in both the public and private sectors in relation to a whole host of activities. Broadly speaking, these include:

- access to the workplace and promotion within it;
- access to vocational training, guidance, and practical work experience;
- employment and working conditions;
- membership of employers', workers', and professional organizations;
- social protection, including social security and health care;
- social advantages;[80]
- education;
- access to supply of goods and services which are available to the public, including housing.[81]

The material remit of the Directive extends well beyond that covered by other EC anti-discrimination behaviour, which has either been employment related, in the case of gender, or, in the case of EU migrants, has not extended to areas such as the supply of goods and services.[82] To be sure, the most serious forms of racial violence are excluded from the Directive, as it does not

---

[79] *Supra* n. 1, Art. 14.

[80] The language seems consciously similar to that in Art. 7(2) of Regulation 1612/68/EEC, OJ 1968, L 257/2.

[81] *Supra* n. 1, Art. 3(1).

[82] There is no provision for this in Regulation 1612/68/EEC, which was previously the most sweeping equal opportunities legislation.

include policing or questions of criminal justice. Yet, it is difficult to think of any other instrument that follows so closely the model for Community intervention, suggested by Weiler, of providing a restraint on the excesses of national life-worlds.[83] University fee arrangements; restrictions on the preparation of Halal meat; allocation of housing by municipal authorities; employer bans on the playing of rap music on grounds of its misogynistic content; bans on wearing of the veil in school; the criminalization of marijuana. These will not only be resolved by reference to Community norms, but ultimate authority will be vested in this regard via reference to the European Court of Justice in the Community institutional machinery.

In all this, however, the Directive still remains an external steering mechanism which recognizes the densities and properties of the subjects it regulates (e.g. the professions, the workplace, centres of education). Attempts are thus made to limit the costs and impediments such legislation might impose on the working of these institutions. As part of its amended proposal, the Commission therefore issued an Impact Assessment Form justifying the proportionality of any costs imposed on enterprises.[84] In addition, these are assumed to have the procedures, internal learning mechanisms, resources, etc. to develop strategies that combat racism with intervention only taking place, as a prima facie exceptional matter, when this has failed to happen. Most obviously, therefore, there is the possibility of implementation through collective agreements between management and labour, if both so request.[85] But, more implicitly, the structure of the Directive, as an instrument of change, is premised upon the assumption that any finding of discrimination will be taken on board by these organizations, absorbed and incorporated into their working practices.

The imposition of duties upon the State for securing the principle of equal treatment creates a bifurcated set of responsibilities for the State. On the one hand, it is responsible for securing non-discrimination as an individual right, by providing for justice and appropriate dispute settlement procedures in individual cases. On the other hand, the principle of equal treatment, as a regulative ideal, requires that the State seek a more general equality, in collective terms, between the different ethnic and racial groups. This collective ideal becomes a regulatory backdrop against which individual disputes take place. Each dispute is no longer simply therefore about individual retribution or justice, but also takes place against the broader context of how it contributes to the more general goal of collective equality.

This is most evident in the judicial machinery set in place by the Directive. The machinery is designed, to be sure, to enable individual access to justice.

---

[83] J. Weiler, *The Constitution of Europe* (1999), esp. 246–56.

[84] See amended proposal for a Council Directive implementing the principle of equal treatment between persons irrespective of racial or ethnic origin, COM (2000) 328 final, at 15–18.

[85] *Supra* n. 1, Art. 16.

Member States are required to ensure that judicial and/or administrative procedures are available to all persons who consider themselves discriminated
under the Directive.[86] Incentives are provided for individual complaints by
the requirement that effective, dissuasive, and proportionate sanctions be
introduced.[87] Furthermore, to ease the path yet further for individual litigation, Member States must provide for anti-victimization measures to be introduced. These must protect individuals from any adverse consequences of
treatment as a result of complaint aimed at enforcing the Directive.[88]

Yet certain structures are put in place to relate the process of judicial settlement to the wider goals of a broader equality of treatment between different
ethnic and racial groups. Member States are therefore required to allow organizations with a 'legitimate interest' in ensuring compliance with the Directive
to bring actions on behalf of an applicant provided they have his or her
approval.[89] This 'test case' provision is not there to secure broader access to
justice for individual applicants. The financial resources of these groups will
be few and the criteria by which they choose which case to support often
opaque and highly instrumental. The 'value' of such groups is precisely in
their targeting of particular litigation to try and secure broad and high-profile
policy change.[90]

The linkage is also present in the burden of proof rules.[91] These provide for
a partial reversal of the burden of proof in cases other than criminal procedures and those where the court has investigative powers.[92] If a complainant
establishes a presumption of direct or indirect discrimination, it shall be for
the respondent to prove that there has been no breach of the equal treatment
principle. The feature of such a rule is that it does not simply facilitate complaints that discrimination has taken place. It also creates new collective
norms of behaviour. In particular, it infers the presence of illegal discrimination wherever patterns emerge over time which suggest one group has been
less favourably treated than another. To be sure, this presumption can be
rebutted by the respondent, but, as it is difficult to prove a negative (e.g. there
has been no discrimination), incentives exist for the respondent to strive for
collective equality of treatment between different groups (albeit in a highly
essentialistic manner) within her area of authority. For if it is shown that there

---

[86] *Supra* n. 1, Art. 7(1). These procedures are, subject to national limitation periods, to be
available after the relationship within which the alleged discrimination occurred has termi-
nated, ibid., Art. 7(1) and (3).

[87] Ibid., Art. 15.   [88] Ibid., Art. 9.   [89] Ibid., Art. 7(2).

[90] The starting point for this within a Community context is, of course, C. Harlow and R.
Rawlings, *Pressure Through Law* (1992).

[91] *Supra* n. 1, Art. 8. This follows the pattern set by Directive 97/80/EC on the burden of
proof in the cases of discrimination based on sex, OJ 1998, L 14/6, Art. 4, as amended by
Directive 98/52/EC, OJ 1998, L 205/66.

[92] Ibid., Art. 8(3) and (5).

is a history of equal treatment, the initial presumption of discrimination cannot take hold. A linkage is thereby drawn between the shadow of individual litigation and more wide-ranging structural change, where the failure to engage in the latter makes the likelihood of the former considerably more imminent.

The treatment of equal treatment as a collective regulative ideal has also led to a diversification in the institutional machinery used to regulate the problem. The question becomes reduced to which set of instruments most 'effectively' contribute to securing equal treatment, with different institutions—each of which configures the issue slightly differently—being laid alongside one another. In addition to the judicial machinery, the Directive proposes three different regulatory routes.

The first is the route of the regulatory agency. Following the model initiated in the United Kingdom, but now followed in a number of Member States,[93] Member States are required to designate a body responsible for promoting the principle of equal treatment of all persons without discrimination on grounds of racial or ethnic origin. Following the myriad of relationships that such bodies have with other organs in the different Member States, the 'independence' of this body and the question of whether it can be submerged into other national human rights agencies is left unresolved. It is required, however, to be charged with providing independent assistance to victims of discrimination in pursuing their complaints; conducting independent surveys concerning discrimination and publishing independent reports and recommendations on discrimination.[94] The advantages of such bodies is that they possess a more focused steering capacity than regulation through ad hoc litigation, but the bureaucratic politics literature suggests that such a model will lead to issues of 'race' becoming tangled with questions of bureaucratic politics. A central feature of such agencies is a tendency to be influenced by a desire to promote their budgets, their prestige, and their problem-solving capacities.[95] This configures not only their tactics, but also the response of other institutional actors who will challenge the legitimacy of certain actions precisely on this basis.

The second route taken is 'regulation by information'. Member States are required to disseminate information about the Directive and implementing provisions to the attention of all persons concerned within their territory. Such 'regulation by information' is a cheap form of regulation, which enables

---

[93] For a discussion of the various national agencies see European Parliament, *From Equal Opportunities Between Women and Men to Combating Racism* (2000) Annex 7.

[94] *Supra* n. 1, Art. 13.

[95] This is, of course, the famous thesis of W. Niskanen, *Bureaucracy and Representative Government* (1971). Within the EU field Majone's writing on the EC's institutional capabilities are premised on similar foundations, e.g. Majone, 'The European Commission as Regulator', in G. Majone, *Regulating Europe* (1996).

desired regulatory effects to be communicated widely and quickly with the hope that societal groups will act upon these in a rationalistic manner to bring about the desired change. Yet any desired message will at best convey bald, highly essentialistic information, which cannot be very context-specific. In such circumstances, it enters the politics of cognition. The interpretation of such information and how it is acted upon will depend upon the recipient's identity, social relations, and the context within which it is received.[96] Some may act upon the information in the required manner. Others, because of their mistrust of EC and national administrative intrusion upon their life-worlds, may act in quite a different direction. Others, because of their existing assumptions about non-discrimination, will assume it has little relevance to them.

The final regulatory route taken is that of 'social dialogue'. Member States shall encourage the two sides of industry to foster equal treatment through the monitoring of workplace practices, collective agreements, codes of conduct, research, exchange of experiences, and good practices.[97] The advantages of this are those of 'reflexive politics'. As the process is one of internal adjustment and the development or adjustment of internal structures, there are few difficulties with minimalist compliance, the possibilities for 'learning' and self-transformation are greater. Yet the place of the employment relationship within the locale of employment and its relationship to broader market-related questions will influence how the problem is conceived and treated. Typically, critics have observed that such processes can preserve asymmetries of power, lack transparency, and can lead, in the worst cases, to the commodification and marginalization of the questions of race and ethnicity.[98]

(iii) Retention of the Institutional Features of the Nation-State

The replacement of the politics of honour by the politics of dignity took place within a discrete set of institutional circumstances, the development of the modern constitutional State. The development of the non-discrimination principle was thus tied to the onset of the principle of citizenship, a concept which, traditionally at least, has been tied very strongly to the

---

[96] The writing on this by social scientists is enormous. A good introduction is contained in P. Macnaughten and J. Urry, *Contested Natures* (1998). For empirical analysis within the environmental field on how social relations modify perception see Grenstad and Selle, 'Cultural Theory, Postmaterialism and Environmental Attitudes', in R. Ellis and E. Thompson (eds), *Culture Matters: Essays in Honour of Aaron Wildavsky* (1997).

[97] *Supra* n. 1, Art. 11.

[98] On the limits of self-regulation and how it leads to the commodification of non-material values see Rehbinder, 'Self-regulation by Industry', in G. Winter (ed.), *European Environmental Law: A Comparative Perspective* (1996).

structures of the nation-State.[99] Within this context, the ambit of the non-discrimination principle has concerned not merely the politics of recognition, but also, equally importantly, the politics of non-recognition. For it has always been an expression of concern for those classes of subjects on whose behalf the State claims to strive to work—an admission of claims against the political settlement. Concerned with the political direction of the State, distinctions have always been drawn between 'desirable' identities, subject to protection, and other identities which can be discriminated against.

The influence of national governments in the decision-making process and national frames of non-discrimination law as models for structuring decision-making have resulted in a replication of this 'inclusion/exclusion' nexus. The most explicit is the exclusion in Article 3(2) of the Directive:

This Directive does not cover difference of treatment based on nationality and is without prejudice to provisions and conditions relating to the entry into and residence of third country nationals and Stateless persons on the territory of the Member States, and to any treatment which arises from the legal status of the third country nationals and stateless persons concerned.

This provision extends beyond the ringfencing of the nation-State's territorial 'monopoly of violence' through granting it full autonomy over whom it lets reside within its territory. The Directive is, above all, not to be used to problematize the Nationhood of the Member States, the belief that the latter are founded on some pre-political community, some pre-existing oneness. Thus, subject to the demands of EU citizenship,[100] the Directive not only permits discrimination against aliens, third-country nationals, who are not members of the political community, it also enables discrimination against individuals for asserting that they belong to political communities within this political community. A pub in London does not only not contravene the Directive when it places a 'No Turks' sign on its entrance, it also fails to breach it with a sign that states 'No Scots or Welsh'.

Apart from the huge bounding problems provoked as to what falls within the ambit of the Directive, both the 'imagined' and 'administrative' structures of nationhood have contributed in a boomerang manner to the problem of racism. On the one hand these structures organize political horizons so subjects organize and construct themselves primarily as nationalized subjects.[101] Within such a scenario an endemic political dialectic thus emerges between 'Them' and 'Us' with pre-political communities becoming ever more idealized and closed. Yet, in addition, the political imagery of the nation-State has also

---

[99] R. Bendix, *Nation-Building and Citizenship* (1964); Bauböck, 'Citizenship and National Identities in the European Union', *Harvard Jean Monnet Working Paper 4/97*.

[100] Art. 17 EC. Case C-274/96 *Bickel* [1998] ECR I–7637.

[101] Miles, *supra* n. 68.

infected racial and ethnicity identities. This has led to the same iconography being adapted by traditionally oppressed ethnic minorities. Gilroy, in particular, has therefore decried the manner in which ultranationalist, fraternalistic, and militaristic discourse is central to some black political identities within both the United States and the United Kingdom.[102]

There is another more powerful dichotomy present within the Directive than that drawn by the nation-State. It is that drawn by the bounding of individuals into different racial and ethnic groups. The division of individuals into 'black' or 'white' groups creates forms of classification, which allow the problem of race/ethnicity to be extricated from broader social relations.[103] Racism becomes reduced to a pathology, which, by its nature, is irrational and marginal, and which can ultimately be traced to the psyche of individuals—a form of 'unfair' behaviour. Decisions taken in accepted 'meritocratic' manners, where the best worker is selected or the best students given the highest grades, become intrinsically non-racist. New identities will be therefore recognized only on the basis that they transform themselves so that they be judged according to the 'rules of the game' of the existing model of political economy, whatever hidden structures or biases it may concern. In short, the right of the Indian not to be discriminated will be recognized under the Directive, but only provided he dresses, speaks, and acts like the Portuguese and like the Portuguese believes the fictional 'reasonable Portuguese' should act.

V. THE CRITIQUE OF THE LIBERAL VISION

It is *de rigueur* to criticize the liberal conception of race and ethnicity. Yet, as a caveat, it is important to note strongly positive features of this vision. It provides markers setting out a reasonably clear irreducible core of behaviour that will not be tolerated, for example, individuals cannot be denied access to employment, education, etc. on grounds of their skin colour. The simplicity and starkness of these markers results in this vision communicating powerful images, which are easily understood by and strongly resonant with many citizens in the territory. It is the power and uncomplicated nature of this imagery that generates a consensus not simply that it is wrong to discriminate on grounds of race and ethnicity, but that such an act is fundamentally wrong. The cardinality of this feeling can evoke, in turn, powerful

---

[102] P. Gilroy, *Against Race: Imagining Political Culture Beyond the Color Line* (2000), at 177–237.

[103] Gilroy, 'The End of Anti-Racism', in W. Ball and J. Solomos (eds), *Race and Local Politics* (1990), at 192–3.

feelings of reflexivity on the part of individuals, which causes them to re-examine their actions through the reinterpretation of this vision.

Yet, for all this, the institutionalization of the liberal vision, be it in Directive 2000/43 or most national anti-discrimination laws, contains many flaws. The critiques follow two paths. One set assumes that the objectives of the liberal vision are legitimate, but still sees a number of institutional failings in this regard.

The first concerns the bounding and identification of those racial and ethnic groups, membership of which acts as the basis for protection under the legislation. As a function of the legal system is that it stabilizes expectations through a system of settled norms, a corollary feature is, that it will be relatively slow to adapt. A feature of legal systems is, therefore, whilst they may confer important recognition upon collective identities, they never pioneer recognition. Typically, therefore, race discrimination laws take a narrow view of which collective identities should be recognized. In the United Kingdom, for example, the recognition of gypsies as an ethnic group whose members are entitled to protection from discrimination only occurred in 1989,[104] twenty-four years after the first race relations legislation. It is still the case that travellers,[105] Rastafarians,[106] and Scots, English and Welsh[107] are not recognized as ethnic or racial groups, so to discriminate against somebody on these grounds does not breach British race relations legislation. Furthermore, the bounding of these groups is done in a monolithic manner. They fail to address identities that cross-cut and exist within these groups. A famous example given of the lack of protection to black women is that it would be almost impossible to establish a case against an employer who employs a proportionate number of women (all white) and a proportionate number of blacks (blacks) but is known to dislike black women. The 'intersectional' person who is both black and female, supposedly the recipient of double protection under two sets of legislation, is, in fact, the most vulnerable.[108]

The second concerns the ascribing of qualities to these groups. General attributes, used often to determine the presence of indirect discrimination, are pegged to a group irrespective of context or circumstance. These are usually highly problematic in the 'average cases' they produce, both because of the manner in which they bound a group together and because of the manner in which these attributes are automatically ascribed to members of these groups. No better example of this can be provided than the use of these for affirmative

---

[104] *CRE v Dutton* [1989] QB 783.

[105] *CRE v Dutton* [1989] QB 783. Portuguese law also refuses to recognize 'nomads' as entitled to protection under this area. European Commission against Racism and Intolerance, *supra* n. 2, at 369.

[106] *Dawkins v Department of the Environment* [1993] IRLR 284.

[107] *Northern Joint Police Board v Power* [1997] IRLR 610.

[108] Delgado and Stefančic, 'Critical Race Theory: Past, Present, and Future', *Current Legal Problems* (1998) 467, at 471–2.

action. Thus, whilst British censuses[109] show that 'Whites' enjoy significant advantages in terms of employment, education, and salaries over 'Non-Whites', in most areas, native-born Whites were outperformed by foreign-born Chinese. An affirmative action programme for 'Blacks' would run into the problem that whilst Black Caribbeans, both native and foreign born, constitute one of the least educated groups, the most educated category of all is Black Africans. This latter group is the one, however, whose socio-economic performance least benefits from educational qualifications. In a parallel manner, African Indians enjoy significantly higher class status than Indian immigrants. If an affirmative action were to be created for 'Bangladeshi Women', possibly the most structurally disadvantaged of all groups in all areas, the central disadvantages to this group seem to stem from the division of labour, which entraps them often in poorly paid and precarious employment, and the lack of educational opportunities. And it would have to be used in these contexts. Affirmative action furthering the highly successful career of a middle-class Bangladeshi woman might generate greater pluralism in certain elite arenas. It in no way addresses the disadvantages of the majority of Bangladeshi women in the United Kingdom for the simple reason that she does not face the structural problems of the others. Indeed, the appropriation of the language of disadvantage by privileged individuals, if anything, heaps further degradation as it deprives the truly disadvantaged of one of the few properties available to them, appropriate recognition of their plight.

It might be argued that these are quibbles. The long-term objective of an equitable distribution of social and economic resources between different ethnic and racial groups justifies these exceptional problems. Yet it is precisely the use of these criteria that entrenches disadvantage. For the separation of racial and ethnic criteria from the other processes that inform choice results in the former being insufficiently adaptive to capture many processes that structure discriminatory choices. Thus, organizational literature suggests that it is 'cultural' racism, which is likely to be most endemic within many organizations. X will rarely be refused a job or promotion explicitly because she is black. More likely, she will be refused because she does not 'fit'. She does not dress or behave appropriately; does not get on sufficiently well with other staff or clients; is insufficiently articulate or extrovert; lacks a good sense of humour, etc. These qualities are normally assessed against hegemonic cultural biases and thus inevitably disadvantage those from other backgrounds.[110] They are

---

[109] For a discussion of this see Model, 'Ethnic Inequality in England: An Analysis Based on the 1991 Census', 22 *Ethnic & Racial Studies* (1999) 966.

[110] McConahay, 'Modern Racism, Ambivalence and the Modern Racism Scale', in J. Dovido and S. Gaertner (eds), *Prejudice, Discrimination and Racism* (1986); Lambert *et al.*, 'Private Versus Public Expressions of Racial Prejudice', 32 *Journal of Experimental Social Psychology* (1996) 437; Wittenbrink *et al.*, 'Evidence for Racial Prejudice at the Implicit Level and its relationship with Questionnaire Measures', 72 *Journal of Personality and Social Psychology* (1997) 262.

further enhanced by organizational structures, which amplify such effects, so that whereas particular managers might not share these biases, they will nevertheless act on them on the basis of the organizational culture.[111] A feature of these belief-structures is that they are implicitly racist. The holder will believe, strongly, that they are not racist. They also cut across questions of class, race, gender, 'merit', collegiality, and are sufficiently fluid for it to be impossible to ascribe them as being possessed (or not) by any group. They become constructed as something in liberal thought that is not 'racial' or 'ethnic' in nature for the simple reason that they do not fit neatly within the schema of classification used.

The above criticisms of the liberal institutionalization of race relations broadly accept its philosophy and aims. The argument is essentially one about methodology. The other set of criticisms are critical, however, of the very beliefs and philosophy of liberal race relations.

The very classification of individuals into different racial and ethnic groups creates, it is argued by its critics, an epistemology of race and ethnicity. It is this epistemology—e.g. the provisions of the distinction between black/ white, Jew/non-Jew—which provides the knowledge that enables racism to occur in the first place.[112] To be sure, legal instruments did not create this epistemology. The ethnic cleansing of the Jews from England in the thirteenth century occurred well before any race relations legislation. It would indeed be irresponsible if legislation ignored the pre-existing empirical reality of racial distinctions and failed to curb the worst excesses.[113] Yet the acknowledgement of this does not prevent this epistemology continuing to generate its own 'false' consciousnesses. The classification allows racist assertions to be transformed into 'social facts', which are then used to ground and foreclose argument. Most infamously, in *The Bell Curve*, this epistemology was used to 'establish' that different racial or ethnic groups had varying levels of IQ. These attributes then became the starting point from which it was reasoned that marginalization was merely an inevitable consequence of this fact, and that little should be done to change this 'natural' state of affairs.[114] Through its acceptance of the black/white distinction as a legitimate, self-standing description of certain social relations, law not only legitimates and entrenches this epistemology, it also problematizes its own claims to counter the latter's disruptive effects. For the construction of racist knowledge which attributes,

---

[111] Brief *et al.*, *supra* n. 59. See also Brief and Hayes, 'The Continuing American Dilemma: Studying Racism in Organizations', in C. Cooper and D. Rousseau (eds), *Trends in Organizational Behaviour* (1997).

[112] The perniciousness of this dualism is most elaborately exposed in F. Fanon, *The Wretched of the Earth* (1963).

[113] C. Guillaumin, *Racism, Sexism, Power and Ideology* (1995), at 99–107.

[114] R. Hernstein and C. Murray, *The Bell Curve: Intelligence and Class Structure in American Life* (1994).

simpliciter, different attributes, skills, etc. to different racial or ethnic groups can never be a basis for legal action, notwithstanding its terribly divisive effects, as it does no more than reiterate the dichotomy in the legislation.[115]

The other, more sweeping, post-structuralist charge is that any measure which is explicitly welfarist in nature is implicitly racist. In this context, non-discrimination legislation may act to curb certain 'old' racisms, but, as a welfarist piece of legislation, it will displace and generate 'new' forms of racism resulting in repression of other sections of society. The basis for such a charge is that a concern with the welfare of the population does not merely structure government action. It is also a regulative ideal that generates norms and modes of conduct as to how people are to behave. Individuals are encouraged to work 'hard', behave 'civically', eat and study 'well', etc. both for their sake and to ensure the welfare of the population as a whole.[116] The 'welfare of the population', thus, became an artifice to be protected, which relied heavily, initially at least, on early myths of the 'symbolics of blood' to legitimize these new forms of intervention:

a whole politics of settlement, family, marriage, education, social hierarchization, and property, accompanied by a series of permanent interventions at the level of the body, conduct, health and everyday life, received their colour and their justification from the mythical concern with protecting the purity of the blood and ensuring the triumph of the race.[117]

To be sure, the presence of this 'scientific racism' has diminished as a basis for intervention. Instead, the emergence of 'cultural racism' has led to preservation of existing ways of life being used increasingly as a basis for exclusion.[118] These structures of 'institutional racism' are replicated within the TEU. Article 29 TEU therefore states:

Without prejudice to the powers of the European Community, the Union's objective shall be to provide citizens *with a high degree of safety* [author's emphasis] within an area of freedom, security and justice by developing common action among the Member States in the fields of police and judicial cooperation in criminal matters and by preventing and combating racism and xenophobia.

In this, Directive 2000/43 will protect members of traditionally discriminated groups who seek to uphold and emulate these life patterns such as the

---

[115] It is not clear therefore that a Member State, which published academic league tables of schools alongside league tables of percentages of ethnic and racial minority pupils within that school, would be in any way breaching the Directive.

[116] M. Foucault, *The History of Sexuality: Volume I* (1978), at 145–53; M. Dean, *Governmentality* (1999), at 134–8; A. Stoler, *Race and the Education of Desire: Foucault's History of Sexuality and the Colonial Order of Things* (1995).

[117] Foucault, *supra* n. 116, at 149.

[118] For an example of such literature in the United States which argues that blacks are not educating themselves sufficiently, showing sufficient initiative or developing strong enough family ties to prosper see N. Glazer and D. Moynihan, *Beyond the Melting Pot* (1970).

studious student, the hard-working worker, the deserving recipient of social security. It does nothing to address the fact that these qualities, as traditionally understood by dominant groups, are, definitionally, in shorter supply amongst structural disadvantaged groups. Moreover, in relation to questions of race and ethnicity, these groups are struck by a double whammy. The 'meritocratic' criteria of the Directive not only sweep socio-economic disadvantage under the carpet as simply a case of 'not being good enough'. They are also highly ethnocentric in their nature. In the field of mental health in the United Kingdom, for example, one finds higher levels of schizophrenia among black men than white counterparts from similar backgrounds[119] and that black men are eight times more likely to be compulsorily admitted to hospital on grounds of mental illness.[120]

VI. MULTICULTURALISM AND THE POLITICS OF THE STRANGER

In no other area has postmodernism kicked at such an open door as in the 'politics of difference'. Through liberalism's creation of norms about what cannot be recognized and through its insistence that within any political settlement there is, ultimately, a single, authoritative lens through which this will be interpreted, it has been particularly susceptible to charges that, contrary to the ideals imminent within it, it fails to recognize or purposively 'misrecognizes' difference. Postmodern starting positions on multiculturalism are that there are not two notional poles, autonomy and dignity, which the political settlement must mediate between. As all choices take place within bounded social contexts, the poles of individual agency and dignity are submerged within the broader paradigm of identity. The politics of difference is about recognition of these identities. This process of identity-formation—the question of 'Who am I'—is something, postmodernists argue, which is knowledge-based. For it is derived from individuals being 'involved directly in constructing every facet of reality'.[121] To be sure, in this, this is not simply a question of Will. Individuals will base their identities on cognitive assumptions about the networks of social relationships within which they locate themselves. Moreover, as individuals are continually reconstructing their life-stories, these identities are continually being renegotiated. Yet, central to all this, is direct

---

[119] Lipwood *et al.*, 'Psychiatric Illness among British Afro-Caribbeans', 296 *British Medical Journal* (1988) 950.

[120] Audini *et al.*, *An Analysis of the Use of Part II of the Mental Health Act Using Existing Local Authority and Health Trust Data and Section 136 using data held by the Metropolitan Police* (London, Department of Health, 2000), at 29–32.

[121] J. Murphy and J. Min Choi, *Postmodernism, Unravelling Racism, and Democratic Institutions* (1997), at 46.

individual involvement. Postmodernists claim, therefore, that any attempt to
prescribe identities for others will inevitably be assimilationist and exclusionary. Multicultural strategies must instead:

focus on the right to choose one's identity as the sole universality of the
citizen/human, on the ultimate, inalienable individual responsibility for the choice.
. . . The chance of human togetherness depends on the rights of the stranger, not on
the question who—the state or the tribe—is entitled to decide who the strangers
are.[122]

On its face, the implications of this for the political settlement seem simply to be a recipe for some form of anarchic libertarianism. In fact, most
multicultural writing on this is a little more sophisticated. Their starting
point is to consider the nature of racism. For them the question of race is
enmeshed with asymmetries of power. It only emerges as a 'social force when
individuals or groups behave toward each other in ways which either reflect
or perpetuate the hegemonic ideology of subordination and the patterns of
inequality in daily life'.[123] Racism differs from other forms of inequality,
however, in that it rationalizes these asymmetries through the identification
of a group and the assertion that certain traits essential to that group justify
its inferiority and consequent marginalization and denigration.[124] The position is further complicated by the manifestations of these asymmetries of
power taking a number of forms.[125]

Multiculturalism sees it as the duty of the political settlement to combat
these forms of racist oppression. More recent arguments recognize, in this
regard, that the State (or the EU in this case) has certain uniquely powerful
coordinating capabilities not possessed by either civil society or economic
agents. It has wide-reaching information-gathering powers. Such information
not only enables monitoring to take place, but generates visioning processes
and horizons, which are still central to how many actors situate themselves.
Through the rule of law and policing institutions, it finally has powerful coercive instruments that others do not have. Only the most extreme would deny

[122] Bauman, 'Making and Unmaking of Strangers', in Z. Fridlizius and A. Peterson (eds),
Stranger or Guest? Racism and Nationalism in Contemporary Europe (1996) 59, at 77.

[123] Marable, 'Beyond Racial Identity Politics: Towards a Liberation Theory for
Multicultural Democracy', in M. Andersen and P. Collins (eds), *Race, Class and Gender*
(1995).

[124] For a discussion of the various views on this see Murphy and Min Choi, *supra* n. 121,
at 85–7.

[125] Young has, famously, detailed five forms of oppressive behaviour. Exploitation is the
transfer of resources from one group to another. Marginalization, by contrast, is a denial of
participatory rights in the activities of social cooperation and access to the means of the
consumption. The third form of powerlessness is a lack of authority and sense of self-worth.
Cultural imperialism, by contrast, is the universalization of a dominant group's experience so
as both to stereotype other groups and render their experiences invisible. Lastly, there is physical violence. I. Young, *Justice and the Politics of Difference* (1990), ch. 2.

that the administration is important for policing, as an ultimate arbiter of conflict and for protecting certain basic liberties. Most would agree that only it has the coordinating powers to counter systemic disadvantage.[126]

Yet, this, alone, is insufficient to protect multiculturalism. The latter also requires that the political settlement:

provide conditions for all persons to learn and use satisfying and expansive skills in socially recognized settings, and enable them to play and communicate with others or express their feelings and perspective on social life in contexts where others can listen.[127]

The political settlement's capability to do this is qualified by both the 'social' and the 'self' being decentred. In this regard, the 'social' is constituted by those horizontal relationships outside the administration, which are treated as a matter for political concern. Within these relationships, however, power is heavily dispersed around a series of sites or nodes of power (e.g. the workspace, the school, the hospital, etc.). These have an autonomy from the administration, but also have a political identity in that their actions will be a subject of political debate and action. Their autonomy renders it impossible for the administration to determine (and therefore have exclusive responsibility for) the asymmetries of power that may exist within them. At best, it can do no more than seek to induce them to remedy these, and even then it must rely on the latter's internal procedures and relays to bring this about.[128] Multiculturalists see it not only as impractical for the administration to try and control the problematic of multiculturalism. They also see it as undesirable. For the 'self' is decentred in that she adopts both multiple and fluid identities, and also multiple subject-positions. Any attempt by the administration to chart and protect these identities against some central regulative ideal inevitably falls into all the assimilative dangers of the liberal model. [129]

They thus argue for a more qualified political strategy, which recognizes the political administration's coercive and cognitive limits. The starting point for this is the feature that postmodernists most admire in liberal political settlements, the practice of reasoned critique. They consider that the political settlement should create a politics of interrogation in which politics above all

---

[126] The above is informed by Young, *Inclusion and Democracy* (2000), at 180–8.

[127] Ibid., at 31–2 and 184.

[128] This is a familiar refrain of post-Foucaudian analyses. In relation to race and ethnicity in particular see Rattansi, ' "Western" Racisms, Ethnicities and Identities in a "Postmodern" Frame', in A. Rattansi and S. Westwood (eds), *Racism, Modernity and Identity* (1994).

[129] The seminal contribution on this is, of course, Stuart Hall. See Hall, 'Old and New Identities: Old and New Ethnicities', in A. King (ed.), *Culture, Globalization and the World System* (1991); Hall, 'Who needs Identity?', in S. Hall and P. Du Gay (eds), *Questions of Cultural Identity* (1996).

becomes a place for questioning.[130] This is to be done through the fostering of multicultural imaginaries.

Imaginaries have both a descriptive and a visioning quality. On the one hand, they describe the way society, its institutions, and practices are imagined by those who live in it. Although particular popular imaginaries are often appropriated and sacralized by political elites, they are thus something which inhabit the *habitus* of ordinary daily lives. In this regard, imaginaries are not expressed in theoretical terms but through images and narratives, which are embedded in and reproduce particular social relations. These images and narratives generate common understandings, which, in turn, create common practices.[131] In this respect, they are not so different from definitions of 'cultures' as interpretative communities based on shared understandings.[132] Yet, on the other hand, imaginaries also describe people's imagination of what they could become. They express desires to overcome 'incompleteness or insufficiency in the construction of identities; they invoke perceptual objectives'.[133] It is this tension within them between 'what I am' and 'what I could be' that leads to a perpetual status of self-interrogation. Future desires and ideals are interpreted and analysed in the light of past experiences. Yet, conversely, an individual's current position is continually being questioned in terms of its potential unsatisfactoriness.

Multicultural imaginaries, as a specific subset, are claimed to have a number of particular qualities. They incorporate, first, a desire to define the absolute limits within which the political settlement is conceived. That is to say that multiculturalism envisages that there are a finite number of identities within the political settlements. No single individual or institution may be able to describe all these, but all the individuals within the political settlement, occupying all the different subject-positions they do, could, and this composite is enclosed within the term multicultural. Secondly, multicultural imaginaries suggest an element of 'incompleteness and discrepancy' about the political settlement.[134] There is therefore an ontological relationship between the nation-State and multiculturalism in that multiculturalism refers to that which is left out of any national political discourse. The discourses of multiculturalism and the nation-State thus condition the invocation and interpretation of each other, but they do so through a dialectic within which each

[130] Hesse, 'It's Your World: Discrepant M/multiculturalisms', in P. Cohen (ed.), *New Ethnicities, Old Racisms?* (1999) 205, at 212–14.

[131] The most banal would be loyalties and support for a common football team. The term 'imaginary' is derived from the psychoanalysis of Lacan, but is acknowledged by even liberal writers as an important feature of multiculturalism. Taylor, 'Modernity and Difference', in P. Gilroy, L. Grossberg, and A. McRobbie (eds), *Without Guarantees: In Honour of Stuart Hall* (2000) 364, at 370–4.

[132] S. Fish, *Is there a Text in This Class?* (1980) 171.

[133] Hesse, *supra* n. 130, at 216–17.   [134] Ibid., at 217.

is in perpetual conflict with the other. Finally, multicultural imaginaries suggest some 'investment or disinvestment in any other social vision' of the political settlement.[135] Young thus talks of multicultural politics imposing a duty on all citizens to enter into communicative engagement with one another.[136] In like vein, Mouffe's theory of agonistic pluralism requires citizens to identify all opponents as adversaries whose existence is legitimate and must be supported.[137] In this manner the descent into cultural relativism is curbed, for it suggests that certain identities—the racist, the bigot, or the xenophobe— are incompatible with multicultural imaginaries as these do not acknowledge any value in alternate identities. Furthermore, as a corollary to this, certain advocates of multicultural politics insist that there is a duty upon holders of all cultural identities to consider how their identities can be transformed to create 'solidarities' between them and other identities. Such processes of reflexive re-examination are not grounded in some rootless, cosmopolitan ideals, but, instead, are said to be possible through reference to shared experiences. Gilroy thus talks of the visioning possibilities of black cosmo-politanism.[138] Bloul, meanwhile, explores the 'transversal solidarities' present in so-called borderland identities (e.g. the Chicanos in the United States or the Beurs in France) which occupy the hinterlands of two or more traditional identities, but whose identity cannot be reduced to either of these.[139]

The institutional implications of multicultural imaginaries are multiple. The decentring of politics, as Mouffe has observed, prevents multiculturalism being identified with one set of institutions. For the processes of com-munication giving meaning to cultural identity are so widely dispersed that it is impossible to bring them together under one unifying principle.[140] Instead, Young has maintained, it is more productive to subject all sites of relational autonomy to the claims of multiculturalism. She notes that autarky rarely exists. Instead, individuals are usually implicated in a series of relationships, made not of their own choosing, in which they can support or thwart the actions of others (and the converse). These sets of relationships, furthermore, are rarely closed, but will inevitably be part of broader, interlocking networks, so that a decision in any one arena will invariably have broader implica-tions.[141] Young argues that structures of deliberative democracy should be built into these relationships wherever possible. It is clearly impractical that every relationship be subject to the claims of democratic process. Young,

---

[135] Ibid.   [136] Young, *supra* n. 126, at 50.
[137] See, most recently, C. Mouffe, *The Democratic Paradox* (2000) 80 et seq.
[138] P. Gilroy, *The Black Atlantic: Modernity and Double Consciousness* (1993); P. Gilroy, *Against Race: Imagining Political Culture Beyond the Color Line* (2000), at 279–326.
[139] Bloul, 'Beyond Ethnic Identity: Resisting Exclusionary Identification', 5 *Social Identities* (1999) 7.
[140] C. Mouffe, *The Return of the Political* (1993), at 144–7.
[141] Young, *supra* n. 126, at 230–3.

instead, suggests that these claims only be applied to all units which possess sufficient historical, geographical, and/or socio-cultural characteristics to make construction of a collective identity possible (e.g. workplace, neighbourhood, school). She states, however, that decentredness requires that such institutions 'take the interests of others into account . . . especially where outsiders make a claim on them that they are affected by the actions and policies of that locale'.[142]

Young appropriates four claims of democratic process that are also features of liberal, deliberative models. Inclusion requires that persons whose options are significantly conditioned by a decision should be included in the process of decision-making. Political equality requires that these be included on equal terms. The requirement of reasonableness requires that participants be disposed to reach agreement and not bind themselves to the authority of unquestionable beliefs. Finally, publicity entails that the decision-making process takes place within a context which enables people to hold one another accountable.[143] Unlike civic republican or Habermasian models, such a model does not consider that deliberation's value lies in its enabling the realization of some idealized conceptions of justice or common or generalizable interests. Deliberative politics is rather perceived as something that, since the members of the *Demos* in Ancient Greece demanded that they be heard by those in power, is a tension between

the structured social body in which every part has its place and 'the part of no part' which unsettles this order . . . the political debate is therefore not a rational debate between multiple interests, but the struggle for one's voice to be heard and recognized as a legitimate partner.[144]

Within this context, deliberation maximizes social knowledge by allowing participants to situate themselves *vis-à-vis* others and to obtain a wider panorama of the processes structuring their experiences. It also facilitates collective decision-making by inducing participants to transform the language of their claims from expressions of self-interest to 'appeals to justice' recognizable by other participants.[145]

As a corollary, multiculturalism imposes more constraints on the deliberative process than liberal models. The norm of reasonableness no longer privileges the 'discourse of reason', where particular views are dismissed as inarticulate or half-baked. Instead, disposition to the claims of others requires that weight be given to other forms of political communication such as narrative and rhetoric. For narrative conveys the situated knowledge of differentiated subject-positions

---

[142] Young, *supra* n. 126, at 233–4. In the context of EU law on this see M. Poiares Maduro, *We, the Court: The European Court of Justice and the European Economic Constitution* (1998), at 164–73.

[143] Ibid., at 21–5.

[144] Žižek, *supra* n. 17, at 188. This is also the point of Mouffe, *supra* n. 137, at 80–107.

[145] Young, *supra* n. 126, at 115–20.

and identities. Whilst rhetoric, whilst not reasoned, is central to political demands as a critique of exclusion and a clamour for inclusion. As a process is one of agonistic pluralism, the norm of inclusion, by contrast, requires that appropriate consideration be given to the proper representation of structurally disadvantaged groups. The norms of inclusion and political equality also problematize the question of representation, a point rarely discussed in liberal models.[146] Young has observed that the condition of representation is a necessary condition of the unavoidable fact that full participation by all those significantly affected by a decision is rarely possible. The norms of political equality and inclusion therefore condition not only the relationships between those participating in the decision-making, but also the relationships between representatives and their consistencies. In particular, she sees them as calling for clear procedures of authorization and accountability, which require representatives to go back and mediate views they have expressed in decision-making procedures with their constituents.[147]

VII. THE MULTICULTURAL IMAGINARIES OF THE EUROPEAN COMMUNITY

The criticisms of multicultural approaches to race and ethnicity, and they are many, will be considered in due course.[148] For the moment, it is worth pausing to note that the structures of the European Community render it more receptive to the claims of multiculturalism than traditional national models.

It is, first, a political settlement that recognizes its cognitive and coercive limits more explicitly than those nation-States still transfixed with their claim to a monopoly of legitimate violence over their territories. Few serious commentators thus argue that the European Union is in imminent danger of creating a new Super-State replicating all the features of the nation-State. A European Polity has, by contrast, emerged, which at a foundational level perceives both political and legal authority as plural, contingent, interdependent, and contested.[149] At a meso-level this is reflected in legislative processes

---

[146] Ibid., ch. 2.   [147] Ibid., ch. 4.

[148] For the most recent outspoken attack see B. Barry, *Culture and Equality* (2000).

[149] The literature on this point is simply enormous. On political authority see Ruggie, 'Territoriality and Beyond: Problematising Modernity in International Relations', 47 *International Organisation* (1993) 139; Capóraso, 'The European Union and Forms of State: Westphalian, Regulatory or Post-Modern?', 34 *Journal of Common Market Studies* (1996) 29; Anderson, 'The shifting stage of politics: new mediaeval and postmodern territorialities?', 14 *Society and Space* (1996) 133; B. Laffan, R. O'Donnell, and M. Smith, *Europe's Experimental Union: Rethinking Integration* (2000). On legal accounts see de Sousa Santos, *supra* n. 57, at 284–8, 376; Bankowski and Christoulidis, 'The European Union as an Essentially Contested Project', 4 *ELJ* (1998) 341; N. McCormick, *Questioning Sovereignty: Law, State and Nation in the European Commonwealth* (1999).

which are so institutionally balkanized that institutional authority is plural and that institutions place a series of 'horizontal' and 'vertical' controls on one another.[150] These procedures are also characterized by the emergence of supplementary, informal networks incorporating both administrative and private actors, who seek to arbitrage between the different points of formal authority.[151]

The consequence of this is a hesitance upon the part of EC institutions, as one set of institutions within this wider polity, to make foundational claims. The process is thus now consciously self-limiting in that every legislative and administrative act is gauged, through its submission to the subsidiarity principle, against whether it exceeds the limits of EC powers.[152] Multiple sources of authority and knowledge are usually acknowledged and deferred to in EC law. Classically, therefore, European economic law has recognized the capacities of each Member State to make separate health, consumer, and environmental assessments. EC social law has always allowed Member States to assert allocative values independent of the legislation.[153] Such limits are not only acknowledged versus administrative actors, but also via the proportionality principle, versus private actors.[154] This principle not only protects the autonomy of private actors and life-worlds from excessive intervention in their activities by the EC. It also allows these life-worlds, in particular, to press certain claims on the EC in the sense that action will not be proportionate if it does not take account of the knowledge-claims and value-judgments of these life-worlds. Thus, the substantive norms of EC health, environmental, or consumer legislation must have reference to science-based claims, legislation relating to 'public morality' (e.g. broadcasting legislation) to the value-judgments

[150] 'Horizontal controls' are those placed between institutions at the same level of governance. Vertical controls are those between institutions at different levels of governance. Héritier, 'Elements of democratic legitimation in Europe: an alternate perspective', 6 *JEPP* (1999) 269.

[151] Kohler Koch, 'Catching Up with Change: the transformation of governance in the European Union' 3 *JEPP* (1996) 359; Marks, Hooghe, and Blank, 'European integration in the 1980's: State-Centric vs Multilevel Governance', 34 *JCMS* (1996) 341; Laffan, 'The European Union: A Distinctive Model of Internationalisation', 1 *EIOP* (1997); K. Armstrong and S. Bulmer, *The Governance of the Single European Market* (1998), at 52–61.

[152] See *Protocol to the EC on the Application of the Principles of Subsidiarity and Proportionality*, paras 9 and 11 in particular.

[153] All legislation in this field is minimum harmonization establishing a 'floor of rights' beyond which Member States may move. Even within this floor, there are many holes allowing national government autonomy. Examples include the ability of Member States to make their own decisions about affirmative action and occupational qualifications, Article 141(4) EC and Directive 76/207/EEC, OJ 1976, L 39/40, Art. 2(2) and (4); the autonomy of Member States to decide whether to apply TUPE obligations to undertakings subject to bankruptcy proceedings, Directive 98/50/EC, OJ 1998, L 201/88, Art. 4a; and whether to extend health and safety protection to the armed forces, the police, and civil protection services, Directive 89/391/EEC, OJ 1989, L 183/1, Art. 2(2).

[154] *Supra* n. 152, para. 9 alinea 3.

of its subjects, financial regulation to the norms and customs of financial markets, etc.

This lack of foundationalism leads to a heightened sense of reflexivity on the part of EC law. The effectiveness of EC law becomes judged therefore not merely by compliance, but by the extent to which it contributes to the tasks it sets itself. Laffan *et al.* have therefore characterized the mode of much EC policy-making as 'learning by monitoring'.[155] This pathology helps explain why, despite the seemingly high hurdles set by the legislative procedures, some areas of EC law are in a state of continual revision. The single market programme can therefore be seen not merely as a project of market integration, but as an on-going process of regulatory reform. The history of the Single Market Programme has thus involved a journey from concern about EC regulatory reform in the development of the 'New Approach to Harmonization',[156] subsidiarity discussions and the Sutherland Report,[157] to being used as a launchpad for more wide-ranging national regulatory reform in the current SLIM programme,[158] and New Strategy for the Single Market.[159]

This anti-foundationalism and commitment to pluralism finds its way into Directive 2000/43. The most limited expressions of this are that the precise definition of racial harassment is left as a matter of national choice,[160] as are the decisions whether to allow affirmative action[161] and differences of treatment based on the occupational requirements of a position.[162] More wide-ranging is the provision in Article 6(1) that:

Member States may introduce or maintain provisions which are more favourable to the protection of the principle of equal treatment than those laid down in this Directive.

On its face this provision seems puzzling. For, as the Directive seems to lay down a prohibition on unequal treatment, it is unclear how national provisions could be more favourable to the principle of equality. This is doubly so since, as affirmative action is dealt with elsewhere in the Directive, it clearly does not refer to that. The only sense that can be given to this provision is that

---

[155] Laffan *et al.*, *supra* n. 149, at 121.

[156] Council Resolution on a new approach to technical harmonization and standards, OJ 1985, C 136/1.

[157] Maher, 'Legislative Review by the EC Commission: Revision without Radicalism', in J. Shaw and G. More (eds), *New Legal Dynamics of European Union* (1995).

[158] Council Resolution on Legislative and Administrative Simplification in the Single Market, OJ 1996, C 224/5; Conclusions of the Vienna European Council 11–12 Dec. 1998, para. 50. On the reaction of the European Parliament see OJ 1998, C 80/292.

[159] EC Commission, *The Strategy for Europe's Internal Market* COM (1999) 464; Weatherill, 'New Strategies for Managing the EC's Internal Market' 53 *Current Legal Problems* (2000) 595.

[160] Directive 2000/43/EC, *supra* n. 1, Art. 2(3).   [161] Ibid., Art. 5.

[162] Ibid., Art. 4.

it is a recognition that there is no 'Universal Pinnacle' from which identities can be recognized and protected, and that visions of multiculturalism are plural. It is thus an admission that there are identities and subject-positions that it will inevitably fail to accommodate, and this should not prevent these being accommodated. To be sure, the pervasive influence of the nation-State will result in only those so protected by national legislation being cherished, and then only within the territorial reaches of that Member State. Yet, notwithstanding this, it suggests a territorial and cultural pluralism not present within any single unitary State.[163]

A second feature of the European Community is its oppositionality. This oppositionality is a discontent with the contours of the existing political settlement, which manifests itself, first, in an oppositionality to the nation-State. The European Community serves to police and curb the activities of national governments. Indeed, it is not simply that it is an alternative locus of administrative power, but that it is one that challenges the manner and capabilities of national governance that leads to the central tensions between it and national governments. It becomes, thereby, a source of opportunities for all those dissatisfied with the status quo. These features are found in abundance, of course, in Directive 2000/43. It provides not only the opportunity for national race relations and other legislation to be overturned on grounds of non-compliance,[164] it also provides opportunities for the Community to monitor more broadly the 'state' of race relations in national territories by requiring the Commission to report on the impact of the Directive and propose any changes necessary five years after the entry into force of the Directive.[165]

Yet the magic of the European Community is that it stands as something that is, simultaneously, not merely external but also internal to national governments in that it is part of the political settlement. Thus, in terms of policy, as liberal governmentalists have never ceased to remind us, use of the opportunity structures provided by the EC are central to national governments' attaining certain welfare-maximizing goals that would otherwise be impossible. In administrative terms, the workings of the European Community have resulted in a 'fusion' of institutional actors.[166] National administrators are, on

---

[163] The Directive therefore states that it is never to be used as a basis for a reduction in the level of protection in a Member State, ibid., Art. 6(2).

[164] Ibid., Art. 14.

[165] Ibid., Art. 17. This report is to be based upon information provided by the national governments, but must take account of the views of the European Monitoring Centre on Racism and Xenophobia as well as those of the social partners and relevant non-governmental organizations.

[166] Wessels and Rometsch, 'Conclusion: European Union and National Institutions', in D. Rometsch and W. Wessels (eds), *The European Union and Member States: Towards Institutional Fusion* (1996); 'An Ever Closer Fusion? A Dynamic Macropolitical View on Integration Processes', 35 *JCMS* (1997) 267; id., 'Comitology: Fusion in Action. Politico-administrative Trends in the EU System', 5 *JEPP* (1998) 209.

the one hand, central to many of the decision-making processes in Brussels. On the other, as national governments responsible for the implementation and management of EC law within their territories, their compliance with EC law is also an assertion of national administrative power against the institutions of civil society and the market. It is this internality of the European Community to national governments that helps to explain the otherwise paradoxical phenomenon of how the expansion of EC law has led not to a decline of central national administrative power, but to its expansion, rationalization, and consolidation.[167] The consequence of this is that the development of EC law is simultaneously an on-going transformation of the nature, extent, and form of national government. Such process involves the creation of new institutions and processes—agencies, collective agreements, new rights of judicial standing in the case of Directive 2000/43—in the regulation of a particular policy field. Yet, as it is also a redefining of government and as the institutions of government enjoy dialectic relationships with the processes they regulate, this transformation inevitably prompts a self-questioning about the aims of government in the field in question.[168] In many cases, this will happen in informal ways. In the case of Directive 2000/43, this process is not to be a narrow one of administrative reflexivity but is to take place within the wider public sphere. Thus, national governments are required by the Directive to encourage dialogue with non-governmental organizations with a legitimate interest in combating discrimination on grounds of racial and ethnic origin with a view to promoting positive change in this field.[169]

The oppositionality of the European Community is also present in its oppositionality to itself. This is captured in its bifurcated relationship with the notion of 'Europeanness'. European identity, as internal to the European Union, is used to legitimate it and distinguish it from both national and more universalist institutions. It is, indeed, the 'Europeanness' of the European Union that, in turn, leads to its actions contributing towards the development of a European identity. Barry has thus noted how the development of EC legislation in fields as diverse as health and safety, consumer protection, the environment, creates 'competitive and cooperative networks' which act as a form of 'signifier' for Europe. Europe becomes associated with health and safety etc. In a parallel manner Directive 2000/43/EC, thus contributes to the idea of the notion of Europe being associated with the fight against racism.[170]

---

[167] Chalmers, 'The Positioning of EU Judicial Politics within the United Kingdom', 23 *WEP* (2000) 169, at 183–7.

[168] For more on this see Weiler, 'Federalism and Constitutionalism, Europe's Sonderweg', *Harvard Jean Monnet Working Paper 10/00.*

[169] *Supra* n. 1, Art. 12.

[170] Barry, 'The European Community and European Government: Harmonization, Mobility and Space', 22 *Economy and Society* (1993) 314, at 321–2.

Yet the idea of Europeanness, as something also perennially external to the European Union, is an irritant acting continually to expose its limits. This is most brutally obvious in the territorial limits of the European Union. The quest for enlargement is driven, in part, by the idea that the Union will not be genuinely pan-European until it extends from the 'Atlantic to the Urals'. Yet Europeanness is also used as a container for any criticism of the current processes, institutions, and policies of the European Union.[171] The heavy normative language of the considerable literature on European constitutional-ism or European citizenship is thus a plea for a process of European self-renewal through which the 'legitimacy deficit' of these institutions can be redressed. The Europeanness of the European Union thus demands from it a continual process of reflexive self-doubt.

This is expressed in Directive 2000/43/EC in a number of ways. There is, of course, the commitment to consider amending the Directive five years after its entry into force.[172] One can also point to the recognition of multiple visions of equality discussed earlier.[173] Perhaps the most deep-seated structure in this regard is the architectonic provision, set out in Article 1, that the purpose of the Directive is, via providing a framework for combating discrimination on grounds of racial or ethnic origin, to put into effect the principle of equal treatment in the Member States. The implication in this is that the principle of equal treatment may be imminent in the Directive, but is an open-ended ambition which can never be fully realized. It is nevertheless an ambition that will be used to critique the provisions and practice of the Directive. By providing a relationship between this Directive and other forms of anti-discrimination legislation, it will also enable this Directive to be used as a bootstrap for legislation to be developed in other fields along the model set out in Directive 2000/43.[174] In short, the implications of all this are that the anti-discrimination structures in the Directive are simultaneously plural, contingent, and universal.

It might be argued that self-limiting and oppositional qualities are not absent from national structures, although whether they are so vividly present as in the Community model is open to doubt. The most telling manner, however, in which the EC model of governance differs from that of the

[171] On the mythical nature of 'Europe' see Hansen and Williams, 'The Myths of Europe: Legitimacy, Crisis and the "Community" of the EU', 37 *JCMS* (1999) 233.
[172] *Supra* n. 1, Art. 17(2).   [173] Ibid., Art. 6(1).
[174] The Commission has therefore proposed amendment of gender equality legislation to bring 'coherence' in the field of anti-discrimination law, generally, both on the concept of indi-rect discrimination and on the need for independent bodies at a national level to promote equal treatment. EC Commission, *Proposal for a Council Directive Amending Directive 76/207/EEC on the Implementation of the Principle of Equal Treatment Between Men and Women as Regards Access to Employment, Working Conditions and Vocational Training* COM (2000) 334 final, para. 8. For the views of the Economic and Social Committee in this regard see OJ 2000, C 204/7, paras 2–3.

nation-State is that it is much more explicitly decentred. The absence of a thick, collective European identity limits the ability of the EC to legitimate itself through reference to input-oriented models of the public sphere. For the absence of a sense of 'Us' gives the losers no reason to accept the collective decisions of deliberative or majoritarian institutions.[175] Self-legitimation is more easily achieved through output-oriented models of political economy which illustrate how EC measures promote common welfare and solve the problems of its subjects.[176] The justifications for EC action are those of rationalization and efficiency, namely that it brings added value to a sphere of government. This has led not only to a heightened concern about how it is managing the problems of its subject, but also, particularly in the absence of strong coercive powers, to a decentring of government where, increasingly, authority is vested in the subjects of government. Private actors become more explicitly engaged in the business of government. This may be through more active involvement in the decision-making process, be it through the setting of substantive norms[177] or through being granted direct responsibility for the application and implementation of EC law. Decentring also occurs through new responsibilities being imposed on certain nodes of power, such as the workplace, the school, the housing authority, etc. Whilst these seem to constrain the autonomy of the latter *vis-à-vis* the administration, they also augment their regulatory capacities through providing new justifications for management of the actors within their justification. Thus, a norm prohibiting discrimination within the workplace obviously prohibits certain forms of behaviour by an enterprise, but it also requires, or at least legitimizes, the enterprise imposing new norms on its staff, carrying out programmes of training and education, involving itself in other private conversations between staff.

The devolution of political responsibilities in this way creates a terrain for the localized negotiation of identities in the manner advocated by Young. Indeed, possibly the most interesting provision of Directive 2000/43 is Article 11:

1. Member States shall, in accordance with national traditions and practice, take adequate measures to promote the social dialogue between the two sides of industry with a view to fostering equal treatment, including through the monitoring of workplace practices, collective agreements, codes of conduct, research or exchange of experiences and good practices.

2. Where consistent with national traditions and practice, Member States shall encourage the two sides of the industry without prejudice to their autonomy to conclude, at the appropriate level, agreements laying down anti-discrimination rules in

---

[175] F. Scharpf, *Governing in Europe* (1999), at 8–9.   [176] Ibid., at 7–10.
[177] e.g. on the role of CEN within the New Approach to Harmonization see E. Vos, *Institutional Frameworks of Community Health and Safety Regulation* (1999), ch. 5.

the fields referred to in Article 3 which fall within the scope of collective bargaining. These agreements shall respect the minimum requirements laid down by this Directive and the relevant national implementing measures.

It is to be regretted that the horizons of this provision seem to have been curtailed by the traditional employment-focused remit of EC anti-discrimination law. In like vein, it is to be hoped that Member States will, unilaterally, enact similar provisions for other points of authority (e.g. schools, hospitals, health and housing authorities, universities, supermarkets) covered by the Directive. Notwithstanding this, two features are salient within this provision. The first is that, by requiring workplace arrangements to foster equal treatment, it is referring to the notion of equality, mentioned earlier, that is contingent, universal, and plural. It opens up the possibility of recognition of identities, subject-positions that are not recognized elsewhere, but which might be particularly acute in that individual context. A crude example is a factory employing a large number of women of Bangladeshi origin. Any code of practice would recognize the intersectionality of their identities, be particularly responsive to the demands of these identities and do all this within the context of a particular industry situated in a particular neighbourhood. The other feature is that the provision provides decentred rather than decentralized governance. The two sides of industry are not free to agree whatever arrangements they choose. The Directive locates any agreement within a set of networks within which it must respect the changing demands of national and EC law. The concept of 'fostering equal treatment', moreover, implies that any such agreement must respect not merely these formal constraints, but must also have regard to its implications for equal opportunities in areas outside its remit, but which might, nevertheless, be significantly affected.

VIII. TRANSCENDING THE MULTICULTURAL/LIBERAL DIVIDE: DIRECTIVE 2000/43/EC AND INTERCULTURAL EVALUATION

By adopting central features of both the liberal and multicultural models the Directive manages to side-step some of the more withering criticisms of the multicultural model. These have noted that the model is so fluid that its central concepts, those of identity and power, are so elastic as to be almost meaningless. In relation to identity, personal idiosyncrasies are elevated to the same level as powerful, traditional, resonant identities. There is, indeed, something extremely distasteful and elitist about suggesting that certain lifestyle identities[178] have as much resonance and should be placed on the same footing as black identities born of a common history of genocide, slavery, and oppression and continued marginalization and oppression. In

[178] e.g. the right to go foxhunting as part of a British 'countryside' identity is an example.

relation to power, by stating that it is everywhere and this renders all situations political, the more postmodern multiculturalists fail to differentiate it sufficiently. Thus, the pluralism of decentred policy-making can result in existing asymmetries of power being insufficiently challenged and local elites pleading self-regulation as a euphemism for maintaining their hegemony.

Both these dangers seem unlikely in the case of Directive 2000/43 precisely because of its liberal foundational bedrocks. A whole range of identities might be fostered and recognized within the workplace and other locales as a result of Article 11, but the national administrations and the EC will only recognize—and judicially protect—some of these under Article 2. This recognition will differentiate these identities from others and bestow a vintage and protection upon them not given to all identities.[179] In this regard, as this is an equal opportunities piece of legislation, the ones most likely to be quickly recognized are those seen as traditionally disadvantaged. In like vein, the judicial prohibition on discrimination in Article 2, whatever the inherent limits of its remit, will cut across and challenge existing asymmetries of power. Individuals and groups will have claims they did not have before and employers, etc. will not be able to exercise certain forms of power.

To be sure, both liberal and multicultural visions are subject to the Marxist critique that they ignore the extent to which racism is embedded in the division of labour. The division of labour, it is argued, is both a source of racist behaviour by pitting Human against Human and a structural source of racism by marginalizing and pigeon-holing certain groups.[180] There may be some truth in this, but it has perhaps less resonance within an EC context than elsewhere. Such an argument is a wide-ranging redistributive one, which calls for a total abandonment of the liberal model of market democracy. Yet as the EC has never had significant redistributive powers, and is unlikely to acquire such powers in the foreseeable future, it would call for such a dramatic transformation of the EC that it would bear little resemblance to its past or current incarnation.

So, has the Directive, through cherry-picking desirable features of both liberal and multicultural models, got the best of all worlds? The difficulty of such a dual regime is that, in the absence of coordination, it could result in the worst of all possible worlds. Each model may, relying upon the other, not become sufficiently developed. Thus, only a very limited range of rights and identities might be judicially protected and very few collective arrangements developed. Alternatively, one model might suffocate the other. An extensive and dogmatic set of rights and identities might be judicially developed, which

---

[179] It seems, to this author at least, quite right that there be a legal obligation that employers arrange working practices so that Jewish employees can always respect the Sabbath but not that the fox-hunting calendar be so respected. In respect of the latter, if this is important to certain employees, it also seems right that it is something that can be negotiated.

[180] S. White, *Political Theory and Postmodernism* (1991), at 115–16.

by laying down something as discrimination, even though it affronts certain other identities, forestalls any incentive for negotiation. Correspondingly, a series of wide-ranging social arrangements, in the absence of judicial guarantees, might just lead to the creation of new outsiders and outcasts.

It is clear therefore that there has to be some architectonic principle, which provides a guiding hand to coordinate these two competing visions. Indeed, it is only through this structure that a development of a genuinely autonomous 'Community method' can emerge that will provide a genuinely new model of multiculturalism rather than a simple repackaging of old structures in new bottles, albeit ones with European labels. The dual nature of the EC regime requires as a prerequisite that any such model give due weight both to those norms of non-discrimination developed by the judiciary and those developed in 'social dialogue' between private parties. In this respect, the author would argue that the model which can be most fruitfully developed is that which contains the central features of the model of 'intercultural evaluation' developed by Bikhu Parekh.

Parekh's starting point is that human beings are articulated at three levels. These are what they share as a common species; what they derive from and share as members of a cultural community and what they succeed in giving themselves as reflective individuals.[181] The presence of all three elements is central, in his view, to any theory of multiculturalism. Excessive concentration on any one is insufficient. Parekh, thus, notes that the first, which he labels 'human identity', may generate certain universal values—a limited number of acts are, after all, almost universally recognized as crimes—but provides too thin a view of identity to generate sufficient understanding of what constitutes the good life.[182] By contrast, he also critiques many multicultural theories on grounds of their uncritical, essentialistic view of cultural identity.[183] For Parekh, cultures are open-ended, dynamic, internally contradictory, and ambiguous. This is, in part, because they enjoy a mutually constitutive relationship with surrounding political, economic, and other institutions, and so change as these change. It is partly because they have overlapping and multiple forms of membership. It is, however, above all because, as reflective and strategic beings, humans are not fully culturally determined. The norms of cultural community are therefore both continually being contested, debated, and changed by members of the community and being shaped by the environment within which members of that community find

---

[181] B. Parekh, *Rethinking Multiculturalism: Cultural Diversity and Political Theory* (2000), at 122–3.

[182] Parekh, 'Is there a Human Nature?', in L. Rouner (ed.), *Is there a Human Nature?* (1997); Parekh, *supra* n. 181, ch. 4.

[183] He understands cultures as 'historically created systems of beliefs and practices in terms of which a group of human beings understand, regulate and structure their individual and collective lives', ibid., at 143.

themselves.[184] Importantly, as this contestation takes place in concrete institutional settings, the claims, 'reform', and development of cultural communities can not be detatched from the material practices and daily lives of their members.[185]

The triple manner in which human beings are constituted leads Parekh to argue for the preservation of cultural diversity, partly on the grounds of preservation of individual cultures, but, primarily, as a source of 'intercultural evaluation'. Cultural diversity alerts individuals to the diversity within their own community. It also enables mutually beneficially dialogues between cultures by providing each with the opportunity to experiment with the other's ideas. Parekh sees these as undoubted benefits, but they are not the central ones. He observes that, with the onset of modernity, Human Beings lack an 'Archimidean' point—a view from nowhere—from which universal values can be derived. Cultural diversity enables individuals to have:

mini-Archimidean standpoints in the form of other cultures that enable them to view their own from outside, tease out its strengths and weaknesses, and deepen their self consciousness. They are able to see the contingency of their culture and relate to it freely rather than as a fate or predicament. Since cultural diversity fosters such vital preconditions of human freedom as self-knowledge, self-transcendence and self-criticism, it is an objective good, a good whose value is not derived from individual choices but from its being an essential condition of human freedom and well-being.[186]

Cultural diversity imposes, therefore, the duty to respect other cultures, but also the duties to criticize and evaluate them as well as the duty to do the same for one's own. The institutional implications of intercultural evaluation drawn by Parekh are the need for a development of a 'multicultural common culture' which would suffuse both the public and private realms. Such a culture would carry, on the one hand, a strong sense of common (usually national) identity. Such an identity is axiomatic to the sustenance of stable, democratic, structures of authority, which allow collective central decision-making, without which such goods as redistributive justice, preservation of law and order, and giving citizens a collective sense of agency are not possible. On the other hand, the requirement of diversity entails recognition of a wide array of collective rights. Meeting these would require that in the private

---

[184] For a study of how new identities emerged through the interaction of different groups in West London see G. Baumann, *Contesting Culture. Discourses of Identity in Multi-Ethnic London* (1996).

[185] *Supra* n. 181, at 142–58. Parekh, 'Minority practices and principles of toleration' 20 *International Migration Review* (1996) 251. This distinguished him from 'dialogic communitarians' who argue for the development of dialogues outside institutional settings, a position that inevitably relapses into the ratified neo-Kantian 'ideal-speech situation' of Habermas. See E. Frazer and N. Lacey, *The Politics of Community: A Feminist Critique of the Liberal–Communitarian Debate* (1993) at 203–214.

[186] *Supra* n. 181, at 167–8.

realm constituent cultural communities engage each other in a climate of dialogue and equality and that the public realm is constituted by plural representation, negotiable political values, and adaptive modes of deliberation. The recognition of both central and cultural identities would lead in Parekh's view to each sustaining the other. Different communities would see themselves as having a stake in the central settlement thereby strengthening the collective sense of 'We', whilst central recognition of different cultural communities would reinforce the rights and status of the latter.[187]

This institutional vision betrays Parekh's strong liberal leanings. Its heavily normative tone provides no answers as to how coordination of these ideals between different systems—legal, economic, political—would be effected or how these ideals might not become suffocated or reified within the administrative capillaries of the State or legal norms. At first glance, it also seems particularly unsuited for the European Community. There is no sufficiently strong political culture within the European Community that has led, at that level, to a defined sense of 'Us'. There is little evidence, either, that it can be synthesized through the imposition of certain common values. Thus, to give an example that will almost undoubtedly come before the Court, it is unclear how a Court of Justice solution to the dispute in France over the *laicisme* of French education, which gives or denies a right to French schoolchildren to wear items of religious dress, will transfer allegiances or 'Europeanize' identities. More probably, it will merely reinforce divisions and rekindle discontent.

If there is a case for strong central liberal values, these, it would seem, must be developed at the national level. It is at this moment that Parekh's theory, paradoxically, opens up strong institutional possibilities for the European Community. As those shared political values sufficient to underpin and legitimate collective decision-making are only obtainable, if at all, at a national level, the European Community is now liberated from having to set these values. It is, thus, free to play a role in this field quite different from that of the nation-State. This role is not that of creating a 'multicultural common culture' but rather requiring the presence of *common multicultural cultures*. The latter involves providing the rules of the game for the process of intercultural evaluation within national arenas.

There are three reasons why the EC is well-suited to policing the rules of the game of intercultural evaluation. First, the claims of supremacy of EC law render the Community well-suited to prescribing meta-norms addressed to decision-makers. Certain rules of the game are pressed on decision-makers which influence divisions of authority at both supranational and infranational levels. Yet, as a highly contingent form of authority open to both national administrative and judicial challenge, a feature of EC law is that it must continually justify its authority for fear of non-compliance. The Court of Justice

---

[187] On all this see Parekh, *supra* n. 181, ch. 7.

has therefore made the authority of EC Instruments subject to a whole series of constraints about respect for fundamental rights, general principles of EC law, division of powers between EC Institutions, and between the Institutions and the Member States. This entails that the EC would have to justify any rules of the game on intercultural evaluation and any justifications it provided that were unacceptable would run the risk of non-compliance. A practical example here might help. If the Court of Justice decided under the Directive, simpliciter, that any attempt to ban the playing of misogynistic rap music in public places was illegal because it violated Directive 2000/43/EC, it is difficult to believe this would not provoke a crisis of authority. The failure to take account of the interests of women of all races and ethnic origin would possibly lead to non-implementation by national judges and, failing this, private action, boycotts, etc. against persons seeking to profit from the ruling. Confronted with this, one would imagine that the Court, in considering such an issue, would have to consider how misogynistic music traditionally played by other races is treated, the public nature of the places involved, the level of offence aimed at women, the level of offence taken, etc. In short, if it allows (or prohibits) the music, it would have to provide a high level of justification. This requirement to justify would moreover act as a continual pressure to create meta-norms that were sensitive to context and not too dogmatic or inflexible.

The second feature is the oppositionality of the Community to the nation-State. Its identity is tied up with prompting reflexivity and suggesting alternative settlements within the national arena. It is the subvert of national totems. The body which suggests that current 'ways of doing things' are not as great as they appear, and that there may be a different manner of mediating interests and values. As a supranational Institution, moreover, it focuses inevitably on the levels of closure within the national settlement. For the supra- in supranationalism inherently points to the limits and exclusion within national settlements, both in their technical capacities and their legitimacy. It thus prompts for new forms of recognition. Yet, conversely, the -nation element in supranationalism points to the inherent multilevel, composite nature of the arrangement. Supranationalism may be a force that can prompt new institutional arrangements and values within the national settlement, it loses its qualities (and its legitimacy) if it tries, however, to supplant this national space. This can occur either where not enough space is left for national governance mechanisms or where solutions are imposed on the latter which suggest that 'The Community Knows Best' rather than 'The Community Knows Differently'. This latter constraint dis-enables the EC from engaging in substantive mediation itself. It cannot decide whether non-Muslim women should be required to observe a Muslim dress code in a Muslim bank, for example, without appearing to engage in excessive centralization. The substantive decision is one better left to national or lower levels of decision-making.

The third feature of the European Community that renders it suitable for providing the rules of the game for intercultural evaluation lies in its oppositionalities to itself. It has already been discussed how this has led to its acceptance, in Directive 2000/43, of the legitimacy of a number of understandings of equal treatment and to an infinite pursuit for self-perfection in this regard. These oppositionalities provide a sensitivity as to how it develops the rules of the game, which are based not merely on the fear of non-compliance, but also have regard to the ethics of the situation. In some circumstances, they might lead to its requirement that interests be taken into account whose consideration might provoke questioning amongst more conservative elements of the national political settlement. At other times, it may involve the questioning of certain strongly held totems within the cultural communities themselves. Yet both these elements are central to any meaningful process of intercultural evaluation.

It is the author's contention that not only do these structures render the EC well-suited to laying down rules of the game for intercultural evaluation, but that, if interpreted in a particular manner, Directive 2000/43 provides the necessary technical means to do so.

The first necessary element is that the Directive imposes a duty that the presence of multiple ethnic and racial identities be recognized in the national settlement. The duty discussed here is not one to determine the content and needs of such identities, but merely a duty to acknowledge that they exist, and that they will have needs and qualities to which the politics of dignity should be extended. This duty is contained, most centrally, in the prohibition of direct discrimination on grounds of racial or ethnic origin and in the prohibition on racial harassment. By rendering a collective identity subject to protection under these provisions, this identity is recognized as having valuable qualities that make it egregious not only to use it as a ground for less favourable treatment, but also give it the right to make certain positive claims on the political settlement. There seems a strong case for this duty to be interpreted widely. A feature of a multicultural society is that a wide variety of cultural communities should be recognized. It seems equally hateful to place a notice on a door banning travellers from a public place as one banning traditionally disadvantaged groups such as Blacks. This duty can be interpreted widely because it does not impose collective views about the attributes of these identities or how disputes between identities should be resolved. The only common value it imposes is that of the value of the multicultural society.

In this regard, a distinction has to be made between overt and covert discrimination, on the one hand, and genuine indirect or structural discrimination, on the other. The former covers both explicit use of racial or ethnic criteria and the use of 'covert' criteria, which, in the words of an earlier draft of the Directive, are 'intrinsically liable to affect persons of a particular racial or ethnic origin and if there is a consequent risk that it will place those persons at a particular disadvantage'.[188] The feature of the latter is that they are direct discrimination in all but name. They are either targeted against particular communities[189] or act to exclude fully a community from a particular activity.[190] Such targeting or exclusion is a denial of the multicultural society. Exclusion suggests certain practices should only be open to some cultural communities and not others. Targeting, meanwhile, suggests a lack of value that inheres to that cultural community, and therefore that its status within society is to some extent impaired. The above differ from the prohibition on indirect or structural discrimination in that it goes further and seeks not merely to establish the presence of a multicultural society, but, through attacking practices that place ethnic or racial groups at a particular disadvantage, to remedy all the disadvantages or identify all the qualities and practices of a particular community. The author is not denying the importance of addressing such matters, but, subject to what will be said later, this provision should, in principle, be interpreted narrowly. One reason is that tackling the problem of indirect discrimination requires the imposition of common political values about the form a particular multicultural society should take, as it involves often mediating between claims of different cultural communities.[191] Another is that the identification of the disadvantages suffered by a group will often involve a claim to identify what 'makes' a particular cultural community.[192] For reasons already set out, it has been suggested that such a task would lead both to an over-extension of the liberal model and would be one for which the institutional set-up of the EC is ill-suited.

The requirement of indirect discrimination is central to the second duty of the protection of *common multicultural cultures*. Intercultural evaluation requires acknowledgement that not all cultures are the same, a claim that a bland requirement of mutual recognition is in danger of making. Acceptance of this difference requires acceptance that different cultures have different forms and different levels of resonance for their members. A culture centred around a religious faith will often intrude more extensively into the lifestyles of its members than one centred more discretely around a particular activity. Similarly, certain racial and ethnic identities carry a resonance others do not have because of a history of disadvantage and

---

[188] *Amended Proposal for a Council Directive Implementing the Principle of Equal Treatment between Persons Irrespective of Racial or Ethnic Origin* COM (2000) 328 final, Art. 2.

[189] e.g. a prohibition on headscarves in French schools.

[190] e.g. a requirement that helmets be worn by motorcycle riders fully excludes Sikhs from these activities.

[191] e.g. a dress code in Islamic banks which requires all women to wear a veil.

[192] e.g. a ban on the smoking of marijuana in the workplace could be seen as discriminating against Rastafarians, but would involve a claim as to how central the smoking of ganja is to the practice of that faith.

oppression. To give a practical example, dress codes do not impinge on all identities equally. A dress code carries implications for some members of the Muslim or Jewish faith that it does not for secular groups. Similarly, it carries implications for Blacks in that it has traditionally been used as a means to discriminate those wearing braids or beads in their hair or traditional African form of dress.

The principle of indirect discrimination is a means of recognizing the positive claims of different cultural communities. Dress codes, working time requirements, vernaculars should not be used as a basis for disadvantaging or preventing the activities of a particular community. The oppositionality of the European Community would also seem to be well-suited to teasing out new recognition by the national settlement of these claims. At first sight, this would seem to contradict what was said above about the danger of imposing a shared political culture. To be sure, at a certain level it does, but it avoids the pitfalls in two ways. First, as the prohibition is based on the resonancy a practice has for a particular community, it is not concerned with identification of all the identities and subject-positions within that community, but only those totems most salient and most dear to it. This does not appear either too challenging or too reifying as a forensic exercise. Secondly, the principle would only apply in the absence of conflict. It would not apply where protecting the practice of one cultural community would offend the customs or beliefs of another cultural community. In this latter circumstance, acceptance of this practice would amount to the imposition of a common culture over the claims of another cultural community. As this suppresses rather than fosters intercultural evaluation, it is clearly inimical to the establishment of 'common multicultural communities'.

It has been argued so far that the safeguarding of 'common multicultural communities' by Directive 2000/43/EC asserts that limited shared political values, which are that the presence of multiple cultural communities be recognized and that their difference and resonance be respected. All this can be done through the judicial machinery applying the provisions in Article 2. These may be the building blocks of the multicultural society, but there is, in addition, the duty of intercultural evaluation. This process is central to the negotiation of cultural conflict. The context within which it occurs will either be where there is a practice central to one cultural community (e.g. polygamy) but not acceptable to others or where an individual makes a claim that a practice she engages in is an important part of her membership of a particular cultural community, but the practice does not have sufficient resonance that it is accepted as such by members of other cultural communities. A feature of cultural conflicts is that they do not exist in the abstract but ground themselves within particular contexts and locales. Parekh's theory of intercultural evaluation requires that the central protagonists within these contexts engage in a process of negotiation where each puts forward not merely the claims of her own culture but agrees to evaluate and reconsider the claims of her own culture in the light of the other culture.[193]

Courts are an unsuitable forum for such evaluation. For it is based upon a logic of negotiation which will be contextually bounded, and will usually be agonistic in nature rather than concerned with establishing truth-claims. The procedures of 'social dialogue' set out in Article 11 of the Directive are much more suited to fostering such a process. Such a process, however, faces procedural hurdles and substantive ones. Procedurally, it is important that there are structures in place which enable the negotiations to take place on the basis of the criteria set out by Young earlier. They should provide for a pattern of dialogue to emerge which respects different forms of expression and commits protagonists to responding to the observations of one another. They should also ensure proper channels of accountability between representatives and their constituencies, and, lastly, they must be decentred in that there must be some mechanism for listening to the voice of interests that would otherwise be excluded. The current procedures are not only merely confined to the workplace, but, even there, are vague and ill-defined in nature. It is thus imperative that models are developed by the Commission or Member States, which set out good practice in detail across all the areas covered by the Directive. Given that there are plural visions of race relations and multiculturalism, there seems, in this regard, little wrong with setting out a variety of models from a number of sources. Rewards should be attached to adoption of these models—in a similar manner to the eco-audit and eco-labels—to encourage their adoption. For example, firms or schools adopting them should be able to advertise themselves as engaging in 'good practice'. Adoption of these models could be considered a relevant factor in the award of government or EC contracts.

All this requires an effort of good will and imagination on the part of the EC and national administrations, but, *per se*, would be insufficient. For the best procedures cannot stop a party negotiating in bad faith or create a starting point for negotiation. In this regard, although not set out by Parekh, the logic of intercultural evaluation would set out the following constraints. To the author it would require each party not only to set out why it was consistent with its beliefs for a practice to be continued/discontinued, but also to explain why, in terms of the other protagonists' cultural identity, it was not significantly offensive.[194] To

---

[193] *Supra* n. 181, at 292–4.

[194] This is a much stronger requirement than that imposed by deliberative democrats that the parties provide reasons for their claims and respond to the reasoning of other protagonists' claims. The latter, by failing to require any party to engage with the congnitive position or interpretive community that lies at the heart of other parties' cultural identities, leads inevitably to a rationalism which excludes the claims of many marginalised groups. On this see Pelizzoni, 'The Myth of the Best Argument: Power, Deliberation and Reason', 52 *British Journal of Sociology* (2001) 59.

take the notorious example of the wearing of headscarves by Muslim children being found to offend the secular tradition of French education. The obligation set out would both require the French authorities to explain how the practice accommodates or could be adjusted to accommodate the beliefs of Muslims, whilst requiring Muslim representatives to explain why the practice would not significantly impair the secular tradition of French education. To be sure, such a process might not result in agreement, but it creates a starting point for negotiation and requires each party to enter and engage with the discursive traditions of the other, and explain itself in terms of those traditions—a process that goes to the heart of multiculturalism.

The key to unlocking this process lies within the provision prohibiting indirect discrimination. Traditional approaches have seen it as a weapon for tackling some forms of structural disadvantages. These therefore examine in a fairly economistic manner whether a group is disadvantaged by a particular practice *vis-à-vis* other groups, and then whether there is a legitimate— usually business-related—reason for such a practice, and whether the means used are proportionate. For reasons already given, the European Community is unsuited to such a 'truth-finding' role, and the indirect discrimination principle would be better interpreted in line with a role promoting intercultural evaluation. Such an interpretation would, moreover, leave untouched national models prohibiting indirect discrimination, which could continue their traditional roles. An interpretation along these lines would require that where a practice appears to disadvantage a particular group, there is a presumption that it cannot be justified unless the defendant has shown that it has entered into a process of intercultural evaluation in which it has responded to the plaintiff's complaints on the plaintiff's terms. Conversely, there would be no finding of indirect discrimination if the plaintiff could not show that they had responded to concerns about the practice in question and justified the practice in the light of these concerns. Such an interpretation would have two advantages. It would address, first, the invidiousness of cultural racism. Promotion procedures based on dress-codes or manners of socialization that appeared to favour dominant groups would now have to justify themselves in the language of other groups. They would have to explain why Jamaican patois or braids were not as acceptable as 'Oxford English' or a short back and sides on the basis that 'Blackness' was the dominant culture rather than 'Whiteness'. Yet, as a corollary, such a process would also challenge the dogmas of minority cultural communities. These would have to explain why particular practices should be acceptable in a wider multicultural society in which many people do not share their beliefs.

IX. CONCLUSIONS

All the above requires that a particular vision, that of intercultural evaluation, be taken of the Directive and that the different administrative institutions at both a national and Community level act on this shared interpretation. It requires therefore that the courts do not over-extend the prohibition on indirect discrimination and that they interpret it in an unprecedented manner. It requires also that administrations develop and recognize negotiating procedures across a wide variety of fora. The author is not optimistic this will happen. The garbage can nature of EC decision-making where particular interests try to subvert one arena by pursuing their interests in other fora render the process far more suited to institutional competition than institutional coordination. The Directive is likely to be subject to the same form of judicial politics as Directive 76/207/EEC, the Gender Equality Directive, where pressure groups cherry-pick 'deserving cases' to try and push through universal change in the manner desired by them.[195] Administrators might resist institutional innovation on the grounds that it, in some symbolic manner, challenges their vested interests. In this regard, the best hope lies in the relatively long transposition time of the Directive, which gives a time for reflection and for visioning in the period up to 19 July 2003.[196] If this is not taken, it is likely that the nettle offered by one of the most radical pieces of EC legislation will not be grasped. And that would be a pity. The European model would follow the tired national models in which we would say that either the Indian should dress like the Portuguese or that he should go naked even into the churches and schools of the Portuguese. The answer suggested here is that each should be free to do what they want and believe provided it talks to the other to discover how it can be adapted so that it does not offend the other.

---

[195] Alter and Vargas, 'Explaining Variation in the Use of European Litigation Strategies: European Community Law and British Gender Equality Policy', 33 *Comparative Political Studies* (2000) 452. Statistics from the United Kingdom suggest the possibility of a blizzard of cases which will exceed that in gender discrimination. Despite constituting a much smaller percentage of the workforce than women, the number of complaints, and successful complaints, from racial and ethnic minorities is much higher. To take the example of the Employment Appeals Tribunal, a pivotal court in making references to the ECJ. In 1998 there were ninety-five appeals to it under gender related discrimination (fourteen successful or remitted to the lower court for reconsideration) and 174 under race legislation (twenty successful or remitted), Lord Chancellor's Department, *Judicial Statistics Annual Report 1998* (1999, Government Statistical Service, London), Table 7.9. The figures for 1999 were more equal, being 119 (20) for gender and 181 (21) for race, Lord Chancellor's Department, *Judicial Statistics Annual Report 1999* (2000, Government Statistical Service, London), Table 7.9.

[196] *Supra* n. 1, Art. 16.

8

International and European Norms Regarding National Legal Remedies for Racial Inequality

CHRISTOPHER McCRUDDEN

I. INTRODUCTION

What are the appropriate national enforcement and remedial structures for tackling racial discrimination by legal means? This chapter considers how far there are international or European legal norms that require, or recommend, to national authorities particular approaches to this difficult issue. The chapter is not concerned primarily with the effectiveness or otherwise of the international mechanisms for enforcement, or with the adequacy of the remedies provided by the international enforcement bodies, or with whether the strategy of making national enforcement the first (sometimes the only) line of defence against racial discrimination is itself appropriate.[1] Rather, the issue considered is what guidance the international community and European regional bodies give to national authorities as to the enforcement institutions and remedies that are appropriately provided at the national level to counter racial discrimination within that country.[2]

II. FUNCTIONS OF LEGAL REQUIREMENTS FOR RACIAL EQUALITY

There is now an increasingly complex web of international norms relating to racial discrimination and racial equality, both treaty-based legal requirements, 'soft-law' standards, and customary international law.[3] Europe has also

[1] For a sceptical reaction to the increasing use of national remedies rather than international remedies, see Evans, 'International Wrongs and National Jurisdiction', in M. D. Evans (ed.), *Remedies in International Law: The Institutional Dilemma* (1998), at 173.

[2] We will not be considering the transnational enforcement of anti-discrimination law.

[3] Among these norms, I include, the International Convention on the Elimination of all Forms of Racial Discrimination, 1966; the International Covenant on Civil and Political Rights, 1966, Articles 2(1), 20(2), and 26; the International Covenant on Economic, Social and Cultural Rights, 1966, Article 2(2); the Refugee Convention, 1951, Article 3; the Convention

adopted a similar range of legal and non-legal norms regarding racial equality under the auspices of the Council of Europe[4] and the European Community.[5] Making these norms 'effective' is a crucial task. However, 'effectiveness' is a problematic concept generally, and this is no less true in the context of assessing the enforcement of anti-discrimination law. For the purposes of this analysis the notion of 'enforcement' will be interpreted broadly to include those mechanisms and strategies devised to implement certain instrumental goals of anti-discrimination law effectively and efficiently. But in identifying this as its goal, we are faced directly with a major issue. Assessing whether a regulatory enforcement regime is effective may be problematic because the goal or goals pursued may be unclear or disputed, or because several different instrumental goals may be pursued at different times in different places. This is, indeed, the case with anti-discrimination law, and important implications for enforcement flow from this.[6]

There is a close connection between the *function* that we attribute to anti-discrimination law, and the enforcement institutions that are thought to be both appropriate and effective. That is true in the context of whether we view the function of anti-discrimination law as symbolic or instrumental, but it is also true in choosing which instruments are appropriate for the enforcement of instrumental functions. Since there are different instrumental functions which anti-discrimination law is frequently thought to serve, which function, or which combination of functions we choose, has important implications for the enforcement mechanisms that will be chosen. There has been very little, if any, discussion of these separate functions at the international or regional levels. For that we need to turn to the national level where a much richer

on the Rights of the Child (1989), Article 2(1); UNESCO Convention Against Discrimination in Education, 1960; UNESCO Declaration on Race and Racial Prejudice, 1978; ILO Convention No. 111 on Discrimination (Employment and Occupation), 1958; United Nations Declaration on the Elimination of All Forms of Racial Discrimination, 1963; Declaration on the Rights of Persons Belonging to National or Ethnic, Religious or Linguistic Minorities, 1992; International Convention on the Protection of the Rights of Migrant Workers and Members of their Families, 1990.

[4] European Convention on Human Rights, 1950, Art. 14; (Revised) European Social Charter (1996); European Convention on the Legal Status of Migrant Workers (1977); European Charter for Regional or Minority Languages (1992); Framework Convention for the Protection of National Minorities (1995); Protocol No. 12 to the European Convention on Human Rights.

[5] Council Directive 2000/43/EC of 29 June implementing the principle of equal treatment between persons irrespective of racial or ethnic origin, OJ 2000 L 180/22, 19.7.2000; Council Directive 2000/78/EC of 27 Nov. 2000 establishing a general framework for equal treatment in employment and occupation, OJ 2000 L 303/23; Charter of Fundamental Rights of the European Union, Articles 20, 21, and 23.

[6] See further McCrudden, 'Assessing Effectiveness, Judging Implementation: Fair Employment in Northern Ireland', 1 *Review of Employment Topics* (1993) 91; id., 'The Effectiveness of European Equality Law', 13 *Oxford Journal of Legal Studies* (1993).

debate is underway about the functions of anti-discrimination law generally, but also in the specific context of racial discrimination.

A central element of this chapter is that how we conceptualize enforcement and remedial structures will be significantly affected by what we think the functions are of the legal prohibitions on racial discrimination. These relate to at least three different conceptions currently attaching to the concept of equality as a political goal in the context of racial and ethnic discrimination. There are several 'equalities' emerging in the current international debates about racism, with each having somewhat different implications for enforcement and remedial structures thought to be appropriate. In this section of the chapter, I sketch out these three models, and some of the institutional and remedial approaches taken to implementing them, drawing on experience at the national level. A better appreciation of the developing debate about legal enforcement and remedies at the international and regional levels will be gained if these emerging international requirements are seen against the background of, and being substantially influenced by, already existing national responses to racial discrimination.[7]

(i) Individual Justice Model

An individual justice model generally aims to secure the reduction of discrimination by eliminating from decisions illegitimate considerations based on race, gender, or other prohibited considerations that have harmful consequences for individuals. Sometimes this model speaks in terms of the 'irrelevance' of certain considerations to decision-taking. This approach concentrates on cleansing the process of decision-making, and is not concerned with the general effect of decisions on groups, except perhaps as an indication of a flawed process. It is markedly individualistic in its orientation: concentrating on securing fairness for the individual. It is generally expressed in universal and symmetrical terms: blacks and whites are equally protected, for example, as are majorities and minorities. It reflects respect for efficiency, 'merit', and achievement and, given the limited degree of intervention permitted, it preserves and possibly enhances the operation of the market. It is 'manageable' in that its aims can be stated with some degree of certainty, and its application does not depend on extensive enquiries and judgements on complex socio-economic facts. It often concentrates on the intention of the perpetrator of the discrimination, and the sense of grievance of the individual

---

[7] See further McCrudden, 'Regulating Discrimination: Advice to a Legislator on Problems Regarding the Enforcement of Anti-Discrimination Law and Strategies to Overcome Them', in T. Loenen and P. R. Rodrigues (eds), *Non-Discrimination Law: Comparative Perspectives* (1999) 295.

arising out of that intention. Particularly in its recent articulations, it is also compatible with and, indeed, an instrument of a movement towards cherishing diversity and protecting different identities equally.

This model is particularly attractive to those who wish to extend the ambit of traditional anti-discrimination law because the traditional grounds of race and sex can be seen as merely an imperfect and partial example of a broader general principle of individual fairness. The individual justice model of equality thus enables those who want to include discrimination against sexual minorities, or discrimination on the ground of age or disability, within the ambit of anti-discrimination law to be able to draw on a principle of general application, indeed, a principle of universal significance, a human rights principle. Not surprisingly, therefore, human rights-talk of equality is increasingly conceptualized in this way.

In very broad terms, three differing approaches are identifiable for enforcing this individual justice model: a criminal justice model, a civil justice model, and a commission (or agency) individual justice model. There are, first, jurisdictions which traditionally treat complaints of discrimination as issues of *criminal* law, whilst others treat them as issues of general civil law. The use of the criminal law is particularly evident as a means of tackling incitement to racial hatred, and related crimes, such as the promotion of genocide.

The civil justice model, at its most unadorned, involves an individual victim making a complaint to an ordinary court exercising a civil (non-criminal) jurisdiction and awarding a remedy to that individual for the discrimination suffered. The crucial parts of this second model, for the purposes of what follows, are the individual focus of the case, the complainant-driven nature of the case, and the adjudicatory (or court-like) nature of the body set up to decide the appropriate degree of culpability, and the remedy. This basic civil justice model described above has been significantly modified in different jurisdictions. We can identify several specific variations on the civil justice theme, for example by shifting the burden of proof, more effective assistance to individual plaintiffs, and providing more effective remedies. Access to justice has been improved by bringing courts and judges to regions or areas which are distant from the main centres has been attempted.[8] Training of judges in racial discrimination issues,[9] and developing greater specialization by judges in equality cases leading to more expertise and greater familiarity with anti-discrimination law, is not uncommon. Two other developments have attracted considerable attention: the use of alternative dispute resolution techniques, and increasing effective assistance to complainants via specialized agencies.

[8] CERD/C/SR.1335 at para. 6 (6 Aug. 1999).
[9] 'Basket of Good Practices: Education & Training': ECRI; <http://www.ecri.coe.int/>.

Third, in several jurisdictions, the mechanism for resolving private complaints is by way of an application to an *enforcement agency* to investigate and resolve the complaint, rather than to the courts. The argument in favour of this approach is often that an investigatory approach is preferable for the complainant who will not be put to the difficulty of proving discrimination.

(ii) Group Justice Model

Despite its obvious attractions, this individual justice model has been criticized as deeply flawed, if it is to be regarded as encapsulating the only meaning of 'equality'. Various arguments tend to recur. The individual justice model is said to misconceive the deep structure of discrimination in some contexts, such as discrimination against black Americans and black South Africans. Such discrimination is as often institutional as individual, it is argued, and therefore there is little likelihood that a highly individualistic model of equality will adequately capture the depth of the problem or the significance of the changes that need to be made to address it. The problem, it is said, is misconceived as being one of intention rather than effect. The individual justice model is said not to take adequately into account the surrounding and re-enforcing nature of disadvantage and membership of certain groups.

Out of these criticisms come various alternative approaches that I will group together under the heading of group justice. Common to such approaches is a view that the aim of anti-discrimination law should be to concentrate more than the individual justice model does on the outcomes of the decision-making processes not just the process itself, and to redistribute resources from the advantaged group to the disadvantaged group. The basic aim is the improvement of the relative position of particular groups, whether to redress past subordination and discrimination, or out of a concern for distributive justice at the present time. These approaches tend to be concerned with the relative position of groups or classes, rather than individuals. They depend on a recognition of social classes or groups. The principle is often expressed in asymmetrical terms as focusing on the betterment of disadvantaged groups and is less concerned with symmetrical protection for non-disadvantaged.

One of the ways in which this idea of group justice has been conceptualized legally is by requiring that discrimination be defined as including the concept of indirect discrimination, which (loosely) involves prohibiting practices that have the effect of disproportionately disadvantaging a particular group and which cannot be justified objectively. Indirect discrimination, in this sense, appears to be increasingly commonly prohibited. European and American law each apply the concept of indirect discrimination to acts of racial discrimination in employment, for example. Another common aspect of this notion of group justice is the concept of group-based remedies. This sometimes takes the form of restitutionary remedies such as is found in those countries where land was discriminatorily taken from indigenous groups. In other countries, affirmative action measures have been developed. For the purpose of this discussion, affirmative action includes preference being accorded to an individual because of his or her membership of a racial minority, in order to redress past discrimination, secure greater distributive justice, or ensure the representativeness of the institution engaged in the affirmative action. Common to both the concept of indirect discrimination and affirmative action is the idea of proportions; often, therefore, statistics are collected in order to monitor the relative position of the disadvantaged group compared with other groups in the society, and to provide information on which indirect discrimination can more easily be identified and affirmative action programmes devised. We see, finally, an important shift in the use of language from the individual justice to the group justice model. In the former, the emphasis is usually on talk of 'discrimination'. In the latter, other terms tend to become predominant: material equality, equality of outcome, disadvantage.

Again, this group justice model has given rise to several different sets of enforcement and remedial structures at the national level. It is not uncommon for mechanisms that seem to have the characteristics associated with the individual justice model to be assessed for their adequacy in delivering aspects of group justice. Several jurisdictions have used mechanisms originally designed to further an apparently individual justice-based approach to advance a group justice approach. The goal of individual justice clearly overlaps with the goal of group justice in significant ways. One of the reasons why so little attention is paid to the distinction, I suspect, is because, tactically, it is thought by those who advocate a group justice model that it can in part be achieved by vigorously pursuing the individual justice model. And, to an extent, this is true in that the demonstration effect of successful individual litigation may well increase the likelihood that methods will be developed to advance the group justice model.

We can point to jurisdictions where classic individual justice enforcement institutions have been adapted to serve group justice aims. Although litigation looks at first like the embodiment of the individual justice model, in some jurisdictions it has (at least in the past) played a significant role in the application of the group justice model, through the adaptation over time of judicial procedure and remedies. So too, the investigation and enforcement by a regulatory agency may serve either of the two models, depending on the extent and nature of the powers given to the agency. Regulatory agency enforcement may begin as a method of securing individual justice but increasingly develop as an important mechanism for achieving group justice.

In some jurisdictions *locus standi* has been accorded to institutional plaintiffs, without the need for an individual victim, such as the standing accorded to public interest groups, trade unions, and equality agencies. Remedies are sometimes made available which apply beyond the individual victim and attempt to redress structural and institutional problems that affect a class. Organizations have, on occasion, been required to produce and disseminate aggregate information relating to pay structures and workforce composition, through monitoring requirements.

Promoting more widespread change throughout different spheres of economic and social life has, however, been considered by several jurisdictions to require specifically tailored group justice mechanisms. In particular, the structure of duties switches from the negative (do not discriminate) to the positive (provide equality of opportunity, or whatever). This has important implications for institutional enforcement. We can point to several approaches that are particularly identified with the implementation of this model. First, the development of agency regulation designed to create pressures for organizations to implement a group justice approach. There are considerable variations as to how such bodies operate in practice to achieve such change.[10] Secondly, we can identify the use of what has been called the state's power of *dominium*, in particular through attaching equality requirements to government contracts. There is considerable variation among the methods of selective purchasing adopted. Thirdly, more explicit restitution to groups is sometimes in evidence, in particular involving land redistribution as compensation for previous discriminatory dispossession.

(ii) Equality as Participation

For some, legal regulation of racism should go several steps further than traditional anti-discrimination law, based on either the individual justice or group justice model, to require government and public bodies to weave policies of equality and non-discrimination into the fabric of decision making across all spheres of government—in short, to 'mainstream' equality issues in public policy, and to do so by involving the affected groups themselves. I shall call this conception of equality the 'participative model' of equality, in order to emphasize the extent to which it addresses the need for those previously excluded to have a voice in public affairs and in the daily decisions of those

---

[10] See, for example, McCrudden, 'The Commission for Racial Equality: Formal Investigations in the Shadow of Judicial Review', in R. Baldwin and C. McCrudden, *Regulation and Public Law* (1987), at 222–66, and *supra* n. 6; id.,'Law Enforcement by Regulatory Agency: the Case of Employment Discrimination in Northern Ireland', 45 *Modern Law Review* (1982) 617.

who shape their life chances. In some ways, this model is apparent in a more limited sphere. Collective bargaining in the employment context has a long history of involvement in tackling racial discrimination. However, there are significant differences between mainstreaming and such collective bargaining strategies, in particular differences relating to the scope of bargaining (main-streaming applies beyond the employment context), and differences in the participants involved (collective bargaining applies mostly to the social partners, employers and unions, not the affected groups themselves, unless separately organized).

Mainstreaming, then, involves government proactively taking equality into account. It is intended to be anticipatory rather than retrospective, to be extensively participatory rather than limited to small groups of the know-ledgeable, and to be integrated into activities of those involved in policy mak-ing. The motivation for mainstreaming lies in the realization that unless special attention is paid to equality in policy making, it becomes too easily sidelined and submerged in the day-to-day concerns of policy-makers who do not view equality as central to their concerns. Mainstreaming, by definition, attempts to address this problem by requiring all government departments to engage directly with equality issues. Mainstreaming should have other, more indirect, benefits. One of these is to encourage greater transparency in deci-sion making since it necessitates defining the likely impact of policies at an earlier stage of policy making, more systematically and to a greater extent than is usually contemplated. It will also encourage greater participation in policy making. Unlike more traditional mechanisms of consultation, mainstreaming requires impact assessments of a degree of specificity that establishes a clear agenda for discussion between policy-makers and those most affected. In combination, impact assessment and participation will develop links between government and 'civil society', encouraging greater participation in decision making by marginal groups and lessening the democratic deficit.

It might be said that there is no conception of equality adopted in this participative model. Rather, there is a recognition that different equalities are in play in different situations and that what is necessary is the ability of the pro-tected groups to be able to engage with policy-makers to help secure the adop-tion of the conception of equality that suits their circumstances. If particular groups prefer a conception of equality closer to the individual justice model, this participative model empowers them to negotiate with policy-makers to make it a reality. If other groups prefer a model of equality that is closer to the group justice model, then they should be empowered to negotiate with policy-makers to make that a reality. What the participative model recognizes, there-fore, is the importance of 'equalities'-talk, rather than 'equality'-talk, because the latter leads to an attempt by each group to try to capture the conception of equality closest to its interests, thus leading to conflict with other groups whose interests are not particularly served by that conception of equality. What emerges, then, is the idea that each group should be free to identify the conception of equality that best serves its interests, a pluralism of equalities.

(iv) Similarities and Differences between the Three Models

It is important not to exaggerate the differences between these three models. In particular, the political perspective of the second and third models is itself often based on background ethical positions, such as distributive justice and the importance of individual self-determination through political action. So too, although the individual justice model appears to stress the importance of the individual more than the other two models, this appearance is somewhat misleading. Both the group justice and participative models are concerned with the individual, but see the ability to make positive changes to the position of the individual as most likely to be made by advancing the position of the group of which the individual is a member. Nor, so far as I am aware, does anyone who advances a group justice model or a participative model want to replace the individual justice model. Rather, they mostly want to complement and supplement the individual justice model. Time after time, advocates of mainstreaming, for example, stress the dangers of giving up traditional anti-discrimination legal approaches. So too, although different institutional mechanisms are identifiably attached to different models, we can see that institutions primarily associated with one model are capable of being used, or adapted, to serve a different model. But nor should we underestimate the tensions between the three conceptions of equality I have sketched out. In particular, although to a significant degree these conceptions overlap, on occasion they do conflict, most dramatically over the permissibility of various forms of affirmative action.

III. DEVELOPING INTERNATIONAL NORMS ON NATIONAL ENFORCEMENT AND REMEDIAL STRUCTURES ON RACIAL EQUALITY

(i) Overview of Organizations Considered

We shall now consider to what extent international law provides any guidance to national authorities on the enforcement and remedial structures for enforcing these conceptions of equality in addition to setting out the substantive norms to which states should adhere. We shall do this by analysing the practice of the most important bodies responsible for interpreting the international legal requirements regarding racial discrimination in order to discern what principles emerge from this regarding the applicable standards applying to domestic enforcement and remedial structures.

Before doing so, however, a brief introduction to the various 'players' to whom we shall make reference is necessary. We can begin by concentrating on developments at the international level. In what follows, we shall be drawing on discussions by international bodies of two main types: treaty monitoring bodies, which are bodies established under specific international treaties and owe their existence solely to that treaty, and Charter-based United Nations bodies, which are established under the Charter of the United Nations.

In the category of international human rights treaty-based bodies we shall consider, in particular, the Committee on the Elimination of Racial Discrimination (CERD), which monitors the International Convention on the Elimination of Racial Discrimination (ICERD). The other relevant treaty monitoring bodies we shall consider will be the Human Rights Committee (HRC), which monitors the implementation of the International Covenant on Civil and Political Rights (ICCPR), and the Committee on Economic, Social, and Cultural Rights (CESCR), which monitors the implementation of the International Covenant on Economic, Social, and Cultural Rights (ICESCR). By adhering to one of these treaties, State Parties agree (amongst other things) to engage in a dialogue with the relevant treaty body. They assume a legal obligation to submit periodic 'State reports' outlining the legislative, judicial, administrative, and other measures they have taken to ensure the enjoyment of the rights contained in the treaty. Treaty bodies normally examine State reports in the presence of representatives of the Government and end with the adoption of 'concluding observations' or 'concluding comments'. In addition, the ICERD and the ICCPR have optional protocols that provide states with the opportunity to permit complaints against the state to be considered by the CERD or the HRC, as appropriate, after exhausting domestic remedies. Each of these treaties has been ratified by a significant number of states, although a noticeably smaller number of states has ratified the optional protocols.

The International Labour Organization was established originally in 1919. Over the years, it has developed a significant body of Conventions and Recommendations on labour rights issues, including in the area of discrimination. Each Convention establishes a mechanism to receive periodic reports on compliance by the member state, and a mechanism by which complaints of non-compliance may be considered. The principal instrument for our discussion is the Discrimination (Employment & Occupation) Convention 1958 (C111) and its associated Recommendation (R111). We shall concentrate on the extent to which the ILO has developed norms relating to national enforcement and remedial structures in that context. More recently, the ILO has also agreed, in 1998, a Declaration on Fundamental Principles and Rights at Work. This marked a renewed universal commitment amongst members, even if they have not ratified the Conventions in question, to respect, promote, and realize certain principles that are regarded as fundamental: freedom of association, effective recognition of the right to collective bargaining, elimination of all forms of forced and compulsory labour, effective abolition of child labour, and (most importantly for our purposes) the elimination of discrimination (including racial discrimination) in respect of employment and occupation. Monitoring the Declaration takes two forms: an 'annual follow-up'[11] and 'global reports'.[12]

Apart from these specific mechanisms, the United Nations has been actively involved more generally. Three 'decades' to combat racism have been proclaimed, in 1973, 1983, and 1993, together with related programmes of action. Over time, the Commission on Human Rights, the Sub-Commission on Prevention of Discrimination and Protection of Minorities (now the Sub-Commission on Promotion and Protection of Human Rights) developed a significant role in the field of racial discrimination. More recently, the United Nations High Commissioner for Human Rights and the Special Rapporteur on Contemporary Forms of Racism, Racial Discrimination, Xenophobia, and Related Intolerance have established themselves as important actors.[13] Much of the activity of the United Nations system (and beyond, as we shall see) is now focused on the forthcoming World Conference against Racism, Racial Discrimination, Xenophobia, and Related Intolerance, which will be held in Durban, South Africa in September 2001.[14] This will be the third such conference, following equivalent conferences in 1978[15] and 1983.[16]

(ii) International Labour Organization

The Discrimination (Employment & Occupation) Convention provides in Article 2 that a member of the ILO for which the Convention is in force

undertakes to declare and pursue a national policy designed to promote, by methods appropriate to national conditions and practice, equality of opportunity and treatment

---

[11] The purpose of the Annual Follow-up is to provide an opportunity to review each year the efforts made in accordance with the Declaration by Members that have not yet ratified all the fundamental Conventions.

[12] The purpose of the Global Reports is to provide a dynamic global picture relating to each category of fundamental principles and rights noted during the preceding four-year period. Thus far, the Global Reports have not focused on discrimination.

[13] The Special Rapporteur on Contemporary Forms of Racism, Racial Discrimination, Xenophobia, and Related Intolerance was established within the United Nations by the Commission on Human Rights (CHR Res. 1993/20, para. 10) to prepare reports for the Human Rights Committee, which are later presented to the General Assembly. The Special Rapporteur discusses allegations he has received and transmitted to the governments concerned and lists his conclusions and recommendations. See, e.g., E/CN.4/2000/16, 10 Feb. 2000.

[14] GA Res 52/111, para. 28.

[15] GA Res 32/129 and the report of the first conference, A/CONF.92/40.

[16] GA Res 35/33, and the report of the second World Conference, A/CONF.119/26.

in respect of employment and occupation, with a view to eliminating any discrimination in respect thereof.

 Article 3 is more specific, providing that a member undertakes, 'by methods appropriate to national conditions and practice', to take various actions. These are: to seek the cooperation of employers' and workers' organizations and other appropriate bodies in promoting the acceptance and observance of this policy; to enact such legislation and to promote such educational programmes as may be calculated to secure the acceptance and observance of the policy; to repeal any statutory provisions and modify any administrative instructions or practices which are inconsistent with the policy; to pursue the policy in respect of employment under the direct control of a national authority; to ensure observance of the policy in the activities of vocational guidance, vocational training, and placement services under the direction of a national authority; and to indicate in its annual reports on the application of the Convention the action taken in pursuance of the policy and the results secured by such action.

 The accompanying Recommendation is more explicit still, although its status is one of soft law at most. Regarding the formulation and application of the policy referred to in Article 2, the Recommendation states that the policy

should be applied by means of legislative measures, collective agreements between representative employers' and workers' organisations or in any other manner consistent with national conditions and practice.[17]

Further, each member should promote the observance of the principles of non-discrimination 'where practicable and necessary' by such methods as making eligibility for contracts involving the expenditure of public funds dependent on observance of the principles, and making eligibility for grants to training establishments and for a licence to operate a private employment agency or a private vocational guidance office dependent on observance of the principles.[18] The Recommendation, unlike the Convention itself, also recommends that '[a]ppropriate agencies . . . should be established for the purpose of promoting application of the policy in all fields of public and private employment'. These agencies should, in particular, take all practicable measures to foster public understanding and acceptance of the principles of non-discrimination; receive, examine, and investigate complaints that the policy is not being observed and, if necessary by conciliation, secure the correction of any practices regarded as in conflict with the policy; and consider further any complaints which cannot be effectively settled by conciliation and render opinions or issue decisions concerning the manner in which discriminatory practices revealed should be corrected.

---

[17] Para. 2.   [18] Para. 3.

(a) Romania Inquiry

One of the more important formal considerations of what these provisions require arose in the 1991 report of the Commission of Inquiry to examine the observance by Romania of the Discrimination (Employment and Occupation) Convention, 1958.[19] The complaint alleged that a significant minority of Romanian citizens of Hungarian origin (more than 2 million persons, or 9.5 per cent of the population) were subjected to particular discrimination in the political, cultural, social, and employment spheres. Members of ethnic minorities, in particular the Hungarian minority, were forcibly dispersed from their places of birth and assigned by the authorities to employment not of their own choosing. Population transfers were carried out as a rule without previous notice and without informing those concerned where they were being sent. Persons of Hungarian origin were barred from a number of cities. Restrictions were deliberately imposed in the field of Hungarian language education; access to higher education and training was restricted. The prohibition of the Hungarian language in public life went hand in hand with the gradual elimination of Hungarian cultural institutions. Youth of the Hungarian ethnic minority as well as those of other minorities (Germans, South Slavs, Slovaks, Ukrainians, Jews, and Gypsies) were discriminated against in education, training and employment. Young people who requested to leave the country were conscripted into the army and sent to unhealthy forced labour camps. The Hungarian minority, with more than 300,000 unemployed, was affected by suppressions of jobs or whole enterprises, as well as restrictions on employment through the use of quotas. Moreover, and as a result of economic difficulties, wages were paid only in part, and Hungarian nationals did not benefit from special premiums paid by way of compensation in enterprises.

The ILO Commission of Inquiry recommended that the Government of Romania adopt a number of measures that could help it to conform fully to the Convention. The Government of Romania should adopt, as soon as possible, measures aimed at ending all discrimination in employment and occupation based on any of the criteria set out in Article 1(a) of the Convention, and in particular on political opinion. It should dismantle all instruments of the policy of assimilation and discrimination against members of minority groups pursued in the past by the Government of the Socialist Republic of Romania. It should put an end to all use of the personal records which workers had to fill out under the former regime and should publicize widely

[19] ILO, Report of the Commission of Inquiry appointed under Article 26 of the Constitution of the International Labour Organization to examine the observance by Romania of the Discrimination (Employment and Occupation) Convention, 1958 (No. 111) following application of the complaints procedure under Articles 24 and 26 of the ILO Constitution (ILO, 1991).

information on the present and future status of such records. It should put an end to the effect of discriminatory measures in employment and restore equal opportunity and treatment with regard to some specific named individuals. It should institute, for all disciplinary measures against workers, a grievance procedure leading to a speedy and impartial settlement. It should guarantee an efficient and impartial follow-up to the requests for medical examinations made by certain named individuals who went on strike, who had been rehabilitated by the courts. It should reinstate the workers who, under the Labour Code provisions on imprisonment for over two months, lost their jobs as a result of being arrested following demonstrations and were not released until after more than two months, despite the absence of evidence. It should adopt all the necessary measures to promote dialogue and an attitude of conciliation between the Romanian majority and minorities. It should adopt a language policy which, without prejudice to the status of Romanian as the official language of the State, would meet the cultural and economic needs of minorities. Through such a policy, it should implement in practice the right of minorities to their cultural identity, traditions and the use of their respective languages. It should aim to achieve an appropriate balance in the teaching of Romanian and minority languages from elementary school through to university, so that all citizens master the Romanian language, while enabling minorities, if they so wish, to engage in trades and professions using their own language. Any distinction in recruitment based on the candidates' language should be prohibited.

In addition, a 'vast campaign' should be undertaken, in collaboration with the political authorities, employers' and workers' organizations, and other appropriate bodies, with a view to eradicating the traditionally negative attitude towards the Roma (Gypsies). The social situation of the Roma should be improved by means of an integrated programme drawn up in collaboration with their representatives, covering education, employment, housing, and the other elements necessary to their progress. The Romanian authorities should step up existing efforts to train teachers of Rom origin and to ensure that children of Rom origin attend school. The maximum available resources should be allocated to enable Rom families to improve the utterly deplorable housing conditions under which many of them live. Programmes of special measures should be drawn up as provided in Article 5 of Convention No. 111 to improve the socio-economic status of the Roma; in particular, creating a programme for the recognition of occupational skills which are not formalized by a diploma. Assistance should be provided to citizens wishing to rebuild their houses destroyed as a result of a policy declared by the previous regime. With regard to the January 1992 census, representatives of minorities should be involved in choices of methodologies, census-taking operations, processing of results, and decisions concerning their publication.

Finally the Committee recommended that Romania inform the supervisory bodies of the ILO of the results achieved as regards reparations[20] for the discrimination suffered by members of national minorities or by persons persecuted for political reasons. Detailed information should be supplied as soon as possible on all developments in the annual reports on the application of Convention No. 111 submitted under Article 22 of the Constitution of the International Labour Organization.

(b) Bosnia-Herzegovina Report

A second interesting example of the approach adopted by ILO bodies regarding appropriate remedies under Convention No. 111 is to be found in the Report of the Committee set up to examine non-observance by Bosnia and Herzegovina of the Discrimination (Employment and Occupation) Convention.[21] Allegations were made that the dismissal of 600 workers from the 'Aluminium' factory and of 950 workers from the 'Soko' factory was motivated solely by the 'nationality'—Bosnian or Serbian—of the workers concerned. No formal dismissal proceedings were initiated. The Labour Inspectorate, which was notified by the trade union organizations concerned, was prevented from doing its work of verifying the truth of the allegations made by the inaction of higher authorities. The Committee found the allegations made concerning the dismissals of workers solely because of their Bosnian or Serbian origin were corroborated by a coherent body of evidence. The persistence of discriminatory practices in employment (based essentially on national extraction and/or religion) in Bosnia and Herzegovina was also corroborated by the 1998 report of the three Ombudsmen for Bosnia and Herzegovina, which confirmed that violations of workers' rights often took the form of discrimination based on ethnic extraction, and that workers had little chance of obtaining protection from the courts.

The Committee emphasized that the primary responsibility of any State that ratifies an ILO Convention is to ensure that it is actually applied. As regards Convention No. 111, simply incorporating the principle of non-

---

[20] On reparations, see also the Report of the Committee set up to examine the representation presented by the National Confederation of Workers of Senegal under Article 24 of the Constitution alleging non-observance by Mauritania of International Labour Conventions Nos. 95, 102, 111, 118, and 122 (12 Nov. 1990) which, *inter alia*, recommended that 'The Government should make every effort to make reparation for the prejudice suffered by Mauritanian nationals against whom there was discrimination, by the restoration to these persons of their rights.'

[21] Report of the Committee set up to examine representations alleging non-observance by Bosnia and Herzegovina of the Discrimination (Employment and Occupation) Convention, 1958 (No. 111), made under Article 24 of the ILO Constitution by the Union of Autonomous Trade Unions of Bosnia and Herzegovina (ILO).

discrimination in employment into the Constitution or legislation is not in itself enough to ensure that the principle is applied in practice; it is also necessary to provide practical guarantees of non-discrimination. The Committee recommended to the Governing Body, *inter alia*, that it invite the Government of Bosnia and Herzegovina to take the necessary measures to ensure that workers dismissed from the 'Aluminium' and 'Soko' factories solely on the grounds of their Bosnian or Serbian extraction or their religion receive adequate compensation for the damage that they have sustained. They should also receive payment of any wage arrears and any other benefits to which they would be entitled if they had not been dismissed. 'As far as possible' they should be reinstated in their posts without losing length of service entitlements. In addition, more generally, the Government should be invited to ensure that a formal dismissal procedure be instituted, in accordance with the provisions of Convention No. 158 which has been ratified by Bosnia and Herzegovina, if the reinstatement of all or some of the workers in question is not possible.

(iii) International Convention on the Elimination of All Forms of Racial Discrimination

(a) *Provisions of the Convention*

The ICERD provides in several different parts of the Convention for national remedial or enforcement structures.[22] Article 2(1) provides that States Parties 'undertake to pursue by all appropriate means and without delay a policy of eliminating racial discrimination'. To this end, the Convention continues, each State Party undertakes to engage in no act or practice of racial discrimination against persons, groups of persons or

---

[22] In addition to those sources discussed subsequently, see also Commission on Human Rights, 'Report of the United Nations seminar to assess the implementation of the International Convention on the Elimination of All Forms of Racial Discrimination with particular reference to articles 4 and 6' (Geneva, 9–13 Sept. 1996); E/CN.4/1997/68/Add.1 (5 Dec. 1996); Preparatory Committee, 'Report of the Consultation on the World Conference against Racism, Racial Discrimination, Xenophobia, and Related Forms of Intolerance held at The Rockefeller Foundation's Study and Conference Center Bellagio, Italy', A/CONF.189/PC.1/10 (8 Mar. 2000); Preparatory Committee, First session, Geneva 1–5 May 2000, 'Proposals for the work of the World Conference against Racism, Racial Discrimination, Xenophobia and Related Intolerance: working paper submitted by Mr. Paulo Sérgio Pinheiro, member of the Sub-Commission, in accordance with Sub-Commission resolutions 1998/6 and 1999/6', A/CONF.189/PC.1/13/Add.1 (6 Mar. 2000); 'United Nations strategies to combat racism and racial discrimination: past experiences and present perspectives'. Background paper prepared by Mr Theodor van Boven, member of the Committee on the Elimination of Racial Discrimination, in accordance with paragraph 51 of Commission resolution 1998/26.

institutions and to ensure that all public authorities and public institutions, national and local, shall act in conformity with this obligation. Each State Party undertakes not to sponsor, defend, or support racial discrimination by any persons or organizations. Each State Party 'shall take' effective measures to review governmental, national, and local policies, and to amend, rescind or nullify any laws and regulations which have the effect of creating or perpetuating racial discrimination wherever it exists. Each State Party 'shall prohibit and bring to an end, by all appropriate means', including legislation as required by circumstances, racial discrimination by any persons, group or organization. Each State Party undertakes to encourage, where appropriate, integrationist multi-racial organizations and movements and other means of eliminating barriers between races, and to discourage anything which tends to strengthen racial division. Article 2(3) provides that States Parties 'shall, when the circumstances so warrant, take, in the social, economic, cultural and other fields, special and concrete measures to ensure the adequate development and protection of certain racial groups or individuals belonging to them, for the purpose of guaranteeing them the full and equal enjoyment of human rights and fundamental freedoms. . . .' Article 3 provides that States Parties 'undertake to prevent, prohibit and eradicate all practices of [racial segregation and apartheid] in territories under their jurisdiction'.

Article 4 provides that States Parties 'undertake to adopt immediate and positive measures designed to eradicate all incitement to, or acts of, such discrimination'. To this end, and with due regard to other human rights, States Parties are obliged to take certain actions. They 'shall declare an offence punishable by law all dissemination of ideas based on racial superiority or hatred, incitement to racial discrimination, as well as all acts of violence or incitement to such acts against any race or groups of persons of another colour or ethnic origin, and also the provision of any assistance to racist activities, including the financing thereof'. They 'shall declare illegal and prohibit organizations, and also organized and all other propaganda activities, which promote and incite racial discrimination, and shall recognize participation in such organizations or activities as an offence punishable by law'. They 'shall not permit public authorities or public institutions, national or local, to promote or incite racial discrimination'.

Article 6 provides for individual remedies. States Parties

shall assure to everyone within their jurisdiction effective protection and remedies, through the competent national tribunals and other State institutions, against any acts of racial discrimination which violate his human rights and fundamental freedoms contrary to this Convention, as well as the right to seek from such tribunals just and adequate reparation or satisfaction for any damage suffered as a result of such discrimination.

(b) General Recommendations

CERD has adopted several general recommendations of relevance. In General Recommendation 26,[23] the Committee notifies the States Parties of its interpretation of Article 6 of CERD regarding the right to seek just and adequate reparation or satisfaction for any damage suffered as a result of discrimination. The Committee is of the opinion that this right 'is not necessarily secured solely by the punishment of the perpetrator of the discrimination'.[24] Courts and other competent authorities 'should consider awarding financial compensation for damage, material or moral, suffered by a victim whenever appropriate',[25] because it believes 'that the degree to which acts of racial discrimination and racial insults damage the injured party's perception of his/her own worth and reputation is often underestimated'.[26] Banton states that to comply with the Convention, a state has to enact laws prohibiting both actions with a discriminatory purpose (direct discrimination) and actions with a discriminatory effect (indirect discrimination). States Parties may provide different penalties to deal with indirect discrimination because it does not spring from a guilty mind.[27]

With regard to the provisions of Article 4, in the view of the Committee the discretion to employ appropriate means as stated in Article 2 is overridden in the case of racial incitement by the wording of Article 4(a) and (b). In saying that certain acts shall be punishable, the Convention requires sanctions under the criminal law. Actions prohibited under other articles of the Convention can be dealt with under other branches of law: administrative law, constitutional law, civil law, labour law, and so on, but not those to which Articles 4(a) and (b) relate.[28] The Committee is of the opinion that incorporating or transforming the Convention into the domestic law of the ratifying state without enacting the necessary legislation stipulated by Article 4 is not sufficient for a full implementation of the article.[29] Even when international treaties automatically become part of domestic law, further legislation is needed to specify the punishment that will follow breach of the obligation under Article 4(a) and to give particular tribunals jurisdiction.[30] CERD has adopted the position that the obligations of Article 4(b) are categoric and unconditional.[31] In reviewing the report of Chile, for example, the Committee stated that the provisions of Article 4, especially 4(b) were mandatory; states should act against racist

---

[23] 24 Mar. 2000. [24] Para. 2.   [25] Para. 2.   [26] Para. 1.

[27] M. Banton, *International Action Against Racial Discrimination* (1996), at 66.

[28] Ibid., at 205.

[29] Commission on Human Rights, 'Report of the United Nations seminar to assess the implementation of the International Convention on the Elimination of All Forms of Racial Discrimination with particular reference to articles 4 and 6' (Geneva, 9–13 Sept. 1996); E/CN.4/1997/68/Add.1 (5 Dec. 1996) at para. 39.

[30] Banton *supra* n. 27, at 196.   [31] Ibid., at 204.

organizations at the earliest possible moment, before any actual incidents of racial discrimination or violence occurred.[32]

(c) Examining National Reports

Banton, in his comprehensive assessment of the practice of CERD in examining National Reports, argues that to assess the extent to which a state meets its obligations under the Convention is much more difficult than looking through the books to see what laws exist on paper. A proper assessment requires, first, an appreciation of the circumstances in which suspicions of racial discrimination might arise in the state in question. Then, secondly, an understanding is necessary of the state's legal order including its provisions regarding discrimination. Thirdly, and no less important, is information about the extent to which the laws are effectively deployed to prevent discrimination or deal with its consequences.[33] Banton asserts that CERD has done much more than compare texts of a country's laws with the obligations set out in the Convention. In accordance with Articles 2 and 9 of the Convention, it has tried to determine whether the state has taken *effective* measures as part of a policy for the elimination of racial discrimination.[34]

Article 2, paragraph 1 of the Convention calls for states to eliminate racial discrimination 'by all appropriate means'. Some reporting states simply stated to the Committee that they had not received any formal complaints, to which the Committee responded that the reason might not be an absence of discrimination, but rather a lack of knowledge, means, courage or determination on the part of its victims. States Parties to the Convention had the obligation to recognize and identify such obstacles.[35] The requirement for evidence of actual implementation of legislative provisions and effective enforcement of those provisions featured in the summary records of reporting states parties. For example, commenting on the report of Azerbaijan, CERD 'would be pleased' if the next periodic report contained more information on the actual implementation of measures against racial discrimination.[36] Regarding Bahrain, the Committee recommended that the State party provide examples of practical implementation of the provisions of the Convention. Guarantees of equality under the Constitution, or the absence of judicial ruling applying provisions of the Convention, should not be taken to imply that racial discrimination within Bahraini society did not exist.[37] Commenting on the question of implementation in Colombia, the Committee recommended that the numerous laws, decrees, and regulations should have a real and practical impact on the situation in the country.[38] The information on remedies in the

---

[32] CERD/C/SR.1347 (17 Aug. 1999) at para. 40.   [33] Banton, *supra* n. 27, at 190.
[34] Ibid., at 307.   [35] Azerbaijan; CERD/C/SR.1359 (26 Aug. 1999) at para. 40.
[36] CERD/C/SR.1359 (26 Aug. 1999) at para. 39.
[37] CERD/C/56/Misc.41/Rev.3 (24 Mar. 2000) at para. 7.
[38] CERD/C/SR.1357 (25 Aug. 1999) at para. 28.

Costa Rican report was too general; the Committee regretted that there were so few examples of prosecution and sentencing.[39] In the Czech Republic, the onus should not be on the victims to lodge complaints.[40]

As van Boven has pointed out, it is in examining reports by States Parties and in drawing up concluding observations that CERD 'focuses on patterns of racial discrimination which affect whole categories of peoples or collectivities and groups'.[41] There was a lack of awareness about recourse procedures among indigenous communities in Guatemala.[42] More expeditious independent investigations were necessary into victims of deaths in custody affecting disproportionately members of minority groups in the United Kingdom.[43] There was a need for equitable solutions for the demarcation, distribution, and restitution of land in Brazil amongst indigenous people, blacks, and mestizos.[44] There was a need for measures of affirmative action for the Roma in Romania.[45]

(d) CERD Consideration of Individual Communications

In several decisions dealing with Communications under Article 14, CERD has commented on national procedures in the context of a decision whether an *individual* had exhausted domestic remedies. The function that the exhaustion of domestic remedies rule plays in the human rights context is by no means uncontroversial, or particularly clear.[46] I have assumed, without wishing to argue the point here, that it provides, in practice if not in theory, an opportunity to the international tribunal to comment on its view of the appropriateness of the national implementation procedures. (Whether a decision by the international tribunal that a particular remedy must be exhausted amounts to a decision that an 'effective remedy' is provided must be open to doubt, although the reverse is probably correct.)

In a case from Australia,[47] although the Committee did not find a contravention, the Committee recommended that every effort should be made to avoid delay in dealing with complaints by the Human Rights and Equal Opportunity Commission. In a second complaint regarding Australia,[48] the State Party claimed that the author had failed to exhaust domestic remedies

---

[39] CERD/C/SR.1321 (17 Mar. 1999) at para. 58.
[40] CERD/C/SR.1321 (17 Mar. 1999) at para. 12.
[41] Theo van Boven, Common Problems Linked to All Remedies Available to Victims of Racial Discrimination, HR/GVA/WCR/SEM.1/2000/BP.5
[42] UN Doc. A/50/18/para. 309.   [43] UN Doc. A/51/18, para. 242.
[44] UN Doc. A/51/18, para. 309.   [45] UN Doc. A/54/18, para. 286.
[46] See T. Haesler, *The Exhaustion of Local Remedies in the Case Law of International Courts and Tribunals* (1968); A. A. C. Trindade, *The Application of the Rule of Exhaustion of Local Remedies in International Law: Its Rational in the International Protection of Human Rights* (1983); C. F. Ameriasinghe, *Local Remedies in International Law* (1990).
[47] Communication No.8/1996 Australia; (10/5/99) [CERD/C/54/D/8/1996].
[48] Australia: Communication No. 7/1995 (29/08/97) [CERD/C/51/D/7/1995].

which were both available and effective, since he could have challenged the decision he complained about in the Supreme Court of South Australia. The author replied that he was not informed of the availability of those remedies, and that the relevant precedents would have made an appeal to the Supreme Court pointless. The Committee noted that the author was legally represented. It would have been incumbent upon his legal representative to inform him of possible avenues of appeal. That the author was not informed of potential judicial remedies by the judicial authorities of South Australia did not absolve him from seeking to pursue avenues of judicial redress. Nor could the impossibility to do so, after expiration of statutory deadlines for the filing of appeals, be attributed to the State Party. The Committee did not consider that the precedents of the Supreme Court of South Australia case were necessarily dispositive of the author's case. In the circumstances, the existence of one judgment, albeit on issues similar to those in the author's case, did not absolve the author from attempting to avail himself of the remedy available. Finally, even if that recourse had failed, it would have been open to the author to appeal to the Federal court. In the circumstances, the Committee concluded that the communication was inadmissible.

In a case from Sweden,[49] the State Party contended that the author's claims were inadmissible for failure to exhaust domestic remedies, since she could have sought the help of the Ombudsman against Ethnic Discrimination in her case. She could also have raised her complaint in a District Court with the possibility of appeal to the Labour Court. The author replied that she was never informed about the possibility of the latter avenue and that appeals to the Ombudsman and the courts would in any event have failed, since the applicable legislation was deficient. The Committee noted that the author was aware of the possibility of a complaint to the Ombudsman against Ethnic Discrimination. She did not avail herself of this possibility, considering it to be futile, and because of alleged previous negative experiences with his office. She learned about the possibility of filing an action with the Labour Court and started preparations to this effect but desisted, apparently because her trade union did not support her in this endeavour as it did not find merits in her claim. She further considered that there was no real possibility of obtaining redress in the District Court because of a negative experience regarding a previous case that she had filed with the District Court. The Committee concluded that, notwithstanding the reservations that the author might have regarding the effectiveness of the current legislation to prevent racial discrimination in the labour market, it was incumbent upon her to pursue the remedies available, including a complaint before a District Court. Mere doubts about the effectiveness of such

---

[49] Sweden: Communication No. 9/1997 (17/08/98) [CERD/C/53/D/9/1997]

remedies, or the belief that the resort to them might incur costs, did not absolve a complainant from pursuing them. The Committee therefore decided that the Communication was inadmissible.

In a case from Denmark,[50] the Committee again considered whether the applicant had exhausted domestic remedies. The applicant claimed that the failure to appeal a judgment against him was due to the negligence of his lawyers. The Committee noted that the author's lawyer was privately retained. In the circumstances, this lawyer's inaction or negligence could not be attributed to the State Party. The Committee went on to note, however, that although the State Party's judicial authorities did provide the author with relevant information on how to file his appeal in a timely manner, it was questionable whether, given the fact that the author alleged himself to be the victim of racial harassment, the authorities had really exhausted all means to ensure that the author could enjoy effectively his rights in accordance with Article 6 of the Convention. However, since the author did not provide prima facie evidence that the judicial authorities were tainted by racially discriminatory considerations and since it was the author's own responsibility to pursue the domestic remedies, the Committee concluded that the Communication was inadmissible.

In two further cases, the issue did not concern the question of exhaustion of domestic remedies but whether the procedures taken by the national authorities themselves breached the Covenant. In a case from Norway,[51] the Committee considered whether the proceedings against the author respected his right to equal treatment before the tribunals, without distinction as to race, colour or national or ethnic origin. The Committee noted that the rule laid down in Article 5(a) applied to all types of judicial proceedings, including trial by jury. The Committee considered that, if a member of a jury was suspected of displaying or voicing racial bias against the accused, it was incumbent upon the national judicial authorities to investigate the issue and to disqualify the juror. However, the competent judicial bodies of Norway had examined the nature of the contested remarks and their potential implications for the course of the trial. The Committee did not consider that it was either the function of the Committee to interpret the Norwegian rules on criminal procedure concerning the disqualification of jurors, or to decide whether the juror had to be disqualified on that basis. The Committee was, therefore, unable to conclude, on the basis of the information before it, that a breach of the Convention had occurred. However, the Committee recommended to the State Party that every effort should be made to prevent any form of racial bias from entering in judicial proceedings which might result in adversely affecting the administration of justice.

[50] Denmark: Communication No. 5/1994: (15/03/95) [CERD/C/46/D/5/1994].
[51] Norway: Communication No. 3/1991 (5/03/94) [CERD/C/44/D/3/1991].

Consequently, the Committee recommended that in criminal cases like the one it had examined due attention be given to the impartiality of juries, in line with the principles underlying Article 5 of the Convention.

In a case against the Netherlands,[52] a Moroccan citizen complained that he had visited a house for which a lease had been offered to him and his family. When he arrived, some twenty people had gathered outside the house. During the visit, the complainant heard several of them both say and shout 'No more foreigners'. Others intimated that if he were to accept the house, they would set fire to it and damage his car. The complainant returned to the Municipal Housing Office and asked the official responsible to accompany them to the street. There, several local inhabitants told the official that they could not accept the complainant as their neighbour, owing to a presumed rule that no more than 5 per cent of the street's inhabitants should be foreigners. Told that no such rule existed, street residents drafted a petition, which noted that the complainant could not be accepted and recommended that another house be allocated to his family. On the same day, the complainant filed a complaint with the municipal police on the ground that he had been the victim of racial discrimination under the Criminal Code. He stated that, initially, the police officer refused to register the complaint, and that it took mediation by a local anti-discrimination group before the police agreed to prepare a report. The complainant's lawyer had apprised the prosecutor of the District Court of the matter and requested access to all the documents on the file. The prosecutor forwarded these documents, but informed the complainant later that the matter had not been registered as a criminal case with his office, because it was not certain that a criminal offence had taken place. The lawyer then requested the Court of Appeal of Amsterdam to order prosecution of the group of residents. The Prosecutor-General at the Court of Appeal asked the court to declare the complaint unfounded or to refuse to hear it on public interest grounds. Before the Court of Appeal, it transpired that only two of the street's inhabitants had actually been summoned to appear. They did not appear personally but were represented. The Court of Appeal dismissed the complainant's case. It held *inter alia*, that the petition was not a document of a deliberately insulting nature, nor a document that was inciting to racial discrimination within the meaning of the Dutch Criminal Code. In the context, the Court of Appeal held that the heading to the petition—which, taking into account statements made during the hearing and to the police, should be interpreted as meaning 'Not accepted because of a fight? Another house for the family please?'— could not be considered to be insulting or as an incitement to racial dis-crimination, however regrettable and undesirable it might have been. As a last resort, the complainant wrote to the Minister of Justice, asking him to order

---

[52] Netherlands: Communication No 4/1991(16/03/93) [CERD/C/42/D/4/1991].

the prosecutor to initiate proceedings in the case. The Minister replied that he could not grant the request, as the Court of Appeal had fully reviewed the case and there was no scope for further proceedings under the Dutch Code of Criminal Procedure. The complainant alleged that the judicial authorities and the public prosecutor did not properly examine all the relevant facts.

The Committee found that, on the basis of the information before it, the investigation into these incidents by the police and prosecution authorities was incomplete. The Committee 'cannot accept any claim that the enactment of law making racial discrimination a criminal act in itself represents full compliance with the obligations of States parties under the Convention'. The Committee reaffirmed its view[53] that

the freedom to prosecute criminal offences—commonly known as the expediency principle—is governed by considerations of public policy and notes that the Convention cannot be interpreted as challenging the raison d'être of that principle. Notwithstanding, it should be applied in each case of alleged racial discrimination in the light of the guarantees laid down in the Convention.

It was incumbent upon the State to investigate with due diligence and expedition. In the instant case, the State Party failed to do this. The Committee recommended that the State should review its policy and procedures concerning the decision to prosecute in cases of alleged racial discrimination, in light of its obligations under Article 4 of the Convention, and provide the complainant with relief commensurate with the moral damage he had suffered.

Delays in the operation of the judicial process have been identified, leading effectively to denial of individual justice. In the concluding observations in its 1996 report, CERD had expressed concern to Denmark about its delay in compensating members of the indigenous population relocated from Thule, the northernmost village in Greenland, in 1953. In August 1999, the Danish Supreme Court handed down a judgment in which it had found that the state was liable to pay the plaintiffs damage for lost hunting rights as well as individual compensation for the transfer of the population. The Government had accepted the judgment, but an appeal had been lodged.[54] In two cases relating to Australia,[55] filed respectively by an Australian citizen of Pakistani origin and an Australian doctor of Indian origin the Committee did not come to the conclusion that the facts submitted disclosed a violation of the Convention. However, the Committee expressed itself in critical terms on the delays and the complexities of the recourse procedures in the State Party. The Committee suggested that the procedures to deal with complaints of racial

[53] As stated in its Opinion on Communication No. 1/1984 of 10 Aug. 1987 (*Yilmaz-Dogan v The Netherlands*)

[54] CERD/C/SR.1377 at para. 13 (14 Mar. 2000).

[55] Communications No. 6/1995 and No. 8/1996.

discrimination be simplified, in particular those in which more than one recourse measure is available, and avoid any delay in the consideration of complaints. The Committee further recommended that Australia should make every effort to avoid any delay in the consideration of all complaints by its agency responsible for adjudicating complaints of discrimination, the Human Rights and Equal Opportunity Commission.[56]

(iv) United Nations Attempts to Systematize Required Remedies

In 1979 the participants of the United Nations Seminar on Recourse Procedures Available to Victims of Racial Discrimination and Activities to be Undertaken at the Regional Level[57] reached a consensus on several issues relating to national remedial structures. States 'should follow or at least consider the example of conciliation procedures in minor cases of racial discrimination, or in the most common cases'. Every country should, 'by all appropriate means, publicize [recourse] procedures and assist victims of racial discrimination to initiate these'. Access to recourse procedures should 'be as broad as possible, [and] . . . in each country all persons, citizens and non-citizens or groups should have access to recourse procedures'. The rules relating to the initiation of complaints should be 'simple and flexible'. There should be reasonable time-limits with regard to the length of investigations. The organs dealing with complaints should be impartial. Victims of racial discrimination should receive legal aid and assistance whether in civil or criminal proceedings. Complaints of racial discrimination should be dealt with expeditiously. Victims should receive 'full and immediate compensation commensurate with the injury sustained'.

Within the framework of the second Programme of Action to Combat Racial Discrimination, the Secretary-General submitted to the General Assembly, at its thirty-ninth session, a Plan of Activities for the Second Decade, in which it was suggested that the General Assembly could consider inviting the Secretary-General to prepare model legislation, which could be used by States as a basis or as guidelines for the enactment or further development of legislation against racial discrimination. In November 1985 the General Assembly requested the Secretary-General to prepare and issue as soon as possible a collection of model legislation for the guidance of Governments in the enactment of further legislation against racial discrimination.[58] In December 1992 the General Assembly requested the Secretary-

---

[56] Prep Com, Background paper prepared by Mr Theo van Boven: HR/GVA/WCR/ SEM.1/2000/BP.5 at 15 (12 Jan. 2000).

[57] UN Doc. ST/HR/SER.A/3, para. 215.

[58] GA Res 39/16, 23 Nov. 1984.

General to revise and finalize the draft model legislation in the light of comments made by CERD and publish and distribute the text.[59]

The text of the Model Legislation, in so far as it considers enforcement and remedial structures, has several important elements. In several respects they reflect, unsurprisingly, the approach taken by CERD. First, 'All human beings are entitled to equal protection of the law against racial discrimination; this includes the right to an effective remedy against racial discrimination, as well as the right to seek just and adequate reparation or other satisfaction for any damage[60] suffered as a result of such discrimination.'[61] Secondly, 'reparation' should be made to victims of racial discrimination by means of 'restitution and/or compensation' which may take the form of a payment for the harm or loss suffered, reimbursement of expenses incurred, provision of services or restoration of rights, as well as other measures taken within a specified period for the purpose of correcting or mitigating the adverse effects on the victims of any of the offences of discrimination. Victims are also entitled to recourse to all other means of satisfaction, such as publication of the judicial decision in an organ having wide circulation at the offender's expense or guarantee of the victim's right of reply by a similar means. Thirdly, individuals or groups of individuals are entitled to make complaints of racial discrimination. Legal persons which came into existence prior to the commission of the offence and whose purpose is to combat racial discrimination are also entitled to enter complaints alleging racial discrimination under the Act, including complaints on behalf (or with the consent) of the victim or alleged victim. Fourthly, complaints regarding alleged acts of racial discrimination may be submitted to the appropriate judicial bodies or be entered in accordance with other domestic recourse procedures. Judicial bodies have automatic jurisdiction with respect to acts of racial discrimination that threaten public order. Fifthly, acts of racial discrimination are criminalized, in particular acts of incitement to racial hatred, but going well beyond this into discrimination in the context of employment, education, housing, and the provision of goods, facilities, and services. These offences 'shall be punished' by imprisonment, fines, suspension of the right to be elected to a public office, and community service. Sixthly, an independent national commission against racial discrimination is established, with such functions as giving advisory opinions to assist in the implementation of the Act, preparing codes of conduct, proposing legislative amendments, providing information and education, receiving complaints from alleged victims, conducting inquiries either on behalf of a complainant or on its own behalf, acting as a mediator either on behalf of a complainant or on its own behalf, bringing legal actions on behalf of a complainant or on its own behalf, and providing legal aid and assistance to alleged victims who have instituted court proceedings under the Act.

---

[59] GA Res 47/77, 16 Dec. 1992, para. 9.
[60] Para. 8 speaks in terms of 'harm'.   [61] Para. 5.

(v) Affirmative Action

The concept of affirmative action 'is generally referred to in international law as "special measures" '.[62] Several international human rights conventions contain provisions envisaging such special measures.[63] In neither the ICCPR nor the ICESCR are such provisions to be found. However, both Committees have given their approval to such measures as compatible with the respective covenants. In the Human Rights Committee's General Comment No. 18 on 'Non-discrimination',[64] the Committee stresses that

the principle of equality sometimes requires States to take affirmative action in order to diminish or eliminate conditions which cause or help to perpetuate discrimination prohibited by the Covenant. For example, in a State where the general conditions of a certain part of the population prevent or impair their enjoyment of human rights, the State should take specific action to correct those conditions. Such action may involve granting for a time to the part of the population concerned certain preferential treatment in specific matters as compared with the rest of the population. However, as long as such action is needed to correct discrimination in fact, it is a case of legitimate differentiation under the Covenant.[65]

The practice of the Human Rights Committee confirms these views.[66]

A similar point is made with regard to Article 27 ICCPR on minority rights. The Committee, in its General Comment No. 23 on 'The rights of minorities',[67] recognizes that the rights protected under Article 27 are individual rights, but stresses that 'positive measures by States may also be necessary to protect the identity of a minority and the rights of its members to enjoy and develop their culture and language and to practise their religion, in community with the other members of the group'.[68] The Committee considers

that such positive measures must respect the provisions of article 2.1 and 26 of the Covenant both as regards the treatment between different minorities and the treatment between the persons belonging to them and the remaining part of the population. However, as long as those measures are aimed at correcting conditions which prevent or impair the enjoyment of the rights guaranteed under article 27, they may constitute a legitimate differentiation under the Covenant, provided that they are based on reasonable and objective criteria.[69]

---

[62] 'The concept and practice of affirmative action': Preliminary report submitted by Mr Marc Bossuyt, Special Rapporteur, in accordance with Sub-Commission resolution 1998/5, Sub-Commission on the Promotion and Protection of Human Rights, E/CN.4/Sub.2/2000/11, 19 June 2000, para. 4.

[63] Art. 1(4) ICERD; Article 4(1) CEDAW; ILO Convention No. 111, Art. 5.

[64] 10 Nov. 1989.   [65] Para. 10.

[66] Sweden, CCPR/C/SR.189, paras 15–16; *Stalla Costa v Uruguay*, Communication No. 198/1985.

[67] 8 Apr. 1994.   [68] Para. 6.2.   [69] Para. 6.2.

Regarding the implementation of the equality and non-discrimination obligation in the context of the ICESCR, Craven has argued that legislative action 'must be considered a necessary first step', but that 'any legislative measures taken, to be effective, should be accompanied by judicial remedies'. Legislation, whilst necessary, is not sufficient, and other measures, 'particularly educational and social' may be appropriate. Where the pursuit of equality of opportunity is in issue, 'extensive measures' may be called for, including the adoption of positive measures 'to promote the position of the vulnerable and disadvantaged groups in society'.[70] The Committee has stated in its General Comment No. 13 that the adoption of temporary special measures intended to bring about de facto equality for disadvantaged groups is not a violation of the right to non-discrimination with regard to equality.[71]

(vi) Three Models of Equality Revisited

We can see, therefore, that of the three models of equality sketched out earlier, the individual justice model and the group justice model are well recognized in general terms in the practice of the bodies we have considered so far. What emerges clearly, however, is the importance of treating the practice of these bodies holistically. Otherwise, there is a considerable risk that a misleading impression will be gained. To focus only on CERD's treatment of individual communications, for example, gives the incorrect impression that it is concerned only with an individual justice model. What is striking also is the almost complete absence of anything recognizably similar to the third model of equality, 'equality as participation'. With the exception of the provisions in the ILO Convention urging collective bargaining as a method of tackling discrimination, participative approaches are almost entirely absent.

IV. DEVELOPING INTERNATIONAL NORMS ON HUMAN RIGHTS REMEDIES GENERALLY

Having examined the bodies primarily involved in developing the international law relating to racial discrimination, we can turn more broadly to see that these approaches are in line with, have influenced, and in turn influence the developing international norms relating to national enforcement of human rights more generally.

---

[70] Quotations from M. Craven, *The International Covenant on Economic, Social, and Cultural Rights* (1995), at 183–4.
[71] General Comment No. 13, paras. 32–3.

(i) A General International Law of (Domestic) Remedies?

An appropriate initial issue is the extent to which there are general international law principles regarding the appropriate type of enforcement and remedial institutions that should exist at the national level, where the domestic application of an international law obligation is required. Is there a developed set of general international law requirements *directly* applicable to domestic structures and remedies where they are required by international obligations? We can say that there appear to be no firm requirements *directly* applicable to domestic structures and remedies, where these are required by international obligations, other (perhaps) than the relatively unspecific principle that states must take steps towards the realization of the obligations of the Treaty.[72] We would be hard put to identify a clear set of more specific general international law requirements (either Treaty- or custom-based) that set out what municipal legal systems must provide by way of enforcement or remedial structures, apart from the more specific requirements discussed below, and leaving aside specific Treaty-based requirements as to national implementation required to comply with the Treaty. That is generally regarded as up to the state concerned. In the terminology of the International Law Commission, international law in general imposes 'obligations of result', rather than 'obligations of conduct'.[73] Provided the state conforms to international law in its dealings with other states, *how* it does so at the domestic level is generally thought to be an exercise of national sovereignty. In principle, a state may choose any domestic methods by which to achieve the obligation undertaken.

The major exception to this arises from human rights obligations. For those parties to the relevant treaties, the appropriate enforcement and remedial structures established in municipal legal systems generally must conform to the requirements that arise from those human rights provisions guaranteeing fair criminal trials and fair legal procedures generally, where those are required, such as arising from Articles 5 and 6 of the European Convention on Human Rights,[74] and Articles 9 and 14 of the ICCPR.[75] These have the effect of precluding elements of racial discrimination in the operation of these procedures.[76] Apart from these requirements, specific treaties also specify the need for effective remedies to be provided in the national legal system, where a breach of human rights has occurred.

---

[72] See *The Case Relative to the Exchange of Greek and Turkish Populations Under the Lausanne Convention VI*, PCIJ (1925), Series B, No. 10 at 20.

[73] Report of the International Law Commission (1977), 2 Yrbk. ILC 20, para. 8.

[74] ECHR on fair trial etc.

[75] See D. McGoldrick, *The Human Rights Committee* (1991), ch. 10.

[76] See, for example, in the context of the European Court of Human Rights *Remli v France*, 23 Apr. 1996; *Gregory v United Kingdom*, 25 Feb. 1997.

(ii) International Covenant on Economic, Social and Cultural Rights

The ICESCR provides in Article 2, paragraph 1, that each State Party

undertakes to take steps, individually and through international assistance and co-operation, especially economic and technical, to the maximum of its available resources, with a view to achieving progressively the full realization of the rights recognized in the present Covenant by all appropriate means, including particularly the adoption of legislative measures.

Craven, in his authoritative study of the Covenant, comments that 'in principle, a State may choose between legislative, administrative, judicial, social, educational, or other methods to undertake the realization' of the rights in the Covenant.[77] Given the variety of different economic, social, and legal systems existing among states that are parties to the Covenant, and their different levels of development, 'it is natural that the approach of each State will vary according to the circumstances in which it finds itself'.[78]

Nevertheless, the CESCR has adopted an important General Comment on 'The domestic application of the Covenant' in December 1998.[79] The Committee considered the states' obligation to give effect to the rights contained in the Covenant 'by all appropriate means'. The duty to give effect to the Covenant in the domestic legal system is reinforced by the rule requiring the exhaustion of domestic remedies. This, the Committee stated, was 'a broad and flexible approach which enables the particularities of the legal and administrative systems of each State, as well as other relevant considerations, to be taken into account'.[80] But alongside this flexibility went the obligation 'to use all the means at its disposal'.[81] The Covenant's norms

must be recognized in appropriate ways within the domestic legal order, appropriate means of redress, or remedies, must be available to any aggrieved individual or group, and appropriate means of ensuring governmental accountability must be put in place.[82]

Although the Committee recognized that the Covenant contained no 'direct counterpart' to the provision of the ICCPR regarding judicial remedies, nevertheless

a State Party seeking to justify its failure to provide any domestic legal remedies for violations of economic, social and cultural rights would need to show either that such remedies are not 'appropriate means' . . . or that, in view of the other means used, they are unnecessary. It will be difficult to show this and the Committee considers that, in many cases, the other 'means' used could be rendered ineffective if they are not reinforced or complemented by judicial remedies.[83]

---

[77] Craven, *supra* n. 70, at 115.   [78] Ibid.   [79] E/C.12/1998/24, 3 Dec. 1998.
[80] Para. 1.   [81] Para. 2.   [82] Ibid.   [83] Para. 3.

In part, this interpretation is justified, according to the Committee, by a 'principle of international law',[84] reflected in Article 8 of the Universal Declaration of Human Rights, according to which 'Everyone has the right to an effective remedy by the competent national tribunals for acts violating the fundamental rights granted him by the constitution or by law.' This right to an effective remedy 'need not be interpreted as always requiring a judicial remedy'.[85] Administrative remedies

will, in many cases, be adequate and those living within the jurisdiction of a State party have a legitimate expectation, based on the principle of good faith, that all administrative authorities will take account of the requirements of the Covenant in their decision-making.

Such administrative remedies 'should be accessible, affordable, timely and effective'.[86] An 'ultimate right of judicial appeal from administrative procedures of this type would also often be appropriate'.[87] But there are some obligations, and the Committee singles out the obligation of non-discrimination, 'in relation to which the provision of some form of judicial remedy would seem indispensable in order to satisfy the requirements of the Covenant'.[88]

(iii) International Covenant on Civil and Political Rights

The ICCPR is somewhat more explicit and detailed as to what is required, although still pretty vague. Article 2(2) provides that

Where not already provided for by existing legislative or other measures, each State Party to the present Covenant undertakes to take the necessary steps, in accordance with its constitutional processes and with the provisions of the present Covenant, to adopt such legislative or other measures as may be necessary to give effect to the rights recognized in the present Covenant.

In its General Comment No. 3, on 'Implementation at the national level',[89] the Committee notes that Article 2 of the Covenant 'generally leaves it to the States parties concerned to choose their method of implementation in their territories within the framework set out in that article'. It goes on, however, to make two important points which limit this apparent flexibility. The first is that 'the implementation does not depend solely on constitutional or legislative enactments, which are often not *per se* sufficient'. The second point is that the State's obligation under the Covenant is not confined 'to the respect of human rights'. States 'have also undertaken to ensure the enjoyment of these rights to all individuals under their jurisdiction. This aspect calls for specific activities by the States parties to enable individuals to enjoy their rights.'[90]

[84] Ibid. [85] Para 9. [86] Ibid. [87] Ibid.
[88] Ibid. [89] 31 July 1981. [90] Para. 1.

Article 2(3) provides specifically for an individualized remedy to be made available. First, each State Party undertakes 'to ensure that any person whose rights or freedoms as herein recognized are violated shall have an effective remedy, notwithstanding that the violation has been committed by persons acting in an official capacity'. Secondly, States Parties also undertake to

ensure that any person claiming such a remedy shall have his right thereto determined by competent judicial, administrative or legislative authorities, or by any other competent authority provided for by the legal system of the State, and to develop the possibilities of judicial remedy.

Thirdly, States Parties undertake to ensure that the competent authorities shall enforce such remedies when granted. In considering the reports of the States Parties, the Committee has 'devoted considerable and painstaking attention' to examining the details of domestic remedies provided.[91] In its examination of communications under the Optional Protocol, the Committee 'has consistently stressed the requirement of an effective remedy in terms of the measures necessary to remedy the violations, pay adequate compensation, and to take steps to ensure that similar violations do not occur in the future.'[92]

(iv) Paris Principles on National Human Rights Institutions

In 1993 the General Assembly adopted an important resolution regarding national institutions for the promotion and protection of human rights,[93] in which it encouraged Member States 'to establish or, where they already exist, to strengthen national institutions for the promotion and protection of human rights'. It welcomed a set of Principles (the 'Paris Principles'), developed in 1991, relating to the status and powers of such bodies, which were annexed to the Resolution. The General Assembly encouraged the establishment and strengthening of national institutions having regard to those Principles, 'recognizing that it is the right of each State to choose the framework that is best suited to its particular needs at the national level'.[94]

---

[91] McGoldrick, *supra* n. 75, at 279.

[92] Ibid., at 285. See also the practice of the HRC in its interpretation of the requirement that to be admissible, applicants must have exhausted domestic remedies, ibid., at 189–96.

[93] GA Res. 48/134 of 20 Dec. 1993, UN Doc. A/Res/48/134, 4 Mar. 1994. See also Commission on Human Rights Resolution 1992/54, 3 Mar. 1992. See also United Nations Centre for Human Rights, *National Human Rights Institutions: A Handbook on the Establishment and Strengthening of National Institutions for the Promotion and Protection of Human Rights*, Professional Training Series No. 4 at 4–6, UN Doc. HR/P/Pt/4 (New York and Geneva, 1995).

[94] Para. 12.

The Resolution further requested that the then Centre for Human Rights of the United Nations Secretariat (later the new United Nations High Commissioner for Human Rights) should promote the establishment of such national institutions.

The Paris Principles have, since that Resolution, served as a set of guidelines that the Office of the UNHCHR uses in its work of encouraging the establishment of national institutions. These Principles are concerned with the competence and responsibilities of such bodies, their composition and guarantees of independence and pluralism, their methods of operation, and their status. Regarding the competence and responsibilities of such bodies, the Principles provide that a national institution should be 'vested with competence to promote and protect human rights'.[95] It should 'be given as broad a mandate as possible', which should be set out 'in a constitutional or legislative text'. It should have several different functions and responsibilities. It should submit to the Government, Parliament, and other competent body (either at the request of the authorities concerned or on its own discretion) opinions, recommendations, proposals, and reports on any matters concerning the promotion and protection of human rights. These should include reports on whether existing or proposed legislation or administrative provisions conform to the fundamental principles of human rights, as well as reports on any violations of human rights which it decides to take up, including the power to draw the attention of the Government to proposals for initiatives to put an end to such situations. The national institution should be empowered to promote and ensure the harmonization of national legislation, regulations, and practices with the international human rights instruments to which the state is a party, and their effective implementation. It should also be able to encourage ratification of international human rights instruments. It should contribute to the reports which states are required to submit to the United Nations and committees, and to regional institutions, and where necessary to express an opinion on the subject. It should be able to cooperate with the United Nations and any other organization in the United Nations system, regional institutions, and the national institutions, of other countries that are competent in the areas of the promotion and protection of human rights. The Principles are also concerned with the composition of, and guarantees of independence for, these national institutions. The procedure of appointment to the national institution should

ensure the pluralist representation of the social forces (of civilian society) involved in the promotion and protection of human rights, particularly by powers which will enable effective cooperation to be established with, or through the presence of, representatives of . . . non-governmental organisations responsible for human rights and efforts to combat racial discrimination . . .

[95] Para. 1.

The institution should have 'adequate funding' to enable it to have its own staff and premises, in order to be independent of the Government and not be subject to financial control which might affect its independence. The Principles provide additional suggestions where a national institution is authorized to hear and consider complaints and petitions concerning individual situations. Such functions, the Principles state, 'may be based' on several principles. These include, seeking an amicable settlement through conciliation or, within the limits prescribed by the law, through binding decisions or, where necessary, on the basis of confidentiality; informing the party who filed the petition of his rights, in particular the remedies available to him, and promoting his access to them; hearing any complaints or petitions or transmitting them to any other competent authority within the limits prescribed by the law; and making recommendations to the competent authority, especially by proposing amendments or reforms of the laws, regulations, and administrative practices especially if they have created difficulties encountered by the persons filing the petitions in order to assert their rights.

These Principles have been significant in influencing the approaches to national enforcement adopted by other international bodies and by national governments.[96] We can point to two in particular. In General Recommendation No. 17 on 'Establishment of national institutions to facilitate the implementation of the Convention',[97] CERD recommends States Parties to establish national commissions or other appropriate bodies, taking into account the Paris Principles, to serve such purposes as: the promotion of respect for the enjoyment of human rights without discrimination, the review of government policy towards protection against racial discrimination, the monitoring of legislative compliance with the provisions of the Convention, the education of the public about the obligations of States Parties, and assisting the Government in the preparation of reports to CERD.

In December 1998 the Committee on Economic, Social and Cultural Rights adopted its General Comment on 'The role of national human rights institutions in the protection of economic, social and cultural rights'.[98] In this, the Committee again considered the states' obligation to give effect to the rights contained in the Covenant 'by all appropriate means'. The Committee noted that one such means is the work of national institutions for the promotion of human rights, and drew attention to the work of the OHCHR in assisting and encouraging states in the establishment of

---

[96] See Relf, 'Building Democratic Institutions: The Role of National Human Rights Institutions in Good Governance and Human Rights Protection', 13 *Harvard Human Rights Journal* (2000) 1.

[97] 19 Mar. 1993.   [98] E/C.12/1998/25, 3 Dec. 1998.

such institutions. Such institutions 'range from national human rights commissions through Ombudsman offices, public interest or other human rights "advocates" to *defenseurs du peuple* and *defensores del pueblo*'.[99] The Committee considered that national institutions 'have a potentially crucial role to play in promoting and ensuring the indivisibility and interdependence of all human rights'. The Comment lists the types of activities that can be and in some instances have already been undertaken in relation to these rights: the promotion of educational and information programmes, scrutinizing existing laws and administrative acts, providing technical advice, conducting research and inquiries, monitoring compliance with specific rights, and examining complaints alleging infringements.[100]

(v) UN Basic Principles and Guidelines on the Right to a Remedy and Reparations

More recently, in April 2000, a set of *Basic Principles and Guidelines on the Right to a Remedy and Reparation for Victims of Violations of International Human Rights and Humanitarian Law* were adopted by the Commission on Human Rights.[101] These *Basic Principles* had a long and tortuous history,[102] demonstrating the difficulty of defining general guidelines on remedial issues. This need not detain us here. It is the substance of the Guidelines that is of particular relevance for our inquiry. The Basic Principles are by far the most detailed general set of international human rights principles relating to the enforcement and remedial structures necessary in domestic law for upholding international human rights law.

The Basic Principles state that states shall ensure, if they have not already done so, that domestic law is consistent with international human rights and humanitarian legal obligations in four ways. States shall ensure that norms of international human rights and humanitarian law are to be incorporated into domestic law, 'or otherwise implemented in their domestic legal system'.[103] States shall ensure that 'appropriate and effective judicial and administrative

---

[99] Para. 2.   [100] Para. 3.

[101] Commission on Human Rights Resolution, 2000/41, The right to restitution, compensation and rehabilitation for victims of grave violations of human rights and fundamental freedoms, E/CN.4/Res/2000/41, 20 Apr. 2000. The Basic Principles are annexed to the final report of the independent expert appointed to revise an earlier draft, see Final report of the Special Rapporteur, Mr M. Cherif Bassiouni, submitted in accordance with Commission resolution 1999/33, E/CN.4/2000/62, 18 Jan. 2000.

[102] See D. Shelton, *Remedies in International Human Rights Law* (1999), at 18–22 (up to 1999).

[103] Art. 2(a).

procedures and other appropriate measures' are adopted 'that provide fair, effective and prompt access to justice'.[104] '[E]ffective and prompt reparation'[105] shall be made available. States shall ensure that if there is a difference between national and international norms, 'that the norm that provides the greatest degree of protection is applied'.[106] In addition, a state has the obligation to ensure respect for and enforce international human rights law in several specified ways. It must 'take appropriate legal and administrative measures to prevent violations'. It must investigate violations and, 'where appropriate, take action against the violator in accordance with domestic and international law'. It must provide victims 'with equal and effective access to justice irrespective of who may be the ultimate bearer of responsibility for the violation.' It must afford appropriate remedies to victims, and it must provide for or facilitate reparation to victims.

Special provisions apply to violations of international human rights and humanitarian law that constitute crimes under international law. Such violations carry the

duty to prosecute persons alleged to have committed these violations, to punish perpetrators adjudged to have committed these violations, and to cooperate with and assist States and appropriate international judicial organs in the investigation and prosecution of these violations.[107]

States 'shall incorporate within their domestic law' appropriate provisions providing for universal jurisdiction over crimes under international law and appropriate legislation to facilitate extradition or surrender of offenders to other states and to international judicial bodies. Statutes of limitations regarding prosecutions should not apply in such cases.

Victims of violations of international human rights and humanitarian law have a right to a remedy. These remedies include the victims, right to access justice, to receive reparation for harm suffered, and to access factual information concerning the violations. We shall examine each in turn. To secure the victims' right to access justice, the state should not have such limitations on prosecution or pursuing civil claims that unduly restrict the ability of a victim to pursue a claim against the perpetrator. Limitations should not apply with respect to periods during which effective remedies did not exist for violations of human rights norms. States should make known, through public and private mechanisms, all available remedies for violations of international human rights law. States should take measures to minimize the inconvenience to victims, protect their privacy 'as appropriate', and ensure their safety before, during, and after any relevant proceedings. All appropriate diplomatic and legal means

---

[104] Art. 2(b).   [105] Art. 2(c).   [106] Art. 2(d).   [107] Art. 4.

to ensure that victims can exercise their rights to a remedy and reparation for violations of international human rights law should be made available. In addition to individual access to justice, 'adequate provision' should also be made to allow 'groups of victims to present collective claims for reparation and to receive reparation collectively'.

Reparation should be adequate, effective, and prompt. Where the State is the violator, it should provide reparation to victims. Where the violation is not attributable to the state, the party responsible for the violation 'should provide reparation to the victim or to the State if the State has already provided reparation to the victim'. In the event that the party responsible for the violation is unable or unwilling to meet these obligations, the state 'should endeavour' to provide reparation 'to victims who have sustained bodily injury or impairment of physical or mental health as a result of these violations and to the families, in particular dependants of persons who have died or become physically or mentally incapacitated as a result of the violation'. The state 'should endeavour' to establish national funds for reparation to victims. A state is required to enforce its domestic judgments for reparation against private individuals or entities responsible for the violations, and 'shall endeavour' to enforce valid foreign judgments for reparations against private individuals or entities responsible for the violations.

Various forms of reparation are to be provided by states to victims of violations of international human rights law, 'taking account of individual circumstances'. These are: restitution, compensation, rehabilitation, and satisfaction and guarantees of non-repetition. The Basic Principles set out what is required under each. Restitution should, 'whenever possible', 'restore the victim to the original situation before the violation of international human rights . . . occurred'. Restitution includes restoration of liberty, legal rights, social status, family life and citizenship, return to one's place of residence, and restoration of employment and return of property. Compensation should be provided for any economically assessable damage resulting from violations of international human rights, such as physical or mental harm (including pain, suffering, and emotional distress), lost opportunities (including education), material damages and loss of earnings (including loss of earning potential), harm to reputation or dignity, and costs required for legal or expert assistance, medicines and medical services, and psychological and social services. Rehabilitation should include medical and psychological care as well as legal and social services. The longest set of provisions relate to what is required regarding satisfaction and guarantees of non-repetition. Where applicable, these should include any or all of a long list of possibilities. These include cessation of continuing violations, verification of the facts, an apology, and preventing the occurrence of violations by such means as the creation of mechanisms for preventive intervention.

(vi) Analogies from State Responsibility?

Can an international law of domestic remedies be seen as arising by analogy with the international law of remedies awarded by international bodies? It is, in general, true to say that, although there has been significant development of an international law governing the application of remedies by international bodies against states, such principles are still remarkably underdeveloped. Writing in 1987, Christine Gray observed that

The question of judicial remedies has generally been regarded as peripheral to the main study of international law; attention has been centred on the substantive rules with little consideration of the consequences of their violation in general or judicial remedies in particular.

This, she wrote,

reflects the lack of any compulsory jurisdiction in the international legal system, the low incidence of modern judicial and arbitral settlement, the decentralized nature of the international legal system, and the predominant role of self-help.[108]

Although these points are somewhat less relevant today, writing in 1998, Malcolm Evans concluded a study of more recent cases regarding remedies at the International Court of Justice that 'the Court . . . has not yet developed a clear pattern of applicable remedies and doubtless much remains to be done in this field'.[109]

This position appears to be changing, however. An important source for emerging principles of the international law of remedies applicable to states before international tribunals is the work of the International Law Commission. In its most recent set of draft articles on state responsibility,[110] the ILC sets out the legal consequences for a state that arise from its internationally wrongful act. Article 30 provides for cessation and a requirement that the state offer appropriate assurances and guarantees of non-repetition. More importantly, however, for the purposes of this study, Article 31 sets out an obligation 'to make full reparation for the injury caused by the internationally wrongful act'. 'Injury' consists 'of any damage, whether material or moral, arising in consequence' of the internationally wrongful act of a state. Articles 35 to 40 set out in greater detail the forms of reparation. Article 35 establishes that '[f]ull reparation for the injury caused . . . shall take the form of restitution, compensation and satisfaction, either singly or in combination . . .'. The various forms of reparation are

---

[108] C. Gray, *Judicial Remedies in International Law* (1987), at 1.

[109] Evans, 'A Practical Look at the International Court of Justice', in M. D. Evans (ed.), *Remedies in International Law: The Institutional Dilemma* (1998) 21, at 26.

[110] International Law Commission, 52nd session, State responsibility: Draft articles provisionally adopted by the Drafting Committee on second reading, A/CN.4?L.600, 11 Aug. 2000.

put in the order of priority. Restitution, which is defined as 're-establish[ing] the situation which existed before the wrongful act was committed, is to be taken first, provided and 'to the extent that' restitution is 'not materially impossible' and would 'not involve a burden out of all proportion to the benefit deriving from restitution instead of compensation'.[111] A state is then obliged to compensate for the damage caused by the internationally wrongful act, 'insofar as such damage is not made good by restitution'.[112] The compensation 'shall cover any financially assessable damage including loss of profits insofar as it is established'.[113] The state is then required to give 'satisfaction . . . insofar as it cannot be made good by restitution or compensation'.[114] Satisfaction 'may consist in an acknowledgement of the breach, an expression of regret, a formal apology or other appropriate modality'.[115] It should not be out of proportion to the injury and 'may not take a form humiliating to the responsible State'.[116] The draft also provides that interest on any principal sum payable as reparation is payable 'when necessary to ensure full reparation'.[117] The interest rate and mode of calculation are to be set so as to achieve that result; interest runs from the date when the sum should have been paid until the date the obligation to pay is fulfilled. Contribution to the damage by 'wilful or negligent action or omission of the injured State or any person or entity in relation to whom reparation is sought' is to be taken into account in the determination of reparation.[118]

(vii) Relevance of Developments for Tackling Racial Inequality

We can see from these developments several features of the evolving landscape of human rights remedies of considerable relevance for considering the appropriate national enforcement and remedial provisions for tackling racial discrimination and inequality. First, there appears to be an increasing challenge to the idea that national remedies, given the extensive differences between jurisdictions and the importance of national sovereignty, are appropriately left entirely to national discretion. Secondly, there is increasingly detailed scrutiny being given by international bodies to the effectiveness in practice of particular national systems of redress, including judicial. Thirdly, the importance of national

[111] Art. 36.   [112] Art. 37(1).   [113] Art. 37(2).   [114] Art. 38(1).
[115] Art. 38(2).   [116] Ibid.   [117] Art. 39(1).
[118] Another source for identifying an international law of remedies are the standards of the various international criminal courts, especially that of the International Criminal Court. The Rome Statute obliges the Court to 'establish principles relating to reparation to, or in respect of, victims, including restitution, compensation and rehabilitation', and obliges the Assembly of States Parties to establish a trust fund for the benefit of victims of crimes within the jurisdiction of the Court and of the families of such victims. It also mandates the Court 'to protect the safety, physical and psychological well-being, dignity and privacy of victims' and to permit the participation of victims at all 'stages of the proceedings determined to be appropriate by the Court'. See also the Yugoslavia and Rwanda Tribunals.

institutions such as independent human rights commissions and their equivalents is increasingly recognized. Fourth, the international community is increasingly systematizing the appropriate remedial armoury that needs to be made available for redressing human rights violations.

V. EUROPEAN NORMS REGARDING ENFORCEMENT STRUCTURES AND NATIONAL REMEDIES

As regards the development of regional norms regarding racial discrimination, we shall concentrate on developments under the auspices of the Council of Europe, particularly the activities of the European Commission against Racism and Intolerance (ECRI), and the European Communities.

(i) European Commission against Racism and Intolerance

Since its creation in 1949, the prime field of competence of the Council of Europe has been the development of a body of rules designed to ensure the protection of fundamental human rights and their effective implementation. As a result of this work, the Organization has accumulated a wealth of experience in promoting human rights. The Council of Europe today comprises over forty member states. The Council of Europe undertakes a wide variety of programmes in the human rights field and many of its other activities, whether in the social, legal, education or cultural field, contain important human rights dimensions. The Council of Europe's most important achievement is the European Convention on Human Rights.

For the purpose of our discussion, however, we shall concentrate on the recommendations developed by the European Commission against Racism and Intolerance (ECRI).[119] This was set up following the Vienna Summit meeting of the Heads of State and of Government of the Council of Europe member States, which took place in October 1993. At this Summit, the Heads of State and of Government expressed their alarm at the rise of

---

[119] No reference is made to the jurisprudence of the European Convention on Human Rights, partly because the limited scope and role given to the anti-discrimination article of the ECHR, Article 14, has meant that the (former) Commission and Court have contributed little specifically to the issue of enforcement and remedial structures at the national level in the context of racial discrimination, although, of course, it has been remarkably significant in its contribution to discussions about the extent to which national implementation procedures satisfy the Convention obligations generally. In part, also, the ECHR is not referred to because the general principles emerging from the Court and Commission have been drawn on by ECRI in drawing up its guidance. The Court will have more of an opportunity to contribute to the evolution of these principles when Protocol No. 12 adds a new provision on discrimination (including racial discrimination) to the ECHR.

racism, xenophobia, anti-Semitism, and intolerance across Europe, and approved a Plan of Action to be implemented by the Council of Europe over the coming months and years. ECRI's terms of reference were decided upon at the Vienna Summit. Its task is to examine and assess the effectiveness of the range of measures (legal, policy, and other) taken by member States to combat racism, xenophobia, anti-Semitism, and intolerance. It was asked to propose further action in this field at local, national, and European level. It should also formulate general policy recommendations to member states and study international legal instruments applicable in this area, with a view to their reinforcement where necessary. ECRI's members are public figures chosen for their high moral authority and recognized expertise in dealing with questions of racism and intolerance. They include parliamentarians, judges and legal experts, sociologists, psychologists, and journalists.

One of the main aspects of ECRI's work over the past few years has been its country-by-country approach. ECRI noted very early in its work that the problems of racism and intolerance across the member states of the Council of Europe were not identical but took different forms requiring different action. It therefore decided that the most useful way to proceed would be, firstly, to examine closely the situation in each country and, secondly, to prepare texts on each country containing suggestions and ideas as to how some of the problems faced by that country might be dealt with. The aim of this exercise is to assist governments by putting forward concrete, specific proposals for action. ECRI accordingly collected information from a variety of sources. It commissioned the Swiss Institute of Comparative Law (in Lausanne) to prepare a study summarizing the legislation in force in each country in the field of combating racism and intolerance. It also sent a questionnaire to governments and to a number of national NGOs in each country in order to obtain a full picture of the problems faced, and legal and policy measures in place. Information was also collected from international NGOs, reports of other international organizations, press, and other sources. Another important input is the process of confidential dialogue that ECRI enters into with a representative of each government—a 'national liaison officer'—in order to refine and complete its draft texts on each country. After this process of dialogue, ECRI finalizes a text containing its proposals and transmits it, through the Committee of Ministers, to the concerned government.

A second main strand of ECRI's current work covers specific issues by means of general recommendations addressed to all member States of the Council of Europe. Following on from the preparation of its guiding principles, setting out in detail the areas which ECRI felt form the basis of a comprehensive approach to combating racism and intolerance, ECRI prepared its General Recommendation No. 1, which recommends action in a certain number of key areas. Its General Recommendation No. 2 deals with the question of specialized bodies existing at national level to combat racism and intolerance, such as commissions or ombudsmen, and sets out practical guidelines and advice on how such institutions might be established and arranged. Alongside these recommendations for governmental action, ECRI is also compiling and publishing a series of 'information sheets' containing brief descriptions of good practices and innovative projects in the various member States to combat racism and intolerance: the first of these publications is entitled 'Combating racism and intolerance: a basket of good practices', and is designed to serve as a source of inspiration and ideas for all those working in the field, both at governmental and non-governmental level.

ECRI General Policy Recommendation No. 1 attempts to assist member States in combating racism by recommending a series of measures. The preliminary paragraphs of the preamble suggest some of the reasoning behind the measures proposed. First, there is a recognition that effective action 'requires a sustained and comprehensive approach reflected in a broad range of measures which complement and reinforce one another, covering all aspects of life'. Secondly, there is a recognition of the social, economic, and legal diversity of member states and the need for specific measures in this field to reflect this diversity. Thirdly, whilst recognizing that racism 'cannot be countered by legal measures alone', ECRI emphasizes 'that legal measures are nevertheless of paramount importance and that non-enforcement of relevant existing legislation discredits action against racism and intolerance in general'.

This discussion concentrates on the section considering law, law enforcement and judicial remedies. Several measures are recommended. The national legal order should enshrine 'at a high level, for example in the Constitution or Basic Law' the commitment of the state to the equal treatment of all persons and to the fight against racism, xenophobia, anti-Semitism, and intolerance. Relevant international instruments should be signed and ratified. Elsewhere, there is a strong emphasis on criminal prosecution of offences of a racist or xenophobic character. Other legal remedies are dealt with more cursorily: adequate legal remedies 'should be made available to victims of discrimination, either in criminal law or in administrative and civil law where pecuniary or other compensation may be secured'. Adequate legal assistance should be made available to victims of discrimination when seeking a legal remedy. Awareness of the availability of legal remedies and the possibilities of access to them should be ensured. Lastly, there are recommendations on the collection of data.

Since it is difficult to develop and effectively implement policies in the areas in question without good data, [it is recommended that Member States] collect, in accordance with European laws, regulations and recommendations on data-protection and protection of privacy, where and when appropriate, data which will assist in assessing and evaluating the situation and experiences of groups which are particularly vulnerable to racism, xenophobia, antisemitism and intolerance.

ECRI's second General Policy Recommendation, on 'Specialized bodies to combat racism, xenophobia, antisemitism, and intolerance at national level', recommends that each member State should consider carefully the possibility of setting up a specialized body to combat racism, antisemitism and intolerance at national level, if such a body does not already exist.[120] In examining this question ECRI recommends that states make use of a set of basic principles annexed to the recommendation 'as guidelines and a source of inspiration presenting a number of options for discussion at national level'. The preamble recognizes that 'the form such bodies might take may vary according to the circumstances of member States and may form part of a body with wider objectives in the field of human rights generally', and this is reflected in Principle 2, as well. Unsurprisingly, the ECRI Principles closely reflect the Paris Principles, except in two major respects. Unlike the Paris Principles, which are framed in such a way that some of the Principles are mandatory and others are voluntary, the ECRI Principles are framed in more qualified terms. So, for example, regarding the functions of the specialized body, the ECRI Principles provide that '[s]ubject to national circumstances, law and practice, specialized bodies should possess as many as possible of [a list of] functions and responsibilities'. The second difference relates to these functions and responsibilities. The ECRI Principles include within the primary list of functions, unlike the Paris Principles, several relating to receiving and adjudicating on complaints from victims of discrimination, and other functions relating to legal enforcement. These include providing aid and assistance to victims, including granting legal aid, in order to secure their rights before institutions and the courts. Such bodies should be able to have recourse to the courts or other judicial authorities as appropriate, subject to the legal framework of the country concerned. They should also be able to hear and consider complaints and petitions concerning specific cases and seek settlements, either through amicable conciliation or through binding and enforceable decision. And finally, the bodies should have appropriate powers to obtain evidence and information in pursuance of this function.

(ii) European Community and Racial Discrimination

Following a long period during which the European Community became increasingly involved in issues of racial equality,[121] but without any clear legal authority to enact anti-discrimination legislation, the Amsterdam Treaty, adopted in 1997, gave the Community new powers to enact legal provisions

---

[120] See also ECRI, *The Place and Role of National Specialised Bodies in Combating Racism: Summary of the Proceedings* (Council of Europe, Strasbourg, 1998) (CRI (98) 85).

[121] See, e.g., European Commission, *The European Institutions in the Fight against Racism: Selected Texts* (1997).

to combat discrimination based on sex, racial, or ethnic origin, religion or belief, disability, age, or sexual orientation.[122] This resulted in a package of proposals from the Commission in 1999. Two Directives were proposed. The first (adopted in November 2000) prohibited discrimination in employment on all the grounds referred to, with the exception of sex and race discrimination. Sex discrimination was already subject to extensive Community legislation dating from the 1970s. A second directive (adopted in June 2000) prohibited discrimination on the grounds of racial and ethnic origin in a wider range of areas than employment, covering fields such as education, access to goods and services, social protection, and social advantages. In addition, an action programme to accompany these directives (adopted by the Council in November 2000)[123] was designed to complement the implementation of the directives through the exchange of information and experiences and the dissemination of best practice in both legislative and non-legislative areas.[124] We shall concentrate on the Directive dealing with racial discrimination.

The debate surrounding the enforcement and remedial structure of the European Community's Race Directive 2000 illustrates the utility of the analysis we have carried out to date, for it brings into sharp relief the relationship between the debate over substance (what vision of equality is adopted?) and enforcement (how is this vision to be implemented?). The substantive provisions of the Directive, as adopted, demonstrate no one clear approach between the three models of equality sketched out above. The focus on discrimination[125] seems to indicate the adoption of the individual justice model, as does the symmetrical nature of the protection provided.[126] The genuine occupational qualification exception, which is drafted in such a way as to indicate that some conception of individual merit is in play,[127] also seems to indicate an individual justice approach. However, a group justice approach seems to be indicated by the adoption of indirect discrimination in the definition of discrimination,[128] and by the adoption of a test of 'disadvantage' within that definition. Also indicative of a group justice approach is the inclusion of a provision on positive action,[129] although it is permitted rather than required, and an exception rather than regarded as integral to a conception of equality. On the basis of the substantive provisions, we would be hard put to choose whether the Directive is aiming to achieve individual justice or group justice. Indeed, it could be said that both are being aimed at, rather than one or the other.

---

[122] Amsterdam Treaty, Article 13.

[123] Council Decision of 27 Nov. 2000 establishing a Community action programme to combat discrimination (2000 to 2006), OJ 2000 L 303/23.

[124] European Commission, An Action Plan Against Racism, Communication from the Commission, COM (1998) 183 final of 25 Mar. 1998.

[125] Art. 1.   [126] Art. 2.   [127] Art. 4.   [128] Art. 2(2)(b).

[129] Art. 5.

The enforcement and remedial provisions, however, as they emerged from the political debate between the Commission, the Parliament, and the Council of Ministers demonstrate a strong preference within the Council of Ministers, (and probably the Commission anticipating the Council's view) for a model of *enforcement* that is clearly individual justice based, with only a faint whiff of the third model (equality as participation). As adopted, the Directive requires judicial and administrative procedures for enforcement to be provided in member States. The approach adopted is one that recognizes some of the limitations of the civil justice model in achieving individual justice. So, for example, a conciliation element is included,[130] broader *locus standi* is provided,[131] the burden of proof is modified,[132] and protection of complainants from victimization is provided.[133] A national body is to be designated for the promotion of equal treatment and this national body is to be empowered to assist individual victims.[134] The sanctions to be provided at the national level must be 'effective, proportionate and dissuasive'[135] but without defining how far the inclusion of 'dissuasion' expands the role of the remedy beyond mere compensation for individuals.

Indeed, the individual justice model adopted is relatively weak with the inclusion of a provision that remedies 'may'[136] comprise the payment of compensation to the victim, rather than apparently making this a requirement. The Commission had proposed an individual justice enforcement model that was noticeably less weak in some respects.[137] In the Commission's original draft, there was less deference accorded to member State procedures. There was no mention of conciliation procedures as an enforcement option. There were fewer restrictions on the role of groups assisting victims, and no exception in the changed burden of proof for investigatory procedures. The European Parliament's approach to individual enforcement was considerably more robust even than the Commission.[138] It had made a clear recommendation that conciliation procedures should be voluntary and not serve as an alternative to judicial remedies,[139] and that the independent bodies to be established should be able to adjudicate on individual complaints.[140]

It is when we come to the enforcement of the group justice dimensions of the Directive, however, that the most significant contrasts between the Commission and the Council on the one hand, and the Parliament on the

---

[130] Art. 7(1), where a member State deems it appropriate.   [131] Art. 7(2).

[132] Art. 8.   [133] Art. 9.   [134] Art. 13.   [135] Art. 15.

[136] Art. 15.

[137] Commission of the European Communities, proposal for a Council Directive implementing the principle of equal treatment between persons irrespective of racial or ethnic origin, COM (1999) 566 final, 25.11.1999.

[138] Report on the proposal for a Council Directive on implementing the principle of equal treatment between persons irrespective of racial or ethnic origin, A5-0136/2000 final, 16 May 2000.

[139] Report, 22–3.   [140] Report, 27–8.

other emerges most clearly. The Parliament's draft is clearly aimed at the recognition that the enforcement of a group justice approach was necessary. There is frequent reference to groups;[141] there is the inclusion of reference to 'institutional racism';[142] the equal treatment principle is interpreted to include 'proportional participation';[143] NGOs were to have the power to initiate 'collective actions' in court,[144] even without individual victims; the independent body was to have extensive investigatory powers;[145] public authorities and employers were to be required to engage in ethnic monitoring;[146] and contract compliance was included as an option.[147] None of these Parliamentary proposals found their way into the Directive as approved by the Council—a clear indication that (to the extent that a group justice approach was adopted) it was to be enforced without special recognition in enforcement mechanisms.

Equality as participation is given very little attention in the Directive as enacted.[148] It is true that collective bargaining implementation is available, but as a way of limiting the individual justice model (a provision the Commission had not suggested), rather than anything more radical. There is no mention of mainstreaming, unlike in the Commission's subsequent proposal for revision of the gender equality directive.[149] 'Dialogue' with NGOs is 'encouraged',[150] but little more. Periodic reports are to be prepared by the Commission on implementation by the Directive, in consultation with social partners and NGOs.[151] 'Social dialogue' is, however, much more prominent. Member States 'shall, in accordance with national traditions and practice, take adequate measures to promote the social dialogue between the two sides of industry with a view to fostering equal treatment. . . '.[152] Indeed, the two sides of industry are to be encouraged to conclude agreements laying down anti-discrimination rules.[153]

(iii) The Three Models of Equality Revisited

The European developments discussed inject a necessary dose of scepticism about some of the international developments discussed in the previous

---

[141] For example, Report, 6, 16.   [142] Report, 11, 13.   [143] Report, 12.
[144] Report, 21–2.   [145] Report, 27.   [146] Report, 23–4.
[147] Report, 24–5.   [148] Art. 16.

[149] Commission of the European Communities, Proposal for a Directive amending Council Directive 76/207/EEC on the implementation of the principle of equal treatment for men and women as regards access to employment, vocational training and promotion, and working conditions, COM(2000) 334 final, 7.6.2000, Article 1(1): 'Member States shall introduce such measures as are necessary to enable them actively and visibly to promote the objective of equality between men and women by its incorporation, in particular, into all laws, regulations, administrative provisions, policies and activities' in the areas covered by the Directive.

[150] Art. 12.   [151] Art. 17.   [152] Art. 11(1).   [153] Art. 11(2).

sections of this chapter. Many of the developments described there are either entirely recommendatory or at most 'soft law'. Where they create enforceable legal obligations, as in the case of communications under the Optional Protocols, remarkably few states (and even fewer large states) have signalled their acceptance. They can, with some justification, be regarded as more often rhetorical than practical in their effect. This is not to underestimate the importance of rhetoric in this area, but to emphasize that when the World Conference is faced with calls for more enforceable norms regarding appropriate national enforcement and remedial structures, it may prove difficult to obtain the necessary acceptance of states.

The European experience bears this out. The (actual or potential) legal significance and relative effectiveness of the various human rights conventions promulgated under the auspices of the Council of Europe, and the even greater legal significance and effectiveness of European Community law in the member States, has contributed to a noticeably more cautious approach being adopted of late in Europe than internationally. The message that European experience sends is that when real legal enforceability is on the horizon, a much less radical vision of racial equality and of the potential for legal remedies becomes apparent. Overwhelmingly, therefore, we can see that an individual justice model of racial equality predominates in European norm creation, combined with considerable unease about national enforcement structures reflecting a group justice model or 'equality as participation' in the racial equality context. We can identify, therefore, a growing gap between international normative rhetoric, and European remedial structures.

VI. EVOLVING POSITIONS IN DISCUSSIONS LEADING TO THE WORLD CONFERENCE ON RACISM

(i) Organization of the World Conference

We have seen that the General Assembly authorized the holding of a World Conference. The responsibility for organizing the Conference has fallen to the Office of the High Commissioner for Human Rights. The High Commissioner for Human Rights, Mary Robinson, has been appointed as Secretary-General of the Conference. The preparations for such conferences involve a considerable range of different types of meetings and events prior to the Conference itself. By the time of writing, in December 2000, four sets of meetings of particular significance for the purpose of this chapter had been held. Four expert seminars had been held: on remedies available to the victims of acts of racism, racial discrimination, xenophobia, and related intolerance, and on good national practices in this

---

[154] Report A/Conf.189/PC.1/8 Geneva, Switzerland, 16–18 Feb. 2000. See also the background papers prepared in preparation of this seminar, summarized in the Report.

field,[154] on the protection of minorities and other vulnerable groups and strengthening human rights capacity at the national level,[155] on the prevention of ethnic and racial conflicts in Africa, [156] and on economic, social, and legal measures to overcome racial discrimination with reference to vulnerable groups.[157] The First Session of the Preparatory Committee for the Conference had met (the Human Rights Commission wearing another hat).[158] The regional meeting organized by the Council of Europe's ECRI had taken place,[159] and its associated non-governmental organizations forum.[160] Still to come, at the time of writing, were the regional meetings for the Americas, Africa and Asia, and their associated NGO forums. The second session of the Preparatory Committee was due to meet between 21 May and 1 June, 2000. The Conference itself was planned for Durban, South Africa between 31 August and 7 September 2001.

(ii) Recognizing 'Equalities' and their Enforcement Dimensions

I argued previously that debates at the international and regional levels have been relatively thin, both in identifying all three models of equality that are in contention, and in drawing the connections between these different models and the type of national enforcement structures and remedies that would be appropriate. The discussions leading up to the World Conference have shown a considerably greater readiness among the participants to become involved in these issues, in part because non-governmental organizations are now becoming much more evident and influential in the debates.

Not surprisingly, detailed consideration of enforcement mechanisms and remedies associated with an individual justice model is evident in the debates. The report of the expert seminar on remedies recommended, for example, that states 'introduce general and comprehensive legislation which provides protection against discrimination on the basis of race, color, national or ethnic origin, religion and gender, and also provides relief in the form of civil damages'.[161] This legislation should apply in both the public and private sector.

---

[154] Report A/Conf.189/PC.1/8 Geneva, Switzerland, 16–18 Feb. 2000. See also the background papers prepared in preparation of this seminar, summarized in the Report.

[155] Report A/Conf.189/PC.2/2 (Regional seminar, Warsaw, 5–7 July 2000).

[156] Regional Seminar of Experts on the Prevention of Ethnic and Racial Conflicts in Africa, 4–6 Oct. 2000, Addis Ababa, Ethiopia, Conclusions and Recommendations (unedited), <https://www.unhchr.ch/html/racism/recomaddis.htm>.

[157] Conclusions and recommendations, Santiago de Chile, Chile, 25–27 Oct. 2000.

[158] Report A/Conf.189/PC.1/21.   [159] Strasbourg, France, 11–13 Oct. 2000.

[160] Report from the Forum of Non-Governmental Organizations, Strasbourg, 10–11 Oct. 2000 (EUROCONF (2000)8).

[161] A/Conf.189/PC.1/8, 44.

The recommendations envisage that 'action against racism will principally be determined in terms of the rule of civil procedure'.[162] Governments should 'undertake information campaign[s] on the rights and procedures relating to remedies available to individuals . . . who are victims of racial discrimination'.[163] Recourse procedures 'should be easily accessible, expeditious and not unduly complicated'.[164] Legal aid and other forms of assistance 'should be provided'.[165] National legislation 'as well as related judicial practices' should be 'reconsidered with regard to the level of proof necessary to establish what constitutes acts of racial discrimination . . . [T]he onus of proof must rest with the respondent to rebut the allegation made by the victim of racism.'[166]

So too, national institutions have featured prominently. The Paris Principles on national institutions were much in evidence in the regional conferences of experts.[167] Victims of racial discrimination should be able to have recourse to 'national institutions, which can play an important role . . . in advising victims of remedies available to them'.[168] Such national institutions 'would be an effective mechanism to provide legal aid as well as non-judicial remedies for the victims'.[169] The expert conference on remedies recommended that they should be given 'a role . . . to undertake alternative methods of resolution of disputes by conciliation and mediation and where necessary, to represent victims in the courts or before other bodies'.[170] Remedies available 'must include procedural mechanisms of recourse against decisions, which constitute or may lead to violations, and of material reparations whenever violations have occurred'.

Victims are entitled to reparations in the form of 'restitution, rehabilitation, satisfaction and guarantees of non-repetition'.[171]

Monetary and non-monetary forms of reparation are equally important in rendering justice to victims of racial discrimination. Non-monetary forms of reparation include measures such as verification of the facts and their public disclosure; official declarations or judicial decisions that restore dignity and rebuild reputation; acknowledgement of the facts and acceptance of responsibility; and commemorations and paying tribute to the victims.

The European Conference conclusions made no similar assumptions concerning the general appropriateness of the use of the civil as opposed to the criminal law in tackling discrimination. Apparently treating them as equally acceptable alternatives, recommendations were made to improve the effectiveness of both criminal and civil law approaches. Regarding the use of the criminal law, the Conference drew attention to a number of measures participating states should consider: that criminal prosecutions of racist offences

---

[162] p. 54.   [163] p. 9.   [164] p. 52.   [165] Ibid.   [166] p. 54.
[167] Santiago Regional Conference of Experts, para. 8.   [168] p. 46.
[169] p. 48.   [170] p. 55.   [171] p. 52.

are given a high priority, that they are 'stringently punished',[172] that racist organizations could be combated, and that the denial of the Holocaust could be made punishable. Regarding access to the courts by complainants, states should consider shifting the burden of proof in certain circumstances, ensuring adequate legal assistance, protecting complainants against victimization, affording the possibility for NGOs to support complainants, and promoting awareness of legal redress. Strong support was given in the European Conference conclusions to the development of national institutions, which were considered 'essential'.[173]

However, there was also evident in the discussion of remedies and national structures an appreciation of the need to include a group justice model of remedies and enforcement institutions.[174] The report of the expert seminar on remedies stressed that 'the perspective of the victim must be the guiding principle'.[175] The recommendations stressed that it is with the most vulnerable that enforcement structures and remedies should be particularly concerned.[176] 'Indigenous peoples, minorities, migrants, refugees, asylum seekers and other non-nationals face special problems more often than other victims of violations do.'[177] The World Conference

should give priority attention to the need for effective remedies for victims of violations among the most vulnerable groups . . . including indigenous peoples and those who suffer discrimination because of structural reasons . . .[178]

There was also a clear recognition of the collective, or group dimension to the problem. 'Effective remedies should be made available for the collective as well as the individual rights of indigenous peoples . . .' Similarly remedies should be made available to members of national or ethnic, religious or linguistic minorities, to address violations of their collective as well as their individual rights. Special measures should be adopted by states to ensure that they enjoy 'equality in law and in fact', and 'remedies should also be available in cases where such special measures are not implemented'.[179] Such special measures should be taken to 'ensure the development and protection of the most disadvantaged racial groups or of persons belonging to these groups'.[180]

So too the subsequent regional seminars stressed the need for affirmative action,[181] the need to collect adequate statistical information,[182] and the need

---

[172] European Conference Report, para. 10.

[173] European Conference Report, para. 21.

[174] One of the background papers prepared for the seminar was particularly strong in this regard, see Theo van Boven, Common problems linked to all remedies available to victims of racial discrimination, HR/GVA/WCR/SEM.1/2000/BP.5, 12 Jan. 2000, esp. 10–11.

[175] p. 43.   [176] p. 45.   [177] p. 48.   [178] p. 47.

[179] p. 49.   [180] p. 45.

[181] A/Conf.189/PC.2/2, para. 21; Santiago Regional Conference of Experts, paras. 58, 60.

[182] A/Conf.189/PC.2/2, para. 57; Santiago Regional Conference of Experts, paras. 7, 38, 39, 66; European Conference, paras. 12, 25.

as a priority to target groups that have suffered systematic discrimination.[183] Particularly interesting additional recommendations emerged from the European Conference. States' legislative frameworks should be kept 'under regular review so as to promote equality and guard against any unintended or inadvertent discriminatory impact which may arise'.[184] Because '[e]qual treatment by itself may not be enough if it does not overcome the weight of accumulated disadvantage suffered by persons belonging to targeted groups', states should consider introducing 'legislative and administrative measures which are necessary to prevent and correct situations of inequality'. This would mean 'a positive duty on public authorities to promote equality and to assess the impact of policy, as well as to prevent and punish violations by any person, organization or enterprise'.[185] The Santiago regional conference of experts also emphasized impact assessments of policies: '[S]ocial impact evaluations of all projects or activities affecting indigenous or Afro-Latin American peoples' should be conducted, 'in order to safeguard their cultural and human aspects'.[186] Additionally, the European Conference suggested that 'public funds [should] not [be] awarded to companies or other organizations which are not committed to non-discriminatory policies'.[187]

The group justice model has not been uncontroversial, however. One of the tasks of the Preparatory Committee was to adopt a set of 'themes' to be included in the provisional agenda of the World Conference. Two are of particular importance for the purposes of this chapter. The first is the 'Provision of effective remedies, recourse, redress, [compensatory] and other measures at the national, regional and international levels.' The second is 'Strategies to achieve *full and effective equality*, including international cooperation and enhancement of the United Nations and other international mechanisms in combating racism . . .' There are several points of interest. A group justice element seems included in the reference to 'full and effective equality'. More importantly, however, it would appear that the broad ramifications of adopting a group justice approach contributed to a public disagreement in the formulation of the 'effective remedies' theme. The word 'compensatory' was put in square brackets because the Committee was unable to agree either to include it, or to leave it out. The group of Western states, together with representatives from Armenia, and Israel reserved the right to 'revisit' whether 'compensation' was appropriately included. The sensitivity of the issue for the Western group appears to have arisen from the sense that the inclusion of the word 'compensatory' opened up the possibility that redress would be claimable by large numbers of people, potentially for discrimination arising

---

[183] A/Conf.189/PC.2/2, para. 21.   [184] European Conference, para. 13.
[185] Ibid., para. 14.   [186] Santiago Regional Conference of Experts, para. 14(c).
[187] European Conference, para. 16.

out of colonialism and slavery.[188] The African group (together with Syria and Cuba) regarded the enclosure of 'compensatory' within square brackets as unacceptable.[189]

Equivalent issues were likely to be discussed in the forthcoming regional meetings.[190] The regional seminar of experts on the prevention of ethnic and racial conflicts in Africa recommended that the World Conference adopted as a theme of its agenda, 'Measures for reparation, restoration and compensation for nations, groups and individuals affected by slavery and the slave trade, colonialism, and economic and political exclusion.'[191] The regional conference of experts in Santiago recommended that measures against discrimination should include 'the establishment of victims' compensation and reparation funds, as appropriate'.[192] The recommendations from the European NGO Forum stated: 'Former colonial powers and other parties involved have the moral duty to grant reparation to victims of slave trade and colonialism. Such reparation may take the form of restitution, compensation, rehabilitation and satisfaction as well as measures which guarantee non-repetition.'[193]

The third model of equality as participation was largely ignored in the background papers prepared for the expert seminar on remedies and in the report of the conclusions of that seminar. The only recognition of this emerging approach is to be found in the conclusions' adoption of an earlier

---

[188] See Xako, 'Third World and West Hit Deadlock on Reparations', *Business Day (South Africa)*, 30 May 2000. There is an active movement attempting to secure reparations for Africa from former colonial and slave-holding countries, see *The Abuja Proclamation* (A declaration of the first Abuja Pan-African Conference on Reparations for African Enslavement, Colonialization and Neo-Colonialization, sponsored by the Organization of African Unity and its Reparations Commission, 27–29 Apr. 1993, Abuja, Nigeria <http://www.innotts.co.uk/~shaka/abujaProclamation.htm>. More recently, an *Accra Declaration on Reparations and Repatriation* has been promulgated, <http://www.tapvideo.com/afrworep.htm>; see 'Commission Reminds UN of Africa's Reparations', Africa News Service, 13 Dec. 1999; 'UN Accused of Hypocrisy Over Enslavement of Africans', Thursday, 14 Dec. 2000. There is also a movement in the United States amongst some black Americans for reparations from the United States government for the effects of slavery and discrimination, see Muwakkil, 'Hot Off the Fringes Tide May Have Finally Changed on Reparations', *Chicago Tribune*, 30 Oct. 2000. See generally, Gifford, 'The Legal Basis of the Claim for Slavery Reparations', 27-*SPG Human Rights*, Spring, 2000, 16.

[189] A/Conf.189/PC.1/21, para. 30.

[190] Capdevila, 'Rights-Americas: Reparations for Victims of Racism Debated', *Interpress Service*, 4 Dec. 2000.

[191] Conclusions and Recommendations, para. 34.

[192] Santiago Regional Conference of Experts, para. 24(b).

[193] Council of Europe and European Commission, Report from the Forum of Non-Governmental Organizations 'End Racism Now!' (Strasbourg, 10–11 Oct. 2000 (EURO-CONF (2000)8) (11 Oct. 2000), para. 9. No equivalent statement is included in either the General Conclusions of the European Conference Against Racism, EUROCONF (2000) 7 final (16 Oct. 2000), or the Political Declaration adopted by Ministers of Council of Europe member States on Friday, 13 Oct. 2000 at the concluding session of the European Conference against Racism (EUROCONF (2000) 1 final (13 Oct. 2000).

ILO recommendation for the involvement of representatives of the minorities themselves in the planning, implementation, monitoring, and evaluation of special measures adopted for their benefit.[194] In the conclusions of the seminar, this became a recommendation that 'Indigenous peoples and minorities should participate both in the establishment and in the operation of remedial mechanisms set up for their special protection'.[195]

The third model of equality was much more apparent, however, in the regional conferences of experts that followed. The conclusions of the Central and Eastern European regional seminar of experts, in addition to reiterating many of the remedial aspects of the individual and group justice models, recommended much more extensive emphasis on effective participation of national minorities in decision-making. The importance was stressed of involving 'representative groups' from all minorities '[i]n designing, implementing and evaluating policies to combat discrimination.'[196] Priority should be given to 'civil society capacity building among minorities and the provision of resource centres and training to facilitate the economic and political participation of minorities'.[197] In the Santiago regional conference of experts, the third model was developed more fully still.

Vulnerable groups should, on an equal basis, participate in, contribute to, and benefit from the right to development. Consequently, development policies should be conducted in ways that reduce the disparities that may exist between different groups. Groups receiving assistance should always be fully consulted with regard to development projects affecting the regions where they live.[198]

Whenever there were investment projects for the exploitation of raw materials, 'those projects [should be] reported to and discussed with the peoples concerned . . .'[199]

The European Conference also stressed the importance of participation by the affected groups. The 'conditions necessary' for the 'effective participation of persons belonging to targeted groups in decision-making processes' should be created by states.[200] It was the European NGO forum that came closest, indeed, to articulating the full 'equality as participation' model. European states, it recommended, should

[m]ainstream the issue of combating racism into all national policies and practices and all sphere of public life, including all stages of decision-making. Mainstreaming involves the application of equality proofing guidelines, participation of groups experiencing racism, positive actions, data collection, proactive monitoring and impact assessment.[201]

---

[194] Affirmative action in the employment of ethnic minorities and persons with disabilities (ILO, 1997), 106, quoted in the background paper by Asbjørn Aide, HR/GVA/WCR/SEM.1/2000/BP.3, 7–8.

[195] p. 49.   [196] A/Conf.189/PC.2/2, para. 27.   [197] Para. 28.

[198] Santiago Regional Conference of Experts, para. 40.   [199] Ibid., para. 14(b).

[200] European Conference, para. 18.   [201] European NGO Forum, para. 41.

VII. CONCLUSION

This chapter has argued, in particular, that decisions as to the type of mechanisms which are thought to be appropriate are likely to be strongly influenced by the aim which the legislator wants to achieve in enacting anti-discrimination law in the first place. While this may seem a relatively straightforward task, it turns out not to be so, and the choice of enforcement instruments thus requires political choices of considerable significance. Some basic propositions emerge with some degree of clarity from the approaches taken by the international and regional bodies we have just examined.

(i) Symbolic and Instrumental Functions of Anti-discrimination Law

The first point relates to the question of whether national anti-discrimination law should serve a primarily symbolic or an instrumental function. Should the purpose of the law be thought to be primarily symbolic, an unequivocal declaration of public policy, aiming to change hearts and minds through making clear what the representative institutions of the society think is inappropriate behaviour, but not much else? To some extent, this symbolic function may be thought to be the primary function that non-discrimination requirements in some national constitutions often seem to serve. Not surprisingly, perhaps, there is remarkable consistency at the international and regional levels that this limited symbolic approach is inadequate, if left as the only function that anti-discrimination law is intended to serve at the national level. International supervisory bodies have become generally dissatisfied with anti-discrimination law that is 'merely' symbolic, considering that the gap between reality and ideal is something which they should actively seek to bridge.

(ii) Voluntarism and Enforcement

A second, closely related, conclusion from the international and regional practice is that whilst we may accept that voluntary action by organizations to achieve equality of opportunity is preferable to the use of legal or non-legal sanctions, it does not effectively implement international or regional standards to expect that the degree of change which is necessary will come about entirely voluntarily, without a legal structure of enforcement and remedies. Not everyone will be sympathetic to the objective of equality of opportunity and some may perceive that providing equality of opportunity would put them at a competitive disadvantage with competitors. Therefore, it is unlikely that all will be prepared to take the necessary steps voluntarily. We should assume, in other words, that organizations will only modify disapproved-of behaviour if faced with sufficient incentives. Where an organization expects to benefit from infringing the law by continuing to act in a certain way, it is unlikely to change its behaviour unless the costs of doing so outweigh the anticipated benefits. To that extent, we should assume that organizations subject to anti-discrimination regulation are amoral pragmatists. Therefore the system of incentives and disincentives to comply is crucial to both the effectiveness and efficiency of anti-discrimination law. There needs to be a clear and comprehensive legal framework to ensure that necessary action will be taken, even if it is not forthcoming voluntarily. That is not to say that voluntary adherence to non-discrimination should not be encouraged.

(iii) Markets and Legal Enforcement

It might be argued that the instrumental goal which anti-discrimination law seeks to further can be realized (indeed, is best realized, some say) without the intervention of state enforcement institutions, by relying on the 'free market' instead. This is indeed an important issue, for it raises the question of what type of conduct the state is aiming to regulate. Does the state regard adverse discrimination as appropriately subject to regulation largely because it is economically inefficient? If so, the most effective way in which to get rid of such adverse discrimination may be to create and maintain a fully functioning free market. Only where that is not possible, for example where there is discrimination by governmental entities that are not subject to market pressures, or there are market failures such as the inadequate provision of information, should legal enforcement be contemplated. Creating and maintaining a free market would involve reducing informational barriers, dealing with market imperfections, and reducing discrimination by natural monopolies; but that is all. The approach taken by the international and regional bodies we have looked at seems at variance with this approach to making the anti-discrimination norm effective.

(iv) The Limits of Anti-discrimination Law

Whilst anti-discrimination law is necessary, the international and regional bodies we have examined have reached a consensus that such laws are unlikely to be a sufficient mechanism for the achievement of racial equality more broadly conceived. Anti-discrimination law largely operates on the *demand* side. Anti-discrimination legislation is generally intended to affect the behaviour (and ultimately the attitudes) of those who are usually in the position of choosing whether to engage in social and economic relations, for example, employers, house owners, etc. In order to implement an equality strategy more fully, several of the international and regional organizations discussed above also advocate that policies which affect the *supply* side be adopted by government to change certain characteristics of those in the position of offering their services such as applicants for jobs, or increase the net amount of opportunities, for example by stimulating the development of new jobs.

(v) Discrimination as a Moral Issue

Anti-discrimination law clearly does not give rise to entirely unique problems of enforcement. On the contrary, the problem of enforcing anti-discrimination often raises issues very similar to the enforcement of social and economic policy requirements more generally. We can view the topic of this chapter, therefore, in part through the lens of regulatory theory.[202] As Karen Yeung has written, '[t]he aim of any form of regulation is to modify the behaviour of those subject to regulation in order to generate a desired outcome',[203] and this is no less true in the context of anti-discrimination law, than it is in the regulation of, for example, monopolies. But it is also true that this regulatory-theory approach does have its limits. Anti-discrimination law, as viewed by the international and regional bodies discussed above, has usually seen the creation of a system of individual rights as one of the most important arrows in the quiver of regulatory instruments, whilst other attempts at enforcing social and economic policy requirements (such as anti-trust regulation) have sometimes not done so. As importantly, in the enforcement of anti-discrimination law the international and regional bodies have eschewed certain regulatory instruments that have proven popular in other areas of regulation. So, for example, corrective taxation (in which the disapproved conduct has not been legally constrained, but if an actor chooses to behave in this undesired way, he or she must pay a tax, thus forcing the internalization of negative externalities) has never been advocated at the international or regional level in the context of anti-discrimination enforcement, whilst it has been widely discussed as a means of controlling environmental pollution, and has been introduced in several countries.[204] What distinguishes the regulation of discrimination from some other regulatory areas, I suggest, is the relatively heavy moral aspect of the equality issue taken by these bodies. That moral dimension constrains the types of regulatory mechanisms that will be regarded as appropriate in order to comply with international and regional standards.

---

[202] For some recent discussions, see C. McCrudden (ed.), *Regulation and Deregulation* (1999).

[203] Yeung, 'The Private Enforcement of Competition Law', in McCrudden, ibid., at 79.

[204] See Ogus, 'Corrective Taxation as a Regulatory Instrument', in McCrudden, ibid., at 15.

(vi) Challenges for the World Conference

What does *not* emerge with any degree of clarity, however, is any consensus at the European or international levels about two crucial issues.

(a) International Supervision vis-à-vis National Procedures

The first is the overarching question of the appropriate role of international supervision *vis-à-vis* national procedures. We can agree with van Boven that

while ensuring effective protection and remedies should basically be a matter of national responsibility, international co-operation and international monitoring are supplementary means to meet the requirements of the relevant international standards.[205]

Where the balance should lie, however, remains deeply contested. A fundamental issue for the World Conference will be whether the international community is prepared to shift that balance more in favour of the formulation of enforceable international standards in the area of enforcement and remedies. The European Community experience is not particularly optimistic for those who wish to see the balance shifted away from the national state.

(b) Which Models of Equality?

The second major issue on which little consensus can be perceived is the equally crucial issue of what model of equality anti-discrimination law should be implementing, and how far this should be reflected in national mechanisms of enforcement and remedies. It has been argued that, although there is some guidance from international and European bodies on these issues, this guidance is remarkably thin and somewhat inconsistent at the present time, concentrating on providing little more than a basic structure for analysis and action. In part, this thinness arises from an unwillingness to be seen to be entering into an area of deep national sensitivities and, indeed, sovereignty. But, as importantly, the thinness derives from an unwillingness to embrace clearly the consequences of adopting a group justice model of anti-discrimination law, or a model of 'equality as participation'. A major contribution of the preparatory work for the World Conference has been to make these issues more visible, and to require that they now be addressed more directly than previously. Again, the *European* experience is hardly promising. How far is the *international* community prepared to go?

---

[205] Van Boven, *supra* n. 174, at 2.

Index

NATIONAL
POLICE
LIBRARY